WPA Outcomes for First-Year Composition	Where *The Allyn & Bacon Guide* Addresses These Outcomes
PROCESSES By the end of first-year composition, students should • Be aware that it usually takes multiple drafts to create and complete a successful text • Develop flexible strategies for generating, revising, editing, and proofreading • Understand writing as an open process that permits writers to use later invention and rethinking to revise their work • Understand the collaborative and social aspects of writing processes • Learn to critique their own and others' works • Learn to balance the advantages of relying on others with the responsibility of doing their part • Use a variety of technologies to address a range of audiences	Part 3, "A Guide to Composing and Revising" Additionally, all Writing Project chapters in Part 2 have substantial process components, including questions for peer review. A variety of technologies is used to produce genres in Part 2.
KNOWLEDGE OF CONVENTIONS By the end of first-year composition, students should • Learn common formats for different kinds of texts • Develop knowledge of genre conventions ranging from structure and paragraphing to tone and mechanics • Practice appropriate means of documenting their work • Control such surface features as syntax, grammar, punctuation, and spelling	Part 1, "A Rhetoric for Writers," Concepts 7, 11, and 12 Part 4, "A Rhetorical Guide to Research" Additionally, all Writing Project chapters in Part 2 explain the format, tone, and style appropriate for a wide range of genres.
COMPOSING IN ELECTRONIC ENVIRONMENTS By the end of first-year composition, students should • Use electronic environments for drafting, reviewing, revising, editing, and sharing texts • Locate, evaluate, organize, and use research material collected from electronic sources, including scholarly library databases; other official databases; and informal electronic networks and Internet sources • Understand and exploit the difference in the rhetorical strategies and in the affordances available for both print and electronic composing processes and texts	Part 4, "A Rhetorical Guide to Research" Additionally, the Writing Project chapters in Part 2 make frequent reference to electronic formats and processes.

Why Do You Need This New Edition?

If you're wondering why you should buy this Concise sixth edition of *The Allyn & Bacon Guide to Writing*, here are 7 great reasons!

1. Coverage of integrating researched sources effectively and ethically has been expanded with new instruction, visual presentations, and examples to help you improve skills fundamental to college readiness and success while avoiding plagiarism (Chapters 13 and 14).

2. MLA and APA coverage is thoroughly updated according to the most recent citation guidelines from each organization, ensuring that you are learning the most current national standards (Chapter 14).

3. A thoroughly revised chapter on image analysis helps you work effectively with the wide variety of visual texts you will encounter in other course areas and outside of college (Chapter 8).

4. New readings offer engaging and contemporary topics for discussion, written response, and exploratory research—including banning laptops and cell phones from classes, sustainable environmental practices, and the growing gap between the rich and the poor.

5. New visual explanations present complex topics clearly so that information is displayed at-a-glance in charts or color-coded samples rather than in long passages of text (Chapters 13 and 14).

6. A new section on presenting data visually to reach different kinds of readers helps you create effective tables, graphs, and charts to support your arguments (Chapter 12).

7. New instruction on creating thesis statements and introductions helps you with parts of the writing process that are often tricky for writers but have a great impact on the efficacy of your writing (Chapter 2).

THE
ALLYN & BACON
GUIDE TO WRITING

Concise Edition

SIXTH EDITION

John D. Ramage
Arizona State University

John C. Bean
Seattle University

June Johnson
Seattle University

Longman

Boston   Columbus   Indianapolis   New York   San Francisco   Upper Saddle River
Amsterdam   Cape Town   Dubai   London   Madrid   Milan   Munich   Paris   Montréal   Toronto
Delhi   Mexico City   São Paulo   Sydney   Hong Kong   Seoul   Singapore   Taipei   Tokyo

Senior Acquisitions Editor: Lauren A. Finn
Senior Development Editor: Marion B. Castellucci
Senior Marketing Manager: Sandra McGuire
Senior Supplements Editor: Donna Campion
Senior Media Producer: Stefanie Liebman
Production Manager: Savoula Amanatidis
Project Coordination, Interior Design, and Electronic
    Page Makeup: Integra
Cover Designer/Manager: Wendy Ann Fredericks
Cover Art: Copyright © Fotalia.com
Photo Researcher: Rebecca Karamehmedovic
Senior Manufacturing Buyer: Roy L. Pickering, Jr.
Printer and Binder: R. R. Donnelley and Sons Company–Crawfordsville
Cover Printer: Lehigh-Phoenix Color Corporation–Hagerstown

For permission to use copyrighted material, grateful acknowledgment is made to the copyright holders on pp. 376–377, which are hereby made part of this copyright page.

Library of Congress Cataloging-in-Publication Data
Ramage, John D.
  The Allyn & Bacon guide to writing/John D. Ramage, John C. Bean, June Johnson.—6th ed.,
  concise ed.
    p. cm.
  ISBN-13: 978-0-205-82314-7 (concise ed. : alk. paper)
  ISBN-10: 0-205-82314-9 (concise ed. : alk. paper)
  1. English language—Rhetoric—Handbooks, manuals, etc.   2. English language—Grammar—
Handbooks, manuals, etc.   3. Report writing—Handbooks, manuals, etc.   4. College readers.
I. Bean, John C.   II. Johnson, June, 1953–   III. Title.   IV. Title: Allyn and Bacon guide to writing.
  PE1408.R18 2010b
  808'.042—dc22

                                                                                    2010050035

    3 4 5 6 7 8 9 10—DOC—14 13 12 11

Longman
is an imprint of

Complete Edition
ISBN-13: 978-0-205-72148-1; ISBN-10: 0-205-72148-6
Brief Edition
ISBN-13: 978-0-205-82315-4; ISBN-10: 0-205-82315-7
Concise Edition
ISBN-13: 978-0-205-82314-7; ISBN-10: 0-205-82314-9

www.pearsonhighered.com

BRIEF CONTENTS

PART 1   A RHETORIC FOR WRITERS

PART 2   WRITING PROJECTS

PART 3   A GUIDE TO COMPOSING AND REVISING

PART 4   A RHETORICAL GUIDE TO RESEARCH

DETAILED CONTENTS

PART 1   A RHETORIC FOR WRITERS

PART 2 WRITING PROJECTS

WRITING TO LEARN

PART 3   A GUIDE TO COMPOSING
AND REVISING

PART 4   A RHETORICAL GUIDE TO RESEARCH

WRITING PROJECTS

THEMATIC CONTENTS

The Allyn & Bacon Guide to Writing contains 22 readings—9 by professional writers and 13 by students. In addition, the text has more than 50 visual texts (such as advertisements, news photographs, posters, and Web sites) that can lead to productive thematic discussions. These readings and visual texts can be clustered thematically in the following ways.

IMMIGRATION

EMPLOYMENT AND OUTSOURCING

VIOLENCE, PUBLIC SAFETY, AND INDIVIDUAL RIGHTS

OTHER PUBLIC POLICY ISSUES

PREFACE

Through five editions of *The Allyn & Bacon Guide to Writing*, users and reviewers have praised the book's ability to explain rhetorical concepts clearly, engage students in critical thinking, and teach reading and composing strategies that lead to thoughtful, interesting, and meaningful student work. In regular, brief, and concise editions, the text has been adopted at a wide range of two- and four-year institutions, where instructors admire its appeal to students, its focus on problem posing, its distinctive emphasis on writing and reading as rhetorical acts, its engaging classroom activities, and its effective writing assignments. Its flexibility enables composition teachers to capitalize on their own strengths and interests to create intellectually stimulating and pedagogically effective courses.

What's New in the Concise Sixth Edition?

While retaining the signature strengths of earlier editions, the sixth edition features the following key changes and improvements:

- **Expanded coverage of integrating researched sources effectively and ethically** includes new instruction, visual presentations, and examples to help students improve skills fundamental to college readiness and success throughout their academic careers (Chapters 13 and 14).

- **A new chapter on proposals** helps students write practical and policy proposals and prepare a proposal speech with visual aids (Chapter 10).

- **A thoroughly revised chapter on image analysis** helps students work effectively with a wide variety of the visual texts they will encounter in other course areas and outside of college (Chapter 8).

- **Four new student models and one new professional text** offer engaging and contemporary topics for discussion, written response, and exploratory research—including banning laptops and cell phones from classes, sustainable environmental practices, and the growing gap between the rich and the poor.

- **MLA and APA coverage is expanded and thoroughly updated** according to the most recent citation guidelines from each organization, ensuring that students are learning up-to-date formats and styles (Chapter 14).

- **New visual pedagogy presents complex topics clearly** and at-a-glance to better suit today's learners and includes new Strategies Charts and new color-coded examples and explanations of incorporating sources using summary, paraphrase, and quotation (Chapters 13 and 14).

- **A new section on presenting data visually** to reach different kinds of readers helps students create effective tables, graphs, and charts to support their arguments (Chapter 12).

- **New instruction helps writers think rhetorically about introductions** (Chapter 2, Concept 6).

- **Chapters 3 and 4 have been extensively revised** to include the previous edition's Chapter 5 and to consolidate the presentation of angle of vision, the ladder of abstraction, and the value of sensory detail.

- **A revised Concept 2 helps writers develop meaningful thesis statements** by showing them how to start by investigating problems rather than topics (Chapter 1).

Distinctive Approach of *The Allyn & Bacon Guide to Writing*

The improvements in the sixth edition enhance the enduring strengths of *The Allyn & Bacon Guide to Writing* that have made this text pedagogically effective for students and intellectually satisfying for instructors. What follows are the distinctive elements of our approach to teaching composition:

- **Integration of rhetorical theory with composition research.** The authors of this text are scholars in rhetoric, composition studies, writing across the curriculum, critical thinking, global cultural studies, and active learning pedagogy. Together, they bring to *The Allyn & Bacon Guide to Writing* a distinctive pedagogical approach that integrates rhetorical theory with composition research by treating writing and reading as rhetorical acts and as processes of inquiry, problem posing, and critical thinking. The text helps students learn important skills that transfer across disciplines and professional fields.

- **Classroom-tested assignments that guide students through all phases of the reading and writing processes and make frequent use of collaboration and peer review.** The Writing Projects promote intellectual growth and stimulate the kind of critical thinking valued in college courses. Numerous "For Writing and Discussion" exercises make it easy to incorporate active learning into a course while deepening students' understanding of concepts. The text's focus on the subject-matter question that precedes the thesis helps students see academic disciplines as fields of inquiry rather than as data banks of right answers.

- **Coverage of a wide range of genres and aims including academic, civic, and professional genres as well as personal and narrative forms.** By placing nonfiction writing on a continuum from closed-form prose (thesis-based) to open-form prose (narrative-based), the text presents students with a wide range of genres and aims, and clearly explains the rhetorical function and stylistic features of different genres. The text focuses on closed-form writing for entering most academic, civic, and professional conversations.

- **Instructional emphases meet the Council of Writing Program Administrators (WPA) guidelines** for outcome goals in first-year composition courses. The correlation of the WPA Outcomes Statement with the sixth edition of *The Allyn & Bacon Guide to Writing* appears on the front endpapers and in the *Instructor's Resource Manual*. In addition to helping instructors plan their courses, these correlations help with program-wide internal and external assessments.

- **Great flexibility for instructors.** Because the chapters on rhetoric, on Writing Projects, and on composing and research strategies have been designed with self-contained modules, users praise the ease with which they can select chapters and sections and order them to fit the goals of their own courses.

- **Use of reader-expectation theory to explain how closed-form prose achieves maximum clarity.** The skills explained in Chapter 12 on composing and revising closed-form prose (such as the reader's need for understanding the problem before encountering the thesis, for forecasting and signposts, for points before particulars, and for old information before new information) are taught as self-contained Skill Lessons that can be easily integrated into a variety of course structures. These explanations show students why certain principles of closed-form prose (such as unified and coherent paragraphs with topic sentences) derive from the psychology of cognition rather than from the rule-making penchant of English teachers.

- **Emphasis on teaching students to read rhetorically.** An often-noted strength of *The Allyn & Bacon Guide to Writing* is its method for teaching students to read rhetorically so that they can summarize complex readings and speak back to them armed with their own powers of analysis and critical thinking. This skill is crucial for undergraduate research in any discipline. In its focus on rhetorical reading, the text teaches students to understand the differences between print and cyberspace sources; to analyze the rhetorical occasion, genre, context, intended audience, and angle of vision of sources; to evaluate sources according to appropriate criteria; and to negotiate the World Wide Web with confidence.

- **A sequenced skill-based approach to research** teaches students expert strategies for conducting academic research in a rhetorical environment.

- **Coverage of visual rhetoric and document design** focuses on Web sites, advertisements, posters, and other texts where words and images work together for rhetorical effect.

- **A friendly, encouraging tone** respects students and treats them as serious learners.

Key Features of *The Allyn & Bacon Guide to Writing*

- **An organization that emphasizes concepts and skills and promotes active learning.** The modular organization offers instructors great flexibility in designing courses and allows students to quickly navigate the text.

- **Twelve rhetorical "Concepts" in Part 1** provide students with memorable takeaway ideas that enable them to situate verbal and visual texts in a rhetorical context and to think critically about how any text tries to persuade its audience.

- **Writing Projects in Part 2,** arranged according to rhetorical aim, teach students the features of a genre while promoting new ways of seeing and thinking. The exploratory exercises for each Writing Project help students develop their skills at posing problems, generating ideas, delaying closure, valuing alternative points of view, and thinking dialectically.

- **Numbered "Skills" in Parts 3 and 4,** designed as modular mini-lessons, teach the compositional and research skills that can be applied to any writing project.

- **Professional and student readings on current and enduring questions** that illustrate rhetorical principles, invite thematic grouping, and provide models for students' own writing.

- **"For Writing and Discussion" exercises,** which appear regularly throughout the text, provide class-tested critical thinking activities that promote conceptual learning or active exploration of ideas.

- **Strategies charts** present suggestions for approaching reading, writing, and research tasks in a handy format for student reference and use.

- **Framework charts for genres and writing assignments** help students understand the structural features of different genres, and serve as flowcharts that promote both idea generation and more purposeful structure.

- **Peer review guidelines for major assignments** help students conduct effective peer reviews of each other's drafts.

Strategies for Using *The Allyn & Bacon Guide to Writing*

The text's organization makes it easy to design a new syllabus or adapt the text to your current syllabus. Although there are many ways to use *The Allyn & Bacon Guide to Writing*, the most typical course design has students reading and discussing selected concepts from Chapters 1–4 (Part 1) during the opening weeks. The brief, informal write-to-learn projects in these chapters can be used either for homework assignments or for in-class discussion. In the rest of the course, instructors typically assign Writing Projects chapters from the array of options available in Part 2. While students are engaged with the Writing Projects in these chapters, instructors can work in mini-lessons on the writing and research "skills" in Parts 3 and 4. Typically during class sessions, instructors move back and forth between classroom exercises related directly to the current Writing Project (invention exercises, group brainstorming, peer review workshops) and discussions focused on instructional matter from the rest of the text. (For more specific suggestions on how to select and sequence materials, see the sample syllabi in the *Instructor's Resource Manual*.)

Supplements for *The Allyn & Bacon Guide to Writing*

The Instructor's Resource Manual, **Sixth Edition,** has been revised by Susan-marie Harrington of the University of Vermont. The *Instructor's Resource Manual* integrates emphases for meeting the Council of Writing Program Administrators' guidelines for outcome goals in first-year composition courses. It continues to offer detailed teaching suggestions to help both experienced and new instructors; practical teaching strategies for composition instructors in a question-and-answer format; suggested syllabi for courses of various lengths and emphases; chapter-by-chapter teaching suggestions; answers to Handbook exercises; suggestions for using the text with nonnative speakers; suggestions for using the text in an electronic classroom; transparency masters for class use; and annotated bibliographies.

 **MyCompLab.** The only online application that integrates a writing environment with proven resources for grammar, writing, and research, MyCompLab gives students help at their fingertips as they draft and revise. Instructors have access to a variety of assessment tools including commenting capabilities, diagnostics and study plans, and an e-portfolio. Created after years of extensive research and in partnership with faculty and students across the country, MyCompLab offers a seamless and flexible teaching and learning environment built specifically for writers.

CourseSmart. Students can subscribe to *The Allyn & Bacon Guide to Writing,* Sixth Edition, as a CourseSmart eText (at CourseSmart.com). The site includes all of the book's content in a format that enables students to search the text, bookmark passages, save their own notes, and print reading assignments that incorporate lecture notes.

Acknowledgments

We wish to give special thanks to the following composition scholars and teachers, who reviewed the fifth-edition text or the manuscript for the sixth edition, helping us understand how they use *The Allyn & Bacon Guide to Writing* in the classroom and offering valuable suggestions for improving the text: Ann Marie Ade, Embry-Riddle Aeronautical University; Terri A. Amlong, De Sales University; Larry Beason, University of Southern Alabama; Lisa Beckelhimer, University of Cincinnati; Linda Bingham, Hawkeye Community College; Rita M. Brown, Sanford-Brown College, Collinsville; Lizbeth A. Bryant, Purdue University Calumet; Allison Carr, University of Cincinnati; Laura Carroll, Abilene Christian University; Virginia Chappell, Marquette University; Jim Dervin, Winstson-Salem State University; Robert Grindy, Richland Community College; Kimberly Harrison, Florida International University; Jen Hazel, Owens Community College; Melissa Ianetta, University of Delaware; Gilda Kelsey, University of Delaware; Lindsay Lewan, Arapahoe Community College; Theresa P. Maue, Embry-Riddle Aeronautical University; Amanda McGuire Rzicznek, Bowling Green State University; MaryGrace N. Paden, John Tyler Community College; Deirdre Pettipiece, University of the Sciences in Philadelphia; Jeanne Purtell, Harrisburg Area Community College, York; Jamey Trotter, Arapahoe

Community College; Scott Warnock, Drexel University; and Derand Wright, Southern Illinois University Carbondale.

Thank you also to the students who reviewed *The Allyn & Bacon Guide to Writing,* telling us about their experiences using the fifth edition: Joseph Derosier, Embry-Riddle Aeronautical University; Roxanne Malick, Harrisburg Area Community College; Lindsey Shiflett, Richland Community College; Chelsea Stevenson, Richland Community College; and Heidi Thomas, Harrisburg Area Community College.

Our deepest thanks and appreciation go to our editor, Lauren Finn, whose comprehensive view of the field, keen insights, and excellent people and communication skills make her a pleasure to work with. We are also particularly grateful to our development editor, Marion Castellucci, who has worked with us through multiple revisions and has become an invaluable part of our team. Her insight, sense of humor, professional experience, and extensive editorial knowledge have once again kept us on track and made the intense work of this revision possible.

We owe special thanks to three people whose expertise inform our new approaches to image analysis in Chapter 8: to Naomi Hume for her experience in teaching the analysis of paintings; to Claire Garoutte for her work on documentary photography; and to Kristopher Johnson for his insights from the fields of advertising and marketing.

We would also like to thank three Seattle University students who provided special research assistance for this edition as well as their perspective on important issues: Jon Carr, Kyle Madsen, and Lydia Wheeler. We'd also like to thank Stephen and Sarah Bean for their research help. Most of all, we are indebted to all our students, who have made the teaching of composition such a joy. We thank them for their insights and for their willingness to engage with problems, discuss ideas, and, as they compose and revise, share with us their frustrations and their triumphs. They have sustained our love of teaching and inspired us to write this book.

Finally, John Bean thanks his wife, Kit, also a professional composition teacher, whose dedication to her students as writers and individuals manifests the sustaining values of our unique profession. John also thanks his children, Matthew, Andrew, Stephen, and Sarah, who have grown to adulthood since he began writing textbooks. June Johnson thanks her husband, Kenneth Bube, for his loving support, his interest in teaching, and his expert understanding of the importance of writing in mathematics and the sciences. Finally, she thanks her daughter, Jane Ellen, who has offered encouragement and support in countless ways.

JOHN D. RAMAGE
JOHN C. BEAN
JUNE JOHNSON

THE
ALLYN & BACON
GUIDE TO WRITING

Concise Edition

PART 1

A RHETORIC FOR WRITERS

As the search for clean, renewable energy to relieve the pressure on oil gains momentum, photographs of wind turbines are appearing more frequently in magazines and newspapers. However, because this source of energy is controversial, *how* these massive technological windmills are depicted varies widely. Do they blend into the landscape or mar it with their industrial presence? Photographers and writers, conscious of the rhetorical effect of photos, carefully plan the impression they want photos of wind power to convey. This low-angle shot of wind turbines, emphasizing their size and power and hinting at barren hills in the background, participates in this public controversy.

This photograph is part of a discussion in Chapter 3, page 59, on the way that visuals make appeals to *logos*, *ethos*, and *pathos*.

1

THINKING RHETORICALLY ABOUT GOOD WRITING

It seems to me, then, that the way to help people become better writers is not to tell them that they must first learn the rules of grammar, that they must develop a four-part outline, that they must consult the experts and collect all the useful information. These things may have their place. But none of them is as crucial as having a good, interesting question.

—Rodney Kilcup, Historian

When new students ask us about the rules for good college writing, they are often surprised by history professor Rodney Kilcup's unexpected advice in the epigraph above. To become a better writer, says Kilcup, the most crucial thing is to have "a good, interesting question." We love Professor Kilcup's advice because we'd like you to think of good writers as critical thinkers who pose questions and problems.

As we show throughout this text, writing is closely allied to critical thinking and to the innate satisfaction you take in exercising your curiosity, creativity, and problem-solving ability. Writing helps you discover and express ideas that you would otherwise never think or say. Unlike speaking, writing gives you time to think deeply and long about an idea. Because you can revise writing, it lets you pursue a problem in stages, with each draft reflecting a deeper, clearer, or more complex level of thought. Moreover, the skills you learn in a writing course are transferable to all majors and to your professional careers. Research has shown that managers, accountants, lawyers, engineers, and other professionals spend, on average, forty-four percent of their professional time writing. In sum, writing has lifelong importance: It stimulates, challenges, and stretches your mental powers while giving you a voice in important academic, civic, and professional conversations.

In this chapter, you will learn three important concepts about writing:

- **CONCEPT 1** Good writing can vary from closed to open forms.
- **CONCEPT 2** Good writers address problems rather than topics.
- **CONCEPT 3** Good writers think rhetorically about purpose, audience, and genre.

CONCEPT I **Good writing can vary from closed to open forms.**

In our experience, beginning college writers are often discomforted by the ambiguity of the rules governing writing. They often wish for some consistent rules: "Never use 'I' in a formal paper" or "Start every paragraph with a topic sentence." The problem is that different kinds of writing have different criteria for effectiveness, leaving the writer with rhetorical choices rather than with hard-and-fast formulas for success. You'll be able to appreciate this insight for yourself through the following exercise.

Read the following short pieces of nonfiction prose. The first is a letter to the editor written by a professional civil engineer in response to a newspaper editorial arguing for the development of wind-generated electricity. The second short piece is entitled "A Festival of Rain." It was written by the American poet and religious writer Thomas Merton, a Trappist monk. After reading the two samples carefully, proceed to the discussion questions that follow.

David Rockwood
A Letter to the Editor

1   Your editorial on November 16, "Get Bullish on Wind Power," is based on fantasy rather than fact. There are several basic reasons why wind-generated power can in no way serve as a reasonable major alternative to other electrical energy supply alternatives for the Pacific Northwest power system.

2   First and foremost, wind power is unreliable. Electric power generation is evaluated not only on the amount of energy provided, but also on its ability to meet system peak load requirements on an hourly, daily, and weekly basis. In other words, an effective power system would have to provide enough electricity to meet peak demands in a situation when the wind energy would be unavailable—either in no wind situations or in severe blizzard conditions, which would shut down the wind generators. Because wind power cannot be relied on at times of peak needs, it would have to be backed up by other power generation resources at great expense and duplication of facilities.

3   Secondly, there are major unsolved problems involved in the design of wind generation facilities, particularly for those located in rugged mountain areas. Ice storms, in particular, can cause sudden dynamic problems for the rotating blades and mechanisms which could well result in breakdown or failure of the generators. Furthermore, the design of the facilities to meet the stresses imposed by high winds in these remote mountain regions, in the order of 125 miles per hour, would indeed escalate the costs.

4   Thirdly, the environmental impact of constructing wind generation facilities amounting to 28 percent of the region's electrical supply system (as proposed in your editorial) would be tremendous. The Northwest Electrical Power system presently has

(continued)

a capacity of about 37,000 megawatts of hydro power and 10,300 megawatts of thermal, for a total of about 48,000 megawatts. Meeting 28 percent of this capacity by wind power generators would, most optimistically, require about 13,400 wind towers, each with about 1,000 kilowatt (one megawatt) generating capacity. These towers, some 100 to 200 feet high, would have to be located in the mountains of Oregon and Washington. These would encompass hundreds of square miles of pristine mountain area, which, together with interconnecting transmission facilities, control works, and roads, would indeed have major adverse environmental impacts on the region.

5   There are many other lesser problems of control and maintenance of such a system. Let it be said that, from my experience and knowledge as a professional engineer, the use of wind power as a major resource in the Pacific Northwest power system is strictly a pipe dream.

Thomas Merton
A Festival of Rain

1   Let me say this before rain becomes a utility that they can plan and distribute for money. By "they" I mean the people who cannot understand that rain is a festival, who do not appreciate its gratuity, who think that what has no price has no value, that what cannot be sold is not real, so that the only way to make something *actual* is to place it on the market. The time will come when they will sell you even your rain. At the moment it is still free, and I am in it. I celebrate its gratuity and its meaninglessness.

2   The rain I am in is not like the rain of cities. It fills the woods with an immense and confused sound. It covers the flat roof of the cabin and its porch with insistent and controlled rhythms. And I listen, because it reminds me again and again that the whole world runs by rhythms I have not yet learned to recognize, rhythms that are not those of the engineer.

3   I came up here from the monastery last night, sloshing through the corn fields, said Vespers, and put some oatmeal on the Coleman stove for supper. ... The night became very dark. The rain surrounded the whole cabin with its enormous virginal myth, a whole world of meaning, of secrecy, of silence, of rumor. Think of it: all that speech pouring down, selling nothing, judging nobody, drenching the thick mulch of dead leaves, soaking the trees, filling the gullies and crannies of the wood with water, washing out the places where men have stripped the hillside! What a thing it is to sit absolutely alone, in a forest, at night, cherished by this wonderful, unintelligible, perfectly innocent speech, the most comforting speech in the world, the talk that rain makes by itself all over the ridges, and the talk of the watercourses everywhere in the hollows!

4   Nobody started it, nobody is going to stop it. It will talk as long as it wants, this rain. As long as it talks I am going to listen.

5   But I am also going to sleep, because here in this wilderness I have learned how to sleep again. Here I am not alien. The trees I know, the night I know, the rain I know. I close my eyes and instantly sink into the whole rainy world of which I am a part, and the world goes on with me in it, for I am not alien to it.

Comparing Rockwood's and Merton's Writing

Working in small groups or as a whole class, try to reach consensus on the following specific tasks:

1. What are the main differences between the two types of writing? If you are working in groups, help your recorder prepare a presentation describing the differences between Rockwood's writing and Merton's writing.
2. Create a metaphor, simile, or analogy that best sums up your feelings about the most important differences between Rockwood's and Merton's writing: "Rockwood's writing is like ..., but Merton's writing is like...."
3. Explain why your metaphors are apt. How do your metaphors help clarify or illuminate the differences between the two pieces of writing?

Now that you have done some thinking on your own about the differences between these two examples, turn to our brief analysis.

Distinctions between Closed and Open Forms of Writing

David Rockwood's letter and Thomas Merton's mini-essay are both examples of nonfiction prose. But as these examples illustrate, nonfiction prose can vary enormously in form and style. From the perspective of structure, we can place nonfiction prose along a continuum that goes from closed to open forms of writing (see Figure 1.1).

Closed-Form Prose   Of our two pieces of prose, Rockwood's letter illustrates tightly closed writing and falls at the far left end of the continuum because it has these elements:

- An explicit thesis in the introduction that informs readers of the point of the whole essay (i.e., wind-generated power isn't a reasonable alternative energy source in the Pacific Northwest)
- Unified and coherent paragraphs (i.e., "First and foremost, wind power is unreliable. ... Secondly, there are major unsolved problems. ... Thirdly, ...")
- Sustained development of that thesis without digressions

Once the thesis is stated, readers know the point of the essay and can predict its structure. (You might note that the five-paragraph essay sometimes taught in high school is a by-the-numbers way to teach closed-form prose.) Because its structure is transparent and predictable, the success of closed-form prose rests entirely on its ideas, which must "surprise" readers by asserting something new, challenging, doubtful, or controversial. It aims to change readers' view of the subject through the power of reason, logic, and evidence. Closed-form prose is what most college professors write in their scholarly research, what they most often expect from their students, and what is most common in professional and business contexts.

FIGURE I.I
A Continuum of
Essay Types:
Closed to Open
Forms

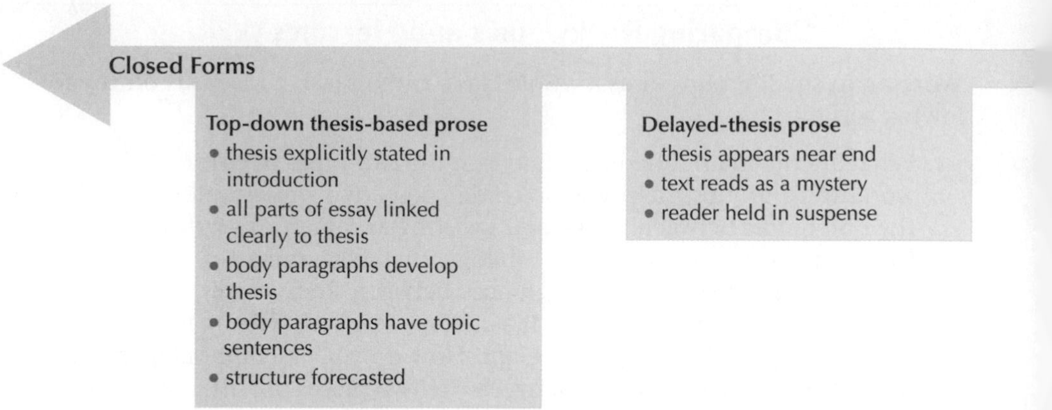

Closed Forms

Top-down thesis-based prose
- thesis explicitly stated in introduction
- all parts of essay linked clearly to thesis
- body paragraphs develop thesis
- body paragraphs have topic sentences
- structure forecasted

Delayed-thesis prose
- thesis appears near end
- text reads as a mystery
- reader held in suspense

Open-Form Prose In contrast, Merton's "A Festival of Rain" falls toward the right end of the closed-to-open continuum because it exhibits these features:

- No reduction to a single, summarizable thesis (Merton clearly opposes the consumer culture that will try to "sell" you the rain, but what exactly does Merton mean by "festival" or by rain's "gratuity and its meaninglessness"?)
- The use of story or narrative as an organizing principle (i.e., the story of Merton's leaving the monastery to sleep in the rain-drenched cabin) through which a point emerges suggestively

Although open-form prose does not announce its thesis and support it with reasons and evidence, it does have a focus. As Merton's piece illustrates, the focus is more like a theme in fiction that readers might discuss and even dispute than like a thesis in argument.

Consider also the extent to which Merton violates the rules for closed-form prose. Instead of using transitions between paragraphs, Merton juxtaposes passages that tell the story of his camping trip ("I came up here from the monastery last night ...") with passages that make cryptic, interpretive comments about his experience ("The rain I am in is not like the rain of cities"). Unlike paragraphs in closed-form prose, which typically begin with topic sentences and are developed with supporting details, the paragraphs in Merton's piece have no clear hierarchical structure; paragraph 4, in fact, is only two lines long. These open-form elements often appear in personal essays, in blogs, in newspaper or magazine feature stories or character profiles, or in professional nonfiction.

Flexibility of "Rules" along the Continuum As you can see from the continuum in Figure 1.1, essays can fall anywhere along the scale. Not all thesis-with-support writing has to be top down, stating its thesis explicitly in the introduction. In some cases writers choose to delay the thesis, creating a more exploratory, open-ended, "let's think through this together" feeling before finally stating the main point late in the essay. In some cases writers explore a problem without *ever* finding a satisfactory thesis, creating an essay that is thesis seeking rather than thesis supporting, an essay aimed at deepening the question, refusing to accept an easy

Open Forms

Thesis-seeking prose
- essay organized around a question rather than a thesis
- essay explores the problem or question, looking at it in many ways
- writer may or may not arrive at thesis

Theme-based narrative
- often organized chronologically or has storylike elements
- often used to heighten or deepen a problem, or show its human significance
- often has an implicit theme rather than a thesis
- often violates rules of closed-form prose by using literary techniques

answer. Such essays may replicate their authors' process of exploring a problem and include digressions, speculations, conjectures, multiple perspectives, and occasional invitations to the reader to help solve the problem. When writers reach the far right-hand position on the continuum, they no longer state an explicit thesis. Instead, like novelists or short story writers, they embed their points in plot, imagery, dialogue, and so forth, leaving their readers to *infer* a theme from the text. This kind of writing is often called "literary nonfiction."

Where to Place Your Writing along the Continuum

Clearly, essays at opposite ends of this continuum operate in different ways and obey different rules. Because each position on the continuum has its appropriate uses, the writer's challenge is to determine which sort of writing is most appropriate in a given situation. Most college papers (but not all) and much professional writing are written in closed form. Thus if you were writing a business proposal, a legal brief, or an academic paper for a scholarly audience, you would typically choose a closed-form structure, and your finished product would include elements such as the following:

- An explicit thesis in the introduction
- Forecasting of structure
- Cohesive and unified paragraphs with topic sentences
- Clear transitions between sentences and between parts
- No digressions

But if you were writing to express your conflicted relationship with, say, a parent or friend or to reflect on your first discovery of racism or homophobia, you would probably move toward the open end of the continuum and violate one or more of these conventions. Instead of a thesis-support structure, you might use the power of compelling stories, vivid characterization, dialogue, and evocative language to convey your ideas.

If we return now to the question about good writing posed at the beginning of this chapter, we can see that having a thesis statement, topic sentences, good transitions, and unified and coherent paragraphs are not qualities of "good prose" but simply of "closed-form prose." What makes a piece of closed-form prose "good," as we will see in the next section, is the extent to which it addresses a problem or question that matters to the reader and brings to the reader something new, surprising, or provocative. In contrast, we have seen that open-form prose can be "good" without having a thesis-driven, hierarchical structure. Open-form prose conveys its pleasures and insights through narrative strategies rather than through thesis-with-support strategies.

FOR WRITING AND DISCUSSION

Thinking Personally about Closed and Open Forms

Do you and your classmates most enjoy writing prose at the closed or at the more open end of the continuum?

Individual task: Recall a favorite piece of writing that you have done in the past. Jot down a brief description of the kind of writing this was (a poem, a personal-experience essay, a piece of workplace writing, a research paper, a newspaper story, a persuasive argument). Where would you place this piece of writing on the closed-to-open continuum? Explore why you like this piece of writing. Are you at your best in closed-form writing that calls for an explicit thesis statement and logical support? Or are you at your best in more open and personal forms?

Small-group or whole-class task: Share the results of the individual tasks. Is there a wide range of preferences in your class? If so, how do you account for this variance? If not, how do you account for the narrow range?

CONCEPT 2 **Good writers address problems rather than topics.**

In the previous section, we explained how the rules for good writing vary along a continuum from closed to open forms. In this section, we return to the close connection between writing and critical thinking. From your previous schooling, you are probably familiar with the term **thesis statement**, which is the main point a writer wants to make in an essay. However, you may not have thought much about the *question* that lies behind the thesis, which is the problem or issue that the writer is wrestling with. Behind every thesis statement is an explicit or implied **thesis question**, which is the problem or issue to which the thesis responds. An essay's thesis statement is actually the writer's proposed answer to this question, and it is this question that has propelled the writer's thinking.

Thus, the problem that matters to engineer David Rockwood is whether wind power can be a viable alternative energy source. Rockwood writes to make his answer ("No!") persuasive to readers. Thomas Merton's question is more complex and subtle, one that leads him to use open-form narrative strategies. His question seems to be: What is the effect of a consumer economy on our understanding of meaning and value? He wants to raise readers' awareness of a problem with corporate capitalism (where corporations want to sell you even the rain), which alienates us from nature and from our deepest selves.

This focus on a writer's motivating problem or question differs somewhat from the common view that writers first choose a topic and then narrow it down. Of course, writers have broad areas of interest (which we might call topics), but what they are seeking isn't the topic itself but a cluster of problems or questions within the topic. Instead of "narrowing a topic," they seek a problem that grips their curiosity and gets them thinking.

Shared Problems Unite Writers and Readers

For college professors, "a good, interesting question" is at the heart of good writing. Professors want students to become gripped by problems because they themselves are gripped by problems. For example, at a workshop for new faculty members, we asked participants to write a brief description of the question or problem that motivated their Ph.D. dissertation or a recent conference paper or article. Here is how a biochemistry professor responded:

> During periods of starvation, the human body makes physiological adaptations to preserve essential protein mass. Unfortunately, these adaptations don't work well during long-term starvation. After the body depletes its carbohydrate storage, it must shift to depleting protein in order to produce glucose. Eventually, this loss of functional protein leads to metabolic dysfunction and death. Interestingly, several animal species are capable of surviving for extensive periods without food and water while conserving protein and maintaining glucose levels. How do the bodies of these animals accomplish this feat? I wanted to investigate the metabolic functioning of these animals, which might lead to insights into the human situation.

As you progress through your college career, you will find yourself increasingly engaged with the kinds of questions that motivate your professors. All around college campuses you'll find clusters of professors and students asking questions about all manner of problems ranging from puzzles in the reproductive cycles of worms and bugs to the use of nanotechnology to fight global warming, from the changing portrayal of race and gender in American films to the impact of digital technology on the dissemination of news. At the heart of all these communities of writers and readers is an interest in common questions and the hope for better or different answers. Writers write because they have something new or surprising or challenging to say in response to a question. Readers read because they share the writer's interest in the problem and want to deepen their understanding.

Where Do Problems Come From?

So where do these problems come from? How does a writer get hooked on a problem? Although this question is complex at a philosophical level, we can offer two relatively simple and helpful answers: Sometimes you encounter a problem that is already "out there" in a conversation already in progress in some human community. Some enduring problems have been sparking conversations that have lasted for thousands of years: Do humans have free will? What constitutes ethical action? What is the origin of the universe? Why do good people have to suffer? Thousands of less sweeping problems are being discussed by human communities all the time. In many of your college courses, you'll be introduced to long-standing problems that you hadn't encountered before and that may hook you and draw you into their spell. In these cases, a problem that is already "out there" initiates your search for a possible answer and invites you to join the conversation.

But sometimes you actually find, pose, or articulate a problem yourself, fresh from your own brain. In this case you start a conversation, rather than join an existing one. (It may turn out later that other people have asked the same question, but you didn't know that at the time.) For example, you find your own problem whenever you see something puzzling in the natural world, note curious or unexplained features in a cultural phenomenon or artifact, or discover conflicts or contradictions within your own way of looking at the world.

In the table below we describe some of the ways that writers can become gripped by a problem that may lead to engaged writing.

TABLE 1.1   How Writers Become Gripped by a Problem

Occasion That Leads to Problem	Your Interior Mental State	Example
	The problem is already "out there." *(You enter a conversation already in progress)*	
You encounter others arguing about a problem, and you don't know where you stand.	• You are equally persuaded by different views or dissatisfied with all the views • Part of you thinks X but another part thinks Y (you feel divided)	I don't know where I stand on the question of whether health care should be rationed. In *To Kill a Mockingbird*, I can't decide whether Atticus Finch is a good father.
You aren't satisfied with a common view of something or you disagree with someone on an issue.	• Your skepticism or intuition pushes against some popular view • You are committed to a view different from someone else's • *Note: You must go beyond simply having an opinion. You aren't gripped by a problem until you have seen the possible strengths of other views and the possible weaknesses of your own.*	My teacher's explanation of the causes for anorexia doesn't seem quite right to me. Shanita says that we should build more nuclear power plants to combat global warming, but I say nuclear power is too dangerous.
Someone gives you a question that you can't yet answer.	• You feel overwhelmed with unknowns • You feel that you can't begin to answer until you do more exploration and research • If you know enough to start proposing hypotheses, you aren't satisfied with any of your approaches	Your boss asks you whether the company should enact the proposed marketing plan. Your history professor asks you, "To what extent does Frederick Jackson Turner's frontier hypothesis reflect a Euro-centric world view?"

TABLE 1.1 *continued*		
Occasion That Leads to Problem	**Your Interior Mental State**	**Example**
	You pose the problem yourself. *(You initiate the conversation)*	
You see something puzzling in a natural or cultural phenomenon.	• Something deviates from what you would expect or is otherwise unexplainable • You begin testing possible solutions or answers. (Often you want to talk to someone—to start a conversation about the problem)	Why is this fungus appearing on some of these tomatoes but not on the others? Why is Twitter more popular among middle-aged adults than teenagers?
You see something unexpected, puzzling, or unexplained in a poem, painting, or other human artifact.	• You can't see why the artist/maker did something in such a way • You wonder why this particular artifact is different from other artifacts that you thought would be similar	Why does Merton call rain "meaningless"? If Hamlet really loves Ophelia, then why does he treat her like a whore in the nunnery scene?
You articulate something inconsistent or contradictory in your own view of the world.	• You feel unsettled by your own inconsistent views or values • You probe more deeply into your own identity and place in the world	I agree with Merton's argument against consumerism, but I really want a large plasma TV. Is consumerism really bad? Am I a materialist?

In each of these cases, the problem starts to spark critical thinking. As we'll explain in more detail in Chapter 2, you are starting to "wallow in complexity."

FOR WRITING AND DISCUSSION

Finding a Problem

This classroom exercise, based on the image in Figure 1.2, will give you the experience of posing a problem for yourself and then participating in a conversation initiated by shared questions from the class. It is designed to help you think about your own thinking as you ask questions and formulate problems that you might want to explore. Figure 1.2 is a photograph of a sculpture, called *The Foundling*, by Australian artist Patricia Piccinini. (The photograph is taken in an art museum; note the spectator walking by in the background.) The sculpture, which is made of silicone, fiberglass, human hair, leather, plywood, and clothing, is part of a larger Piccinini exhibit of similar life-size figures. Imagine that you came across this sculpture while visiting a museum. Consider the sculpture's title as well as its appearance and its effect on viewers.

Individual task: Working individually, spend several minutes writing down one or more thought-provoking questions that emerge from your looking

(continued)

FIGURE 1.2 The Foundling

at the photo of the front view of this sculpture. By "thought-provoking," we mean questions that don't have simple "right answers" but that invite "possible answers" supported by different lines of reasoning, speculation, and argument.

Task for group or whole class discussion: Working in small groups or as a whole class, share your individual questions. Then speculate about possible answers to several of them. The best questions will lead to alternative responses—the feeling of a genuine conversation with different points of view. Each individual should now write down new questions that emerge from the conversation.

Individual reflection: To what extent did the activities provoked by this exercise help you think about where questions come from? How did the questions that you initially posed for yourself evolve as you participated in a conversation about the sculpture? Identify one question that now particularly intrigues you and explain why you find it a good question. (If you would like to find out more about Patricia Piccinini, a quick Web search will yield many results, including statements of her philosophy of art and photographs of her other works.)

CONCEPT 3 Good writers think rhetorically about purpose, audience, and genre.

So far, we have used the term "rhetoric"—as in "A Rhetoric for Writers" (the title of Part 1 of this text) or "thinking rhetorically"—without defining it. Now is the time for us to explain what we mean by *rhetoric*.

What Is Rhetoric?

At the broadest level, **rhetoric** is the study of how human beings use language and other symbols to influence the attitudes, beliefs, and actions of others. One prominent twentieth-century rhetorician, Kenneth Burke, calls rhetoric "a symbolic means of inducing cooperation in beings that by nature respond to symbols." To understand what Burke means by "symbols," consider the difference in flirting behavior between peacocks and humans. When male peacocks flirt, they spread their fantastic tail feathers, do mating dances, and screech weirdly to attract females, but the whole process is governed by instinct. Peacocks don't have to choose among different symbolic actions such as buying an Armani tail versus buying a knockoff from Wal-Mart or driving to the mating grounds in the right car. Unlike a peacock, however, a flirting human must make symbolic choices, all of which have meaning. Consider the different flirting messages humans send to each other by their choice of clothes, their method of transportation, their choice of major, their favorite music. Even word choices (for example, academic jargon words versus street slang) or texting behavior give further hints of a person's identity, values, and social groups. Rhetoricians study, among other things, how these symbols arise within a given culture and how they influence others.

In a narrower sense, rhetoric is the art of making messages persuasive. Perhaps the most famous definition of rhetoric comes from the Greek philosopher Aristotle, who defined rhetoric as "the ability to see, in any particular case, all the available means of persuasion." An effective speaker's task, in Aristotle's view, is to persuade listeners to accept the speaker's views on a question of action or belief. But to do so, the speaker must first understand all the arguments on all sides of the question ("all the available means of persuasion"). If we imagine the interaction of several speakers, each proposing different answers to a question, and if we imagine all the speakers listening to each other respectfully and open-mindedly, we can see how productive human conversation could emerge. The study of rhetoric can therefore help people write, speak, read, and listen more effectively.

At an operational level, writers can be said to "think rhetorically" whenever they are consciously aware of writing to an audience for a purpose within a genre. (A *genre*, to be explained in more detail shortly, is a recurring type of writing with distinguishing features and conventions such as a letter to the editor, a scholarly article, a business memo, or a blog.) To think rhetorically, writers consider questions like these:

- ***Purpose:*** What am I trying to accomplish in this paper? What do I want my readers to know, believe, see, or do?
- ***Audience:*** Who are my intended readers, and what are their values and assumptions? What do they already know or believe about my subject? How much do they care about it?
- ***Genre:*** What kind of document am I writing? What are its requirements for structure, style, and document design?

Let's look more closely at each of these components of a writer's rhetorical context.

How Writers Think about Purpose

In this section, we want to help you think more productively about your purpose for writing, which can be examined from several different perspectives: your rhetorical aim, the motivating occasion that gets you going, and your desire to change your reader's view. All three perspectives will help you make your awareness of purpose work for you and increase your savvy as a writer. Let's look at each in turn.

Purpose as Rhetorical Aim   One powerful way to think about purpose is through the general concept of "rhetorical aim." In this text, we identify six different rhetorical aims of writing: to express, to explore, to inform, to analyze and synthesize, to persuade, and to reflect. Thinking of each piece of writing in terms of one or more of these rhetorical aims can help you understand typical ways that your essay can be structured and developed and can help you clarify your relationship with your audience. The writing projects in Part 2 of this text are based on these rhetorical aims. Table 1.2 gives you an overview of each of the six rhetorical aims and sketches out

TABLE 1.2   Purpose as Rhetorical Aim

Rhetorical Aim	Focus of Writing	Relationship to Audience	Forms and Genres
Express or share (Chapter 6) May also include an artistic aim (Chapter 18)	Your own life, personal experiences, reflections	You share aspects of your life; you invite readers to walk in your shoes, to experience your insights	**Form:** Has many open-form features **Sample genres:** journal, blog, personal Web site, or online profile; personal essays or literacy narratives, often with artistic features
Explore or inquire (Chapter 7)	A significant subject-matter problem that puzzles you	You take readers on your own intellectual journey by showing your inquiry process (raising questions, seeking evidence, considering alternative views)	**Form:** Follows open form in being narrative based; is thesis seeking rather than thesis supporting **Sample genres:** freewriting; research logs; articles and books focused on process of discovery
Inform or explain (Chapter 8)	Factual knowledge addressing a reader's need or curiosity	You provide knowledge that your readers need or want, or you arouse curiosity and provide new, surprising information. You expect readers to trust your authority	**Form:** Usually has a closed-form structure **Sample genres:** encyclopedia articles; instruction booklets; sales reports; technical reports; informative magazine articles; informative Web sites

TABLE 1.2 *continued*			
Rhetorical Aim	**Focus of Writing**	**Relationship to Audience**	**Forms and Genres**
Analyze, synthesize, or interpret (Chapters 9–12)	Complex subject matter that you can break down into parts and put together in new ways for greater understanding	Using critical thinking and possibly research, you challenge readers with a new way of understanding your subject. Skeptical readers expect you to support your thesis with good particulars.	**Form:** Typically has a closed-form structure **Sample genres:** scholarly articles; experimental reports; many kinds of college research papers; public affairs magazine articles; many kinds of blogs
Persuade (Chapters 13–15)	Subject-matter questions that have multiple controversial answers	You try to convince readers, who may not share your values and beliefs, to accept your stance on an issue by providing good reasons and evidence and attending to alternative views.	**Form:** Usually closed form, but may employ many open-form features for persuasive effect **Sample genres:** letters to the editor; op-ed pieces; advocacy pieces in public affairs magazines; advocacy Web sites; researched academic arguments
Reflect (Chapter 24)	Subject matter closely connected to your interests and experience; often involves self-evaluation of an experience	Writing for yourself as well as for a reader, you seek to find personal meaning and value in an experience or course of study. You assume a sympathetic and interested reader.	**Form:** Anywhere on the closed-to-open-form continuum **Sample genres:** memoirs, workplace self-evaluations; introductory letter for a portfolio; personal essays looking back on an experience

how the subject matter differs from aim to aim, how the writer's task and relationship to readers differ according to aim, and how a chosen aim affects the writing's genre and its position on the spectrum from open to closed forms.

Purpose as a Response to a Motivating Occasion Another important way to think about purpose is to think about each piece of writing as a response to a particular motivating occasion. Almost all writing is compelled by some sort of motivating occasion or exigency.* This exigency can be external (someone giving you a task and setting a deadline) or internal (your awareness of a problem stimulating your desire to bring about some change in people's views). Thus, when engineer David Rockwood read a newspaper editorial supporting wind-power projects, his own belief in the impracticality of wind power motivated him to write a letter to the editor in rebuttal (see pp. 5–6). But he also knew that he had to write the letter

---

*An *exigency* is an urgent or pressing situation requiring immediate attention. Rhetoricians use the term to describe the event or occasion that causes a writer to begin writing.

within one or two days or else it stood no chance of being published. His exigency thus included both internal and external factors.

College students' motivations for writing can be equally mixed: In part, you write to meet an assignment deadline; in part, you write to please the teacher and get a good grade. But ideally you also write because you have become engaged with an intellectual problem and want to say something significant about it. Our point here is that your purposes for writing are always more complex than the simple desire to meet an assignment deadline.

Purpose as a Desire to Change Your Reader's View Perhaps the most useful way to think about purpose is to focus on the change you want to bring about in your audience's view of the subject. When you are given a college writing assignment, this view of purpose engages you directly with the intellectual problem specified in the assignment. This view of purpose will be developed further in Concept 5 when we explain the importance of surprise as a measure of what is new or challenging in your essay. For most essays, you can write a one-sentence, nutshell statement about your purpose.

See Chapter 2, Concept 5, for an explanation of surprise in thesis statements.

> My purpose is to give my readers a vivid picture of my difficult struggle with Graves' disease.
> My purpose is to explain how Thoreau's view of nature differs in important ways from that of contemporary environmentalists.
> My purpose is to persuade the general public that wind-generated electricity is not a practical energy alternative in the Pacific Northwest.

Chapter 12, Skill 12.4, shows you how purpose statements can be included in closed-form introductions.

In closed-form academic articles, technical reports, and other business and professional pieces, writers often place explicit purpose statements in their introductions along with the thesis. In most other forms of writing, the writer uses a behind-the-scenes purpose statement to achieve focus and direction but seldom states the purpose explicitly. Writing an explicit purpose statement for a paper is a powerful way to nutshell the kind of change you want to bring about in your reader's view of the subject.

How Writers Think about Audience

In our discussion of purpose, we have already had a lot to say about audience. What you know about your readers—their familiarity with your subject matter, their reasons for reading, their closeness to you, their values and beliefs—affects most of the choices you make as a writer.

In assessing your audience, you must first determine who that audience is— a single reader (for example, your boss), a select group (a scholarship committee; attendees at an undergraduate research conference), or a general audience. If you imagine a general audience, you will need to make some initial assumptions about their views and values. Doing so creates an "implied audience," giving you a stable rather than a moving target so that you can make decisions about your own essay. Once you have identified your audience, you can use the following strategies for analysis.

To appreciate the importance of audience, consider how a change in audience can affect the content of a piece. Suppose you want voters to approve a bond

Strategies for Analyzing Audience

Questions to Ask about Your Audience	Reasons for Asking the Question
How busy are my readers?	• Helps you decide on length, document design, and open versus closed features • In workplace writing, busy readers often require closed-form prose with headings that allow for skimming
What are my readers' motives for reading?	• If the reader has requested the document, you need only a short introduction • In most cases, your opening must hook your reader's interest
What is my relationship with my readers?	• Helps you decide on a formal or informal style • Helps you select tone—polite and serious or loose and slangy
What do my readers already know about my topic? Do my readers have more or less expertise than I have, or about the same expertise?	• Helps you determine what will be old/familiar information for your audience versus new/unfamiliar information • Helps you decide how much background and context to include • Helps you decide to use or avoid in-group jargon and specialized knowledge
How interested are my readers in my topic? Do my readers already care about it?	• Helps you decide how to write the introduction • Helps you determine how to make the problem you address interesting and significant to your reader
What are my readers' attitudes toward my thesis? Do my readers share my beliefs and values?	• Helps you make numerous decisions about tone, structure, reference to alternative views, and use of evidence • Helps you decide on the voice and persona you want to project

issue to build a new baseball stadium. If most voters are baseball fans, you can appeal to their love of the game, the pleasure of a new facility, and so forth. But non-baseball fans won't be moved by these arguments. To reach them, you must tie the new stadium to their values. You can argue that it will bring new tax revenues, clean up a run-down area, revitalize local businesses, or stimulate tourism. Your purpose remains the same—to persuade taxpayers to fund the stadium—but the content of your argument changes if your audience changes.

In college, you often seem to be writing for an audience of one—your instructor. However, most instructors try to read as a representative of a broader audience. To help college writers imagine these readers, many instructors try to design writing assignments that provide a fuller sense of audience. They may ask you to write for the readers of a particular magazine or journal, or they may create case assignments with built-in audiences (for example, "You are an accountant in the firm of Numbers and Fudge; one day you receive a letter from …"). If your instructor does not specify an audience, you can generally assume the audience to be what we like to call "the generic academic audience"—student peers who have approximately the same level of knowledge and expertise in the field as you do, who are engaged by the question you address, and who want to read your writing and be surprised in some way.

How Writers Think about Genre

The term *genre* refers to categories of writing that follow certain conventions of style, structure, approach to subject matter, and document design. Table 1.3 shows different kinds of genres.

The concept of genre creates strong reader expectations and places specific demands on writers. How you write any given letter, report, or article is influenced by the structure and style of hundreds of previous letters, reports, or articles written in the same genre. If you wanted to write for *Reader's Digest*, for example, you would have to use the conventions that appeal to its older, conservative readers: simple language, subjects with strong human interest, heavy reliance on anecdotal evidence in arguments, an upbeat and optimistic perspective, and an approach that reinforces the conservative *ethos* of individualism, self-discipline, and family. If you wanted to write for *Seventeen* or *Rolling Stone*, however, you would need to use quite different conventions.

TABLE 1.3   Examples of Genres

Personal Writing	Academic Writing	Popular Culture	Public Affairs, Civic Writing	Professional Writing	Literature
Letter	Scholarly article	Articles for magazines such as *Seventeen*, *Ebony*, or *Vibe*	Letter to the editor	Cover letter for a job application	Short story
Diary/journal	Research paper		Newspaper editorial	Résumé	Novel
Memoir	Scientific report			Business memo	Graphic novel
Blog	Abstract or summary	Advertisements	Op-ed piece	Legal brief	Play
Text message		Hip-hop lyrics	Advocacy Web site	Brochure	Sonnet
E-mail	Book review	Fan Web sites			Epic poem
Facebook profile	Essay exam	Bumper stickers	Political blog	Technical manual	Literary podcast
Personal essay	Annotated bibliography	Reviews of books, films, plays, music	Magazine article on civic issue	Instruction booklet	
Literacy narrative	Textual analysis			Proposal	
				Report	
				Press release	

To illustrate the relationship of a writer to a genre, we sometimes draw an analogy with clothing. Although most people have a variety of different types of clothing in their wardrobes, the genre of activity for which they are dressing (Saturday night movie date, job interview, wedding) severely constrains their choice and expression of individuality. A man dressing for a job interview might express his personality through choice of tie or quality and style of business suit; he probably wouldn't express it by wearing a Hawaiian shirt and sandals. Even when people deviate from a convention, they tend to do so in a conventional way. For example, teenagers who do not want to follow the genre of "teenager admired by adults" form their own genre of purple hair and pierced body parts. The concept of genre raises intriguing and sometimes unsettling questions about the relationship of the unique self to a social convention or tradition.

These same kinds of questions and constraints perplex writers. For example, academic writers usually follow the genre of the closed-form scholarly article. This highly functional form achieves maximum clarity for readers by orienting them quickly to the article's purpose, content, and structure. Readers expect this format, and writers have the greatest chance of being published if they meet these expectations. In some disciplines, however, scholars are beginning to publish more experimental, open-form articles. They may slowly alter the conventions of the scholarly article, just as fashion designers alter styles of dress.

Thinking about Purpose, Audience, and Genre

FOR WRITING AND DISCUSSION

1. This exercise, which is based on Table 1.2 on pages 16–17, will help you appreciate how rhetorical aim connects to choices about subject matter as well as to audience and genre. As a class, choose one of the following topic areas or another provided by your instructor. Then imagine six different writing situations in which a hypothetical writer would compose an essay about the selected topic. Let each situation call for a different aim. How might a person write about the selected topic with an expressive aim? An exploratory aim? An informative aim? An analytic aim? A persuasive aim? A reflective aim? How would each essay surprise its readers?

automobiles	animals	hospices or nursing homes
homelessness	music	dating or marriage
advertising	energy crisis	sports injuries

Working on your own or in small groups, create six realistic scenarios, each of which calls for prose in a different category of aim. Then share your results as a whole class. Here are two examples based on the topic "hospices."

Expressive Aim   Working one summer as a volunteer in a hospice for dying cancer patients, you befriend a woman whose attitude toward death changes your life. You write an autobiographical essay about your experiences with this remarkable woman.

(continued)

Analytic Aim   You are a hospice nurse working in a home care setting. You and your colleagues note that sometimes family members cannot adjust psychologically to the burden of living with a dying person. You decide to investigate this phenomenon. You interview "reluctant" family members in an attempt to understand the causes of their psychological discomfort so that you can provide better counseling services as a possible solution. You write a paper for a professional audience analyzing the results of your interviews.

2. Working in small groups or as a whole class, develop a list of the conventions for one or more of the following genres:
   - Cell phone text messages as typically created by teenagers
   - A Facebook profile
   - The home page for a college or university Web site

Chapter Summary

This chapter has introduced you to three transferable rhetorical concepts aimed at deepening your thinking about "good writing" in college.

- ***Concept 1: Good writing can vary from closed to open forms.*** Closed-form prose has an explicit thesis statement, topic sentences, unified and coherent paragraphs, and good transitions. At the other end of the continuum is open-form prose, which often uses narrative techniques such as storytelling, evocative language, surprising juxtapositions, and other features that violate the conventions of closed-form prose. Closed-form prose is "good" only if its ideas bring something new, provocative, or challenging to the reader.
- ***Concept 2: Good writers address problems rather than topics.*** Writers write because they have something surprising or challenging to say in response to a question that matters to the reader. Writers can pose their own problematic questions about a subject or become engaged in controversies or issues that are already "out there."
- ***Concept 3: Good writers think rhetorically about purpose, audience, and genre.*** In thinking about purpose, writers consider their rhetorical aim, their motivating occasion, or their desire to bring about change in their readers' view. They also think about their audience, analyzing how much their readers already know about (and care about) their subject and assessing their readers' values, beliefs, and assumptions. Writers attend to genre by thinking about the conventions of content, structure, and style associated with the kind of document they are writing.

BRIEF WRITING PROJECT I

Two Messages for Different Purposes, Audiences, and Genres

The purpose of this brief write-to-learn assignment is to let you experience first-hand how rhetorical context influences a writer's choices. The whole assignment, which has three parts, should not be more than two double-spaced pages long.

1. ***A Text Message to a Friend.*** Write a text message to a friend using the abbreviations, capitalization, and punctuation style typically used for text messages. Explain that you are going to miss an upcoming social event (movie, football game, dance, trip to the local diner or coffee house) because you are feeling sick. Then ask your friend to text you during the event to schedule another get-together. (Make up details as you need them.)

2. ***An E-Mail Message to a Professor.*** Compose an e-mail message to your professor explaining that you cannot meet an assignment deadline because you are sick and asking for an extension. (Use the same sickness details from Part 1.) Create a subject line appropriate for this new context.

3. ***Reflection on the Two Messages.*** Using items 1 and 2 as illustrative examples, explain to someone who has not read Chapter 1 of this text why a difference in your rhetorical context caused you to make different choices in these two messages. In your explanation, use the terms "purpose," "audience," and "genre." Your goal is to teach your audience the meanings of these terms.

| A Letter to Your Professor about What You Learned in Chapter 1 | **BRIEF WRITING PROJECT 2** |

Write a letter to your instructor in which you reflect on the extent to which the ideas in this opening chapter are new to you or have caused you to think about writing in new or different ways. Structure your letter in the following way:

- Describe for your instructor a piece of writing you did in high school or elsewhere that represents your most engaged work or about which you are most proud. Explain the context of this piece of writing (class or professional setting, nature of the assignment, length, and so forth) and provide a brief summary of your intentions and argument. Explain why this piece of writing particularly engaged you.
- Then analyze this piece of writing and your own thinking processes in producing it in light of the following three questions from this chapter:
  - Where would you place this piece of writing on the continuum from closed to open forms? Why?
  - To what extent was this piece of writing rooted in a "good, interesting question"? Explain.
  - To what extent did you think about purpose, audience, and genre as you wrote this piece?
- Finally, explain to your instructor the extent to which this chapter caused you to think about writing in any new or different ways.

2 THINKING RHETORICALLY ABOUT YOUR SUBJECT MATTER

"In management, people don't merely 'write papers,' they solve problems," said [business professor A. Kimbrough Sherman]. ... He explained that he wanted to construct situations where students would have to "wallow in complexity" and work their way out, as managers must.

—A. Kimbrough Sherman, Management Professor, Quoted by

Barbara E. Walvoord and Lucille P. McCarthy

In the previous chapter we explained how the rules for good writing vary along a continuum from closed to open forms, how writers become engaged with subject-matter questions, and how they think rhetorically about their purpose, audience, and genre. In this chapter we show how writers think rhetorically about their "subject matter"—that is, how they think about what is unknown, puzzling, or controversial in their subject matter and about how their view of the subject might be different from their audience's.

Because this chapter concerns academic writing, we focus on closed-form prose—the kind of thesis-governed writing most often required in college courses and often required in civic and professional life. As we will show, thesis-governed writing requires a behind-the-scenes ability to think rigorously about a problem and then to make a claim* based on your own solution to the problem. This claim should bring something new, interesting, useful, or challenging to readers.

In this chapter, you will learn four concepts of significant explanatory power:

- **CONCEPT 4** To determine their thesis, writers must often "wallow in complexity."
- **CONCEPT 5** A strong thesis surprises readers with something new or challenging.
- **CONCEPT 6** In closed-form prose, a typical introduction starts with the problem, not the thesis.
- **CONCEPT 7** Thesis statements in closed-form prose are supported hierarchically with points and particulars.

*In this text we use the words *claim* and *thesis statement* interchangeably. In courses across the curriculum, instructors typically use one or the other of these terms. Other synonyms for *thesis statement* include *proposition, main point,* or *thesis sentence.*

CONCEPT 4 **To determine their thesis, writers must often "wallow in complexity."**

As we explained in the previous chapter, the starting point of academic writing is a "good, interesting question." At the outset, we should say that these questions may lead you toward new and unfamiliar ways of thinking. Beginning college students typically value questions that have right answers. Students ask their professors questions because they are puzzled by confusing parts of a textbook, a lecture, or an assigned reading. They hope their professors will explain the confusing material clearly. Their purpose in asking these questions is to eliminate misunderstandings, not to open up controversy and debate. Although basic comprehension questions are important, they are not the kinds of inquiry questions that lead to strong college-level writing and thinking.

Instead, the kinds of questions that stimulate the writing most valued in college are open-ended questions that focus on unknowns or uncertainties (what educational researcher Ken Bain calls "beautiful problems") rather than factual questions that have single, correct answers.* Good open-ended questions invite multiple points of view or alternative hypotheses; they stimulate critical thinking and research. We don't mean to make this focus on problems sound scary. Indeed, humans pose and solve problems all the time and often take great pleasure in doing so. Psychologists who study critical and creative thinking see problem solving as a productive and positive activity. According to one psychologist, "Critical thinkers are actively engaged with life.... They appreciate creativity, they are innovators, and they exude a sense that life is full of possibilities."** Our way of thinking about problems has been motivated by the South American educator Paulo Freire, who wanted his students (often poor, illiterate villagers) to become *problematizers* instead of memorizers. Freire opposed what he called "the banking method" of education, in which students deposit knowledge in their memory banks and then make withdrawals during exams. The banking method, Freire believed, left third world villagers passive and helpless to improve their situations in life. Using the banking method, students being taught to read and write might learn the word *water* through drill-and-skill workbook sentences such as, "The water is in the well." With Freire's problematizing method, students might learn the word *water* by asking, "Why is the water dirty and who is responsible?" Freire believed that good questions have stakes and that answering them can make a difference in the world.

*Cognitive psychologists call these beautiful problems "ill-structured." An ill-structured problem has competing solutions, requiring the thinker to argue for the best solution in the absence of full and complete data or in the presence of stakeholders with different backgrounds, assumptions, beliefs, and values. In contrast, a "well-structured" problem eventually yields a correct answer. Math problems that can be solved by applying the right formulae and processes are well structured. That's why you can have the correct answers in the back of the book.
**Academic writers regularly document their sources. Two standard methods for documenting sources in student papers and in many professional scholarly articles are the MLA and APA citation systems explained in Chapter 14. In this text we have cited our sources in an "Acknowledgments" section. To find our source for this quotation (or the quotations from Kilcup or Kimbrough in the epigraphs or the "beautiful problem" quotation from Ken Bain), see the Acknowledgments at the end of the text.

Learning to Wallow in Complexity

This focus on important problems explains why college professors want students to go beyond simply understanding course concepts as taught in textbooks and lectures. Such comprehension is important, but it is only a starting point. As management professor A. Kimbrough Sherman explains in the epigraph to this chapter, college instructors expect students to wrestle with problems by applying the concepts, data, and thought processes they learn in a course to new situations. As Sherman puts it, students must learn to "wallow in complexity" and work their way out. To put it another way, college professors want students to "earn" their thesis. (Earning a thesis is very different from simply stating your opinion, which might not be deeply examined at all.) Because college professors value this kind of complex thinking, they often phrase essay exam questions or writing assignments as open-ended problems that can be answered in more than one way. They are looking not for the right answer, but for well-supported arguments that acknowledge alternative views. A C paper and an A paper may have the same "answer" (identical thesis statements), but the C writer may have waded only ankle deep into the mud of complexity, whereas the A writer wallowed in it and worked a way out.

What skills are required for successful wallowing? Specialists in critical thinking have identified the following:

CRITICAL THINKING SKILLS NEEDED FOR "WALLOWING IN COMPLEXITY"

- The ability to pose problematic questions
- The ability to analyze a problem in all its dimensions—to define its key terms, determine its causes, understand its history, appreciate its human dimension and its connection to one's own personal experience, and appreciate what makes it problematic or complex
- The ability (and determination) to find, gather, and interpret facts, data, and other information relevant to the problem (often involving library, Internet, or field research)
- The ability to imagine alternative solutions to the problem, to see different ways in which the question might be answered and different perspectives for viewing it
- The ability to analyze competing approaches and answers, to construct arguments for and against alternatives, and to choose the best solution in light of values, objectives, and other criteria that you determine and articulate
- The ability to write an effective argument justifying your choice while acknowledging counterarguments

We discuss and develop these skills throughout this text.

Seeing Each Academic Discipline as a Field of Inquiry and Argument

In addition to these general thinking abilities, critical thinking requires what psychologists call "domain-specific" skills. Each academic discipline has its own characteristic ways of approaching knowledge and its own specialized habits of mind. The questions asked by psychologists differ from those asked by historians or anthropologists; the evidence and assumptions used to support arguments in literary analysis differ from those in philosophy or sociology. As illustrations, here are some examples of how different disciplines might pose different questions about hip-hop:

- *Psychology:* To what extent do hip-hop lyrics increase misogynistic or homophobic attitudes in male listeners?
- *History:* What was the role of urban housing projects in the early development of hip-hop?
- *Sociology:* How does the level of an individual's appreciation for rap music vary by ethnicity, class, age, geographic region, and gender?
- *Rhetoric/Composition:* What images of urban life do the lyrics of rap songs portray?
- *Marketing and Management:* How did the white media turn a black, urban phenomenon into corporate profits?
- *Women's Studies:* What influence does hip-hop music have on the self-image of African-American women?
- *Global Studies:* How are other countries adapting hip-hop to their cultures?

As these questions suggest, when you study a new discipline, you must learn not only the knowledge that scholars in that discipline have acquired over the years, but also the processes they used to discover that knowledge. It is useful to think of each academic discipline as a network of conversations in which participants exchange information, respond to each other's questions, and express agreement and disagreement. As each discipline evolves and changes, its central questions evolve also, creating a fascinating, dynamic conversation that defines the discipline. Table 2.1 provides examples of questions that scholars have debated over the years as well as questions they are addressing today.

TABLE 2.1	**Scholarly Questions in Different Disciplines**	
Field	**Examples of Current Cutting-Edge Questions**	**Examples of Historical Controversies**
Anatomy	What is the effect of a pregnant rat's alcohol ingestion on the development of fetal eye tissue?	In 1628, William Harvey produced a treatise arguing that the heart, through repeated contractions, causes blood to circulate through the body. His views were attacked by followers of the Greek physician Galen.
Literature	To what extent does the structure of a work of literature, for example, Conrad's *Heart of Darkness*, reflect the class and gender bias of the author?	In the 1920s, a group of New Critics argued that the interpretation of a work of literature should be based on close examination of the work's imagery and form and that the intentions of the writer and the biases of the reader were not important. These views held sway in U.S. universities until the late 1960s, when they came increasingly under attack by deconstructionists and other postmoderns, who claimed that author intentions and reader's bias were important parts of the work's meaning.

(continued)

TABLE 2.1   *continued*

Field	Examples of Current Cutting-Edge Questions	Examples of Historical Controversies
Rhetoric/ Composition	How does hypertext structure and increased attention to visual images in Web-based writing affect the composing processes of writers?	Prior to the 1970s, college writing courses in the United States were typically organized around the rhetorical modes (description, narration, exemplification, comparison and contrast, and so forth). This approach was criticized by the expressivist school associated with the British composition researcher James Britton. Since the 1980s, composition scholars have proposed various alternative strategies for designing and sequencing assignments.
Psychology	What are the underlying causes of gender identification? To what extent are differences between male and female behavior explainable by nature (genetics, body chemistry) versus nurture (social learning)?	In the early 1900s under the influence of Sigmund Freud, psychoanalytic psychologists began explaining human behavior in terms of unconscious drives and mental processes that stemmed from repressed childhood experiences. Later, psychoanalysts were opposed by behaviorists, who rejected the notion of the unconscious and explained behavior as responses to environmental stimuli.

Using Exploratory Writing to Help You Wallow in Complexity

One of the important discoveries of research in rhetoric and composition is the extent to which experienced writers use writing to generate and discover ideas. Not all writing, in other words, is initially intended as a final product for readers. The very act of writing—often without concern for audience, structure, or correctness—can stimulate the mind to produce ideas. Moreover, when you write down your thoughts, you'll have a record of your thinking that you can draw on later. In Chapter 11 we explain this phenomenon more fully, showing you how to take full advantage of the writing process for invention of ideas and revision for readers. In this section we describe five strategies of exploratory writing and talking: freewriting; focused freewriting; idea mapping; dialectic talk in person, in class discussions, or in electronic discussion boards; and playing the believing and doubting game.

Freewriting *Freewriting*, also sometimes called *nonstop writing* or *silent, sustained writing*, asks you to record your thinking directly. To freewrite, put pen to paper (or sit at your computer screen, perhaps turning *off* the monitor so that you can't see what you are writing) and write rapidly, *nonstop*, for ten to fifteen minutes at a stretch. Don't worry about grammar, spelling, organization, transitions, or other features of edited writing. The object is to think of as many ideas as possible. Some freewriting looks like stream of consciousness. Some is more organized and focused, although it lacks the logical connections and development that would make it suitable for an audience of strangers.

Many freewriters find that their initial reservoir of ideas runs out in three to five minutes. If this happens, force yourself to keep your fingers moving. If you can't think of anything to say, write, "Relax" over and over (or "This is stupid" or "I'm stuck") until new ideas emerge.

What do you write about? The answer varies according to your situation. Often you will freewrite in response to a question or problem posed by your instructor. Sometimes you will pose your own questions and use freewriting to explore possible answers or simply generate ideas.

The following freewrite, by student writer James Gardiner, formed the starting point for his later exploration of issues connected to online social networks such as MySpace.com and Facebook.com. It was written in response to the prompt "What puzzles you about the new digital age?" We will return to James's story occasionally throughout this text. You can read his final paper in Chapter 14, pages 362–370, where he argues that online social networks can have unexpected detrimental effects on many users. You can also read his earlier exploratory paper (Chapter 6, pp. 144–148), which narrates the evolution of his thinking as he explored the popularity of MySpace and Facebook.

JAMES GARDINER'S INITIAL FREEWRITE

Hmm, what puzzles me about the new digital age? Let's see, let's see, OK I'm puzzled by what life used to be like before there was so much technology. I'm amazed by the growing role that technology has on the lives of people my age. It seems that my generation is spending an increasing amount of time surfing the net, talking on cell phones, listening to MP3 players, playing video games, and watching digital television. I wonder what type of effect these new technologies will have on our society as a whole and if the positive aspects that they bring into the lives of their users outweigh the negative aspects. Are kids happier now that they have all this technology? Hmm. What is the effect of text-messaging rather than talking directly to people? Also what about online social networks like Myspace and Facebook? A lot of my friends have a profile on these sites. I've never joined one of these networks or created a profile. What is my reason for avoiding them? Think. Think. OK, for one thing, I have seen how much time people can spend on these sites and I already feel that I spend enough time checking emails and voicemails. Here's another thing—I am a little hesitant to display personal information about myself on a website that can be viewed by anyone in the world. I feel I am a generally private person and there is something about posting personal details of my life in cyberspace that makes me a little uneasy. As these online social networks increase in popularity and membership, I am puzzled by how my generation will be affected by them. Although people use the sites to communicate with one another, they are usually (physically) alone at their computer. I wonder how this new type of online communication will affect other forms of interpersonal communication skills in the "real world." I also question whether young people should be encouraged to limit their time on these networks and what specifically they should use these sites for. [out of time]

Note how this freewrite rambles, moving associatively from one topic or question to the next. Freewrites often have this kind of loose, associative structure. The value of such freewrites is that they help writers discover areas of interest or rudimentary beginnings of ideas. When you read back over one of your freewrites, try to find places that seem worth pursuing. Freewriters call these places "hot spots," "centers of interest," "centers of gravity," or simply "nuggets" or "seeds." Because we believe this technique is of great value to writers, we suggest that you use it to generate ideas for class discussions and essays.

Focused Freewriting Freewriting, as we have just described it, can be quick and associational, like brainstorming aloud on paper. Focused freewriting, in contrast, is less associational and aimed more at developing a line of thought. You wrestle with a specific problem or question, trying to think and write your way into its complexity and multiple points of view. Because the writing is still informal, with the emphasis on your ideas and not on making your writing grammatically or stylistically polished, you don't have to worry about spelling, punctuation, grammar, or organizational structure. Your purpose is to deepen and extend your thinking on the problem. Some instructors will create prompts or give you specific questions to ponder, and they may call this kind of exploratory writing "focused freewriting," "learning log responses," "writer's notebook entries," or "thinking pieces."

Idea Mapping Another good technique for exploring ideas is *idea mapping*, a more visual method than freewriting. To make an idea map, draw a circle in the center of a page and write down your broad topic area (or a triggering question or your thesis) inside the circle. Then record your ideas on branches and subbranches that extend out from the center circle. As long as you pursue one train of thought, keep recording your ideas on subbranches off the main branch. But as soon as that chain of ideas runs dry, go back and start a new branch.

Often your thoughts will jump back and forth between one branch and another. This technique will help you see them as part of an emerging design rather than as strings of unrelated ideas. Additionally, idea mapping establishes at an early stage a sense of hierarchy in your ideas. If you enter an idea on a subbranch, you can see that you are more fully developing a previous idea. If you return to the hub and start a new branch, you can see that you are beginning a new train of thought.

An idea map usually records more ideas than a freewrite, but the ideas are not as fully developed. Writers who practice both techniques report that they can vary the kinds of ideas they generate depending on which technique they choose. Figure 2.1 shows a student's idea map made while he was exploring issues related to the grading system.

Dialectic Talk Another effective way to explore the complexity of a topic is through face-to-face discussions with others, whether in class, over coffee in the student union, or late at night in bull sessions. Not all discussions are productive; some are too superficial and scattered, others too heated. Good ones are *dialectic*—participants with differing views on a topic try to understand each other and resolve their differences by examining contradictions in each person's position. The key to dialectic conversation is careful listening, which is made possible by an openness to each other's views. A dialectic discussion differs from

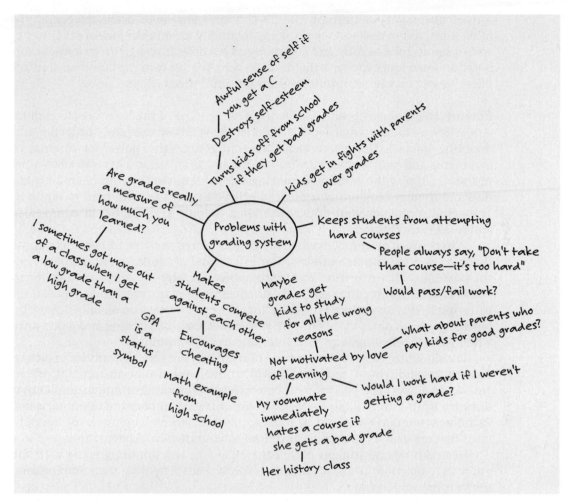

FIGURE 2.1 Idea Map on Problems with the Grading System

a talk show shouting match or a pro/con debate in which proponents of opposing positions, their views set in stone, attempt to win the argument. In a dialectic discussion, participants assume that each position has strengths and weaknesses and that even the strongest position contains inconsistencies, which should be exposed and examined. When dialectic conversation works well, participants scrutinize their own positions more critically and deeply, and often alter their views. True dialectic conversation implies growth and change, not a hardening of positions.

Dialectic discussion can also take place in electronic discussion boards, chat rooms, blogs, or other digital sites for informal exchange of ideas. If your goal is to generate ideas, your stance should be the exact opposite of the flamer's stance. A flamer's intention is to use brute rhetorical power (sometimes mindlessly obscene or mean, sometimes clever and humorous) to humiliate another writer and shut off further discussion. In contrast, the dialectician's goal is to listen respectfully to other ideas, to test new ways of thinking, to modify ideas in the face of other views, and to see an issue as fully and complexly as possible. If you go on to a discussion board to learn and change, rather than to defend your own position and shut off other views, you will be surprised at how powerful this medium can be.

Playing the Believing and Doubting Game One of the best ways to explore a question is to play what writing theorist Peter Elbow calls the "believing and doubting game." This game helps you appreciate the power of alternative arguments and points of view by urging you to formulate and explore alternative positions. To play the game, you imagine a possible answer to a problematic question and then systematically try first to believe that answer and then to doubt it. The game stimulates your critical thinking, helping you wallow in complexity and resist early closure.

When you play the believing side of this game, you try to become sympathetic to an idea or point of view. You listen carefully to it, opening yourself to the possibility that it is true. You try to appreciate why the idea has force for so many people; you try to accept it by discovering as many reasons as you can for believing it. It is easy to play the believing game with ideas you already believe in, but the game becomes more difficult, sometimes even frightening and dangerous, when you try believing ideas that seem untrue or disturbing.

The doubting game is the opposite of the believing game. It calls for you to be judgmental and critical, to find fault with an idea rather than to accept it. When you doubt a new idea, you try your best to falsify it, to find counterexamples that disprove it, to find flaws in its logic. Again, it is easy to play the doubting game with ideas you don't like, but it, too, can be threatening when you try to doubt ideas that are dear to your heart or central to your own worldview.

Here is how one student played the believing and doubting game with the following assertion from professional writer Paul Theroux that emphasizing sports is harmful to boys.

> Just as high school basketball teaches you how to be a poor loser, the manly attitude towards sports seems to be little more than a recipe for creating bad marriages, social misfits, moral degenerates, sadists, latent rapists and just plain louts. I regard high school sports as a drug far worse than marijuana.

Believing and Doubting Paul Theroux's Negative View of Sports

Believe

1   Although I am a woman I have a hard time believing this because I was a high school basketball player and believe high school sports are *very* important. But here goes. I will try to believe this statement even though I hate it. Let's see. It would seem that I wouldn't have much first-hand experience with how society turns boys

into men. I do see though that Theroux is right about some major problems. Through my observations, I've seen many young boys go through humiliating experiences with sports that have left them scarred. For example, a 7-year-old boy, Matt, isn't very athletic and when kids in our neighborhood choose teams, they usually choose girls before they choose Matt. I wonder if he sees himself as a sissy and what this does to him? I have also experienced some first-hand adverse effects of society's methods of turning boys into men. In our family, my dad spent much of his time playing football, basketball, and baseball with my brother. I've loved sports since I was very young so I was eager to play. In order to play with them, I had to play like a boy. Being told you threw or played like a girl was the worst possible insult you could receive. The phrase, "be tough" was something I heard repeatedly while I was growing up. Whenever I got hurt, my dad would say, "Be tough." It didn't matter how badly I was hurt, I always heard the same message. Today, I think, I have a very, very difficult time opening up and letting people get to know me, because for so long I was taught to keep everything inside. Maybe sports does have some bad effects.

Doubt

2   I am glad I get to doubt this too because I have been really mad at all the sports bashing that has been going on in class. I think much of what Theroux says is just a crock. I know that the statement "sports builds character" is a cliché, but I really believe it. It seems to me that the people who lash out at sports clichés are those who never experienced these aspects of athletics and therefore don't understand them. No one can tell me that sports didn't contribute to some of my best and most meaningful friendships and growing experiences. I am convinced that I am a better person because through sports I have had to deal with failure, defeat, frustration, sacrificing individual desires for the benefit of the team, and so on. After my last high school basketball game when after many years of mind games, of hating my coach one minute and the next having deep respect for him, of big games lost on my mistakes, of hours spent alone in the gym, of wondering if the end justifies the means, my coach put his arm around me and told me he was proud. Everything, all the pain, frustration, anxiety, fear, and sacrifice of the past years seemed so worthwhile. You might try to tell me that this story is hackneyed and trite, but I won't listen because it is a part of me, and some thing you will never be able to damage or take away. I think athletes share a special bond. They know what it is like to go through the physical pain of practice time and again. They understand the wide variety of emotions felt (but rarely expressed). They also know what a big role the friendships of teammates and coaches play in an athlete's life.

We admire this writer a great deal—both for the passion with which she defends sports in her doubting section and for the courage of walking in a sports basher's shoes in the believing section. This exercise clearly engaged and stretched her thinking.

Using Exploratory Writing and Talking to Generate Ideas

Background: In our discussion of problem posing in the last chapter (Concept 2: "Good writers address problems rather than topics," pp. 10–14), we explain two main ways that you can become gripped by a problem: (1) You can become engaged by a question or issue that is already "out there"—that is, already being examined or debated in some academic or civic community; or (2) you can pose your own question based on your observation of a puzzling phenomenon or artifact. You might have tried out these strategies in your thinking about the sculpture in Figure 1.2, page 14. Now in Concept 4, we have shown how exploratory writing and talking can help you learn to wallow in complexity. For this exercise we give you for analysis a poem by e. e. cummings and a pair of historical graphs on life expectancy and causes of death in the twentieth century.

next to of course god america i

"next to of course god america i
love you land of the pilgrims' and so forth oh
say can you see by the dawn's early my
country 'tis of centuries come and go

and are no more what of it we should worry
in every language even deafanddumb
thy sons acclaim your glorious name by gorry
by jingo by gee by gosh by gum
why talk of beauty what could be more beautiful than these heroic happy dead
who rushed like lions to the roaring slaughter
they did not stop to think they died instead
then shall the voice of liberty be mute?"

He spoke. And drank rapidly a glass of water

—e. e. cummings

1. ***Generating questions using freewriting and discussion***
   Individual task: Read e. e. cummings' poem three or four times, trying to make as much sense of it as you can. Then freewrite for five minutes in response to this prompt: *What do you find puzzling or thought provoking about this poem?* Let the ideas flow through your fingers. You are trying to identify aspects of the poem that you personally find puzzling or thought provoking while also trying to recall memories of conversations already "out there" about issues raised in the poem. While freewriting, you can also explore how you might try to "answer" some of these questions.
   Small-group or whole-class task: Share some of the questions or ideas raised in your freewrites and see how such "dialectic conversation" inspires more ideas.

2. ***Generating questions using idea mapping and discussion***
   Repeat the same process, but this time look at the graphs in Figures 2.2 and

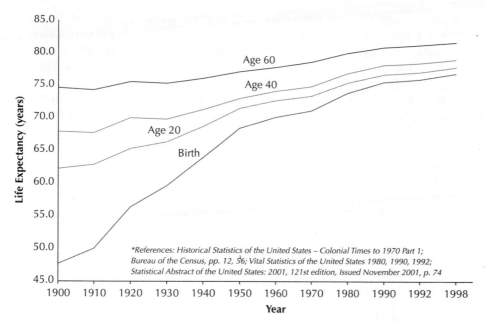

FIGURE 2.2 U.S. Life Expectancy at Birth, Age 20, Age 40, and Age 60, 1900–1998

2.3, and use idea mapping rather than freewriting. Address the question, *What do you find puzzling or thought provoking in these graphs about changes in life expectancy and causes of death in the twentieth century?* On spokes coming out from the center of the idea map, write some questions or ideas raised by

FIGURE 2.3 U.S. Death Rates for Selected Causes, 1900–2000

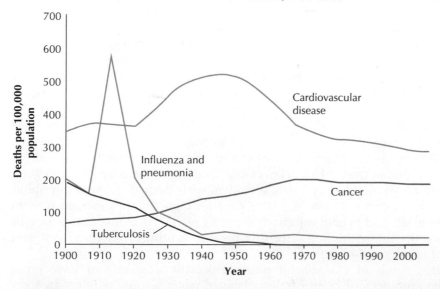

(continued)

the graphs. Then pursue ideas from each of these spokes so that you begin making a branching map of thoughts. Then share your maps with class-mates, using them to spark problem-centered conversations. Finally, discuss which technique works better for you, freewriting or idea mapping. How are they similar or different in the way they stimulate thinking?

3. ***Using freewriting or idea mapping to move from topics to problems*** Another valuable use of exploratory writing and talking is to turn broad topic areas such as "poverty," "music," "globalization," "climate change," "animal rights," or "food" into problematic questions that invite alterna-tive points of view and opportunities for analysis or argument. Using freewriting or idea mapping, start with a broad topic area (either something that interests you or something that your instructor assigns) and explore it in search of questions or problems. Try to recall all the conversations about this topic that you have heard where people expressed confusion or dis-agreement. Also think of puzzling questions that might emerge from your own personal experiences with the topic area. Your goal is to find a ques-tion that interests you and eventually to discover a thesis that gives you an entry into the conversation.

CONCEPT 5   A strong thesis statement surprises readers with something new or challenging.

The strategies for exploring ideas that we offered in the previous section can pre-pare you to move from posing problems to proposing your own solutions. Your answer to your subject-matter question becomes your **thesis statement**. In this section we show that a good thesis surprises its readers either by bringing some-thing new to the reader or by pushing against other possible ways to answer the writer's question.

Thus, a strong thesis usually contains an element of uncertainty, risk, or chal-lenge. A strong thesis implies a naysayer who could disagree with you. According to composition theorist Peter Elbow, a thesis has "got to stick its neck out, not just hedge or wander. [It is] something that can be quarreled with." Elbow's sticking-its-neck-out metaphor is a good one, but we prefer to say that a strong thesis *surprises* the reader with a new, unexpected, different, or challenging view of the writer's topic. By surprise, we intend to connote, first of all, freshness or newness for the reader. Many kinds of closed-form prose don't have a sharply contestable thesis of the sticking-its-neck-out kind highlighted by Elbow. A geol-ogy report, for example, may provide readers with desired information about rock strata in an exposed cliff, or a Web page for diabetics may explain how to coordinate meals and insulin injections during a plane trip across time zones. In these cases, the information is surprising because it brings something new and significant to intended readers.

In other kinds of closed-form prose, especially academic or civic prose addressing a problematic question or a disputed issue, surprise requires an argu-mentative, risky, or contestable thesis. In these cases also, surprise is not inherent in the material but in the intended readers' reception; it comes from the writer's providing an adequate or appropriate response to the readers' presumed question or problem.

In this section, we present two ways of creating a surprising thesis: (1) trying to change your reader's view of your subject; and (2) giving your thesis tension.

Trying to Change Your Reader's View of Your Subject

To change your reader's view of your subject, you must first imagine how the reader would view the subject *before* reading your essay. Then you can articulate how you aim to change that view. A useful exercise is to write out the "before" and "after" views of your imagined readers:

Before reading my essay, my readers think this way about my topic: _____

_____

After reading my essay, my readers will think this different way about my topic:

_____

You can change your reader's view of a subject in several ways.* First, you can enlarge it. Writing that enlarges a view is primarily informational; it provides new ideas and data to add to a reader's store of knowledge about the subject. For example, suppose you are interested in the problem of storing nuclear waste (a highly controversial issue in the United States) and decide to investigate how Japan stores radioactive waste from its nuclear power plants. You could report your findings on this problem in an informative research paper. (Before reading my paper, readers would be uncertain how Japan stores nuclear waste. After reading my paper, my readers would understand the Japanese methods, possibly helping us better understand our options in the United States.)

Second, you can clarify your reader's view of something that was previously fuzzy, tentative, or uncertain. Writing of this kind often explains, analyzes, or interprets. This is the kind of writing you do when analyzing a short story, a painting, an historical document, a set of economic data, or other puzzling phenomena or when speculating on the causes, consequences, purpose, or function of something. Suppose, for example, that you are analyzing the persuasive strategies used in various clothing ads. You are intrigued by a jeans ad that you "read" differently from your classmates. (Before reading my paper, my readers will think that this jeans ad reveals a liberated woman, but after reading my paper they will see that the ad fulfills traditional gender stereotypes.)

Another kind of change occurs when an essay actually restructures a reader's whole view of a subject. Such essays persuade readers to change their minds or make decisions. For example, engineer David Rockwood, in his letter to the editor that we reprinted in Chapter 1 (pp. 5–6), wants to change readers' views about

*Our discussion of how writing changes a reader's view of the world is indebted to Richard Young, Alton Becker, and Kenneth Pike, *Rhetoric: Discovery and Change* (New York: Harcourt Brace & Company, 1971).

wind power. (Before reading my letter, readers will believe that wind-generated electricity can solve our energy crisis, but after reading my letter they will see that the hope of wind power is a pipe dream.)

Surprise, then, is the measure of change an essay brings about in a reader. Of course, to bring about such change requires more than just a surprising thesis; the essay itself must persuade the reader that the thesis is sound as well as novel. Later in this chapter (Concept 7), we talk about how writers support a thesis through a network of points and particulars.

Giving Your Thesis Tension through "Surprising Reversal"

Another element of a surprising thesis is tension. By *tension* we mean the reader's sensation of being pulled away from familiar ideas toward new, unfamiliar ones. A strategy for creating this tension—a strategy we call "surprising reversal"—is to contrast your surprising answer to a question with your targeted audience's common answer, creating tension between your own thesis and one or more alternative views. Its basic template is as follows:

> *"Many people believe X (common view), but I am going to show Y (new, surprising view)."*

The concept of surprising reversal spurs the writer to go beyond the commonplace to change the reader's view of a topic.

One of the best ways to employ this strategy is to begin your thesis statement with an "although" clause that summarizes the reader's "before" view or the counterclaim that your essay opposes; the main clause states the surprising view or position that your essay will support. You may choose to omit the *although* clause from your actual essay, but formulating it first will help you achieve focus and surprise in your thesis. The examples that follow illustrate the kinds of tension we have been discussing and show why tension is a key requirement for a good thesis.

Question	What effect has the cell phone had on our culture?
Thesis without Tension	The invention of the cell phone has brought many advantages to our culture.
Thesis with Tension	Although the cell phone has brought many advantages to our culture, it may also have contributed to an increase in risky behavior among boaters and hikers.
Question	Do reservations serve a useful role in contemporary Native American culture?
Thesis without Tension	Reservations have good points and bad points.
Thesis with Tension	Although my friend Wilson Real Bird believes that reservations are necessary for Native Americans to preserve their heritage, the continuation of reservations actually degrades Native American culture.

In the first example, the thesis without tension (cell phones have brought advantages to our culture) is a truism with which everyone would agree and hence lacks surprise. The thesis with tension places this truism (the reader's "before" view) in an *although* clause and goes on to make a surprising or contestable assertion. The idea that the cell phone contributes to risky behavior among outdoor enthusiasts alters our initial, complacent view of the cell phone and gives us new ideas to think about.

In the second example, the thesis without tension may not at first seem tension-less because the writer sets up an opposition between good and bad points. But *almost anything* has good and bad points, so the opposition is not meaningful, and the thesis offers no element of surprise. Substitute virtually any other social institution (marriage, the postal service, the military, prisons), and the statement that it has good and bad points would be equally true. The thesis with tension, in contrast, is risky. It commits the writer to argue that reservations have degraded Native American culture and to oppose the counterthesis that reservations are needed to *preserve* Native American culture. The reader now feels genuine tension between two opposing views.

Tension, then, is a component of surprise. The writer's goal is to surprise the reader in some way, thereby bringing about some kind of change in the reader's view. As you are wallowing in complexity about your subject-matter problem, try the following strategies for bringing something new, surprising, or challenging to your targeted readers:

Strategies for Creating a Thesis with Tension or Surprise

How You Became Gripped with a Problem	Example of a Problem	Your Strategy While You "Wallow in Complexity"	Possible Thesis with Tension or Surprise
The problem is already "out there." *(You enter a conversation already in progress)*			
You don't know where you stand on an issue.	Should health care be rationed?	Look at all sides of the issue, including all the available data, to determine where you stand based on your own examined values.	Although rationing health care at first seems inhumane, it may be the only ethical way to provide affordable health care to all citizens.
You do know where you stand on an issue. *[You need to move from an opinion to an earned thesis.]*	Shanita says that we should build more nuclear power plants to combat global warming, but I say nuclear power is too dangerous.	Research the strengths of the opposing views and the weaknesses of your own view. (*Note: You may change your mind.*)	Although nuclear power poses danger from storage of waste or possible meltdown, the benefits of reducing greenhouse gases and cutting coal pollution outweigh the dangers.

(continued)

How You Became Gripped with a Problem	Example of a Problem	Your Strategy While You "Wallow in Complexity"	Possible Thesis with Tension or Surprise
Someone gives you a question that you can't yet answer.	Your boss asks you whether the company should enact the proposed marketing plan.	Do the research, critical thinking, and analysis needed to propose the "best solution" to the boss's question.	The marketing team's proposal, despite its creative use of advertising, is too risky to undertake at this time.
You pose the problem yourself. *(You initiate the conversation)*			
You see something puzzling in a natural phenomenon or a cultural activity or artifact.	Why does Merton call rain "meaningless"?	Through critical thinking and research, try to figure out a plausible "best solution" to your question.	Merton's puzzling use of "meaningless" in reference to the rain can perhaps be explained by his admiration for Buddhism.
You discover something inconsistent or contradictory in your own view of the world.	I agree with Merton's argument against consumerism, but I really want a large plasma TV. Is consumerism really bad? Am I a materialist?	Reflect on your own values and beliefs; try to achieve a consistent stand with regard to enduring social or ethical issues.	Although Merton makes me consider the potential shallowness of my desire for a huge plasma TV, I don't think I'm necessarily a materialist.

FOR WRITING AND DISCUSSION

Developing Thesis Statements Out of Questions

It is difficult to create thesis statements on the spot because a writer's thesis grows out of an exploratory struggle with a problem. However, in response to a question one can often propose a claim and treat it as a tentative thesis statement for testing. You may have already done some exploratory talking and writing in response to a problem provided by your instructor or about problems supplied so far in this text: the sculpture in Figure 1.2 (p. 14), the e. e. cummings poem (p. 34), or the graphs in Figures 2.2 and 2.3 (p. 35). Working individually, spend ten minutes considering possible thesis statements that you might make in response to one or more of the questions you have already been thinking about. (Remember that these are tentative thesis statements, done for practice, that you might abandon after doing research or more critical thinking.) Identify a possible audience for your thesis statement, and try to explain why this audience would find your thesis new, surprising, or challenging. Then, working in small groups or as a whole class, share your thesis statements. Select one or two thesis statements that your small group or class thinks are particularly effective and brainstorm the kinds of evidence that would be required to support the thesis.

Alternatively, your instructor might use the following exercises:

1. To what extent should the public support genetically modified foods? (possible audiences: readers of health food magazines; general public concerned about food choices; investors in companies that produce genetically modified seeds)
2. Should the government mandate more fuel-efficient cars? If so, how? (possible audiences: SUV owners; conservative legislators generally in favor of free markets; investors in the automobile industry)

Here is an example:

Problematic question: What can cities do to prevent traffic congestion?

One possible thesis: Although many people think that building light-rail systems won't get people out of their cars, new light-rail systems in many cities have attracted new riders and alleviated traffic problems.

Intended audience: Residents of cities concerned about traffic congestion but skeptical about light-rail

Kinds of evidence needed to support thesis: Examples of cities with successful light-rail systems; evidence that many riders switched from driving cars; evidence that light-rail alleviated traffic problems

CONCEPT 6 **In closed-form prose, a typical introduction starts with the problem, not the thesis.**

So far we've talked about the importance of finding a good problem and exploring its complexity. Eventually, however, your goal is to contribute to the conversation by stating and supporting your own thesis. First, however, readers need to know what problem your thesis addresses. One of the principles of closed-form prose—which we describe in detail later in this text—is that readers' need to attach new information to old information. In other words, before they can understand an answer, they must first understand the question. One function of the introduction in most closed-form prose is to show your readers what the problem is and to motivate their interest in it. This introduction can be long or short depending on whether your targeted audience is already familiar with the problem or already cares about it. Once readers know what problem you intend to address, they are prepared for your thesis statement.

For more on the old/new contract, see Skill 12.7.

A Protypical Introduction

To show you how academic writers typically begin by asking a question, we will illustrate with several "prototype" examples.* In the following introduction by student writer Jackie Wyngaard, note how the author first presents a question and then moves, at the end of the introduction, to her thesis statement.

Provides background on EMP

Begins to turn topic area (EMP) into a problem by showing that it has been controversial

Establishes her own purposes and expectations: She expects EMP to teach her about music history.

Implies her question: Is EMP a good place to learn about the history of rock music?

States her thesis

EMP: MUSIC HISTORY OR MUSIC TRIVIA?

Along with other college students new to Seattle, I wanted to see what cultural opportunities the area offers. I especially wanted to see billionaire Paul Allen's controversial Experience Music Project (known as EMP), a huge, bizarre, shiny, multicolored structure that is supposed to resemble a smashed guitar. Brochures say that EMP celebrates the creativity of American popular music, but it has prompted heated discussions among architects, Seattle residents, museum goers, and music lovers, who have questioned its commercialism and the real value of its exhibits. My sister recommended this museum to me because she knows I am a big music lover and a rock and roll fan. Also, as an active choir member since the sixth grade, I have always been intrigued by the history of music. I went to EMP expecting to learn more about music history from exhibits that showed a range of popular musical styles, that traced historical connections and influences, and that enjoyably conveyed useful information. However, as a museum of rock history, EMP is a disappointing failure.

Features of a Good Introduction

Wyngaard's introduction, which shares the structure of many professionally written closed-form introductions, includes the following prototypical features:

- **Background needed to identify the topic area and provide context.** Readers need early on to know the specific topic area of the paper they are about to read—in this case a paper about the Experience Music Project in Seattle rather than, say, shower mold or medieval queenship. Sometimes writers also use a startling scene or statistic as an "attention grabber" as part of the opening background.
- **A direct or implied question.** As soon as possible, readers need to sense the problem, question, or issue that the writer will examine. In this case, Jackie Wyngaard implies her question: Will my expectations about EMP be fulfilled? Note that her question appears directly in her title: "EMP: Music History [her expectations] or Music Trivia [her claim]?"
- **An indication of how the question invites tension or is otherwise problematic.** An effective question or problem supposes the possibility of

*A *prototype* is the most typical or generic instance of a class and doesn't constitute a value judgment. For example, a prototype bird might be a robin or blackbird (rather than an ostrich, chicken, hummingbird, or pelican) because these birds seem to exhibit the most typical features of "birdiness." Likewise, a prototype dog would be a medium-sized mutt rather than a St. Bernard or toy poodle.

alternative points of view, different perspectives in tension with each other. In many cases, a writer summarizes alternative arguments sparked by the question or summarizes a particular point of view that the writer intends to oppose. Because Jackie initiates the conversation about EMP's status as a rock museum, she evokes this tension by contrasting her initial expectations with her later disappointment.

- *An indication of how the question is significant or worth examining.* In order to avoid a "so what?" response, writers must motivate readers' interest in the question. Somebody might say, "Who cares about EMP anyway?" Jackie's strategy is to imagine an audience who shares her interest in rock and roll music and her love of music history. These are the readers who will care whether it is worth big bucks to spend an afternoon in EMP. Readers who identify with Jackie's enthusiasm for rock history will share her engagement with the question. Other strategies for showing a question's significance include pointing to the good or bad consequences of a particular way of answering the question ("If we could understand why the crime rate in New York City dropped dramatically in the 1990s, we could apply these same principles to other cities today") or by showing how an answer to a smaller question might help readers begin to answer a larger question ("If we could better understand the role of the witches in *Macbeth*, we would better understand the ways gender was constructed in Shakespeare's time").

- *The writer's thesis, which brings something new to the audience.* Once readers are hooked on the writer's question, they are ready for the writer's answer. In this case, Jackie makes the claim that EMP fails as a rock history museum.

- *[optional] A purpose statement ("The purpose of this paper is ... ") along with a mapping statement forecasting the content and shape of the rest of the article ("First I discuss X, then Y, and finally Z").* Because her paper is short, Jackie ends the introduction with her thesis. An alternative strategy, common among longer closed-form essays, is to include a purpose statement along with a forecasting passage that maps what is coming. This strategy is used by student writer James Gardiner at the end of his introduction to a paper about the consequences of using online social networks like Facebook. Note how he poses his problematic question and then moves to a purpose statement and mapping statement.

For more on thesis statements, purpose statements, and blueprint statements, see Skill 12.4. See also James Gardiner's full essay on pp. 362–370.

... While "Facebook Trance" might describe only an occasional and therefore harmless phenomenon, it gives rise to an important question: What are the possible negative consequences of OSNs [online social networks]? What should youthful users be watchful for and guard against? The purpose of this paper is to identify the possible harms of OSNs. I will suggest that overuse of OSNs can be a contributing factor to a decline in grades as well as to other problems such as a superficial view of relationships, an increase in narcissism, and possible future embarrassment.

States directly the question his paper will address

Purpose statement

Maps out the argument's structure while motivating readers' interest in question

For a fuller look at the ways a writer can introduce readers to the problem he or she is addressing, consider the following strategies chart:

Strategies for Introducing Your Problem to Targeted Readers	
Situation	**Strategies**
The problem is already "out there" *(You enter a conversation already in progress)*	*If readers are already familiar with the problem and care about it, use a mix of the following strategies:* • Provide background where needed • State the problem directly (often as a grammatical question ending with a question mark) or imply the question through context • Summarize the different points of view on the problem (or) • Summarize the particular point of view you intend to "push against" *If readers are less familiar with the problem:* • Summarize controversy in more depth • Explain why the problem is problematic (show why there are no easy answers to the problem; point out weaknesses in proposed answers; show the history of attempts to solve the problem) *If readers don't already care about the problem:* • Show why the problem is important (answer the "so what?" question) • Show how solving the problem will bring good consequences (or) • Show how answering the question will help us begin to answer a larger question
You pose the problem yourself *(You initiate the conversation)*	• Describe the artifact or phenomenon you are writing about and point to the specific features where you see an inconsistency, gap, or puzzle • State the problem directly (often as a grammatical question ending with a question mark) • Show how there isn't any immediate, easy answer to the question or problem or how the question can invite controversy/discussion; you can often employ a template such as the following: 　• Some people might think…, but closer observation shows that…. 　• At first I thought…, but later I saw that…. 　• Part of me thinks…, but another part of me thinks that…. 　• I expected … ; but what I actually found was…. • Show why the problem is important (answer the "so what?" question) • Show how solving the problem will bring good consequences (or) • Show how answering this question will help us begin to answer a larger question

Examining Problem-Thesis Structure of Introductions

Background: As we explained in Concept 1, good writing can vary along a continuum from closed to open forms. Although academic essays are typically closed form, they can vary significantly along the continuum. Likewise, the introductions to closed-form essays don't always follow the prototypical structure we just described. But many do. In this exercise, we invite you to analyze additional introductions.

   Task: Look at the following introductions. In each case, analyze the extent to which the introduction follows or varies from the prototypical introductions we have described in Concept 6.

1. Paragraphs 1–2 of Ross Taylor's "Paintball: Promoter of Violence or Healthy Fun?" (pp. 234–36)
2. Paragraphs 1–4 of "No to Nukes," a *Los Angeles Times* editorial (p. 241)
3. Paragraphs 1–6 of Shannon King's "How Clean and Green Are Hydrogen Fuel-Cell Cars?" (pp. 165–70)

CONCEPT 7 **Thesis statements in closed-form prose are supported hierarchically with points and particulars.**

Of course, a surprising thesis is only one aspect of an effective essay. An essay must also persuade the reader that the thesis is believable as well as surprising. Although tabloid newspapers have shocking headlines ("Cloning Produces Three-Headed Sheep"), skepticism quickly replaces surprise when you look inside and find the article's claims unsupported. A strong thesis, then, must both surprise the reader and be supported with convincing particulars.

   In fact, the particulars are the flesh and muscle of writing and comprise most of the sentences. In closed-form prose, these particulars are connected clearly to points, and the points precede the particulars. In this section, we explain this principle more fully.

How Points Convert Information to Meaning

When particulars are clearly related to a point, the point gives meaning to the particulars, and the particulars give force and validity to the point. Particulars constitute the evidence, data, details, examples, and subarguments that develop a point and make it convincing. By themselves, particulars are simply information—mere data without meaning.

   In the following example, you can see for yourself the difference between information and meaning. Here is a list of information:*

- In almost all species on earth, males are more aggressive than females.
- Male chimpanzees win dominance by brawling.

*The data in this exercise are adapted from Deborah Blum, "The Gender Blur," *Utne Reader* Sept. 1998: 45–48.

- To terrorize rival troops, they kill females and infants.
- The level of aggression among monkeys can be manipulated by adjusting their testosterone levels.
- Among humans, preliminary research suggests that male fetuses are more active in the uterus than female fetuses.
- Little boys play more aggressively than little girls despite parental efforts to teach gentleness to boys and aggression to girls.

To make meaning out of this list of information, the writer needs to state a point—the idea, generalization, or claim—that this information supports. Once the point is stated, a meaningful unit (point with particulars) springs into being:

Point

Particulars

> Aggression in human males may be a function of biology rather than culture. In almost all species on earth, males are more aggressive than females. Male chimpanzees win dominance by brawling; to terrorize rival troops, they kill females and infants. Researchers have shown that the level of aggression among monkeys can be manipulated by adjusting their testosterone levels. Among humans, preliminary research suggests that male fetuses are more active in the uterus than female fetuses. Also, little boys play more aggressively than little girls despite parental efforts to teach gentleness to boys and aggression to girls.

Once the writer states this point, readers familiar with the biology/culture debate about gender differences immediately feel its surprise and tension. This writer believes that biology determines gender identity more than does culture. The writer now uses the details as evidence to support a point.

To appreciate the reader's need for a logical connection between points and particulars, note how readers would get lost if, in the preceding example, the writer included a particular that seemed unrelated to the point ("Males also tend to be taller and heavier than women"—a factual statement, but what does it have to do with aggression?) or if, without explanation, the writer added a particular that seemed to contradict the point ("Fathers play more roughly with baby boys than with baby girls"—another fact, but one that points to culture rather than biology as a determiner of aggression).

Obviously, reasonable people seek some kind of coordination between points and particulars, some sort of weaving back and forth between them. Writing teachers use a number of nearly synonymous terms for expressing this paired relationship: *points/particulars, generalizations/specifics, claims/evidence, ideas/ details, interpretations/data, meaning/support.*

How Removing Particulars Creates a Summary

What we have shown, then, is that skilled writers weave back and forth between generalizations and specifics. The generalizations form a network of higher-level and lower-level points that develop the thesis; the particulars (specifics) support each of the points and subpoints in turn. In closed-form prose, the network of points is easily discernible because points are clearly highlighted with transitions, and main points are placed prominently at the heads of paragraphs. (In open-form prose, generalizations are often left unstated, creating gaps where the reader must actively fill in meaning.)

If you remove most of the particulars from a closed-form essay, leaving only the network of points, you will have written a summary or abstract of the essay. As an example, reread the civil engineer's letter to the editor arguing against the feasibility of wind-generated power (pp. 5–6). The writer's argument can be summarized in a single sentence:

> Wind-generated power is not a reasonable alternative to other forms of power in the Pacific Northwest because wind power is unreliable, because there are major unsolved problems involved in the design of wind-generation facilities, and because the environmental impact of building thousands of wind towers would be enormous.

What we have done in this summary is remove the particulars, leaving only the high-level points that form the skeleton of the argument. The writer's thesis remains surprising and contains tension, but without the particulars the reader has no idea whether to believe the generalizations or not. The presence of the particulars is thus essential to the success of the argument.

Being able to write summaries and abstracts of articles is an important academic skill. See Chapter 5 on strategies for writing summaries and strong responses, pp. 98–109.

Analyzing Supporting Particulars

FOR WRITING AND DISCUSSION

Compare the civil engineer's original letter with the one-sentence summary just given and then note how the engineer uses specific details to support each point. How do these particulars differ from paragraph to paragraph? How are they chosen to support each point?

How to Use Points and Particulars When You Revise

The lesson to learn here is that in closed-form prose, writers regularly place a point sentence in front of detail sentences. When a writer begins with a point, readers interpret the ensuing particulars not as random data but rather as *evidence* in support of that point. The writer depends on the particulars to make the point credible and persuasive.

This insight may help you understand two of the most common kinds of marginal comments that readers (or teachers) place on writers' early drafts. If your draft has a string of sentences giving data or information unconnected to any stated point, your reader is apt to write in the margin, "What's your point here?" or "Why are you telling me this information?" or "How does this information relate to your thesis?" Conversely, if your draft tries to make a point that isn't developed with particulars, your reader is apt to write marginal comments such as "Evidence?" or "Development?" or "Could you give an example?" or "More details needed."

Don't be put off by these requests; they are a gift. It is common in first drafts for main points to be unstated, buried, or otherwise disconnected from their details and for supporting information to be scattered confusingly throughout the draft or missing entirely. Having to write point sentences obliges you to wrestle with your intended meaning: Just what am I trying to say here? How can I nutshell that in a point? Likewise, having to support your points with particulars causes you to wrestle with the content and shape of your argument: What particulars will make this point convincing? What further research do I need to do to find these particulars? In Part 3 of this text, which is devoted to advice about composing and revising, we show how the construction and location of point sentences are essential for reader clarity. Part 3 also explains various composing and revising strategies that will help you create effective networks of points and particulars.

Chapter Summary

This chapter has introduced you to four concepts that will enable you to think about your subject matter from a rhetorical perspective.

- *Concept 4: To determine their thesis, writers must often "wallow in complexity."* What typically initiates the writing process is a problematic question that invites the writer to explore the problem's complexity. To do so, experienced writers often use exploratory techniques such as freewriting, idea mapping, dialectic talk, and the believing and doubting game to generate ideas.
- *Concept 5: A strong thesis surprises readers with something new or challenging.* A good thesis tries to change the reader's view of the subject and often creates tension by pushing against alternative views.
- *Concept 6: In closed-form prose, a typical introduction starts with the problem, not the thesis.* Readers need to be engaged with the writer's question before they can understand the thesis.
- *Concept 7: Thesis statements in closed-form prose are supported hierarchically with points and particulars.* Points give meaning to particulars; particulars make points persuasive. If you remove the particulars from a writer's argument and keep the points, you will have created a summary.

BRIEF WRITING PROJECT

Playing the Believing and Doubting Game

Part 1. The Game.   Play the believing and doubting game with one of the assertions listed here (or with another assertion provided by your instructor) by freewriting your believing and doubting responses. Spend ten minutes believing and then ten minutes doubting the assertion, for a total of twenty minutes. When you believe an assertion, you agree, support, illustrate, extend, and apply the idea. When you doubt an assertion, you question, challenge, rebut, and offer counterreasons and counterexamples to the assertion. Note that when students first learn to do exploratory writing, they often run out of ideas quickly and want to stop. But the best ideas often happen when you push through that wall. If you run out of ideas, let your mind follow a tangent. Particularly explore your personal experiences with the subject. Eventually you will get back on track with new ideas.

1. Grades are an effective means of motivating students to do their best work.
2. Facebook is a good way to make new friends.
3. In recent years, advertising has made enormous gains in portraying women as strong, independent, and intelligent.
4. If there is only one kidney available for transplant and two sick persons need it, one in her thirties and one in her sixties, the kidney should go to the younger person.
5. The United States should reinstate the draft.
6. Humans have free will.
7. Fencing at the U.S.–Mexico border is not an effective immigration policy.
8. If students in a large lecture course can listen to a lecture and surf the Web or check e-mail at the same time, then they should be allowed to do so.

Part 2. Reflection. Write a reflective paragraph in which you assess the extent to which the believing and doubting game extended or stretched your thinking. Particularly, answer these questions:

- What was difficult about this writing activity?
- To what extent did it make you take an unfamiliar or uncomfortable stance?
- How can believing and doubting help you wallow in complexity?

3

THINKING RHETORICALLY ABOUT HOW MESSAGES PERSUADE

A way of seeing is also a way of not seeing.

—*Kenneth Burke, Rhetorician*

Every time an Indian villager watches the community TV and sees an ad for soap or shampoo, what they notice are not the soap and shampoo but the lifestyle of the people using them, the kind of motorbikes they ride, their dress and their homes.

—*Nayan Chanda, Indian-Born Editor of YaleGlobal Online Magazine*

In Chapters 1 and 2 we have focused on writing as a rhetorical act: When writers think rhetorically, they write to an audience for a purpose within a genre. We have also shown how academic writers pose subject-matter questions that engage their audience's interests, and then propose solutions to those problems that bring something new, surprising, or challenging to their audiences.

In this chapter we expand your understanding of a writer's choices by showing how messages persuade. We'll use the word *message* in its broadest sense to include verbal texts and nonverbal texts such as photographs and paintings or consumer artifacts such as clothing. When you understand how messages achieve their effects, you will be better prepared to analyze and evaluate those messages and to make your own choices about whether to resist them or accede to them.

In this chapter, you will learn three more important rhetorical concepts:

- **CONCEPT 8**   Messages persuade through their angle of vision.
- **CONCEPT 9**   Messages persuade through appeals to *logos, ethos,* and *pathos.*
- **CONCEPT 10** Nonverbal messages persuade through visual strategies that can be analyzed rhetorically.

CONCEPT 8 **Messages persuade through their angle of vision.**

One way that messages persuade is through their **angle of vision**, which causes a reader to see a subject from one perspective only—the writer's. Writers create an angle of vision through strategies such as the following:

- Stating point of view directly
- Selecting some details while omitting others
- Choosing words or figures of speech with intended connotations
- Creating emphasis or de-emphasis through sentence structure and organization

The writer's angle of vision—which might also be called a lens, a filter, a perspective, or a point of view—is persuasive because it controls what the reader "sees." Unless readers are rhetorically savvy, they can lose awareness that they are seeing the writer's subject matter through a lens that both reveals and conceals.

A classic illustration of angle of vision is the following thought exercise:

THOUGHT EXERCISE ON ANGLE OF VISION

Suppose you attended a fun party on Saturday night. (You get to choose what constitutes "fun" for you.) Now imagine that two people ask what you did on Saturday night. Person A is a close friend who missed the party. Person B is your parent. How would your descriptions of Saturday night differ?

Clearly there isn't just one way to describe this party. Your description will be influenced by your purpose and audience. You will have to decide:

- What image of myself should I project? (For your friend you might construct yourself as a party animal; for your parent, as a more detached observer.)
- How much emphasis do I give the party? (You might describe the party in detail for your friend while mentioning it only in passing to your parent, emphasizing instead all the homework you did over the weekend.)
- What details should I include or leave out? (Does my parent really need to know that the neighbors called the police?)
- What words should I choose? (The slang you use with your friend might not be appropriate for your parent.)

You'll note that our comments about your rhetorical choices reflect common assumptions about friends and parents. You might actually have a party-loving parent and a geeky friend, in which case your party descriptions would be altered accordingly. In any case, you are in rhetorical control; you choose what your audience "sees" and how they see it.

Recognizing the Angle of Vision in a Text

This thought exercise illustrates a key insight of rhetoric: There is always more than one way to tell a story, and no single way of telling it constitutes the whole truth. By saying that a writer writes from an "angle of vision," we mean that the writer cannot take a godlike stance that allows a universal, unfiltered, totally unbiased or objective way of knowing. Rather, the writer looks at the subject from a certain location, or, to use another metaphor, the writer wears a lens that colors or filters the topic in a certain way. The angle of vision, lens, or filter determines what part of a topic gets "seen" and what remains "unseen," what gets included or excluded, what gets emphasized or de-emphasized, and so forth. It even determines what words get chosen out of an array of options—for example, whether the writer says "panhandler" or "homeless person," "torture" or "enhanced interrogation," "universal health care" or "socialized medicine."

As an illustration of angle of vision, consider the cartoon in Figure 3.1, which shows different ways that stakeholders "see" sweatshops. For each stakeholder, some aspects of sweatshops surge into view, while other aspects remain unseen or invisible. An alert reader needs to be aware that none of these stakeholders can portray sweatshops in a completely "true" way. Stockholders and corporate leaders emphasize reduced labor costs and enhanced corporate profits and retirement portfolios while de-emphasizing (or omitting entirely) the working conditions in sweatshops or the plight of American workers whose jobs have been outsourced to

FIGURE 3.1 Different Angles of Vision on "Sweatshops"

developing countries. Consumers enjoy abundant low-cost goods made possible by sweatshops and may not even think about where or how the products are made. Opponents of sweatshops focus on the miserable conditions of sweatshop workers, their low wages, the use of child labor, and the "obscene" profits of corporations. Meanwhile, as the American union worker laments the loss of jobs in the United States, third world workers and their children may welcome sweatshops as a source of income superior to the other harsh alternatives such as scavenging in dumps or prostitution. The multiple angles of vision show how complex the issue of sweatshops is. In fact, most issues are equally complex, and any one view of the issue is controlled by the writer's angle of vision.

To get a hands-on feel for how a writer creates an angle of vision, try doing the following U. R. Riddle activity, which invites you to write a letter of recommendation for a student.

U. R. Riddle Letter

FOR WRITING AND DISCUSSION

Background: Suppose that you are a management professor who regularly writes letters of recommendation for former students. One day you receive a letter from a local bank requesting a confidential evaluation of a former student, Uriah Rudy Riddle (U. R. Riddle), who has applied for a job as a management trainee. The bank wants your assessment of Riddle's intelligence, aptitude, dependability, and ability to work with people. You haven't seen U. R. for several years, but you remember him well. Here are the facts and impressions you recall about Riddle:

- Very temperamental student, seemed moody, something of a loner
- Long hair and very sloppy dress—seemed like a misplaced street person; often twitchy and hyperactive
- Absolutely brilliant mind; took lots of liberal arts courses and applied them to business
- Wrote a term paper relating different management styles to modern theories of psychology—the best undergraduate paper you ever received. You gave it an A+ and remember learning a lot from it yourself.
- Had a strong command of language—the paper was very well written
- Good at mathematics; could easily handle all the statistical aspects of the course
- Frequently missed class and once told you that your class was boring
- Didn't show up for the midterm. When he returned to class later, he said only that he had been out of town. You let him make up the midterm, and he got an A.
- Didn't participate in a group project required for your course. He said the other students in his group were idiots.
- You thought at the time that Riddle didn't have a chance of making it in the business world because he had no talent for getting along with people.
- Other professors held similar views of Riddle—brilliant, but rather strange and hard to like; an odd duck.

(continued)

You are in a dilemma because you want to give Riddle a chance (he's still young and may have had a personality transformation of some sort), but you also don't want to damage your own professional reputation by falsifying your true impressions.

Individual task: Working individually for ten minutes or so, compose a brief letter of recommendation assessing Riddle; use details from the list to support your assessment. Role-play that you have decided to take a gamble with Riddle and give him a chance at this career. Write as strong a recommendation as possible while remaining honest. (To make this exercise more complex, your instructor might ask half the class to role-play a negative angle of vision in which you want to warn the bank against hiring Riddle without hiding his strengths or good points.)

Task for group or whole-class discussion: Working in small groups or as a whole class, share your letters. Then pick representative examples ranging from the most positive to the least positive and discuss how the letters achieve their different rhetorical effects. If your intent is to support Riddle, to what extent does honesty compel you to mention some or all of your negative memories? Is it possible to mention negative items without emphasizing them? How?

Analyzing Angle of Vision

Just as there is more than one way to describe the party you went to on Saturday night or to write about sweatshops, there is more than one way to write a letter of recommendation for U. R. Riddle. The writer's angle of vision determines what is "seen" or "not seen" in a given piece of writing—what gets slanted in a positive or negative direction, what gets highlighted, what gets thrown into the shadows. As rhetorician Kenneth Burke claims in the first epigraph for the chapter, "A way of seeing is also a way of not seeing." Note how the writer controls what the reader "sees." As Riddle's former professor, you might in your mind's eye see Riddle as long-haired and sloppy, but if you don't mention these details in your letter, they remain unseen to the reader. Note too that your own terms "long-haired and sloppy" interpret Riddle's appearance through the lens of your own characteristic way of seeing—a way that perhaps values business attire and clean-cut tidiness. Another observer might describe Riddle's appearance quite differently, thus seeing what you don't see.

In an effective piece of writing, the author's angle of vision often works so subtly that unsuspecting readers—unless they learn to think rhetorically—will be drawn into the writer's spell and believe that the writer's prose conveys the "whole picture" of its subject rather than a limited picture filtered through the screen of the writer's perspective.

Contrasting Angles of Vision in Two Texts Consider the differences in what gets seen in the following two descriptions of the Arctic National Wildlife Refuge in Alaska (the ANWR), where proponents of oil exploration are locked in a fierce battle with anti-exploration conservationists. The first passage is from a pro-exploration advocacy group called Arctic Power; the second is from former President Jimmy Carter.

ARCTIC POWER'S DESCRIPTION OF THE ANWR

On the coastal plain [of the ANWR], the Arctic winter lasts for 9 months. It is dark continuously for 56 days in midwinter. Temperatures with the wind chill can reach –110 degrees F. It's not pristine. There are villages, roads, houses, schools, and military installations. It's not a unique Arctic ecosystem. The coastal plain is only a small fraction of the 88,000 square miles that make up the North Slope. The same tundra environment and wildlife can be found throughout the circumpolar Arctic regions. The 1002 Area [the legal term for the plot of coastal plain being contested] is flat. That's why they call it a plain. […]

Some groups want to make the 1002 Area a wilderness. But a vote for wilderness is a vote against American jobs.

JIMMY CARTER'S DESCRIPTION OF THE ANWR

Rosalynn [Carter's wife] and I always look for opportunities to visit parks and wildlife areas in our travels. But nothing matches the spectacle of wildlife we found on the coastal plain of America's Arctic National Wildlife Refuge in Alaska. To the north lay the Arctic Ocean; to the south rolling foothills rose toward the glaciated peaks of the Brooks Range. At our feet was a mat of low tundra plant life, bursting with new growth, perched atop the permafrost.

As we watched, 80,000 caribou surged across the vast expanse around us. Called by instinct older than history, this Porcupine (River) caribou herd was in the midst of its annual migration. To witness this vast sea of caribou in an uncorrupted wilderness home, and the wolves, ptarmigan, grizzlies, polar bears, musk oxen and millions of migratory birds, was a profoundly humbling experience. We were reminded of our human dependence on the natural world.

Sadly, we were also forced to imagine what we might see if the caribou were replaced by smoke-belching oil rigs, highways and a pipeline that would destroy forever the plain's delicate and precious ecosystem.

How Angle of Vision Persuades To understand more clearly how angle of vision persuades, you can analyze the language strategies at work. Some of these strategies—which writers employ consciously or unconsciously to achieve their intended effects—are described in the following strategies chart.

Strategies for Constructing an Angle of Vision		
Strategy	**ANWR Example**	**U. R. Riddle Example**
State your intention directly.	• Earlier passages directly state Arctic Powers' pro-drilling and Carter's anti-drilling stances.	• You might say "Riddle would make an excellent manager" or "Riddle doesn't have the personality to be a bank manager."
Select details that support your intentions; omit or de-emphasize others.	• Arctic Power writer (AP) "sees" the cold, barren darkness of the ANWR; Carter sees the beauty.	• A positive view of Riddle would select and emphasize Riddle's good traits and de-emphasize or omit his bad ones.

(continued)

Strategy	ANWR Example	U. R. Riddle Example
	• AP spotlights the people who live on the coastal plain while making the animals invisible; Carter spotlights the caribou while omitting the people. • To AP, drilling means jobs; to Carter it means destructive oil rigs.	• A negative view would take opposite the tack.
Choose words that frame your subject in the desired way or have desired connotations.	• AP frames the ANWR as the dreary "1002 Area"; Carter frames it as a "spectacle of wildlife," a unique "delicate and precious ecosystem." • Arctic Power uses words with negative connotations ("wind chill"); Carter uses words connoting life and growth ("a mat of low tundra plant life").	• "Riddle is an independent thinker who doesn't follow the crowd" (frames him positively in value system that favors individualism). • "Riddle is a loner who thinks egocentrically" (frames him negatively in value system favoring consensus and social skills). • You could say, "Riddle is forthright" or "Riddle is rude"—positive versus negative connotations.
Use figurative language (metaphors, similes, and analogies) that conveys your intended effect.	• AP avoids figurative language, claiming objective presentation of facts. • Carter uses positive metaphors to convey ANWR's vitality (tundra "bursting with new growth") and negative metaphors for drilling ("smoke-belching oil rigs").	• To suggest that Riddle has outgrown his alienating behavior, you could say, "Riddle is a social late bloomer." • To recommend against hiring Riddle while still being positive, you could say, "Riddle's independent spirit would feel caged in by the routine of a bank."
Use sentence structure to emphasize and de-emphasize your ideas. *(Emphasize an idea by placing it at the end of a long sentence, in a short sentence, or in a main clause.)*	• AP uses short sentences to emphasize main points: "It's not pristine." It's not a unique ecosystem." "That's why they call it a plain." • Carter uses longer sentences for description, with an occasional short sentence to make a point: "We were reminded of our human dependence on the natural world."	Consider the difference between the following: • "Although Riddle had problems relating to other students, he is a brilliant thinker." • "Although Riddle is a brilliant thinker, he had problems relating to other students in the class."

CONCEPT 9 **Messages persuade through appeals to *logos*, *ethos*, and *pathos*.**

Another way to think about the persuasive power of texts is to examine the strategies writers or speakers use to sway their audiences toward a certain position on an issue. To win people's consideration of their ideas, writers or speakers can appeal to what the classical philosopher Aristotle called *logos, ethos*, and *pathos.* Developing the habit of examining how these appeals are functioning in texts and being able to employ these appeals in your own writing will enhance your ability to read and write rhetorically. Let's look briefly at each:

A fuller discussion of these classical appeals appears in Chapter 9, "Writing a Classical Argument."

- *Logos* **is the appeal to reason.** It refers to the quality of the message itself— to its internal consistency, to its clarity in asserting a thesis or point, and to the quality of reasons and evidence used to support the point.
- *Ethos* **is the appeal to the character of the speaker/writer.** It refers to the speaker/writer's trustworthiness and credibility. One can often increase one's *ethos* in a message by being knowledgeable about the issue, by appearing thoughtful and fair, by listening well, and by being respectful of alternative points of view. A writer's accuracy and thoroughness in crediting sources and professionalism in caring about the format, grammar, and neat appearance of a document are part of the appeal to *ethos.*
- *Pathos* **is the appeal to the sympathies, values, beliefs, and emotions of the audience.** Appeals to *pathos* can be made in many ways. *Pathos* can often be enhanced through evocative visual images, frequently used in Web sites, posters, and magazine or newspaper articles. In written texts, the same effects can be created through vivid examples and details, through connotative language, and through empathy with the audience's beliefs and values.

To see how these three appeals are interrelated, you can visualize a triangle with points labeled *Message, Audience,* and *Writer* or *Speaker.* Rhetoricians study how effective communicators consider all three points of this *rhetorical triangle.* (See Figure 3.2.)

We encourage you to ask questions about the appeals to *logos, ethos,* and *pathos* every time you examine a text. For example, is the appeal to *logos* weakened by the writer's use of scanty and questionable evidence? Has the writer made a powerful appeal to *ethos* by documenting her sources and showing that she is an authority on the issue? Has the writer relied too heavily on appeals to *pathos* by using numerous heart-wringing examples? Later chapters in this textbook will help you use these appeals competently in your own writing as well as analyze these appeals in others' messages.

CONCEPT 10 **Nonverbal messages persuade through visual strategies that can be analyzed rhetorically.**

Chapter 8 deals extensively with visual rhetoric, explaining how visual elements work together to create a persuasive effect.

Just as you can think rhetorically about texts, you can think rhetorically about photographs, drawings, and other images as well as artifacts such as clothing or cars.

Message
Logos: How can I make my ideas internally consistent and logical? How can I find the best reasons and support them with the best evidence?

Audience
Pathos: How can I make the readers open to my message? How can I best engage my readers' emotions and imaginations? How can I appeal to my readers' values and interests?

Writer or Speaker
Ethos: How can I present myself effectively? How can I enhance my credibility and trustworthiness?

FIGURE 3.2 Rhetorical Triangle

Visual Rhetoric

Consider, for example, the persuasive power of famous photographs from the war in Iraq. Early in the war, several widely publicized images, particularly the film footage of the toppling of the statue of Saddam Hussein and the "Mission Accomplished" photograph of former President George W. Bush wearing a pilot's flight suit on the deck of the aircraft carrier *Abraham Lincoln*, served to consolidate public support of the war. Later, certain images began eating away at public support. For example, an unauthorized picture of flag-draped coffins filling the freight deck of a military transport plane focused attention on those killed in the war. Particularly devastating for supporters of the war were the images of American guards sexually humiliating Iraqi prisoners in the Abu Ghraib prison. Images like these stick in viewers' memories long after specific texts are forgotten.

What gives images this persuasive power? For one thing, they can be apprehended at a glance, condensing an argument into a memorable scene or symbol that taps deeply into our emotions and values. Images also persuade by appealing to *logos, ethos*, and *pathos*. They make implicit arguments (*logos*) while also appealing to our values and emotions (*pathos*) and causing us to respond favorably or unfavorably to the artist or photographer (*ethos*). Like verbal texts, images have an angle of vision, which can be crafted by selecting, manipulating, and often photoshopping images to control what viewers see and thus influence what they think. (Note that "angle of vision" is itself a visual metaphor.) Through the location and angle of the camera, the distance from the subject, and the framing, cropping, and filtering of the image, the photographer steers us toward a particular view of the subject, influencing us to forget, at least momentarily, that there are other ways of seeing the same subject.

Although images can have powerful rhetorical effects, these effects may be less controllable and more audience-dependent than those of verbal texts. Consider, for example, the wind farm photograph on page 3. In this striking image, the dominance of the whirling turbines could convey several implicit arguments. Some viewers might find that this photo fuels their objections to wind farms. They might zero in on how intrusive, massive, and unattractive wind turbines are. The blurred blades of the gigantic turbines might strike them as frightening or menacing. These same viewers, though, might respond more positively to a longdistance photo of wind turbines against a scarlet sunset over the hills. In contrast, other viewers might interpret these wind turbines in motion as an argument for the plentiful energy that wind farms generate. For these viewers, the photograph's angle of vision, which emphasizes the size and power of these wind towers against a background of barren hills and blue sky, could be used to counter David Rockwood's argument in his letter to the editor in Chapter 1 (pp. 5–6) that wind power is unreliable and destroys the "pristine wilderness." Instead, to these viewers the photograph suggests that wind farms make productive use of arid or barren land. Interpreted this way, this photo could be seen to use *pathos* to appeal to environmentalists' concerns (preserve beautiful landscape; don't harm wildlife) while evoking positive feelings about technology. In either case, viewers would agree that the photographer is obviously a professional, who uses an upward camera placement to emphasize the technological power of the wind turbines. One's feelings toward the photograph and the photographer may also depend on how much the photograph seems "natural" as opposed to being framed for artistic or political effect. Because images are somewhat open in the way they create visual arguments, writers of texts that include images should anticipate viewers' possible alternative interpretations.

Analyzing Visual Messages

FOR WRITING AND DISCUSSION

The following exercise asks you to think about how rhetorical effects of images can create implicit arguments. Figures 3.3–3.6 depict the controversial northernmost part of Alaska—the Arctic National Wildlife Refuge and the North Slope near the Brooks Range that Arctic Power and Jimmy Carter described on page 55. This region figures prominently in public debates about the United States' energy independence, climate change, environmental preservation, and unexplored sources of oil. Note that oil drilling has long been established in the North Slope but is currently forbidden in the adjacent ANWR. Working in small groups or as a whole class, explore the rhetorical effect of images by doing the following two tasks.

(continued)

1. ***Analyzing the Photos.*** Explore the rhetorical effect of these images, noting how the effect may differ from person to person.
   a. In each photograph, on what details has the photographer chosen to focus? How do the details contribute to a dominant impression conveyed by the whole photograph? How does the photograph affect you emotionally? How does it make you feel about the ANWR/North Slope?
   b. Place your impression of the ANWR/North Slope, as conveyed by each of these images, on a continuum from ugly/forbidding to beautiful/fascinating or from barren/empty of animal life to biologically rich.
2. ***Using the Photos.*** Now imagine that you are creating a flyer for each of the following audiences and purposes. Which photo would you use to make the most compelling argument (consider *logos, ethos,* and *pathos*) for each audience? Explain your reasoning. Note that there is no "right answer" for these questions. If you think that none of the photographs would be

FIGURE 3.3 Caribou Crossing a River in the Arctic National Wildlife Refuge

FIGURE 3.4 Caribou Grazing Near Oil Pipeline in the Arctic North Slope

FIGURE 3.5 The ANWR Coastal Plain in Winter

FIGURE 3.6 Oil-Extraction Plant, North Slope

appropriate for the designated audience and purpose, what kind of photograph would be more effective?

a. *Audience:* tourists
   Purpose: to invite people to buy tour packages to the Arctic National Wildlife Refuge and the North Slope

b. *Audience*: political leaders and voters
   Purpose: to persuade decision makers to take a pro-environment, anti-business stand on this region

c. *Audience*: political leaders and voters
   Purpose: to persuade decision makers to see this region as remote, empty, and therefore available for oil exploration and business development

d. *Audience*: undecided voters who want both more oil and a preserved environment
   Purpose: to persuade people to see that economic development in the ANWR can be compatible with preserving the region's unique natural beauty and wildlife

The Rhetoric of Clothing and Other Consumer Items

Not only do photographs, paintings, and drawings have rhetorical power, but so do the images projected by many of our consumer choices. Consider, for example, the rhetorical thinking that goes into our choice of clothes. We choose our clothes not only to keep ourselves covered and warm but also to project visually our identification with certain social groups and subcultures. For example, if you want to be identified as a skateboarder, a preppy socialite, a geek, a NASCAR fan, or a junior partner in a corporate law firm, you know how to select clothes and accessories that convey that identification. The way you dress is a code that communicates where you fit (or how you want to be perceived as fitting) within a class and social structure.

How do these symbolic codes get established? They can be set by fashion designers, by advertisers, or by trendy groups or individuals. The key to any new clothing code is to make it look different in some distinctive way from an earlier code or from a code of another group. Sometimes clothing codes develop to show rebellion against the values of parents or authority figures. At other times they develop to show new kinds of group identities.

Clothing codes are played on in conscious ways in fashion advertisements so that consumers become very aware of what identifications are signaled by different styles and brands. This aspect of consumer society is so ubiquitous that one of the marks of growing affluence in third world countries is people's attention to the rhetoric of consumer goods. Consider the second epigraph to this chapter, which indicates that villagers in India watching TV ads notice not only the soap or shampoo being advertised but also the brands of motorbikes and the lifestyles of the people in the ads. Buying a certain kind of consumer good projects a certain kind of status or group or class identity. Our point, from a rhetorical perspective, is that in making a consumer choice, many people are concerned not only with the quality of the item itself but also with its rhetorical symbolism. Note that the same item can send quite different messages to different groups: A Rolex watch might enhance one's credibility at a corporate board meeting while undercutting it at a barbecue for union workers.

Clothing as Visual Arguments

The rhetorical power of clothing especially comes into play in the workplace. This exercise asks to you think about workplace dress codes, which are enforced by peer pressure and peer modeling as well as by company policies. Figures 3.7 to 3.10 show four different workplace environments. Working in small groups or as a whole class, consider the rhetoric of workplace clothing by sharing your responses to the following questions:

1. How would you describe the differences in dress codes in each of these environments?
2. If you were employed in one of these workplaces, how much do you think you could vary your style of dress without violating workplace codes?

FIGURE 3.7 Engineering Firm

FIGURE 3.8 Warehouse

FIGURE 3.9 Associates, Law Firm

FIGURE 3.10 Espresso Bar

3. Suppose that you are interviewing for a job in one of these workplaces. What clothing would be appropriate for your interview and why? (Note that how you dress for an interview might be different from how you dress once you have the job.) Share your rhetorical thinking about clothing choices aimed at making the best first impression on the people who interview you. Be as specific as possible for all items of clothing including shoes and accessories.
4. To what extent are dress codes for women more complex than those for men?

Chapter Summary

In this chapter we have looked briefly at rhetorical theory in order to explain the persuasive power of both verbal and visual texts.

- *Concept 8: Messages persuade through their angle of vision.* Any text necessarily looks at its subject from a perspective—an angle of vision—that selects and emphasizes some details while omitting or minimizing others. You can analyze writers' angle of vision by considering their direct statements of intention, their selection of details, their word choice, their figures of speech, and their manipulation of sentence structure to control emphasis.
- *Concept 9: Messages persuade through appeals to* **logos, ethos,** *and* **pathos.** *Logos* refers to the power of the writer's reasons and evidence; *pathos* to the way the writer connects to the reader's sympathies, emotions, values, and beliefs; and *ethos* to the way the writer portrays himself or herself as trustworthy and credible.
- *Concept 10: Nonverbal messages persuade through visual strategies that can be analyzed rhetorically.* Like verbal texts, visual texts have an angle of vision created by the way the image is framed and by the perspective from which it is viewed. Images also make implicit arguments (*logos*), appeal to the viewer's emotions and values (*pathos*), and suggest the creator's character and trustworthiness (*ethos*). One can also analyze consumer choices (clothing, jewelry, cars) rhetorically because such choices make implicit arguments about the consumer's desired identity.

Analyzing Angle of Vision in Two Passages about Nuclear Energy	BRIEF WRITING PROJECT

Background and Readings

This brief writing project will give you practice at analyzing the angle of vision in different texts. The assignment focuses on two passages about nuclear power plants.

The first passage is from the home page of NuclearPowerNow, a nuclear power advocacy site. It was posted in 2008.

Nuclear Power Now

Nuclear power is the world's largest source of emission-free energy. Nuclear power plants produce no controlled air pollutants, such as sulfur and particulates, or greenhouse gases. The use of nuclear power in place of other energy sources helps to keep the air clean, preserve the Earth's climate, avoid ground-level ozone formation and prevent acid rain.

Nuclear power has important implications for our national security. Inexpensive nuclear power, in combination with fuel cell technology, could significantly reduce our dependency on foreign oil.

Nuclear power plants have experienced an admirable safety record. About 20% of electricity generated in the U.S. comes from nuclear power, and in the last forty years of this production, not one single fatality has occurred as a result of the operation of a civilian nuclear power plant in the United States. In comparison, many people die in coal mining accidents every year and approximately ten thousand Americans die every year from pollution related to coal burning.

The nuclear power industry generates approximately 2,000 tons of solid waste annually in the United States. In comparison, coal fueled power plants produce 100,000,000 tons of ash and sludge annually, and this ash is laced with poisons such as mercury and nitric oxide.

Even this 2,000 tons of nuclear waste is not a technical problem. Reprocessing of nuclear fuel, and the implementation of Integral Fast Reactor technology, will enable us to turn the vast majority of what is currently considered waste into energy.

Unfortunately, the voting public has been victimized by forty years of misinformation regarding the safety of nuclear power. The graphs on nuclear energy showing it to be safe, economical, and in our national interest are countered by anti-nuclear activists using fear tactics to frighten the electorate into inaction.

Until we can successfully educate the American electorate on the real pros and cons of nuclear power, we will not be able to engage in a healthy national discussion on the topic.

The second passage is by Carl Pope, the executive director of the Sierra Club. This brief article was posted in September 2009 on the "Great Debate" blog site hosted by Reuters, a news service focused on business and industry.

Nuclear Power Is Not the Way Forward

Nuclear power is not a responsible choice and makes no sense as part of America's clean energy future. We can meet our energy needs through energy efficiency and renewable energy, and have a clean and healthy world without nuclear power.

There are four insurmountable problems with nuclear power.

First, nuclear power produces highly dangerous radioactive waste. Every nuclear reactor generates about 20 tons of highly radioactive spent nuclear fuel and additional low-level radioactive waste per year. The waste can kill at high doses and cause cancer and birth defects at low doses. Nuclear waste remains dangerous to humans for 200 thousand years.

Worse, we don't know what to do with this waste once it is generated. Some propose dumping nuclear waste in Yucca Mountain, NV; however, the mountain is seismically active. An earthquake in the 1990's caused over $1 million damage to a

Department of Energy (DOE) facility at the site. In addition, a Department of Energy panel of scientists has found that the nuclear material may leak from the containment vessels over time and will contaminate groundwater. On its way to Yucca Mountain, the waste would also pass through thousands of cities and towns and present multiple exposure risks.

Second, nuclear power is prohibitively expensive. The method is not anywhere near cost effective; nuclear plants in the states of Oregon, New York, Maine, Illinois, and Connecticut have been shut down because the owners found it was too expensive to keep them going.

American taxpayers are also subsidizing the nuclear industry. According to the Congressional Research Service, the industry has cost taxpayers tens of billions of dollars in research and development subsidies.

Third, an accident at a coal plant is a problem, but an accident at a nuclear plant can be a disaster. Because human beings operate plants and drive the trucks that transport nuclear waste, accidents can and will happen. The danger with nuclear power is that the stakes in accidents are extremely high. Anyone exposed to radiation leaks or accidents will likely sicken or die from that exposure.

And finally, there is a risk that nuclear material will fall into the wrong hands. Some have recommended that we consider "reprocessing" of spent nuclear fuel, a method that consolidates waste into weapons-usable plutonium. The government has elaborate plans to prevent rogue nations and terrorists from stealing the nuclear fuel or waste to make nuclear bombs. The more nuclear reactors, the more risk of radioactive material being stolen to make bombs.

Nuclear power is not the way forward. America deserves a safer, cleaner, and cheaper energy future.

Your task: Contrast the differences in angle of vision in these two passages by analyzing how they create their different rhetorical effects. Consider factors such as overt statements of meaning, selection/omission of details, connotations of words and figures of speech, and sentence emphasis. To help guide your analysis, review the strategies chart ("Strategies for Constructing an Angle of Vision") on pages 55–56. Your goal here is to explain to your readers how these two passages create different impressions of nuclear power.

4

THINKING RHETORICALLY ABOUT STYLE AND DOCUMENT DESIGN

Style is everything, and nothing. It is not that, as is commonly supposed, you get your content and soup it up with style; style is absolutely embedded in the way you perceive.

—*Martin Amis, Author*

... [C]larity and excellence in thinking is very much like clarity and excellence in the display of data. When principles of design replicate principles of thought, the act of arranging information becomes an act of thought.

—*Edward Tufte, Visual Design Researcher and Consultant*

In Chapters 1, 2, and 3, we explained the importance of rhetorical thinking for writers. In this chapter, we focus on the rhetorical effect of different writing styles and document designs and suggest ways to increase the power and effectiveness of your prose. As our two epigraphs suggest, style and document design are not decorative add-ons to jazz up dull content but rather means of guiding an audience to see what matters. Style and document design are thus "acts of thought."

To build on your understanding of rhetorical effectiveness, in this chapter you will learn two new concepts:

- **CONCEPT 11** Good writers make purposeful stylistic choices.
- **CONCEPT 12** Good writers make purposeful document design choices.

CONCEPT 11 **Good writers make purposeful stylistic choices.**

You can gain power as a writer by understanding the rhetorical effect of different writing styles.

Factors That Affect Style

Style refers to analyzable features of language that work together to create different effects. As shown in Figure 4.1, style can be thought of as a mixture of four factors:

- *Ways of shaping sentences,* such as length or complexity of sentence structure
- *Word choice,* such as abstract versus concrete or formal versus colloquial
- *Voice, or persona,* which refers to the reader's impression of the writer as projected from the page: expert versus layperson or scholarly voice versus popular voice
- *Tone,* which refers to the writer's attitude toward the subject matter or toward the reader, such as cold or warm, humorous or serious, detached or passionate

What style you adopt depends on your purpose, audience, and genre. Consider, for example, the differences in style in two articles about the animated sitcom *South Park.* The first passage comes from an academic journal in which the author analyzes how race is portrayed in *South Park.* The second passage is from a popular magazine, where the author argues that despite *South Park*'s vulgarity, the sitcom has a redeeming social value.

PASSAGE FROM SCHOLARLY JOURNAL

In these cartoons, multiplicity encodes a set of nonwhite identities to be appropriated and commodified by whiteness. In the cartoon world, obscene humor and satire mediate this commodification. The whiteness that appropriates typically does so by virtue of its mobile positioning between and through imagined boundaries contrarily shown as impassible to black characters or agents marked as black. Let me briefly turn to an appropriately confusing example of such a character in *South Park*'s

FIGURE 4.1 Ingredients of Style

Ways of shaping sentences	Types of words	Voice or persona	Tone
Long/short Simple/complex Many modifiers/few modifiers Normal word order/frequent inversions or interruptions Mostly main clauses/many embedded phrases and subordinate clauses	Abstract/concrete Formal/colloquial Unusual/ordinary Specialized/general Metaphorical/literal Scientific/literary	Expert/layperson Scholar/student Outsider/insider Political liberal/conservative Neutral observer/active participant	Intimate/distant Personal/impersonal Angry/calm Browbeating/sharing Informative/entertaining Humorous/serious Ironic/literal Passionately involved/aloof

scatological hero extraordinaire, Eric Cartman. ... Eric Cartman's yen for breaking into Black English and interactions with black identities also fashion him an appropriator. However, Cartman's voice and persona may be seen as only an avatar, one layer of textual identity for creator Trey Parker, who may be regarded in one sense as a "blackvoice" performer.

—Michael A. Chaney, "Representations of Race and Place in *Static Shock, King of the Hill,* and *South Park*"

PASSAGE FROM POPULAR MAGAZINE

Despite the theme song's chamber of commerce puffery, *South Park* is the closest television has ever come to depicting hell on earth. Its inhabitants are, almost without exception, stupid, ignorant or venal—usually all three. Its central characters are four eight-year-olds: Stan, the high-achiever, Kyle, the sensitive Jew, Kenny, whose grisly death each week prompts the tortured cry, "Oh my God! They've killed Kenny! Those bastards!" and Eric Cartman, who has become the Archie Bunker of the '90s, beloved by millions. My 12-year-old son informs me that many of his schoolmates have taken to speaking permanently in Cartman's bigoted and usually furiously inarticulate manner. A (mild) sample: any display of human sensitivity is usually met by him with the rejoinder: "Tree-hugging hippie crap!" This has led to predictable calls for *South Park*, which is usually programmed late in the evening, to be banned altogether.

—Kevin Michael Grace, "*South Park* Is a Snort of Defiance Against a World Gone to Hell"

FOR WRITING AND DISCUSSION

Analyzing Differences in Style

Working in small groups or as a whole class, analyze the differences in the styles of these two samples.

1. How would you describe differences in the length and complexity of sentences, in the level of vocabulary, and in the degree of formality?
2. How do the differences in styles create different voices, personas, and tones?
3. Based on clues from style and genre, who is the intended audience of each piece? What is the writer's purpose? How does each writer hope to surprise the intended audience with something new, challenging, or valuable?
4. How are the differences in content and style influenced by differences in purpose, audience, and genre?

In the sections that follow, we highlight some ways of thinking about style that will be particularly relevant to you in your college writing.

Four Powerful Strategies for Improving Your Style

The preceding section has given you an overview of vocabulary and concepts for analyzing style. In this section we offer four powerful tips for making your own style forceful, clear, and effective. Of all the advice given about style in various handbooks, these four tips are usually regarded as essential—so much so that they rise to the level of rhetorical principles.

Streamline Your Prose by Cutting Deadwood In early drafts, writers often produce wordy, convoluted prose where unneeded words and roundabout expressions take up space without adding meaning. When they revise, experienced writers cut deadwood and use other strategies to make their prose as efficient and economical as possible. Their aim is to create streamlined sentences that keep the reader on track. In the following examples, consider how cutting words creates a leaner, more streamlined style:

Wordy/Verbose	Streamlined
As a result of the labor policies established by Bismarck, the working-class people in Germany were convinced that revolution was unnecessary for the attainment of their goals and purposes.	Bismarck's labor policies convinced the German working class that revolution was unnecessary.
In recent times a new interest has been apparent among many writers to make the language as it is used by specialists in the areas of government, law, and medicine more available to be understood and appreciated by readers who are not specialists in the aforementioned areas.	Recently writers have tried to make the language of government, law, and medicine more accessible to nonspecialist readers.

Control Emphasis with Sentence Structure Experienced writers vary the length and structure of their sentences to create a rhythm that emphasizes main ideas. For example, you can emphasize an idea by placing it in a main clause or by placing it in a short sentence surrounded by longer sentences. We illustrated this phenomenon in our discussion of the U. R. Riddle exercise (pp. 53–54), where variations in sentence structure created different emphases on Riddle's good or bad points:

> Although Riddle is a brilliant thinker, he had problems relating to other students in my class. (Emphasizes Riddle's personal shortcomings.)
> Although Riddle had problems relating to other students in my class, he is a brilliant thinker. (Emphasizes Riddle's intelligence.)

Neither of these effects would have been possible had the writer simply strung together two simple sentences:

> Riddle had problems relating to other students in my class. He is also a brilliant thinker.

In this version, both points about Riddle are equally emphasized, leaving the reader uncertain about the writer's intended meaning.

Our point is that subordinate structures help the reader distinguish between main and subordinate ideas. If you string together a long sequence of short sentences—or simply join them with words like *and, or, so,* or *but*—you create a choppy effect that fails to distinguish between more important and less important material. Consider the differences in the following examples.

Every Idea Equally Emphasized	Main Ideas Emphasized	Comment
Hisako usually attends each lab meeting. However, she missed the last one. She took the train to Boston to meet her sister. Her sister was arriving from Tokyo.	Although Hisako usually attends each lab meeting, she missed the last one because she took the train to Boston to meet her sister, who was arriving from Tokyo.	Sentence now focuses on main idea—why Hisako missed the lab.
I am a student at Sycamore College, and I live in Watkins Hall, and I am enclosing a proposal that concerns a problem with dorm life. There is too much drinking, so nondrinking students don't have an alcohol-free place to go, and so the university should create an alcohol-free dorm, and they should strictly enforce this no-alcohol policy.	As a Sycamore College student living in Watkins Hall, I am enclosing a proposal to improve dorm life. Because there is too much drinking on campus, there is no place for nondrinking students to go. I propose that the university create an alcohol-free dorm and strictly enforce the no-alcohol policy.	The fact that the writer is a Sycamore College student living in Watkins Hall is needed background information but not a main point. Focus of passage is now a crisp summary of the problem and her proposed solution.

In each of the above examples, the revised passage is easier to process because it subordinates less important material, focusing the reader's attention on main ideas.

Use Specific Details, Where Appropriate, to Stay Low on the Ladder of Abstraction In previous writing courses, you might have been offered advice such as "Show, don't tell" or "Use concrete, specific language." Our advice in this section follows the same spirit: to write as low on the ladder of abstraction as your context allows.

We use the metaphor of a ladder to show how words can vary along a continuum from the abstract ("crime") to the more specific and concrete ("aggravated assault with brass knuckles"). As a general rule, when you move from points to particulars in your prose, the more specific you can make these particulars, the more vivid the rhetorical effect on a reader. As an illustration, consider Figure 4.2, which depicts a "ladder of abstraction" descending from abstract terms at the top toward more specific ones at the bottom.

Choosing words low on the ladder of abstraction is particularly effective for descriptive writing, where your goal is to create a vivid mental image for readers. Writing teachers often express this advice through the maxim "Show, don't tell." *Tell* words interpret a scene or tell readers what to feel about a scene without describing it. ("The dog looked angry.") In contrast, *show* words describe a scene through sensory details. ("The neighbor's Doberman, growling and baring his

Level on Ladder	Clothing Example	Global Problem Example	Gendered Play Example
High level: Abstract or general	• She chose new footwear.	• Should farmers in developing countries produce traditional crops or commercial crops?	• Sam exhibited traditionally gendered play behavior.
Middle level	• She chose new flip-flops.	• In India, should farmers plant traditional crops or genetically engineered crops?	• Sam played with trucks and fire engines.
Low level: Specific or concrete	• She chose new purple platform flip-flops with rhinestones.	• For sale on the global market, should farmers of Northern India plant traditional mandua and jhangora or genetically modified soy beans?	• Sam gleefully smashed his toy Tonka fire engine into the coffee table.

FIGURE 4.2 The Ladder of Abstraction: From Abstract to Specific

teeth, lunged against his chain.") The description itself evokes the desired effect without requiring the writer to interpret it overtly. This difference in rhetorical effect can be seen in the following examples of descriptive writing:

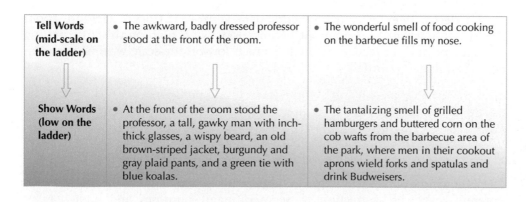

Tell Words (mid-scale on the ladder)	• The awkward, badly dressed professor stood at the front of the room.	• The wonderful smell of food cooking on the barbecue fills my nose.
Show Words (low on the ladder)	• At the front of the room stood the professor, a tall, gawky man with inch-thick glasses, a wispy beard, an old brown-striped jacket, burgundy and gray plaid pants, and a green tie with blue koalas.	• The tantalizing smell of grilled hamburgers and buttered corn on the cob wafts from the barbecue area of the park, where men in their cookout aprons wield forks and spatulas and drink Budweisers.

Of course, not all writing needs to be this low on the ladder of abstraction. Our advice, rather, is to descend as low on the ladder as your context allows. Even the most abstract kind of prose will move up and down between several rungs on the ladder. In closed-form prose writers need to make choices about the level of specificity that will be most effective based on their purpose, audience, and genre. Note the differences in the levels of abstraction in the following passages:

PASSAGE 1: FAIRLY HIGH ON LADDER OF ABSTRACTION

Point sentence

Particulars high on ladder of abstraction

> Although lightning produces the most deaths and injuries of all weather-related accidents, the rate of danger varies considerably from state to state. Florida has twice as many deaths and injuries from lightning strikes as any other state. Hawaii and Alaska have the fewest.

—Passage from a general interest informative article on weather-related accidents

PASSAGE 2: LOWER ON LADDER OF ABSTRACTION

Point sentence

Particulars at midlevel on ladder

Particulars at lower level on ladder

> Florida has twice as many deaths and injuries from lightning strikes as any other state, with many of these casualties occurring on the open spaces of golf courses. Florida golfers should carefully note the signals of dangerous weather conditions such as darkening skies, a sudden drop in temperature, an increase in wind, flashes of light and claps of thunder, and the sensation of an electric charge on one's hair or body. In the event of an electric storm, golfers should run into a forest, get under a shelter, get into a car, or assume the safest body position. To avoid being the tallest object in an area, if caught in open areas, golfers should find a low spot, spread out, and crouch into a curled position with feet together to create minimal body contact with the ground.

—Passage from a safety article aimed at Florida golfers

See Rockwood's letter to the editor, pp. 5–6.

Both of these passages are effective for their audience and purpose. The first passage might be compared to a distant shot with a camera, giving an overview of lightning deaths in the United States, while the second zooms in for a more detailed look at a specific case, Florida golf courses. Sometimes, low-on-the-ladder particulars consist of statistics or quotations rather than sensory details. For example, civil engineer David Rockwood uses low-on-the-ladder numerical data about the size and number of wind towers to convince readers that wind generation of electricity entails environmental damage. Your rhetorical decisions about level of abstraction are important because too much high-on-the-scale writing can become dull for readers, while too much low-on-the-scale writing can seem overwhelming or pointless.

FOR WRITING AND DISCUSSION

Choosing Details for Different Levels on the Ladder of Abstraction

The following exercise will help you appreciate how details can be chosen at different levels of abstraction to serve different purposes and audiences. Working in small groups or as a whole class, invent details at appropriate positions on the ladder of abstraction for each of the following point sentences.

1. *Yesterday's game was a major disappointment.* You are writing an e-mail message to a friend who is a fan (of baseball, football, basketball, another sport) and missed the game; use midlevel details to explain what was disappointing.

2. *Although the game stank, there were some great moments.* Switch to low-on-the-ladder specific details to describe one of these "great moments."
3. *Advertising in women's fashion magazines creates a distorted and unhealthy view of beauty.* You are writing an analysis for a college course on popular culture; use high-to-midlevel details to give a one-paragraph overview of several ways these ads create an unhealthy view of beauty.
4. *One recent ad, in particular, conveys an especially destructive message about beauty.* Choose a particular ad and describe it with low-on-the-ladder, very specific details.

Use a Voice Matched to Your Purpose, Audience, and Genre   College students often wonder what style—and particularly, what voice—is appropriate for college papers. For most college assignments, we recommend that you approximate your natural speaking voice to give your writing a conversational academic style. By "natural," we mean a voice that strives to be plain and clear while retaining the engaging quality of a person who is enthusiastic about the subject.

Of course, as you become an expert in a discipline, you may need to move toward a more scholarly voice. For example, the prose in an academic journal article can be extremely dense with technical terms and complex sentence structure, but expert readers in that field understand and expect this voice. Students sometimes try to imitate a dense academic style before they have achieved the disciplinary expertise to make the style sound natural. The result can seem pretentiously stilted and phony—an "inflated" style. At the other extreme, students sometimes adopt an overly informal or street slang voice that doesn't fit an academic context. Writing with clarity and directness within your natural range will usually create the most effective and powerful voice. Consider the difference in the following examples:

Inflated Voice	Natural Speaking Voice	Overly Informal Voice
As people advance in age, they experience time-dependent alterations in their ability to adapt to environmental change. However, much prior research on the aging process has failed to differentiate between detrimental changes that result from an organism's aging process itself and detrimental changes resulting from a disease process that is often associated with aging.	As people get older, they are less able to adapt to changes in their environment. Research on aging, however, hasn't always distinguished between loss of function caused by aging itself and loss caused by diseases common among older people.	Old folks don't adapt well to changes in their environments. Some scientists who studied the cane and walker crowd found out that it was hard to tell the difference between bad stuff caused by age versus bad stuff caused by disease.

Although the "natural voice" style is appropriate for most college papers, especially those written for lower-division courses, many professors construct assignments asking you to adopt different voices and different styles. It is thus important to understand the professor's assignment and to adopt the style and voice appropriate for the assigned rhetorical situation.

Revising Passages to Create a More Effective Style

Working individually or in small groups, try to improve the style of the following passages by cutting deadwood, by combining sentences to subordinate less important ideas and emphasize main points, or by achieving a more natural voice.

1. It is unfortunate that the mayor acted in this manner. The mayor settled the issue. But before he settled the issue he made a mistake. He fostered a public debate that was very bitter. The debate pitted some of his subordinates against each other. These subordinates were in fact key subordinates. It also caused many other people to feel inflamed passions and fears as a result of the way the mayor handled the issue.
2. Cheerleading should be seen as a sport. It should not be regarded as just sexy dancing. This issue is especially important to women. It is often the desire of junior high school girls to want to become cheerleaders, but their role models for achieving this desire are the Dallas Cowboys cheerleaders, but instead the vision they should strive to achieve is a vision of cheerleaders as athletes. Such athletes in order to become cheerleaders must be able to do very athletic moves and stunts such as handstands, cartwheels, handsprings, high jumps, and the splits. A great cheerleader is not a girl who makes suggestive moves like a pop star in an MTV video, but instead it is a girl who can participate in routines that are complex like lifts, tosses, flips, catches, and other gymnastic moves.

CONCEPT 12 **Good writers make purposeful document design choices.**

Document design refers to the format of a text including use of charts, illustrations, or visual images. The "look" of a document can signal to readers its purpose, its genre, its intended audience, and the writer's intended (or unintended!) *ethos*. Writers need to distinguish between document design appropriate for manuscripts—a category that includes most of the kinds of writing you will do in college—and document design for published works.

Document Design for Manuscripts and Papers

As a writer in an academic setting, you will usually be producing manuscript (keyboarded pages of typed text held together with a staple or folder, or submitted electronically) rather than a publication-ready document. Your document design choices mainly concern margins, font style and size, material in headers or footers (page number, document identification), and line spacing. Generally these choices are dictated by the style guidelines of an academic discipline such as the Modern

Language Association (MLA) or by the conventions established in a business or professional setting. If you deviate from the expected document design, readers will assume that you are doing so on purpose and will wonder what that purpose is. (If you use scripted font or design a personalized cover page for an academic paper, you'd make a "notice me" statement, analogous to wearing a green jumpsuit to a business meeting—you might want to do so, but there's a risk.)

Attention to document design and the appearance of your manuscripts thus signals your membership in an academic or professional community. An inappropriately formatted or sloppy paper can hurt your *ethos* and may send a message that you are unprofessional. Figure 4.3 illustrates the first- and second-page manuscript formats for MLA and APA (American Psychological Association) style papers.

Document Design for Published Works

In contrast to manuscripts and college papers, published works require elaborate decisions about document design. The original manuscripts for a scholarly article, an article for a popular magazine, a newspaper op-ed piece, and a Web page may have all been double-spaced, typed documents with one-inch margins, but the published products look totally different, as you can see in Figure 4.4. Today's writers, especially in professional settings, often use desktop-publishing software to produce print-ready or Web-ready documents that have a professional visual appeal. For published documents, design is closely related to genre and involves decisions about type, use of space and layout, color, and graphics or images. Let's look at each in turn.

Type Type comes in different typeface styles, or **fonts**, that are commonly grouped in three font families:

1. **Serif fonts** have tiny extensions on the letters, which make them easier to read in long documents.
2. **Sans serif fonts** lack the extensions on the letters and are good for labels, headings, and short documents.
3. **Specialty fonts,** often used for decorative effect, include script fonts and special symbols.

Fonts also come in different sizes and can be formatted with **boldface**, *italics*, <u>underlining</u>, or shading.

In published documents, font use varies by genre. Scholarly print publications usually employ conservative typography: a consistently sized, plain, highly readable font like Times New Roman with variations mainly reserved for titles, headings, notes, and bibliography. Popular magazines, on the other hand, tend to use fonts playfully and artistically; they vary font styles and sizes to attract readers' attention and to make articles look pleasingly decorative on the page. Although the body text of articles is usually the same font throughout, the opening page often uses a variety of fonts and sizes. Font variations may highlight key ideas for readers who are reading casually or rapidly.

FIGURE 4.3 Manuscript Format for MLA and APA Papers

MLA Manuscript, page 1

Gardiner 1

James Gardiner

Professor Johnson

Writing Seminar: Inquiry and Argument

15 May 2007

Why *Facebook* Might Not Be Good For You:

Some Dangers of Online Social Networks

Walk into any computer lab located at any college campus across the country and you'll see dozens of students logged onto an online social network (OSN). In the last few years, the use of these networks has skyrocketed among Internet users, especially young adults. These new virtual communities are significantly influencing the way young people communicate and interact with one another. A report titled "E-Expectations: The Class of 2007" went so far as to label upcoming college freshmen "the Social-Networking Generation" (qtd. in Joly).

In late 2006, the Pew Internet Project, a nonpartisan, nonprofit research group that examines the social impact of the Internet, reported that 55 percent of online teens have created a personal profile on OSNs and that 48 percent of teens visit social networking Web sites daily, with 22 percent visiting several times a day (Lenhart and Madden 2). The two most popular OSNs are *MySpace* and *Facebook. MySpace* is a general networking site that allows anyone to join, develop a profile, and display personal information. In less than four years of existence, *MySpace* has exploded to become the third most visited Web site on the Internet behind only *Google* and *Yahoo* ("Top Sites") with more than 100 million members (Joly). *Facebook* is geared more toward college students (until recently it required that a person attend a university to join the network) and is the number one site accessed by 18- to 24-year-olds. According to research studies cited in an article in the *Toronto Star*, 90 percent of all undergraduates

APA Manuscript, page 1

A Comparison of Gender Stereotypes in *SpongeBob SquarePants* and a 1930s

Mickey Mouse Cartoon

Lauren Campbell, Charlie Bourain, and Tyler Nishida

November 10, 2006

MLA Manuscript, page 2

Gardiner 2

has also experienced unprecedented growth in its relatively short existence and now ranks as the seventh most visited site on the Internet ("Top Sites") and has a member base of more than 19 million (Joly).

With the use of OSNs increasing among young people, the term "Facebook trance" has emerged to describe a person who loses track of all time and stares at the screen for hours (Copeland). While "Facebook trance" might describe only an occasional and therefore harmless phenomenon, it gives rise to important questions: What are the possible negative consequences of OSNs? What should youthful users be watchful for and guard against? The purpose of this paper is to identify the possible harms of OSNs. I will suggest that overuse of OSNs can be a contributing factor to a decline in grades as well as to other problems such as a superficial view of relationships, an increase in narcissism, and possible future embarrassment.

I don't mean to deny that OSNs have positive consequences for young people. For one thing, they provide a "virtual hangout" that acts as a convenient and cost-effective way to stay in close contact with friends and family. According to the Pew survey, 91 percent of users use OSNs to keep in touch with their regularly seen friends, while 82 percent use the sites to stay in touch with distant friends (Lenhart and Madden). OSNs let young people regularly view their friends' profiles, leave short messages or comments, and share personal information. OSN researcher Danah Boyd also claims that these sites give young people a platform on which to experiment with identities, voice their opinions, and practice how they present themselves through personal data, pictures, and music placed in their profiles (Bowley). OSNs also assist them in learning more about people they've met offline. Used as an investigative tool, OSNs offer quick ways to get additional background information on someone. For example, a student could use an OSN to decide whom

APA Manuscript, page 2

Abstract

Researchers in gender identity have continually argued whether gender differences are biological or social. Because television is a prime place for teaching children gender differences through socialization, we studied the extent of gender stereotyping in two 1930s Mickey Mouse cartoons and two recent *SpongeBob SquarePants* cartoons. We analyzed the cartoons in one-minute increments and recorded the number of gender stereotypical and gender-non-stereotypical actions in each increment. Our results confirmed our hypothesis that *SpongeBob SquarePants* would have fewer gender stereotypes than Mickey Mouse. This study is significant because it shows that in at least one contemporary cartoon males and females have a range of acceptable behaviors that go beyond traditional gender stereotypes.

FIGURE 4.4 Examples of Published Documents

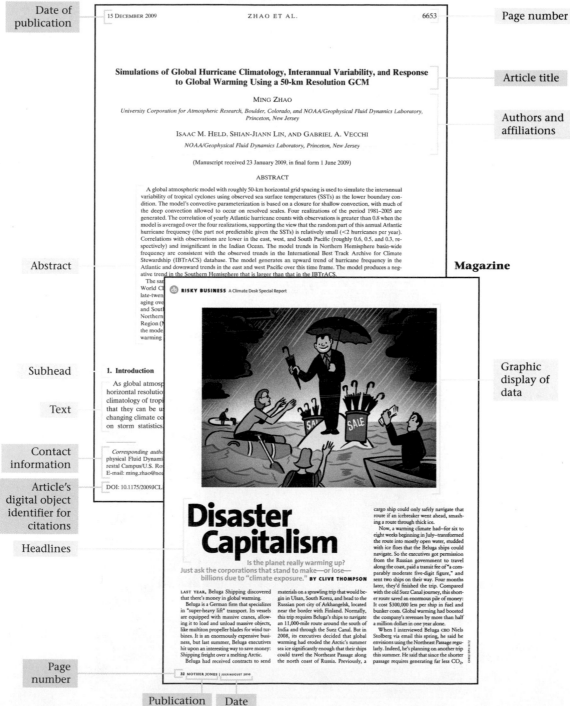

Scholarly Journal

Date of publication — 15 DECEMBER 2009 — ZHAO ET AL. — 6653 — Page number

Simulations of Global Hurricane Climatology, Interannual Variability, and Response to Global Warming Using a 50-km Resolution GCM — Article title

MING ZHAO

University Corporation for Atmospheric Research, Boulder, Colorado, and NOAA/Geophysical Fluid Dynamics Laboratory, Princeton, New Jersey

ISAAC M. HELD, SHIAN-JIANN LIN, AND GABRIEL A. VECCHI

NOAA/Geophysical Fluid Dynamics Laboratory, Princeton, New Jersey — Authors and affiliations

(Manuscript received 23 January 2009, in final form 1 June 2009)

ABSTRACT

A global atmospheric model with roughly 50-km horizontal grid spacing is used to simulate the interannual variability of tropical cyclones using observed sea surface temperatures (SSTs) as the lower boundary condition. The model's convective parameterization is based on a closure for shallow convection, with much of the deep convection allowed to occur on resolved scales. Four realizations of the period 1981–2005 are generated. The correlation of yearly Atlantic hurricane counts with observations is greater than 0.8 when the model is averaged over the four realizations, supporting the view that the random part of this annual Atlantic hurricane frequency (the part not predictable given the SSTs) is relatively small (<2 hurricanes per year). Correlations with observations are lower in the east, west, and South Pacific (roughly 0.6, 0.5, and 0.3, respectively) and insignificant in the Indian Ocean. The model trends in Northern Hemisphere basin-wide frequency are consistent with the observed trends in the International Best Track Archive for Climate Stewardship (IBTrACS) database. The model generates an upward trend of hurricane frequency in the Atlantic and downward trends in the east and west Pacific over this time frame. The model produces a negative trend in the Southern Hemisphere that is larger than that in the IBTrACS. — Abstract

1. Introduction — Subhead

As global atmosp[...] horizontal resolutio[...] climatology of tropi[...] that they can be u[...] changing climate co[...] on storm statistics. — Text

Corresponding autho[...] physical Fluid Dynami[...] restal Campus/U.S. Ro[...] E-mail: ming.zhao@noa[...] — Contact information

DOI: 10.1175/2009JCL[...] — Article's digital object identifier for citations

Magazine

RISKY BUSINESS A Climate Desk Special Report — Graphic display of data

Disaster Capitalism
Is the planet really warming up? Just ask the corporations that stand to make—or lose—billions due to "climate exposure." **BY CLIVE THOMPSON** — Headlines

LAST YEAR, Beluga Shipping discovered that there's money in global warming.

Beluga is a German firm that specializes in "super-heavy lift" transport. Its vessels are equipped with massive cranes, allowing it to load and unload massive objects, like multiton propeller blades for wind turbines. It is an enormously expensive business, but last summer, Beluga executives hit upon an interesting way to save money: Shipping freight over a melting Arctic.

Beluga had received contracts to send materials on a sprawling trip that would begin in Ulsan, South Korea, and head to the Russian port city of Arkhangelsk, located near the border with Finland. Normally, this trip requires Beluga's ships to navigate an 11,000-mile route around the south of India and through the Suez Canal. But in 2008, its executives decided that global warming had eroded the Arctic's summer sea ice significantly enough that their ships could travel the Northeast Passage along the north coast of Russia. Previously, a

cargo ship could only safely navigate that route if an icebreaker went ahead, smashing a route through thick ice.

Now, a warming climate had—for six to eight weeks beginning in July—transformed the route into mostly open water, studded with ice floes that the Beluga ships could navigate. So the executives got permission from the Russian government to travel along the coast, paid a transit fee of "a comparably moderate five-digit figure," and sent two ships on their way. Four months later, they'd finished the trip. Compared with the old Suez Canal journey, this shorter route saved an enormous pile of money: It cost $300,000 less per ship in fuel and bunker costs. Global warming had boosted the company's revenues by more than half a million dollars in one year alone.

When I interviewed Beluga CEO Niels Stolberg via email this spring, he said he envisions using the Arctic's warmer regularly. Indeed, he's planning on another trip this summer. He said that since the shorter passage requires generating far less CO_2,

32 MOTHER JONES | JULY/AUGUST 2010 — Page number — Publication — Date

Newspaper

Op Ed Page

Date and page number

Author biography

Headline

Author

Web Page

Links to main section of museum's site

Link to blog

Site sponsor

Site title

Links to sections of site

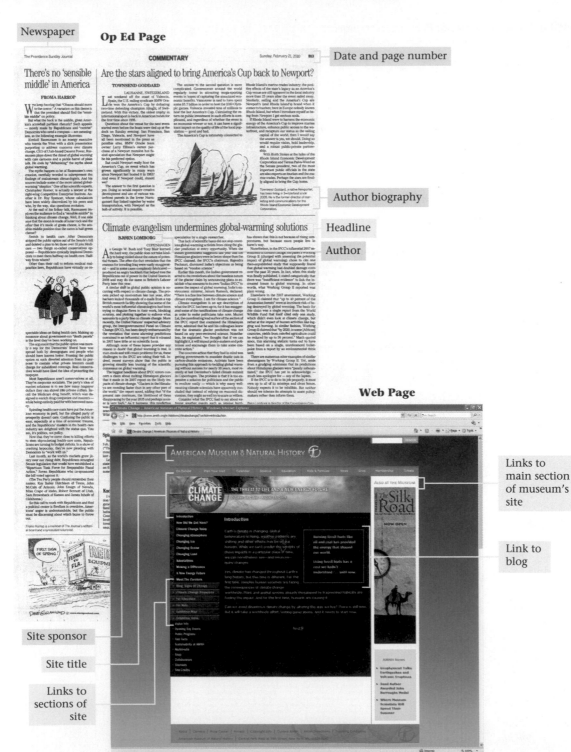

Space and Layout **Layout** refers to how the text is formatted on the page. Layout includes the following elements:

- Page size, margin size, proportion of text to white space
- Arrangement of text on the page (single or multiple columns, spaces between paragraphs)
- Use of justification (alignment of text with the left or right margins or both margins)
- Placement of titles, use of headings and subheadings, and spacing before and after headings
- Use of numbered or bulleted lists or of boxes and sidebars to highlight ideas or break text into visual units

Academic and scholarly publications, both in print and on the Web, use simple, highly functional document layouts. Most scholarly print journals use single or double columns of text that are justified at both margins to create a regular, even look. The layout of scholarly journals strikes a balance between maximizing the amount of text that fits on a page and ensuring readability.

In contrast, text layout in popular magazines and Web sites is more varied and playful, with text often wrapped around charts, sidebars, photographs, or drawings. While readability is important, so is visual appeal and entertainment: Readers must enjoy looking at the pages. For example, many popular print magazines try to blur the distinction between content and advertising so that ads become part of the visual appeal. This is why the table of contents is often buried a dozen or more pages into the magazine. The publisher wants to coax readers to think of the ads as part of the content. In contrast, the table of contents for most academic print journals is on the cover.

Color Colors make powerful appeals, even affecting moods. Whereas manuscripts are printed entirely in black ink, published documents often use color to identify and set off main ideas or important information. Color-tinted boxes can indicate special features or allow different but related articles to appear on the same page.

Academic and scholarly articles, books, and Web sites use color minimally, relying instead on different font styles and sizes to make distinctions in content. Popular magazines and Web sites, on the other hand, use colors playfully, artistically, decoratively, and strategically to enhance their appeal. They often vary colors of type or background for different kinds of content to give variety to the whole publication.

Graphics and Images **Graphics** include visual displays of information such as tables, line graphs, bar graphs, pie charts, maps, cartoons, illustrations, and photos.

As with the use of type, space, and color, the use of graphics indicates the focus, seriousness, function, and complexity of the writing. In scientific articles and books, many of the important findings may be displayed in complex, technical graphs and tables. Sources of information for these graphics are usually prominently stated, with key variables clearly labeled. In the humanities and social sciences, content-rich photos and drawings also tend to be vital parts of an article, even the subject of the analysis.

Popular publications typically use simple numeric visuals (for example, a colorful pie chart or a dramatic graph) combined with decorative use of **images**, especially photos. If photos appear, it is worthwhile to consider their rhetorical function. For example, some photos may be unscripted, realistic, and spontaneous, like news photos of a disaster scene or a sports highlight. Some may aim to look like news photos, but are in fact scripted and posed. Still others are concept (thematic) photos meant to illustrate an idea in an article. For example, an article on health care costs may include a photoshopped picture of a woman in a hospital gown surrounded by images of pills, doctors, expensive medical equipment, and wrangling employers and insurance agents.

FOR WRITING AND DISCUSSION

Analyzing Rhetorical Effect

Working individually or in small groups, analyze how genre and document design are interrelated in the examples shown in Figure 4.4.

1. How does the design of each document—its use of fonts, layout, color, and graphics—identify each piece as a scholarly article, an article in a popular magazine, a newspaper op-ed piece, or a Web page?
2. When you download an article from an electronic database (unless it is in pdf format), you often lose visual cues about the article's original genre. Even when an article is in pdf format, you lose cues about its original print context—the kind of magazine or journal the article appeared in, the magazine's layout and advertisements, and its targeted audience. Likewise, when you print a document from a Web site, you lose contextual cues about the original Web environment. How do document design and other visual features in the original print or Web source provide important contextual information for reading the article and using it in your own research?

Chapter Summary

In this chapter we have looked at how writers think rhetorically about style and document design.

- *Concept 11: Good writers make purposeful stylistic choices.* Style refers to analyzable language features—such as sentence structure, word choice, voice, and tone—that work together to create different rhetorical effects. You can improve your style by learning to cut deadwood, use sentence structure for emphasis, write low on the ladder of abstraction, and achieve a natural voice in your writing.
- *Concept 12: Good writers make purposeful document design choices.* Document design issues differ for manuscripts and published works. In producing manuscripts, expert writers follow the guidelines of their academic or professional communities, thereby signaling insider status. Design features for published documents concern type sizes and styles; layout and spacing; use of color; and use of graphics or images. Academic articles generally adopt a conservative design while more popular genres approach design playfully and artistically.

Two Contrasting Descriptions of the Same Scene

This brief writing project is a write-to-learn task that will help you appreciate how writers construct an "angle of vision" (see Concept 8) and how aspects of style (particularly writing low on the ladder of abstraction) have strong rhetorical effects (Concept 11).

> Write two descriptions of the same scene, from contrasting angles of vision. Here is the catch: Your first description must convey a favorable impression of the scene, making it appear pleasing or attractive. The second description must convey a negative or unfavorable impression, making the scene appear unpleasant or unattractive. Both descriptions must contain only factual details and must describe exactly the same scene from the same location at the same time. It's not fair, in other words, to describe the scene in sunny weather and then in the rain or otherwise to alter factual details. Each description should be one paragraph long (approximately 125–175 words).
>
> Your instructor may ask you to discuss how you sought to create different rhetorical effects in these descriptions.

Establishing a Context

To get into the spirit of this unusual assignment, you need to create a personal rationale for why you are writing two opposing descriptions. Our students have been successful imagining any one of the following three rationales:

- ***Different moods.*** Pretend that you are observing this scene in different moods. How could you reflect a "happy" view of this scene and then a "sad" view? Let the mood determine your selection and framing of details, but don't put yourself into the scene. The reader should infer your mood from the description.
- ***Verbal game.*** Here you see yourself as a word wizard trying consciously to create two different rhetorical effects for readers. In this scenario, you don't worry how you feel about the scene but how you want your readers to feel. Your focus is on crafting the language to influence your audience in different ways.
- ***Different rhetorical purposes.*** In this scenario, you imagine your description in service of some desired action. You might dislike a certain space (for example, a poorly designed library reading room) and describe it in a way that highlights its bad features. This description is *the way you really feel.* Your next task is to see this same scene from an opposing perspective—perhaps that of the architect who designed the reading room.

Observing and Taking Notes

Once you have chosen your scene, you'll need to observe and take notes for fifteen or twenty minutes in preparation for writing the focused descriptions of the scene using specific, concrete, sensory details. You need to compose descriptions that are rich in sensory detail—sights, sounds, smells, textures, even on occasion tastes—all contributing to a dominant impression that gives the description focus.

You can train yourself to notice sensory details by creating a two-column sensory chart and noting details that appeal to each of the senses. Then try describing them, first positively (left column) and then negatively (right column). One student, observing a scene in a local tavern, made these notes in her sensory chart:

Positive Description	Negative Description
Taste	
salted and buttered popcorn	salty, greasy popcorn
frosty pitchers of beer	half-drunk pitchers of stale, warm beer
big bowls of salted-in-the-shell peanuts on the tables	mess of peanut shells and discarded pretzel wrappers on tables and floor
Sound	
hum of students laughing and chatting	din of high-pitched giggles and various obnoxious frat guys shouting at each other
the jukebox playing oldies but goodies from the early Beatles	jukebox blaring out-of-date music

Student Example

We conclude with a student example of this assignment.

DESCRIPTION 1—POSITIVE EFFECT

Light rain gently drops into the puddles that have formed along the curb as I look out my apartment window at the corner of 14th and East John. Pedestrians layered in sweaters, raincoats, and scarves and guarded with shiny rubber boots and colorful umbrellas sip their steaming hot triple-tall lattes. Some share smiles and pleasant exchanges as they hurry down the street, hastening to work where it is warm and dry. Others, smelling the aroma of French roast espresso coming from the coffee bar next to the bus stop, listen for the familiar rumbling sound that will mean the 56 bus has arrived. Radiant orange, yellow, and red leaves blanket the sidewalk in the areas next to the maple trees that line the road. Along the curb a mother holds the hand of her toddler, dressed like a miniature tugboat captain in yellow raincoat and pants, who splashes happily in a puddle.

DESCRIPTION 2—NEGATIVE EFFECT

A solemn grayness hangs in the air, as I peer out the window of my apartment at the corner of 14th and East John. A steady drizzle of rain leaves boot-drenching puddles for pedestrians to avoid. Bundled in rubber boots, sweaters, coats, and rain-soaked scarves, commuters clutch Styrofoam cups of coffee as a defense against the biting cold. They lift their heads every so often to take a small sip of caffeine, but look sleep-swollen nevertheless. Pedestrians hurry past each other, moving quickly to get away from the dismal weather, the dull grayness. Some nod a brief hello to a familiar face, but most clutch their overcoats and tread grimly on, looking to avoid puddles or spray from passing cars. Others stand at the bus stop, hunched over, waiting in the drab early morning for the smell of diesel that means the 56 bus has arrived. Along the curb an impatient mother jerks the hand of a toddler to keep him from stomping in an oil-streaked puddle.

PART 2

WRITING PROJECTS

This poster, one of hundreds created by the United States' Office of War Information during World War II, enlisted Americans' communal efforts, particularly women's help at home, in conserving resources to support the production for the war being fought on two fronts—the Pacific and Europe. This poster taps the urgency of that historical moment just as Michael Pollan's article, "Why Bother?", in Chapter 5 speaks to our current environmental problems. Think about how choice of words, images, color, and design in this poster work together to create an emotionally intense argument. Consider how you would design a poster to convey Pollan's argument or some other timely environmental message.

5

READING RHETORICALLY
The Writer as Strong Reader

Many new college students are surprised by the amount, range, and difficulty of reading they have to do in college. Every day they are challenged by reading assignments ranging from scholarly articles and textbooks on complex subject matter to primary sources such as Plato's dialogues or Darwin's *Voyage of the Beagle*.

To interact strongly with challenging texts, you must learn how to read them both with and against the grain. When you read *with the grain* of a text, you see the world through its author's perspective, open yourself to the author's argument, apply the text's insights to new contexts, and connect its ideas to your own experiences and personal knowledge. When you read *against the grain* of a text, you resist it by questioning its points, raising doubts, analyzing the limits of its perspective, or even refuting its argument.

We say that readers read *rhetorically* when they are aware of the effect a text is intended to have on them. Strong rhetorical readers analyze how a text works persuasively and they think critically about whether to enter into or challenge the text's intentions. The two writing projects in this chapter, both of which demand rhetorical reading, introduce you to several of the most common genres of academic writing: the summary, and various kinds of strong response essays, which usually incorporate a summary of the text to which the writer is responding. Thus, our goal is to help you become a more powerful reader of academic texts, prepared to take part in the conversations of the disciplines you study.

In this chapter, you will learn to:

- listen carefully to a text, recognize its parts and their functions, and summarize its ideas
- formulate strong responses to texts by interacting with them, either by agreeing with, interrogating, or actively opposing them

---

Exploring Rhetorical Reading

As an introduction to rhetorical reading, we ask you to imagine that you are investigating different strategies that individual Americans might take to protect the environment. You have come across the 2008 article "Why Bother?" by Michael Pollan in the *New York Times Magazine*. Pollan, a professor of journalism at the

University of California Berkeley's Graduate School of Journalism, is known for his popular books on reforming our food-production system for the benefit of humans, animals, and the environment: *The Omnivore's Dilemma: A Natural History of Four Meals* (2007), *In Defense of Food: An Eater's Manifesto* (2009), and *Food Rules* (2010). Before reading Pollan's article, respond to the following opinion survey, using a 1 to 5 scale, with 1 meaning "strongly agree" and 5 meaning "strongly disagree."

Item	Strongly agree	Agree	Neutral	Disagree	Strongly disagree
1. Global warming is a very serious problem.	1	2	3	4	5
2. Going green in my own lifestyle will have no effect on climate change—the magnitude of the problem is too great.	1	2	3	4	5
3. The only way to make a real difference in climate change is through hugely expensive actions taken by governments and businesses.	1	2	3	4	5
4. The best way to combat global warming is for individual Americans to go green in their own consumer choices.	1	2	3	4	5
5. Environmentally conscious people should change the way they eat.	1	2	3	4	5

When you have finished rating your degree of agreement with these statements, read Pollan's article, using whatever note-taking, underlining, or highlighting strategies you normally use when reading for a class. When you have finished reading, complete the exercises that follow.

Michael Pollan
Why Bother?

1   **Why bother?** That really is the big question facing us as individuals hoping to do something about climate change, and it's not an easy one to answer. I don't know about you, but for me the most upsetting moment in *An Inconvenient Truth* came long after Al Gore scared the hell out of me, constructing an utterly convincing case that the very survival of life on earth as we know it is threatened by climate change. No, the really dark moment came during the closing credits, when we are asked to ... change

(continued)

our light bulbs. That's when it got really depressing. The immense disproportion between the magnitude of the problem Gore had described and the puniness of what he was asking us to do about it was enough to sink your heart.

2   But the drop-in-the-bucket issue is not the only problem lurking behind the "why bother" question. Let's say I do bother, big time. I turn my life upside-down, start biking to work, plant a big garden, turn down the thermostat so low I need the Jimmy Carter* signature cardigan, forsake the clothes dryer for a laundry line across the yard, trade in the station wagon for a hybrid, get off the beef, go completely local. I could theoretically do all that, but what would be the point when I know full well that halfway around the world there lives my evil twin, some carbon-footprint *doppelgänger* in Shanghai or Chongqing who has just bought his first car (Chinese car ownership is where ours was back in 1918), is eager to swallow every bite of meat I forswear and who's positively itching to replace every last pound of CO2 I'm struggling no longer to emit. So what exactly would I have to show for all my trouble?

3   A sense of personal virtue, you might suggest, somewhat sheepishly. But what good is that when virtue itself is quickly becoming a term of derision? And not just on the editorial pages of the *Wall Street Journal* or on the lips of the vice president,* who famously dismissed energy conservation as a "sign of personal virtue." No, even in the pages of the *New York Times* and the *New Yorker*, it seems the epithet "virtuous," when applied to an act of personal environmental responsibility, may be used only ironically. Tell me: How did it come to pass that virtue—a quality that for most of history has generally been deemed, well, a virtue—became a mark of liberal softheadedness? How peculiar, that doing the right thing by the environment—buying the hybrid, eating like a locavore—should now set you up for the Ed Begley Jr.* treatment.

4   And even if in the face of this derision I decide I am going to bother, there arises the whole vexed question of getting it right. Is eating local or walking to work really going to reduce my carbon footprint? According to one analysis, if walking to work increases your appetite and you consume more meat or milk as a result, walking might actually emit more carbon than driving. A handful of studies have recently suggested that in certain cases under certain conditions, produce from places as far away as New Zealand might account for less carbon than comparable domestic products. True, at least one of these studies was co-written by a representative of agribusiness interests in (surprise!) New Zealand, but even so, they make you wonder. If determining the carbon footprint of food is really this complicated, and I've got to consider not only "food miles" but also whether the food came by ship or truck and how lushly the grass grows in New Zealand, then maybe on second thought I'll just buy the imported chops at Costco, at least until the experts get their footprints sorted out.

5   There are so many stories we can tell ourselves to justify doing nothing, but perhaps the most insidious is that, whatever we do manage to do, it will be too little too late. Climate change is upon us, and it has arrived well ahead of schedule.

*Jimmy Carter was the Democratic president (1977–1981) who supported environmental policies, world peace, and human rights.
*Pollan is referring to Dick Cheney who served as George W. Bush's vice president from 2001–2009.
*Ed Begley, Jr., is a prominent television star who has his own green living reality TV show, *Living with Ed*. Begley has explored such topics as tapping the energy produced by people using exercise equipment.

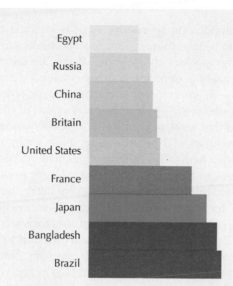

High Anxiety?
Percentage of people by country
who view global warming as a
"very serious" problem.

Scientists' projections that seemed dire a decade ago turn out to have been unduly optimistic: the warming and the melting is occurring much faster than the models predicted. Now truly terrifying feedback loops threaten to boost the rate of change exponentially, as the shift from white ice to blue water in the Arctic absorbs more sunlight and warming soils everywhere become more biologically active, causing them to release their vast stores of carbon into the air. Have you looked into the eyes of a climate scientist recently? They look really scared.

So do you still want to talk about planting gardens?

I do.

Whatever we can do as individuals to change the way we live at this suddenly very late date does seem utterly inadequate to the challenge. It's hard to argue with Michael Specter,* in a recent *New Yorker* piece on carbon footprints, when he says: "Personal choices, no matter how virtuous [N.B.!], cannot do enough. It will also take laws and money." So it will. Yet it is no less accurate or hardheaded to say that laws and money cannot do enough, either; that it will also take profound changes in the way we live. Why? Because the climate-change crisis is at its very bottom a crisis of lifestyle—of character, even. The Big Problem is nothing more or less than the sum total of countless little everyday choices, most of them made by us (consumer spending represents 70 percent of our economy), and most of the rest of them made in the name of our needs and desires and preferences.

For us to wait for legislation or technology to solve the problem of how we're living our lives suggests we're not really serious about changing—something our politicians cannot fail to notice. They will not move until we do. Indeed, to look to leaders and experts, to laws and money and grand schemes, to save us from our predicament represents precisely the sort of thinking—passive, delegated, dependent

---

*Michael Specter is a staff writer for the *New Yorker* and a national science reporter, who has most recently written a book, *Denialism*, about people's refusal to accept scientific evidence.

for solutions on specialists—that helped get us into this mess in the first place. It's hard to believe that the same sort of thinking could now get us out of it.

10   Thirty years ago, Wendell Berry, the Kentucky farmer and writer, put forward a blunt analysis of precisely this mentality. He argued that the environmental crisis of the 1970s—an era innocent of climate change; what we would give to have back *that* environmental crisis!—was at its heart a crisis of character and would have to be addressed first at that level: at home, as it were. He was impatient with people who wrote checks to environmental organizations while thoughtlessly squandering fossil fuel in their everyday lives—the 1970s equivalent of people buying carbon offsets to atone for their Tahoes and Durangos. Nothing was likely to change until we healed the "split between what we think and what we do." For Berry, the "why bother" question came down to a moral imperative: "Once our personal connection to what is wrong becomes clear, then we have to choose: we can go on as before, recognizing our dishonesty and living with it the best we can, or we can begin the effort to change the way we think and live."

11   For Berry, the deep problem standing behind all the other problems of industrial civilization is "specialization," which he regards as the "disease of the modern character." Our society assigns us a tiny number of roles: we're producers (of one thing) at work, consumers of a great many other things the rest of the time, and then once a year or so we vote as citizens. Virtually all of our needs and desires we delegate to specialists of one kind or another—our meals to agribusiness, health to the doctor, education to the teacher, entertainment to the media, care for the environment to the environmentalist, political action to the politician.

12   As Adam Smith and many others have pointed out, this division of labor has given us many of the blessings of civilization. Specialization is what allows me to sit at a computer thinking about climate change. Yet this same division of labor obscures the lines of connection—and responsibility—linking our everyday acts to their real-world consequences, making it easy for me to overlook the coal-fired power plant that is lighting my screen, or the mountaintop in Kentucky that had to be destroyed to provide the coal to that plant, or the streams running crimson with heavy metals as a result.

13   Of course, what made this sort of specialization possible in the first place was cheap energy. Cheap fossil fuel allows us to pay distant others to process our food for us, to entertain us and to (try to) solve our problems, with the result that there is very little we know how to accomplish for ourselves. Think for a moment of all the things you suddenly need to do for yourself when the power goes out—up to and including entertaining yourself. Think, too, about how a power failure causes your neighbors—your community—to suddenly loom so much larger in your life. Cheap energy allowed us to leapfrog community by making it possible to sell our specialty over great distances as well as summon into our lives the specialties of countless distant others.

14   Here's the point: Cheap energy, which gives us climate change, fosters precisely the mentality that makes dealing with climate change in our own lives seem impossibly difficult. Specialists ourselves, we can no longer imagine anyone but an expert, or anything but a new technology or law, solving our problems. Al Gore asks us to change the light bulbs because he probably can't imagine us doing anything much more challenging, like, say, growing some portion of our own food. We can't imagine it, either, which is probably why we prefer to cross our fingers and talk about the

promise of ethanol and nuclear power—new liquids and electrons to power the same old cars and houses and lives.

15   The "cheap-energy mind," as Wendell Berry called it, is the mind that asks, "Why bother?" because it is helpless to imagine—much less attempt—a different sort of life, one less divided, less reliant. Since the cheap-energy mind translates everything into money, its proxy, it prefers to put its faith in market-based solutions—carbon taxes and pollution-trading schemes. If we could just get the incentives right, it believes, the economy will properly value everything that matters and nudge our self-interest down the proper channels. The best we can hope for is a greener version of the old invisible hand. Visible hands it has no use for.

16   But while some such grand scheme may well be necessary, it's doubtful that it will be sufficient or that it will be politically sustainable before we've demonstrated to ourselves that change is possible. Merely to give, to spend, even to vote, is not to do, and there is so much that needs to be done—without further delay. In the judgment of James Hansen, the NASA climate scientist who began sounding the alarm on global warming 20 years ago, we have only 10 years left to start cutting—not just slowing—the amount of carbon we're emitting or face a "different planet." Hansen said this more than two years ago, however; two years have gone by, and nothing of consequence has been done. So: eight years left to go and a great deal left to do.

17   Which brings us back to the "why bother" question and how we might better answer it. The reasons not to bother are many and compelling, at least to the cheap-energy mind. But let me offer a few admittedly tentative reasons that we might put on the other side of the scale:

18   If you do bother, you will set an example for other people. If enough other people bother, each one influencing yet another in a chain reaction of behavioral change, markets for all manner of green products and alternative technologies will prosper and expand. (Just look at the market for hybrid cars.) Consciousness will be raised, perhaps even changed: new moral imperatives and new taboos might take root in the culture. Driving an S.U.V. or eating a 24-ounce steak or illuminating your McMansion like an airport runway at night might come to be regarded as outrages to human conscience. Not having things might become cooler than having them. And those who did change the way they live would acquire the moral standing to demand changes in behavior from others—from other people, other corporations, even other countries.

19   All of this could, theoretically, happen. What I'm describing (imagining would probably be more accurate) is a process of viral social change, and change of this kind, which is nonlinear, is never something anyone can plan or predict or count on. Who knows, maybe the virus will reach all the way to Chongqing and infect my Chinese evil twin. Or not. Maybe going green will prove a passing fad and will lose steam after a few years, just as it did in the 1980s, when Ronald Reagan took down Jimmy Carter's solar panels from the roof of the White House.

20   Going personally green is a bet, nothing more or less, though it's one we probably all should make, even if the odds of it paying off aren't great. Sometimes you have to act as if acting will make a difference, even when you can't prove that it will. That, after all, was precisely what happened in Communist Czechoslovakia and Poland, when a handful of individuals like Václav Havel and Adam Michnik resolved that they would

simply conduct their lives "as if" they lived in a free society. That improbable bet created a tiny space of liberty that, in time, expanded to take in, and then help take down, the whole of the Eastern bloc.

21   So what would be a comparable bet that the individual might make in the case of the environmental crisis? Havel himself has suggested that people begin to "conduct themselves as if they were to live on this earth forever and be answerable for its condition one day." Fair enough, but let me propose a slightly less abstract and daunting wager. The idea is to find one thing to do in your life that doesn't involve spending or voting, that may or may not virally rock the world but is real and particular (as well as symbolic) and that, come what may, will offer its own rewards. Maybe you decide to give up meat, an act that would reduce your carbon footprint by as much as a quarter. Or you could try this: determine to observe the Sabbath. For one day a week, abstain completely from economic activity: no shopping, no driving, no electronics.

22   But the act I want to talk about is growing some—even just a little—of your own food. Rip out your lawn, if you have one, and if you don't—if you live in a high-rise, or have a yard shrouded in shade—look into getting a plot in a community garden. Measured against the Problem We Face, planting a garden sounds pretty benign, I know, but in fact it's one of the most powerful things an individual can do—to reduce your carbon footprint, sure, but more important, to reduce your sense of dependence and dividedness: to change the cheap-energy mind.

23   A great many things happen when you plant a vegetable garden, some of them directly related to climate change, others indirect but related nevertheless. Growing food, we forget, comprises the original solar technology: calories produced by means of photosynthesis. Years ago the cheap-energy mind discovered that more food could be produced with less effort by replacing sunlight with fossil-fuel fertilizers and pesticides, with a result that the typical calorie of food energy in your diet now requires about 10 calories of fossil-fuel energy to produce. It's estimated that the way we feed ourselves (or rather, allow ourselves to be fed) accounts for about a fifth of the greenhouse gas for which each of us is responsible.

24   Yet the sun still shines down on your yard, and photosynthesis still works so abundantly that in a thoughtfully organized vegetable garden (one planted from seed,

nourished by compost from the kitchen and involving not too many drives to the garden center), you can grow the proverbial free lunch—CO2-free and dollar-free. This is the most-local food you can possibly eat (not to mention the freshest, tastiest and most nutritious), with a carbon footprint so faint that even the New Zealand lamb council dares not challenge it. And while we're counting carbon, consider too your compost pile, which shrinks the heap of garbage your household needs trucked away even as it feeds your vegetables and sequesters carbon in your soil. What else? Well, you will probably notice that you're getting a pretty good workout there in your garden, burning calories without having to get into the car to drive to the gym. (It is one of the absurdities of the modern division of labor that, having replaced physical labor with fossil fuel, we now have to burn even more fossil fuel to keep our unemployed bodies in shape.) Also, by engaging both body and mind, time spent in the garden is time (and energy) subtracted from electronic forms of entertainment.

25   You begin to see that growing even a little of your own food is, as Wendell Berry pointed out 30 years ago, one of those solutions that, instead of begetting a new set of problems—the way "solutions" like ethanol or nuclear power inevitably do—actually beget other solutions, and not only of the kind that save carbon. Still more valuable are the habits of mind that growing a little of your own food can yield. You quickly learn that you need not be dependent on specialists to provide for yourself—that your body is still good for something and may actually be enlisted in its own support. If the experts are right, if both oil and time are running out, these are skills and habits of mind we're all very soon going to need. We may also need the food. Could gardens provide it? Well, during World War II, victory gardens supplied as much as 40 percent of the produce Americans ate.

26   **But there are sweeter** reasons to plant that garden, to bother. At least in this one corner of your yard and life, you will have begun to heal the split between what you think and what you do, to commingle your identities as consumer and producer and citizen. Chances are, your garden will re-engage you with your neighbors, for you will have produce to give away and the need to borrow their tools. You will have reduced the power of the cheap-energy mind by personally overcoming its most debilitating weakness: its helplessness and the fact that it can't do much of anything that doesn't involve division or subtraction. The garden's season-long transit from seed to ripe fruit—*will you get a load of that zucchini?!*—suggests that the operations of addition and multiplication still obtain, that the abundance of nature is not exhausted. The single greatest lesson the garden teaches is that our relationship to the planet need not be zero-sum, and that as long as the sun still shines and people still can plan and plant, think and do, we can, if we bother to try, find ways to provide for ourselves without diminishing the world.

THINKING CRITICALLY
about "Why Bother?"

1. In three to four sentences, summarize Pollan's main points.

2. Freewrite a response to this question: In what way has Pollan's article caused me to reconsider one or more of my answers to the opinion survey on page 87?

3. Working in small groups or as a whole class, compare the note-taking strategies you used while reading this piece. (a) How many people wrote marginal notes? How many underlined or highlighted? (b) Compare the contents of these notes. Did people highlight the same passages or different ones? (c) Individually, look at your annotations and highlights and try to decide why you wrote or marked what you did. Share your reasons for making these annotations. The goal of this exercise is to make you more aware of your thinking processes as you read.

4. Working as a whole class or in small groups, share your responses to the questionnaire and to the postreading questions. What were the most insightful or provocative points in this article? To what extent did this article change people's thinking about the value of individual actions or about the impact of our individual lifestyles on climate change? As a result of Pollan's argument, are you more apt to try growing some of your own vegetables either now or in the future?

Understanding Rhetorical Reading

In this section, we explain why college-level reading is often difficult for new students and offer suggestions for improving your reading process based on the reading strategies of experts.

What Makes College-Level Reading Difficult?

The difficulty of college-level reading stems in part from the complexity of new subject matter. Whatever the subject—from international monetary policies to the intricacies of photosynthesis—you have to wrestle with new and complex materials that might perplex anyone. But in addition to the daunting subject matter, several other factors contribute to the difficulty of college-level reading:

- *Vocabulary.* Many college-level readings contain unfamiliar technical language such as the economic terms *assets, opportunity costs,* or *export subsidy* or the philosophic terms *hermeneutics* or *Neo-Platonism.* Even nontechnical readings and civic writing for the general public can contain unfamiliar terms. For example, in the Pollan article, the literary term *doppelgänger* or the ecological terms *feedback loops* or *pollution-trading systems* may have given you pause. In academia, words often carry specialized meanings that evoke a whole history of conversation and debate that may be inaccessible, even through a specialized dictionary. Good examples might be *postmodernism, string theory,* or *cultural materialism.* You will not fully understand these terms until you are initiated into the disciplinary conversations that gave rise to them.
- *Unfamiliar rhetorical context.* As we explained in Part 1, writers write to an audience for a purpose arising from some motivating occasion. Knowing an author's purpose, occasion, and audience will often clarify confusing parts

of a text. For example, Pollan's article was published in the *New York Times Magazine*, which attracts a liberal, well-educated audience. Pollan assumes that his audience already believes in global warming and takes climate change seriously. In fact, they may be so overwhelmed with the problem that they are ready to give up, shrug, and say, "Why bother?" His purpose is to motivate them to action. A text's internal clues can sometimes help you fill in the rhetorical context, but often you may need to do outside research.

- *Unfamiliar genre.* In your college reading, you will encounter a range of genres such as textbooks, trade books, scholarly articles, scientific reports, historical documents, newspaper articles, op-ed pieces, and so forth. Each of these makes different demands on readers and requires a different reading strategy.
- *Lack of background knowledge.* Writers necessarily make assumptions about what their readers already know. For example, Pollan makes numerous references to popular culture (Al Gore's *An Inconvenient Truth*; "the Ed Begley Jr. treatment"; "imported chops at Costco") or to general liberal arts knowledge (references to the economist Adam Smith or to the recent history of Communist Czechoslovakia and Poland). The more familiar you are with this cultural background, the more you will understand Pollan's argument on first reading.

Appreciating the Importance of Background Knowledge

FOR WRITING AND DISCUSSION

The importance of background knowledge is easily demonstrated any time you dip into past issues of a newsmagazine or try to read articles about an unfamiliar culture. Consider the following passage from a 1986 *Newsweek* article. How much background knowledge do you need before you can fully comprehend this passage? What cultural knowledge about the United States would a student from Ethiopia or Indonesia need?

> Throughout the NATO countries last week, there were second thoughts about the prospect of a nuclear-free world. For 40 years nuclear weapons have been the backbone of the West's defense. For almost as long American presidents have ritually affirmed their desire to see the world rid of them. Then, suddenly, Ronald Reagan and Mikhail Gorbachev came close to actually doing it. Let's abolish all nuclear ballistic missiles in the next 10 years, Reagan said. Why not all nuclear weapons, countered Gorbachev. OK, the president responded, like a man agreeing to throw in the washer-dryer along with the house.
>
> What if the deal had gone through? On the one hand, Gorbachev would have returned to Moscow a hero. There is a belief in the United States that the Soviets need nuclear arms because nuclear weapons are what make them a superpower. But according to Marxist-Leninist doctrine, capitalism's nuclear capability (unforeseen by Marx and Lenin) is the only thing that can prevent the inevitable triumph of communism. Therefore, an end to nuclear arms would put the engine of history back on its track.
>
> On the other hand, Europeans fear, a nonnuclear United States would be tempted to retreat into neo-isolationism.

—Robert B. Cullen, "Dangers of Disarming," *Newsweek*

(continued)

Working in small groups or as a class, identify words and passages in this text that depend on background information or knowledge of culture for complete comprehension.

Using the Reading Strategies of Experts

In Chapter 11, we describe the differences between the writing processes of experts and those of beginning college writers. There are parallel differences between the reading processes of experienced and inexperienced readers, especially when they encounter complex materials. In this strategies chart we describe some expert reading strategies that you can begin applying to your reading of any kind of college-level material.

Strategies for Reading Like an Expert		
Strategies	**What to Do**	**Comments**
Reconstruct the rhetorical context.	Ask questions about purpose, audience, genre, and motivating occasion.	If you read an article that has been anthologized (as in the readings in this textbook), note any information you are given about the author, publication, and genre. Try to reconstruct the author's original motivation for writing.
Take notes.	Make extensive marginal notes as you read.	Expert readers seldom use highlighters, which encourage passive, inefficient reading.
Get in the dictionary habit.	Look up words whose meaning you can't get from context.	If you don't want to interrupt your reading, check off words to look up when you are done.
Match your reading speed to your goals.	Speed up when skimming or scanning for information. Slow down for complete comprehension or detailed analysis.	Robert Sternberg, a cognitive psychologist, discovered that novice readers tend to read everything at about the same pace, no matter what their purpose. Experienced readers know when to slow down or speed up.

Strategies	What to Do	Comments
Read a complex text in a "multidraft" way.	Read a text two or three times. The first time, read quickly, skimming ahead rapidly, looking at the opening sentences of paragraphs and at any passages that sum up the writer's argument or clarify the argument's structure. Pay particular attention to the conclusion, which often ties the whole argument together.	Rapid "first-draft reading" helps you see the text's main points and structure, thus providing background for a second reading. Often, experienced readers reread a text two or three times. They hold confusing passages in mental suspension, hoping that later parts of the essay will clarify earlier parts.

Reading with the Grain and Against the Grain

The reading and thinking strategies that we have just described enable skilled readers to interact strongly with texts. Your purpose in using these strategies is to read texts both *with the grain* and *against the grain*, a way of reading that is analogous to the believing and doubting game we introduced in Chapter 2. This concept is so important that we have chosen to highlight it separately here.

For an explanation of the believing and doubting game, see Chapter 2, Concept 4.

When you read with the grain of a text, you practice what psychologist Carl Rogers calls "empathic listening," in which you try to see the world through the author's eyes, role-playing as much as possible the author's intended readers by adopting their beliefs and values and acquiring their background knowledge. Reading with the grain is the main strategy you use when you summarize a text, but it comes into play also when you develop a strong response. When making with-the-grain points, you support the author's thesis with your own arguments and examples, or apply or extend the author's argument in new ways.

When you read against the grain of a text, you question and perhaps even rebut the author's ideas. You are a resistant reader who asks unanticipated questions, pushes back, and reads the text in ways unforeseen by the author. Reading against the grain is a key part of creating a strong response. When you make against-the-grain points, you challenge the author's reasoning, sources, examples, or choices of language. You present alternative lines of reasoning, deny the writer's values, or raise points or specific data that the writer has omitted. Strategies for thinking with the grain and against the grain are shown in the following chart, along with particular occasions when each is helpful.

Strategies for Reading with and Against the Grain

Reading with the Grain	Reading Against the Grain
• Listen to the text, follow the author's reasoning, and withhold judgment.	• Challenge, question, and resist the author's ideas.

(continued)

Reading with the Grain	Reading Against the Grain
• Try to see the subject and the world from the author's perspective. • Add further support to the author's thesis with your own points and examples. • Apply the author's argument in new ways.	• Point out what the author has left out or overlooked; note what the author has *not* said. • Identify what assumptions, ideas, or facts seem unsupported or inaccurate. • Rebut the author's ideas with counterreasoning and counterexamples.
Occasions When Most Useful	**Occasions When Most Useful**
• In writing summaries, you listen to a text without judgment to identify the main ideas. • In writing analyses, you seek to understand a text to determine points to elaborate on and discuss. • In synthesizing ideas from sources, you determine what ideas to adopt and build on. • In writing arguments, you inhabit an author's viewpoint to deepen your understanding of an issue and to understand alternative views so you can represent them fairly.	• In writing an initial strong response, you determine the ways in which your beliefs, values, and views might be different from the author's. • In writing analyses, you identify limitations in the author's view. • In synthesizing, you determine which ideas to reject, replace, or go beyond. • In writing arguments, you develop refutations and rebuttals to the author's views.

Strong readers develop their ability to read in both ways—with the grain and against the grain. Some readers prefer to separate these approaches by first reading a text with the grain and then rereading it with more against-the-grain resistance. Throughout the rest of this chapter, we show you different ways to apply these strategies in your reading and writing.

Understanding Summary Writing

A **summary** (often called an **abstract**) is a condensed version of a text that extracts and presents main ideas in a way that does justice to the author's intentions. As fairly and objectively as possible, a summary states the main ideas of a longer text, such as an article or even a book. Although the words "summary" and "abstract" are often used interchangeably, the term "abstract" is usually used for a stand-alone summary at the head of a published article. Scholars often present "abstracts" of their own work (that is, a summary of their argument) for publication in a conference program.

Usefulness of Summaries

Students often report later in their academic careers how valuable summary writing skills are. Summary writing fosters a close engagement between you and the text and demonstrates your understanding of it. By forcing you to distinguish between main and subordinate points, summary writing is a valuable tool for improving your reading comprehension. Summary writing is also useful in other ways. For example, summaries at the beginning of articles, in prefaces to books, and on book jackets help readers determine if they want to read the article or book. To participate in conferences, your professors—and perhaps you also—send abstracts of proposed papers to conference committees in hopes of getting the paper accepted for presentation. Engineers and business executives place "executive summaries" at the beginning of proposals of major reports. In the "literature review" section of scientific papers, summaries of previous research are used to demonstrate gaps in knowledge that the present researchers will try to fill. Finally, writing summaries is a particularly important part of research writing, where you often present condensed views of other writers' arguments, either in support of your own view or as alternative views that you are analyzing or responding to.

The Demands that Summary Writing Makes on Writers

Even though summaries are short, they are challenging to write. You must distinguish between the main and subordinate points in a text, and you must provide even coverage of the text. You must also convey clearly the main ideas—ideas that are often complex—in a limited number of words. Often, summaries are written to certain specifications, say, one-tenth of the original article, or 200 words, or 100 words.

One of the biggest challenges of summarizing is framing the summary so that readers can easily tell your own ideas from those of the author you are summarizing. Often, you are incorporating a summary into a piece of writing as a basis of your own analysis or argument, so this distinction is particularly important. You make this distinction by using frequent **attributive tags** (sometimes called "signal phrases") such as "Pollan claims," "according to Pollan," or "Pollan says"; by putting quotation marks around any passages that use the writer's original wording; and by citing the article using the appropriate documentation style. Typically, writers also introduce the summary with appropriate contextual information giving the author's name and perhaps also the title and genre (in research writing, this information is repeated in the "Works Cited" or "References" list). The first sentence of the summary typically presents the main idea or thesis of the entire article. Here is an example summary of the Pollan article using MLA citation and documentation style.

Chapter 13 provides additional instruction in summarizing, paraphrasing, and quoting sources. It also explains how to incorporate sources smoothly into your own writing and avoid plagiarism.

Summary of "Why Bother?"

In "Why Bother?" published in the *New York Times Magazine*,

environmental journalist Michael Pollan asks why, given the

magnitude of the climate change problem, any individual should

bother to go green, and argues that an individual's actions can bring

Identification of the article, journal, and author

Gives overview summary of whole article

Attributive tag

multiple rewards for individuals, society, and the environment. Explaining that "the warming and the melting" (90) are occurring much faster than earlier models had predicted, Pollan acknowledges the apparent powerlessness of individuals to make a difference. Not only are we uncertain what actions to take to preserve the planet, but we realize that whatever we do will be offset by growing carbon emissions from emerging

Short quotations from article, MLA documentation style; number in parentheses indicates page number of original article where quotation is found

nations. Our actions will be "too little too late" (89). He asserts that our environmental problem is a "crisis of lifestyle"—"the sum total of countless little everyday choices" (90) made possible by cheap fossil fuel, which has led to our increasingly specialized jobs. Nevertheless, to counteract our practical and moral distance from the environment caused by this specialization, Pollan urges individuals to go green. Although he concedes that "'laws and money'" (90) are necessary, he still believes that individual actions may be influential by setting off a "process of viral social change" (92). A particularly powerful act, he claims, is to convert yards into vegetable gardens. Growing your own vegetables, he argues, will help us overcome "specialization," eat locally, reduce carbon emissions, get healthy exercise, reconnect with neighbors, and restore our relationship with the earth. (227 words)

Work Cited

Bibliographic citation for Pollan's article using MLA style. In a formal paper, the "Works Cited" list begins on a new page at the end of the paper.

Pollan, Michael. "Why Bother?" *New York Times Magazine* 20 Apr. 2008: 19+. Rpt. in *The Allyn and Bacon Guide to Writing.* John D. Ramage, John C. Bean, and June Johnson. 6th ed. New York: Pearson, 2012. 88–94. Print.

Note in this example how the use of attributive tags, quotation marks, and citations makes it easy to tell that the writer is summarizing Pollan's ideas rather than presenting his own. Note too the writer's attempt to remain neutral and objective and not to impose his own views. To avoid interjecting your own opinions, you need to choose your verbs in attributive tags carefully. Consider the difference between "Smith argues" and "Smith rants" or between "Brown asserts" and "Brown leaps to the conclusion that. . . ." In each pair, the second verb, by moving beyond neutrality, reveals the writer's judgment of the author's ideas.

In an academic setting, then, think of summaries as short, tightly written pieces that retain an author's main ideas while eliminating the supporting details. In the writing projects for this chapter, we'll explain the strategies you can use to write a good summary. The following chart lists the criteria for incorporating a summary effectively into your own prose.

CRITERIA FOR AN EFFECTIVE SUMMARY INCORPORATED INTO YOUR OWN PROSE

- Represents the original article accurately and fairly.
- Is direct and concise, using words economically.
- Remains objective and neutral, not revealing the writer's own ideas on the subject, but, rather, only the original author's points.
- Gives the original article balanced and proportional coverage.
- Uses the writer's own words to express the original author's ideas.
- Distinguishes the summary writer's ideas from the original author's ideas by using attributive tags (such as "according to Pollan" or "Pollan argues that").
- Uses quotations sparingly, if at all, to present the original author's key terms or to convey the flavor of the original.
- Is a unified, coherent piece of writing in its own right.
- Cites and documents the text the writer is summarizing and any quotations used according to an appropriate documentation system.

Determining What Is a Good Summary

FOR WRITING AND DISCUSSION

This exercise asks you to work with the "Criteria for an Effective Summary Incorporated into Your Own Prose" (above) as you analyze the strengths and weaknesses of three summaries of the same article: "Protect Workers' Rights" by Bruce Raynor, published in the *Washington Post* on September 1, 2003. Imagine three student writers assigned to summarize this editorial in approximately 200 words. The first of the summaries below we have rated as excellent. Read the excellent summary first and then determine how successful the other summaries are.

SUMMARY 1 (AN EXCELLENT SUMMARY OF THE RAYNOR ARTICLE)

In Bruce Raynor's op-ed article "Protect Workers' Rights," originally published in the *Washington Post* on September 1, 2003, union official Raynor argues that workers everywhere are threatened by the current rules of globalization that allow corporations and governments to seek out the cheapest and least regulated labor around the world. Using the example of the Pillowtex Corporation that recently shut down its plant in Kannapolis, North Carolina, he shows how ending manufacturing that has played a long and major role in the economies of towns leaves workers without severance pay, medical insurance, money to pay taxes and mortgages, and other options for employment. According to Raynor, in the last three years, millions of jobs have been lost in all branches of American manufacturing. While policymakers advise these workers to seek education to retool for

(continued)

white-collar jobs, Raynor points out that fields such as telemarketing and the computer industry are also losing millions of jobs. Furthermore, outsourcing has caused a drop in wages in the United States. The same dynamic of jobs moving to countries with cheaper and less stringent safety and health regulation has recently caused Mexican and Bangladeshi workers to lose their jobs to Chinese workers. Raynor concludes with a call to protect the rights of workers everywhere by rewriting the "rules for the global economy" (A25). (214 words)

Work Cited

Raynor, Bruce. "Protect Workers' Rights." *Washington Post* 1 Sept. 2003: A25. Print.

SUMMARY 2

The closing of the Pillowtex Corporation's factories in the United States represents a loss of sixteen textile plants and about 6,500 jobs, according to Bruce Raynor, president of UNITE, a union of textile workers.

The workers left in Kannapolis, North Carolina, former home of one of the largest Pillowtex plants, are experiencing financial problems as they are unable to buy medical insurance, pay their taxes or mortgages or find other jobs.

Raynor argues that the case of the Pillowtex workers is representative of workers in other industries such as metals, papers, and electronics and that "this is the longest decline since the Great Depression" with about three million jobs gone in the last three years.

He then explains that white-collar jobs are not safe either because millions of jobs in telemarketing, claims adjusting, and even government are predicted to go overseas in the next five years. Furthermore, Raynor states that the possibility of outsourcing jobs leads to lowering of wages within the United States, as "outsourcing has forced down hourly wage rates by 10 percent to 40 percent for many U.S. computer consultants" (A25).

However, according to Raynor, the developing countries like Mexico and Bangladesh that have acquired manufacturing jobs are also threatened by countries like China who can offer employees who are willing to work for even lower wages and under worse conditions.

Raynor concludes that "a prosperous economy requires that workers be able to buy the products that they produce" (A25) and that workers everywhere need to be protected. (251 words)

Work Cited

Raynor, Bruce. "Protect Workers' Rights." *Washington Post* 1 Sept. 2003: A25. Print.

SUMMARY 3

In his article "Protect Workers' Rights," Bruce Raynor, president of UNITE, a textile workers' union, criticizes free trade and globalization for taking away workers' jobs. Using the Pillowtex Corporation's closing of its plant in Kannapolis, North Carolina, as his prime example, Raynor claims that outsourcing has destroyed the economy of this town and harmed workers across the United States. Raynor threatens that millions of white-collar jobs are also being lost and going to be lost in the next five years. Raynor complains that the whole national and global economy is falling apart and is going to get worse. He implies that the only solution is to keep jobs here in the United States. He maintains that workers around the world are also suffering when factories are moved from one developing country to another that has even more favorable conditions for the corporations. Raynor naively fails to factor in the role of consumers and the pressures on corporations into his defense of workers' rights. Clearly, Raynor loves unions and hates corporations; he probably fears that he is going to lose his own job soon. (183 words)

Understanding Strong Response Writing

We have said that the summary or abstract is an important academic genre and that summary writing is an essential academic skill. Equally important is strong response writing in which you identify and probe points in a text, sometimes by examining how a piece is written and often by inserting your own ideas into the text's conversation. "Strong response" is an umbrella term that incorporates a wide variety of ways that you can speak back to a text. In all cases, you are called on to do your own critical thinking by generating and asserting your own responses to the text.

In this section we will explain four different genres of strong response writing:

- Rhetorical critique
- Ideas critique
- Reflection
- Blended version of all three of these

Strong Response as Rhetorical Critique

A strong response as **rhetorical critique** analyzes a text's rhetorical strategies and evaluates how effectively the author achieves his or her intended goals. When writing a rhetorical critique, you discuss how a text is constructed, what rhetorical strategies it employs, and how effectively it appeals to *logos*, *ethos*, and *pathos*. In other words, you closely analyze the text itself, giving it the same close attention that an art critic gives a painting, a football coach gives a game video, or a biologist gives a cell formation. The close attention can be with the grain, noting the effectiveness of the text's rhetorical strategies, or against the grain, discussing what is ineffective or problematic about these strategies. Or an analysis might point out both the strengths and weaknesses of the text's rhetorical strategies.

For example, suppose that you are writing a rhetorical critique of an article from a conservative business journal advocating oil exploration in the Arctic National Wildlife Refuge (ANWR). You might analyze the article's rhetorical strategies by asking questions like these:

- How is the argument shaped to appeal to a conservative, business-oriented audience?
- How has the writer's angle of vision influenced the selection of evidence for his or her argument?
- How does the writer make himself or herself seem credible to this audience?

You would also evaluate the *logos* of the argument:

- How sound is the logic of the argument?
- Is the evidence accurate and current?
- What are the underlying assumptions and beliefs on which the argument is based?

Rhetorical critiques are usually closed-form, thesis-driven essays. The essay has a thesis that captures the writer's overall assessment of the text and maps out the specific points that the writer will develop in the analysis. When you are writing a rhetorical critique, your goal is to find a few rhetorical points that you find particularly intriguing, important, or disturbing to discuss and probe. Typically, your analysis zeroes in on some key features that you, the writer, find noteworthy. In the following strategies chart, we suggest the kinds of questions you can ask about a text to construct a rhetorical critique.

Question-Asking Strategies for Writing a Rhetorical Critique

Ask Questions about Any of the Following:	Examples
Audience and purpose: • Who is the intended audience? • What is the writer's purpose? • How well does the text suit its particular audience and purpose?	Examine how Michael Pollan writes to the well-educated audience of the *New York Times Magazine*, who are aware of climate change debates and most likely concerned about the problems ahead. Consider how Pollan writes to move these readers beyond good intentions to action. Examine how the text's structure, language, and evidence support this purpose.
Influence of genre on the shape of the text: • How has the genre affected the author's style, structure, and use of evidence?	Examine how the genre of the feature editorial for a highbrow magazine accounts for the length, structure, and depth of Pollan's argument. Examine how his references to political and intellectual figures (Al Gore, then Vice President Cheney, Adam Smith, Wendell Berry, and so forth) carry weight in this magazine's investigation of contemporary issues.
Author's style: • How do the author's language choices and sentence length and complexity contribute to the impact of the text?	Examine how Pollan's casual and cordial connections with readers (use of "I," "you," and "we"), his urgency, and his use of questions contribute to the article's effect.
Appeal to *logos*, the logic of the argument: • How well has the author created a reasonable, logically structured argument?	Examine how well Pollan uses logical points to support his claim and make his claim persuasive.

Ask Questions about Any of the Following:	Examples
Use of evidence: • How reputable, relevant, current, sufficient, and representative is the evidence?	Examine how Pollan uses references to scientific articles, newspaper accounts, and his own experiences to develop his points.
Appeal to *ethos* and the credibility of the author: • How well does the author persuade readers that he/she is knowledgeable, reliable, credible, and trustworthy?	Examine how Pollan conveys his knowledge of environmentalism, economics, and social trends. Examine the effects of genre and style in creating this *ethos*. Examine whether this *ethos* is effective for readers who are not familiar with Pollan's other writing, are skeptical of climate change, or are less in tune with environmental activism.
Appeal to *pathos*: • How well does the writer appeal to readers' emotions, sympathies, and values?	Examine how Pollan seeks to tap his audience's values and feelings. Consider how he conveys his familiarity with the everyday choices and decisions facing his readers.
Author's angle of vision: • How much does the author's angle of vision or interpretive filter dominate the text, influencing what is emphasized or omitted?	Examine how Pollan's angle of vision shapes his perspective on climate change, his choice of activist solutions, and his development of solutions. Consider how Pollan's reputation as the author of a number of books on food system reform influences his focus in this argument.

For a rhetorical critique, you would probably not choose all of these questions but would instead select three or four to highlight. Your goal is to make insightful observations about how a text works rhetorically and to support your points with examples and short quotations from the text.

Strong Response as Ideas Critique

A second kind of strong response, the **ideas critique,** focuses on the ideas at stake in the text. Rather than treat the text as an artifact to analyze rhetorically (as in a rhetorical critique), you treat it as a voice in a conversation—one perspective on an issue or one solution to a problem or question. Your strong response examines how the ideas of the original author mesh or conflict with your own. Based on your own critical thinking, personal experiences, and research, to what extent do you agree or disagree with the writer's thesis? A with-the-grain reading of a text would support all or some of the text's ideas, while also supplying additional evidence or extending the argument, perhaps applying it in a new context. An against-the-grain reading would challenge the writer's ideas, point out flaws and holes in the writer's thinking, and provide counterexamples and rebuttals. You might agree with some ideas and disagree with others in the text. In any case, in an ideas critique you speak back to the text from your own experience, background, reading, and thoughtful wrestling with the writer's ideas.

As an example, let's return to the article from the conservative business journal on drilling for oil in the ANWR. For an ideas critique, you would give your own views on oil exploration in the ANWR to support or challenge the writer's views, to raise new questions, and otherwise to add your voice to the ANWR conversation.

- You might supply additional reasons and evidence for drilling.
- You might oppose drilling in the ANWR by providing counterreasoning and counterexamples.
- You might propose some kind of synthesis or middle ground, where you would allow drilling in the ANWR but only under certain conditions.

When you write an ideas critique you are thus joining an important conversation about the actual subject matter of a text. Because much academic and professional writing focuses on finding the best solution to complex problems, this kind of strong response is very common. Usually this genre requires closed-form, thesis-governed prose. The following strategies chart suggests questions you can ask about a text to enter into its conversation of ideas.

Question-Asking Strategies for Writing an Ideas Critique

Questions to Ask	Examples
Where do I agree with this author? (with the grain)	Consider how you might amplify or extend Pollan's ideas. Build on his ideas by discussing examples where you or acquaintances have tried to change your lifestyle to lower carbon emissions. Show how these changes might have inspired others to do so.
What new insights has this text given me? (with the grain)	Explore Pollan's ideas that the environmental crisis is at heart a "crisis of lifestyle" or that specialization leads to a disjuncture between our everyday acts and their environmental consequences. Explore Pollan's argument that individual actions may lead to a social revolution. Think of how your eating habits or relationship to gardens has or could contribute to reform.

Questions to Ask	Examples
Where do I disagree with this author? (against the grain)	Challenge Pollan's assumptions about the magnitude of the problem. Challenge Pollan's idea that individuals can make a difference. Challenge his assumptions that technological solutions won't work because we still will face a crisis of lifestyle. Challenge the practicality and value of his main solution—growing gardens.
What points has the author overlooked or omitted? (against the grain)	Recognize that Pollan overlooks the constraints that would keep people from gardening. Consider that Pollan chooses not to focus on problems of overpopulation, water shortage, or economic disruption caused by environmentalism.
What new questions or problems has the text raised? (with or against the grain)	Explain how Pollan minimizes the economic impact of environmental action and downplays the role of government and business. Consider how we might need to "change the system" rather than just change ourselves. Consider his apparent lack of interest in technological solutions to the energy crisis.
What are the limitations or consequences of this text? (with or against the grain)	Consider ways that Pollan excludes some of his readers even while reaching out to others. Consider how Pollan, given his books on food and his passion for replacing industrial food production with local food, has written a predictable argument. Consider what new ideas he brings to his readers.

Because critiques of ideas appear in many contexts where writers search for the best solutions to problems, this kind of thinking is essential for academic research. In writing research papers, writers typically follow the template "This other writer has argued A, but I am going to argue B." Often the writer's own view (labeled "B") results from the writer's having wrestled with the views of others. Because this kind of dialectic thinking is so important to academic and professional life, we treat it further in Chapter 6 on exploratory writing and in Chapter 10 on classical argument. Each of these chapters encourages you to articulate alternative views and respond to them.

Strong Response as Reflection

A third kind of strong response is often called a "reflection" or a "reflection paper." (An instructor might say, for example, "Read Michael Pollan's article on climate change and write a reflection about it.") Generally, a **reflection** is an introspective genre; it invites you to connect the reading to your own personal experiences, beliefs, and values. In a reflection paper, the instructor is particularly interested in how the reading has affected you personally—what memories it has triggered, what personal experiences it relates to, what values and beliefs it has challenged, what dilemmas it poses, and so forth. A **reflection paper** is often more exploratory, open-ended, musing, and tentative than a rhetorical critique or an ideas critique, which is usually closed form and thesis governed.

To illustrate, let's consider how you might write a reflection in response to the article in the conservative business journal on drilling for oil in the ANWR. One approach might be to build a reflection around a personal conflict in values by exploring how the reading creates a personal dilemma:

- You might write about your own wilderness experiences, musing about the importance of nature in your own life.
- But at the same time, you might reflect on the extent to which your own life depends on cheap oil and acknowledge your own reluctance to give up owning a car.

In short, you want pristine nature and the benefits of cheap oil at the same time. Another quite different approach might be to reflect on how this article connects to discussions you are having in your other courses, say, the economic cost of individuals' and companies' going green. Here are some strategies you can use to generate ideas for a reflective strong response:

Question-Asking Strategies for Writing a Reflective Strong Response	
Questions to Ask	**Examples**
What personal memories or experiences does this text trigger?	Explore how Pollan's article evokes memories of your own frustrations about or successes with "green" living. Have you ever tried to change your habits for environmental reasons? If so, how did you go about doing it? Would your changes have met Berry's and Pollan's criteria for a change of "lifestyle"?
What personal values or beliefs does this text reinforce or challenge?	Explore the extent to which you can or can't identify with Pollan, Al Gore, and others who are proclaiming the seriousness of climate change and advocating changes in lifestyle. To what extent does Pollan as a person of conviction spark your admiration?

Questions to Ask	Examples
What questions, dilemmas, or problems does this text raise for me?	Explore how Pollan has challenged readers to take actions that may be difficult for them. For instance, you may have arrived at other solutions or know groups or organizations that are contributing positively in other ways. Perhaps Pollan's level of commitment or his particular approach to living green disturbs you in some way.
What new insights, ideas, or thoughts of my own have been stimulated by this text?	Explore any moments of enlightenment you had while reading Pollan. For example, perhaps his focus on individual action rather than on "laws and money" seems problematic to you. Perhaps there are other causes besides the environment that spur you to concern or to action. Perhaps you are now interested in exploring what inspires people to make major changes in how they live.

As you can tell from these questions, a reflective strong response highlights your own personal experiences and beliefs in conversation with the text. Whereas the focus of a rhetorical critique is on analyzing the way the text works rhetorically and the focus of an ideas critique is on taking a stance on the ideas at stake in the text, a reflective response focuses on the personal dimension of reading the text. Reflections call for a degree of self-disclosure or self-exploration that would be largely absent from the other kinds of strong responses.

Strong Response as a Blend

It should be evident that the boundaries among the rhetorical critique, ideas critique, and reflection overlap and that a strong response could easily blend features of each. In trying to decide how to respond strongly to a text, you often don't have to confine yourself to a pure genre but can mix and match different kinds of responses. You can analyze and critique a text's rhetorical strategies, show how the text challenges your own personal values and beliefs, and also develop your own stance on the text's ideas. In writing a blended response, you can emphasize what is most important to you, while not limiting yourself to only one approach.

Before we turn to the writing project for this chapter, we show you an example of a student's summary/strong response that is a blend of rhetorical critique, ideas critique, and personal reflection. Note that the essay begins by conveying the writer's investment in environmental conservation. It then summarizes Pollan's article. Following the summary, the student writer states his thesis, followed by his strong response, which contains both rhetorical points and points engaging Pollan's ideas.

Kyle Madsen (student)
Can a Green Thumb Save the Planet?
A Response to Michael Pollan

When I was a child, our household had one garbage can, in which my family and I would deposit all of our cardboard, plastic, glass, and paper waste. No one on my block had ever heard of recycling or using energy saving bulbs, and we never considered turning down our thermostats during the frozen winters and ice storms that swept our region from November to March. It wasn't that we didn't care about what we were doing to our environment. We just didn't know any better. However, once I got to college all that changed. My university's policies requested that students separate glass bottles and pizza boxes from plastic candy wrappers and old food containers. Thanks in large part to the chilling success of Al Gore's documentary *An Inconvenient Truth*, many of my old neighbors were starting to catch on as well, and now my home town is as devoted to its recycling as any major metropolitan area. Still, even though we as a country have come a long way in just a few years, there is a long way to go. Environmental journalist Michael Pollan in his article "Why Bother?" for the *New York Times Magazine* examines why working to slow the threat of climate change is such a daunting task.

In "Why Bother?" Michael Pollan explores how we have arrived at our current climate change crisis and argues why and how we should try to change our individual actions. Pollan sums up the recent scientific evidence for rapid climate change and then focuses on people's feeling overwhelmed in the face of this vast environmental problem. He presents his interpretation of how we have contributed to the problem and why we feel powerless. Pollan asserts that the climate-change crisis is "the sum total of countless everyday choices" made by consumers globally and that it is "at its very bottom a crisis of lifestyle—of character, even" (90). Our reliance on "cheap fossil fuel" has contributed to both the problem and to our sense of helplessness. In the final part of his article, Pollan concedes that "laws and money" (90) are necessary to create change, but he still advocates acting on our values and setting an example, which might launch a green social revolution.

According to Pollan, "The idea is to find one thing to do in your life that does not involve spending or voting ... that will offer its own rewards" (93). He concludes by encouraging readers to plant gardens in order to reduce carbon emissions, to lessen our "sense of dependence and dividedness" (93)—to empower ourselves to contribute positively to our environment.

Although Pollan has created an argument with strong logical, ethical, and emotional appeals, his very dominant angle of vision—seen in his assumptions, alarmist language, and exclusive focus on garden-growing—may fail to win neutral readers. I also think Pollan's argument loses impact by not discussing more realistic alternatives such as pursuing smart consumerism and better environmental education for children.

Pollan builds a forceful case in his well-argued and knowledgeable interpretation of our climate-change problem as a "crisis of lifestyle—of character, even" (90).

His frank confrontation of the problem of how to motivate people is compelling, especially when he admits the contrast between "the magnitude of the problem" and the "puniness" of individual action (89). Pollan both deepens his argument and constructs a positive ethos by drawing on the ideas of environmental ethicist Wendell Berry and classical economist Adam Smith to explain how modern civilization has developed through the division of labor (specialization), which has brought us many advantages but also cut us off from community and environmental responsibility. In this part of his argument, Pollan helps readers understand how our dependence on cheap oil and our lifestyle choices have enhanced our roles as limited, specialized producers and major consumers. Pollan's development of his theory of the "cheap-energy mind" (92) and his reasonable support of this idea are the strongest part of his argument and the most relevant to readers like me. I have thought that we have become small cogs in an overbearing machine of consumption and only larger cogs such as the government can have enough influence on the overall system to make change happen. From time to time, I have wondered what I as one person could really do. This sense of insignificance, which Pollan theorizes, has made me wait until my regular light bulbs burned out before considering replacing them with energy-efficient ones.

    Another strength of Pollan's argument is the way he builds bridges to his audience through his appeals to *pathos*. He understands how overwhelmed the average person can feel when confronted with the climate-change problem. Pollan never criticizes his readers for not being as concerned as he is. Instead he engages them in learning with him. He explores with readers the suggestion of walking to work, a task on par with light bulb changing, when he writes, even if "I decide that I am going to bother, there arises the whole vexed question of getting it right. Is eating local or walking to work really going to reduce my carbon footprint?" (89). By asking questions like these, he speaks as a concerned citizen who tries to create a dialogue with his audience about the problem of climate change and what individuals can do.

    However, despite his outreach to readers, Pollan's angle of vision may be too dominant and intense for some readers. He assumes that his *New York Times Magazine* readers already share his agreement with the most serious views of climate change held by many scientists and environmentalists, people who are focusing on the "truly terrifying feedback loops" (90) in weather and climate. He also assumes that his readers hold similar values about local food and gardening. This intense angle of vision may leave out some readers. For example, I am left wondering why gardening is more effective than, say, converting to solar power. He also tries to shock his readers into action with his occasional alarmist or overly dramatic use of language. For example, he tries to invoke fear: "Have you looked into the eyes of a climate scientist recently? They look really scared" (90). However, how many regular people have run-ins with climate scientists?

    In addition, after appearing very in tune with readers in the first part of his argument, in the final part he does not address his readers' practical concerns. He describes in great detail the joys of gardening—specifically how it will connect readers not only to the earth, but to friends and neighbors as well—yet he glosses over the amount of work necessary to grow a garden. He writes, "Photosynthesis still works so abundantly that in a

With-the-grain rhetorical point focused on the logos and ethos of Pollan's argument

Brief reflective comment

With-the-grain rhetorical point focused on the pathos of Pollan's argument

Against-the-grain rhetorical point focused on angle of vision

Transition to ideas critique, an against-the-grain point critiquing Pollan's ideas—Pollan

doesn't acknowledge the impracticality of expecting people to grow their own vegetables.

thoughtfully organized vegetable garden (one planted from seed, nourished by compost from the kitchen and involving not too many drives to the gardening center), you can grow the proverbial free lunch" (93–4). However, not everyone has a space for a garden or access to a public one to grow tomatoes themselves, and it takes hours of backbreaking labor to grow a productive vegetable garden—hardly a free lunch. Average Americans work upwards of sixty hours per week, so it is unrealistic to expect them to spend their free time working in a garden. In not addressing readers' objections to gardening or suggesting other ways to mend our cheap oil values, I think Pollan proposes simply another situation for semi-concerned individuals to again say, "Why bother?"

Another point critiquing Pollan's ideas. Madsen proposes sustainable consumerism as an alternative to gardening.

Also, besides gardens, I think Pollan could emphasize other avenues of change such as sustainable consumerism. In different places in the article, he mentions that individuals can use their consumer lifestyles to achieve a more sustainable way of life, but he chooses to insist that gardening be the main means. I would have liked him to discuss how we as consumers could buy more fuel-efficient cars, avoid plastic packaging, drink tap water, and buy products from green industries. This "going green" trend has already taken root in many of America's top industries—at least in their advertising and public relations campaigns. We can't leave a Starbucks without inadvertently learning about what they are doing to offset global warming. But we consumers need to know which industries really are going green in a significant way so that we can spend our shopping dollars there. If Pollan is correct, environmentally conscientious consumers can demand a change from the corporations they rely on, so why not use the same consumerism that got us into this mess to get us out?

Another point addressing Pollan's ideas—environmental education in the schools as an alternative to gardening.

Besides sustainable consumerism, I think we should emphasize the promotion of better environmental education for our children. Curriculum in K–12 classrooms presented by teachers rather than information from television or newspapers will shape children's commitment to the environment. A good example is the impact of Recycle Now, an organization aimed at implementing recycling and global awareness in schools. According to Dave Lawrie, a curriculum expert featured on their Web site, "Recycling at school is a hands-on way to show pupils that every single person can help to improve the environment. Everyone in our school has played a part in making a difference." With serious education, kids will learn the habits of respecting the earth, working in gardens, and using energy-saving halogen bulbs, making sustainability and environmental stewardship a way of life.

Short conclusion bringing closure to the essay.

While Pollan is correct in pushing us into action now, asking Americans to grow a garden, when changing a light bulb seems daunting, is an unrealistic and limited approach. However, Pollan persuasively addresses the underlying issues in our attitudes toward the climate crisis and works to empower readers to become responsible and involved. Whether it be through gardening, supporting green businesses, or education, I agree with Pollan that the important thing is that you learn to bother for yourself.

Works Cited

Citation of works cited in the essay using MLA format

Lawrie, Dave. "Bringing the Curriculum to Life." *School Success Stories. RecycleNow* 11 Nov. 2009. Web. 28 Feb. 2010.

Pollan, Michael. "Why Bother?" *New York Times Magazine* 20 Apr. 2008: 19+. Rpt. in *The Allyn and Bacon Guide to Writing.* John D. Ramage, John C. Bean, and June Johnson. 6th ed. New York: Pearson, 2012. 88–94. Print.

In the student example just shown, Kyle Madsen illustrates a blended strong response that includes both a rhetorical critique of the article and some of his own views. He analyzes Pollan's article rhetorically by pointing out both the persuasive features of the argument and the limiting angle of vision of a worried environmentalist and extremely committed gardening enthusiast. He seconds some of Pollan's points with his own examples, but he also reads Pollan against the grain by suggesting how Pollan's word choice and fixation on gardening as a solution prevent him from developing ideas that might seem more compelling to some readers.

A Summary

Write a summary of an article assigned by your instructor for an audience who has not read the article. Write the summary using attributive tags and providing an introductory context as if you were inserting it into your own longer paper (see the model on p. 99). The word count for your summary will be specified by your instructor. Try to follow all the criteria for a successful summary listed on page 101, and use MLA documentation style, including a Works Cited entry for the article that you are summarizing. (Note: Instead of an article, your instructor may ask you to summarize a longer text such as a book or a visual-verbal text such as a Web page or an advocacy brochure. We address these special cases at the end of this section.)

Generating Ideas: Reading for Structure and Content

Once you have been assigned an article to summarize, your first task is to read it carefully a number of times to get an accurate understanding of it. Remember that summarizing involves the essential act of reading with the grain as you figure out exactly what the article is saying. In writing a summary, you must focus on both a text's structure and its content. In the following steps, we recommend a process that will help you condense a text's ideas into an accurate summary. As you become a more experienced reader and writer, you'll follow these steps without thinking about them.

Step 1: The first time through, read the text fairly quickly for general meaning. If you get confused, keep going; later parts of the text might clarify earlier parts.

Step 2: Read the text carefully paragraph by paragraph. As you read, write gist statements in the margins for each paragraph. A *gist statement* is a brief indication of a paragraph's function in the text or a brief summary of a paragraph's content. Sometimes it is helpful to think of these two kinds of gist statements as "what it does" statements and "what it says" statements.* A "what

*For our treatment of "what it does" and "what it says" statements, we are indebted to Kenneth A. Bruffee, *A Short Course in Writing*, 2nd ed. (Cambridge, MA: Winthrop, 1980).

it does" statement specifies the paragraph's function—for example, "summarizes an opposing view," "introduces another reason," "presents a supporting example," "provides statistical data in support of a point," and so on. A "what it says" statement captures the main idea of a paragraph by summarizing the paragraph's content. The "what it says" statement is the paragraph's main point, in contrast to its supporting ideas and examples.

When you first practice detailed readings of a text, you might find it helpful to write complete *does* and *says* statements on a separate sheet of paper rather than in the margins until you develop the internal habit of appreciating both the function and content of parts of an essay. Here are *does* and *says* statements for selected paragraphs of Michael Pollan's article on climate change activism.

Paragraph 1: ***Does:*** Introduces the need for environmental action as a current problem that readers know and care about and sets up the argument. ***Says:*** We as individuals often wonder if our small, minor actions are worth doing in light of the magnitude of the climate change problem.

Paragraph 2: ***Does:*** Explores another reason why individuals may doubt whether individual actions could make a difference. ***Says:*** People willing to change their lifestyles to combat climate change may be discouraged by the increase in a carbon-emissions lifestyle in other parts of the world such as China.

Paragraph 8: ***Does:*** Expresses an alternative view, partially concedes to it, and asserts a counterview. ***Says:*** Although big money and legislation will be important in reversing climate change, the problem at its heart is a "crisis of lifestyle—of character" (90), and therefore will require the effort of individuals.

Paragraph 18: ***Does:*** Presents and develops one of Pollan's main reasons that concerned individuals should take personal action to fight climate change. ***Says:*** Setting an example through our own good environmental choices could exert moral influence here and abroad, on individuals and big business.

Writing a *says* statement for a paragraph is sometimes difficult. You might have trouble, for example, deciding what the main idea of a paragraph is, especially if the paragraph doesn't begin with a closed-form topic sentence. One way to respond to this problem is to formulate the question that you think the paragraph answers. If you think of chunks of the text as answers to a logical progression of questions, you can often follow the main ideas more easily. Rather than writing *says* statements in the margins, therefore, some readers prefer writing *says* questions. *Says* questions for the Pollan text may include the following:

- What are some of the biggest obstacles that discourage people from undertaking individual actions to fight climate change?
- Despite our excuses not to act, why is individual action still necessary?
- How is the problem of climate a "crisis of lifestyle"?
- What are the reasons we should "bother"?
- Why is growing one's own vegetable garden a particularly powerful individual act?

No matter which method you use—*says* statements or *says* questions—writing gist statements in the margins is far more effective than underlining or highlighting in helping you recall the text's structure and argument.

Step 3: Locate the article's main divisions or parts. In longer closed-form articles, writers often forecast the shape of their essays in their introductions or use their conclusions to sum up main points. For example, Pollan's article uses some forecasting and transitional statements to direct readers through its parts and main points. The article is divided into several main chunks as follows:

- Introductory paragraphs, which establish the problem to be addressed and describe the reasons that people don't take action to help slow climate change (paragraphs 1–5)
- Two short transitional paragraphs (a one-sentence question and a two-word answer) stating the author's intention to call for individual action in spite of the obstacles. These two paragraphs prepare the move into the second part of the article (paragraphs 6 and 7).
- A paragraph conceding to the need for action beyond the individual (laws and money) followed by a counterclaim that the climate change problem is a "crisis of lifestyle" (paragraph 8)
- Eight paragraphs developing Pollan's "crisis of lifestyle" claim, drawing on Wendell Berry and explaining the concepts of specialization and the "cheap-energy mind" that have led us into both the climate change problem and our feelings of inadequacy to tackle it (paragraphs 9–16)
- A transitional paragraph conceding that reasons against individual action are "many and compelling," but proposing better ways to answer the "why bother" question. (paragraph 17)
- Two paragraphs developing Pollan's reasons for individual action—how individuals will influence each other and broader communities and lead to "viral social change" (paragraphs 18–19)
- Two paragraphs elaborating on the possibility of viral social change based on analogy to the end of Communism in Czechoslovakia and Poland and to various ways individuals might make significant changes in their lifestyles (paragraphs 20–21)
- Five paragraphs detailing Pollan's choice for the best solution for people to reduce their carbon emissions and make a significant environmental statement: grow gardens (paragraphs 22–26)

Instead of listing the sections of your article, you might prefer to make an outline or tree diagram of the article showing its main parts.

Drafting and Revising

Once you have determined the main points and grasped the structure of the article you are summarizing, combine and condense your *says* statements into clear sentences that capture the gist of the article. These shortened versions of your *says* statements will make up most of your summary, although you might mention the structure of the article to help organize the points. For example, you might say, "[Author's name] makes four main points in this article. ... The article concludes with a call to action. … " Because representing an article in your own words in a greatly abbreviated form is a challenge, most writers revise their sentences to find the clearest, most concise way to express the article's ideas accurately. Choose and use your words carefully to stay within your word limit.

The procedures for summarizing articles can work for book-length texts and visual-verbal texts as well. For book-length texts, your *does* and *says* statements may cover chapters or parts of the book. Book introductions and conclusions as well as chapter titles and introductions may provide clues to the author's thesis and subthesis to help you identify the main ideas to include in a book summary. For verbal-visual texts such as a public affairs advocacy ad, product advertisement, Web page, or brochure, examine the parts to see what each contributes to the whole. In your summary, help your readers visualize the images, comprehend the parts, and understand the main points of the text's message.

Plan to create several drafts of all summaries to refine your presentation and wording of ideas. Group work may be helpful in these steps.

FOR WRITING AND DISCUSSION

Finding Key Points in an Article

If the whole class or a group of students is summarizing the same article, brainstorm together and then reach consensus on the main ideas that you think a summary of that article should include to be accurate and complete. Then reread your own summary and check off each idea.

When you revise your summary, consult the criteria on page 101 in this chapter as well as the Questions for Peer Review that follow.

Questions for Peer Review

In addition to the generic peer review questions explained in, Skill 16.4, ask your peer reviewers to address these questions:

1. In what way do the opening sentences provide needed contextual information and then express the overall thesis of the text? What information could be added or more clearly stated?
2. How would you evaluate the writer's representation and coverage of the text's main ideas in terms of accuracy, balance, and proportion? What ideas have been omitted or overemphasized?
3. Has the writer treated the article fairly and neutrally? If judgments have crept in, where could the writer revise?
4. How could the summary use attributive tags more effectively to keep the focus on the original author's ideas?
5. Has the writer used quotations sparingly and cited them accurately? Has the writer translated points into his or her own words? Has the writer included a Works Cited?
6. Where might the writer's choice of words and phrasing of sentences be revised to improve the clarity, conciseness, and coherence of the summary?

A Summary/Strong Response Essay

In response to a text assigned by your instructor, write a "summary/strong response" essay that incorporates a 150–250-word summary of the article. In your strong response to that reading, speak back to its author from your own critical thinking, personal experience, values, and, perhaps, further reading or research. Unless your instructor assigns a specific kind of strong response (rhetorical critique, ideas critique, or reflection), write a blended response in which you are free to consider the author's rhetorical strategies, your own agreement or disagreement with the author's ideas, and your personal response to the text. Think of your response as your analysis of how the text tries to influence its readers rhetorically and how your wrestling with the text has expanded and deepened your thinking about its ideas. As you work with ideas from the text, remember to use attributive tags, quotation marks for any quoted passages, and MLA documentation to distinguish your own points about the text from the author's ideas and language.

Exploring Ideas for Your Strong Response

Earlier in the chapter we presented the kinds of strong responses you may be asked to write in college. We also provided examples of the questions you can ask to generate ideas for different kinds of strong response. Your goal now is to figure out what you want to say. Your first step, of course, is to read your assigned text with the grain, listening to the text so well that you can write a summary of its argument. Use the strategies described in the previous writing project to compose your summary of the assigned text.

After you have written your summary, which demonstrates your full understanding of the text, you are ready to write a strong response. Because your essay cannot discuss every feature of the text or every idea the text has evoked, you will want to focus on a small group of points that enable you to bring readers a new, enlarged, or deepened understanding of the text. You may decide to write a primarily with-the-grain response, praising, building on, or applying the text to a new context, or a primarily against-the-grain response, challenging, questioning, and refuting the text. If your strong response primarily agrees with the text, you must be sure to extend it and apply the ideas rather than simply make your essay one long summary of the article. If your strong response primarily disagrees with the text and criticizes it, you must be sure to be fair and accurate in your criticisms. Here we give you some specific rereading strategies that will stimulate ideas for your strong response, as well as an example of Kyle Madsen's marginal response notes to Pollan's article (Figure 5.1).

See Chapter 1, Concept 3, for a discussion of audience analysis.

Strategies for Rereading to Stimulate Ideas for a Strong Response

Strategies	What to Do	Comments
Take notes.	Make copious marginal notes while rereading, recording both with-the-grain and against-the-grain responses.	Writing a strong response requires a deep engagement with texts. For example, in Figure 5.1, observe how Kyle Madsen's notes incorporate with-the-grain and against-the-grain responses and show him truly talking back to and interacting with Pollan's text.
Identify "hot spots" in the text.	Mark all hot spots with marginal notes. After you've finished reading, find these hot spots and freewrite your responses to them in a reading journal.	By "hot spot" we mean a quotation or passage that you notice because you agree or disagree with it or because it triggers memories or other associations. Perhaps the hot spot strikes you as thought provoking. Perhaps it raises a problem or is confusing yet suggestive.
Ask questions.	Write several questions that the text caused you to think about. Then explore your responses to those questions through freewriting, which may trigger more questions.	Almost any text triggers questions as you read. A good way to begin formulating a strong response is to note these questions.
Articulate your difference from the intended audience.	Decide who the writer's intended audience is. If you differ significantly from this audience, use this difference to question the author's underlying assumptions, values, and beliefs.	Your gender, age, class, ethnicity, sexual orientation, political and religious beliefs, interests, values, and so forth, may cause you to feel estranged from the author's imagined audience. If the text seems written for straight people and you are gay, or for Christians and you are a Muslim or an atheist, or for environmentalists and you grew up in a small logging community, you may well resist the text. Sometimes your sense of exclusion from the intended audience makes it difficult to read a text at all.

Michael Pollan

Why Bother?

This idea is very direct and clear.

Why bother? That really is the big question facing us as individuals hoping to do something about climate change, and it's not an easy one to answer. I don't know about you, but for me the most upsetting moment in *An Inconvenient Truth* came long after Al Gore scared the hell out of me, constructing an utterly convincing case that the very survival of life on earth as we know it is threatened by climate change. No, the really dark moment came during the closing credits, when we are asked to ... change our light bulbs. That's when it got really depressing. The immense disproportion between the magnitude of the problem Gore had described and the puniness of what he was asking us to do about it was enough to sink your heart.

Informal speech.

Sounds like Pollan is talking to readers.

How I felt when I saw this film.

Short sentence sounds casual.

Another very informal statement.

But the drop-in-the-bucket issue is not the only problem lurking behind the "why bother" question. Let's say I do bother, big time. I turn my life upside-down, start biking to work, plant a big garden, turn down the thermostat so low I need the Jimmy Carter signature cardigan, forsake the clothes dryer for a laundry line across the yard, trade in the station wagon for a hybrid, get off the beef, go completely local. I could theoretically do all that, but what would be the point when I know full well that halfway around the world there lives my evil twin, some carbon-footprint *doppelgänger* in Shanghai or Chongqing who has just bought his first car (Chinese car ownership is where ours was back in 1918), is eager to swallow every bite of meat I forswear and who's positively itching to replace every last pound of CO2 I'm struggling no longer to emit. So what exactly would I have to show for all my trouble?

Helpful examples.

Good word choice? Sounds prejudiced and alarmist.

Look up this word.

Exaggerated statement?

This paragraph shows Pollan's liberal perspective.

A sense of personal virtue, you might suggest, somewhat sheepishly. But what good is that when virtue itself is quickly becoming a term of derision? And not just on the editorial pages of the *Wall Street Journal* or on the lips of the vice president, who famously dismissed energy conservation as a "sign of personal virtue." No, even in the pages of the *New York Times* and the *New Yorker*, it seems the epithet "virtuous," when applied to an act of personal environmental responsibility, may be used only ironically. Tell me: How did it come to pass that virtue—a quality that for most of history has generally been deemed, well, a virtue—became a mark of liberal softheadedness? How peculiar, that doing the right thing by the environment—buying the hybrid, eating like a locavore—should now set you up for the Ed Begley Jr.* treatment.

Former Vice President Cheney?

What's the definition of this term?

FIGURE 5.1 Kyle Madsen's Marginal Response Notes

Practicing Strong Response Reading Strategies

What follows is a short passage by writer Annie Dillard in response to a question about how she chooses to spend her time. This passage often evokes heated responses from our students.

> I don't do housework. Life is too short. ... I let almost all my indoor plants die from neglect while I was writing the book. There are all kinds of ways to live. You can take your choice. You can keep a tidy house, and when St. Peter asks you what you did with your life, you can say, "I kept a tidy house, I made my own cheese balls."

Individual task: Read the passage and then briefly freewrite your reaction to it.

Group task: Working in groups or as a whole class, develop answers to the following questions:

1. What values does Dillard assume her audience holds?
2. What kinds of readers are apt to feel excluded from that audience?
3. If you are not part of the intended audience for this passage, what in the text evokes resistance?

Articulate Your Own Purpose for Reading

Although you usually read a text because you are joining the author's conversation, you might occasionally read a text for an entirely different purpose from what the author intended. For example, you might read the writings of nineteenth-century scientists to figure out what they assumed about nature (or women, or God, or race, or capitalism). Or suppose that you examine a politician's metaphors to see what they reveal about her values, or analyze *National Geographic* for evidence of political bias. Understanding your own purpose will help you read deeply both with and against the grain.

Writing a Thesis for a Strong Response Essay

See Chapter 2, Concept 5, for a discussion of surprising thesis statements.

A thesis for a strong response essay should map out for readers the points that you want to develop and discuss. These points should be risky and contestable; your thesis should surprise your readers with something new or challenging. Your thesis might focus entirely on with-the-grain points or entirely on against-the-grain points, but most likely it will include some of both. Avoid tensionless thesis statements such as "This article has both good and bad points."

Here are some thesis statements that students have written for strong responses in our classes. Note that each thesis includes at least one point about the rhetorical strategies of the text.

EXAMPLES OF SUMMARY/STRONG RESPONSE THESIS STATEMENTS

- In "The Beauty Myth," Naomi Wolf makes a very good case for her idea that the beauty myth prevents women from ever feeling that they are good enough;

however, Wolf's argument is geared too much toward feminists to be persuasive for a general audience, and she neglects to acknowledge the strong social pressures that I and other men feel to live up to male standards of physical perfection.

- Although Naomi Wolf in "The Beauty Myth" uses rhetorical strategies persuasively to argue that the beauty industry oppresses women, I think that she overlooks women's individual resistance and responsibility.

- Although the images and figures of speech that Thoreau uses in his chapter "Where I Lived, and What I Lived For" from *Walden* wonderfully support his argument that nature is spiritually renewing, I disagree with his antitechnology stance and with his extreme emphasis on isolation as a means to self-discovery.

- In "Where I Lived, and What I Lived For" from *Walden*, Thoreau's argument that society is missing spiritual reality through its preoccupation with details and its frantic pace is convincing, especially to twenty-first century audiences; however, Thoreau weakens his message by criticizing his readers and by completely dismissing technological advances.

- Although the booklet *Compassionate Living* by People for the Ethical Treatment of Animals (PETA) uses the design features of layout, color, and image powerfully, its extreme examples, its quick dismissal of alternative views, and its failure to document the sources of its information weaken its appeal to *ethos* and its overall persuasiveness.

Examining Thesis Statements for Strong Response Critiques

FOR WRITING AND DISCUSSION

Working individually or in groups, identify the points in each of the thesis statements in the preceding section and briefly state them. Think in terms of the ideas you are expecting the writers to develop in the body of the essay. As a follow-up to this exercise, you might share in your groups your own thesis statements for your strong response essays. How clearly does each thesis statement lay out points that the writer will probe? As a group, discuss what new, important perspectives each thesis statement promises to bring to readers and how each thesis suits a rhetorical critique, ideas critique, or some combination of these.

Shaping and Drafting

Most strong response essays call for a short contextualizing introduction to set up your analysis. In the essay on pages 110–112, student writer Kyle Madsen begins by reflecting on personal and societal changes in environmental awareness and then raises the question that Pollan will address: What challenges confront us in changing how we live? Student writer Stephanie Malinowski (pp. 124–126) uses a similar strategy. She begins by tapping into her readers' experiences with outsourcing, and then poses the question that Thomas Friedman addresses in his op-ed piece: Should Americans support or question the practice of outsourcing?

Both student writers introduce the question addressed by the article they are critiquing, and both include a short summary of the article that gives readers a foundation for the critique before they present the points of the article they will address in their strong responses.

Each of the thesis statements in the preceding section as well as Kyle's and Stephanie's thesis statements identifies and maps out two or more points that readers will expect to see developed and explained in the body of the essay. In a closed-form, thesis-driven strong response, readers will also expect the points to follow the order in which they are presented in the thesis. If your strong response is primarily a rhetorical critique, your evidence will come mainly from the text you are analyzing. If your strong response is primarily an ideas critique, your evidence is apt to come from personal knowledge of the issue or from further reading or research. If your strong response is primarily reflective, much of your evidence will be based on your own personal experiences and inner thoughts. A blended response, of course, can combine points from any of these perspectives.

Each point in your thesis calls for a lively discussion, combining general statements and specifics that will encourage readers to see this text your way. Just as you do in your summary, you must use attributive tags to distinguish between the author's ideas and your own points and responses. In addition, you must document all ideas gotten from other sources as well as place all borrowed language in quotation marks or block indentations according to MLA format and include a Works Cited in MLA format. Most strong response essays have short conclusions, just enough commentary to bring closure to the essay.

Revising

In a summary/strong response essay, you may want to work on the summary separately before you incorporate it into your whole essay. Use the peer review questions for summaries (p. 116) for that part of your essay. You will definitely want to get feedback from readers to make your strong response as clear, thorough, and compelling as possible.

Questions for Peer Review

In addition to the generic peer review questions explained in Skill 16.4, ask your peer reviewers to address these questions:

1. How appealingly do the title and introduction of the essay set up the topic of critique, convey the writer's interest, and lay a foundation for the summary of the article and the writer's thesis?
2. How could the writer's thesis statement be clearer in presenting several focused points about the text's rhetorical strategies and ideas?
3. How could the body of the strong response follow the thesis more closely?
4. Where do you, the reader, need more clarification or support for the writer's points? How could the writer develop with-the-grain or against-the-grain points more appropriately?
5. Where could the writer work on the effectiveness of attributive tags, quotations, and documentation?

The readings for this chapter address the issue of outsourcing, the practice of moving jobs from developed countries like the United States to developing countries, which have a cheaper workforce. This practice affects available jobs for college graduates and American workers as well as the progress and vitality of the economies of many countries. Outsourcing continues to spark fiery debates about job creation and unemployment in the United States, about the distribution of benefits and harm, and about global economic competition. The readings that follow address these points from multiple perspectives. The questions for analysis have been omitted from all but the student essay by Stephanie Malinowski so that you can do your own independent thinking in preparation for writing your own summary/strong response essay.

Our first reading is an op-ed piece by prominent journalist Thomas L. Friedman, published in the *New York Times* on February 29, 2004. Friedman is known for his pro–free trade enthusiasm and his three books on globalization, *The Lexus and the Olive Tree* (1999), *The World Is Flat: A Brief History of the Twenty-First Century* (2005), and *Hot, Flat, and Crowded* (2008).

Thomas L. Friedman
30 Little Turtles

1   Indians are so hospitable. I got an ovation the other day from a roomful of Indian 20-year-olds just for reading perfectly the following paragraph: "A bottle of bottled water held 30 little turtles. It didn't matter that each turtle had to rattle a metal ladle in order to get a little bit of noodles, a total turtle delicacy. The problem was that there were many turtle battles for less than oodles of noodles."

2   I was sitting in on an "accent neutralization" class at the Indian call center 24/7 Customer. The instructor was teaching the would-be Indian call center operators to suppress their native Indian accents and speak with a Canadian one—she teaches British and U.S. accents as well, but these youths will be serving the Canadian market. Since I'm originally from Minnesota, near Canada, and still speak like someone out of the movie "Fargo," I gave these young Indians an authentic rendition of "30 Little Turtles," which is designed to teach them the proper Canadian pronunciations. Hence the rousing applause.

3   Watching these incredibly enthusiastic young Indians preparing for their call center jobs—earnestly trying to soften their t's and roll their r's—is an uplifting experience, especially when you hear from their friends already working these jobs how they have transformed their lives. Most of them still live at home and turn over part of their salaries to their parents, so the whole family benefits. Many have credit cards and have become real consumers, including of U.S. goods, for the first time. All of them seem to have gained self-confidence and self-worth.

4   A lot of these Indian young men and women have college degrees, but would never get a local job that starts at $200 to $300 a month were it not for the call centers. Some do "outbound" calls, selling things from credit cards to phone services to Americans and Europeans. Others deal with "inbound" calls—everything from tracing lost luggage for U.S. airline passengers to solving computer problems for U.S. customers. The calls are transferred here by satellite or fiber optic cable.

5   I was most taken by a young Indian engineer doing tech support for a U.S. software giant, who spoke with pride about how cool it is to tell his friends that he just spent the day helping Americans navigate their software. A majority of these call center workers are young women, who not only have been liberated by earning a decent local wage (and therefore have more choice in whom they marry), but are using the job to get M.B.A.'s and other degrees on the side.

6   I gathered a group together, and here's what they sound like: M. Dinesh, who does tech support, says his day is made when some American calls in with a problem and is actually happy to hear an Indian voice: "They say you people are really good at what you do. I am glad I reached an Indian." Kiran Menon, when asked who his role model was, shot back: "Bill Gates—[I dream of] starting my own company and making it that big." I asked C. M. Meghna what she got most out of the work: "Self-confidence," she said, "a lot of self-confidence, when people come to you with a problem and you can solve it—and having a lot of independence." Because the call center teams work through India's night—which corresponds to America's day—"your biological clock goes haywire," she added. "Besides that, it's great."

7   There is nothing more positive than the self-confidence, dignity and optimism that comes from a society knowing it is producing wealth by tapping its own brains—men's and women's—as opposed to one just tapping its own oil, let alone one that is so lost it can find dignity only through suicide and "martyrdom."

8   Indeed, listening to these Indian young people, I had a déjà vu. Five months ago, I was in Ramallah, on the West Bank, talking to three young Palestinian men, also in their 20's, one of whom was studying engineering. Their hero was Yasir Arafat. They talked about having no hope, no jobs and no dignity, and they each nodded when one of them said they were all "suicide bombers in waiting."

9   What am I saying here? That it's more important for young Indians to have jobs than Americans? Never. But I am saying that there is more to outsourcing than just economics. There's also geopolitics. It is inevitable in a networked world that our economy is going to shed certain low-wage, low-prestige jobs. To the extent that they go to places like India or Pakistan—where they are viewed as high-wage, high-prestige jobs—we make not only a more prosperous world, but a safer world for our own 20-year-olds.

Our second reading is a summary/strong response essay by student writer Stephanie Malinowski in response to the Friedman article. It follows primarily a "rhetorical critique" strategy for the strong response.

Stephanie Malinowski

Questioning Thomas L. Friedman's Optimism in "30 Little Turtles"

1   You are struggling to fix a problem that arises when you are downloading new computer software on to your computer. You're about to give up on the whole thing when an idea hits you: call the software company itself to ask for assistance. Should

you be surprised when the person who answers the phone to help you is based in India? Should Americans support or question outsourcing?

2   In "30 Little Turtles," an op-ed piece that appeared in the *New York Times* on February 29, 2004, journalist and foreign affairs columnist Thomas L. Friedman argues that outsourcing call center jobs from the Western world to India is transforming the lives of Indian workers and benefiting geopolitics. Friedman supports his argument by detailing his experience visiting a call center in India. He claims that the Indians working to serve Canadian and American markets are happy with how their work has improved their lives. Friedman points out that the working Indian women feel liberated now that they are making a decent wage and can afford such things as a college education. He describes Indian workers' view of their jobs, using words such as "self-confidence" and "independence." At the end of his article, Friedman states that he doesn't favor Indian employment over American employment but that outsourced jobs in countries like India or Pakistan create both prosperity and global security. Although Friedman's article clearly conveys to its audience how some Indian workers are benefiting from outsourcing, his argument relies heavily on personal experience and generalizations. I also think his condescending attitude hurts his argument, and he concludes his article too abruptly, leaving readers with questions.

3   Friedman succeeds in portraying the positive side of outsourcing to his *New York Times* readers who may be questioning the rationale for outsourcing. Friedman interviews the recipients of American jobs to see outsourcing from their perspective and enlightens Americans trying to understand how outsourcing is benefiting workers in other countries. Friedman's opening is vivid and captures the readers' interest by detailing his experience inside an Indian call center. He quotes the Indian workers expressing the joys of working for American and Canadian people. These workers testify to the financial and personal gains these jobs have brought. One woman says that she feels good about her job and herself "when people come to you with a problem and you can solve it" (125). The article is so full of optimism that the reader can't help but empathize with the Indians and feel happy that outsourcing has transformed their lives. Through these emotional appeals, Friedman succeeds in making readers who may have big reservations about outsourcing think about the human dimension of outsourcing.

4   However, Friedman also makes large generalizations based on his few personal experiences, lessening the credibility of his article. The first sentence of the article reads, "Indians are so hospitable." So are *all* Indians "so hospitable"? Friedman seems to make this generalization about national character based on the fact that he was applauded by a room full of Indians after reading a tongue twister paragraph in a perfect Canadian accent. I can see why Friedman appreciates his warm reception, but "feel good" moments can hardly provide evidence for the soundness of global economic policies. Friedman generalizes further about what he sees and hears in the call center room. He talks about the Indian employees in these terms: "All of them seem to have gained self-confidence and self-worth" (124). From this single observation, Friedman makes the assumption that almost every Indian working an outsourcing job must be gaining, and that the overall experience has done wonders for their lives. However, other articles that I have read have mentioned that call center work is basically a

deadend job and that $200 a month is not a big salary. Later in his conclusion, Friedman states that "we make not only a more prosperous world, but a safer world for our own 20-year-olds" (125). Can this conclusion be drawn from one visit to a call center where Indians expressed gratitude for their outsourcing work?

5   An even bigger problem with Friedman's article is the condescending way in which he describes the Indian workers. I think he portrays the culture as being incompetent before the American and Canadian outsourcing jobs came to improve their accents and their lives. One statement that conveys condescension is this remark: "Watching these incredibly enthusiastic young Indians preparing for their call center jobs—earnestly trying to soften their t's and roll their r's—is an uplifting experience … " (124). This passage reminds me of the delight and pride of parents witnessing their children's growth milestones. Friedman is casting the accent neutralization of the Indian workers as overcoming a barrier in order to reach success. Friedman's condescending tone is apparent again when he restates the words of one American caller to an Indian worker, "They say you people are really good at what you do. I am glad I reached an Indian" (125). I see Friedman's reason for including this quote; he wants the reader to know that Indian workers are being valued for their work. However, the words that the American uses, which Friedman deliberately chooses to include in his article, "you people," suggest that Indians are a whole other kind of people different from American workers in their skills. Friedman's condescension also appears when he says that these are "low-wage, low-prestige jobs" (125). This remark is full of problems because it puts down the Indians taking the jobs and the Americans who have lost them, and it misrepresents the outsourcing scene that now includes many highly skilled prestigious jobs.

6   I also think that Friedman weakens his article by concluding abruptly and introducing new ideas to readers that leave them with unanswered questions. Friedman asks the reader, "What am I saying here? That it's more important for young Indians to have jobs than Americans?" (125). This point seems like a relevant question to investigate, but its weakness is that Friedman never even mentions any place in his article the loss that American workers are experiencing. At the end of the article, readers are left with questions. For example, the last sentence reads, "we make not only a more prosperous world, but a safer world for our own 20-year-olds" (125). Although Friedman is implying that outsourcing improves our relationships with other countries and enhances our national safety, nowhere in the article does he substantiate this claim. He seems to have thrown this statement into the conclusion just to end the article on a happy note.

7   Giving a human face to outsourcing is a good idea; however, Friedman does not support his main argument well, and this article comes across as a simplistic, unexplored view of outsourcing. I and other readers are left needing to look for answers to serious questions about outsourcing elsewhere.

Work Cited

Friedman, Thomas L. "30 Little Turtles." *New York Times* 29 Feb. 2004. Rpt. in *The Allyn & Bacon Guide to Writing.* John D. Ramage, John C. Bean, and June Johnson. 6th ed. New York: Pearson, 2012. 124–5. Print.

THINKING CRITICALLY
about "Questioning Thomas L. Friedman's Optimism in '30 Little Turtles'"

1. What rhetorical points has Stephanie Malinowski chosen to analyze?

2. What examples and quotations from Friedman's article work particularly well as support for her points? Where might she have included more support?

3. Where does Stephanie use attributive tags effectively?

4. If you were to write a rhetorical critique of Friedman's article, what points would you select to analyze?

5. If you were to write an ideas critique, what would you choose to focus on? Where would you agree and disagree with Friedman?

Our third reading is a political cartoon that tells a story about employment and outsourcing. As you read, identify the character, the story line, the angle of vision, and the argument. The cartoon, by Mike Lane, a well-known liberal cartoonist, appeared in the *Baltimore Sun* in 2003.

Mike Lane
Labor Day Blues

6

WRITING AN EXPLORATORY ESSAY OR ANNOTATED BIBLIOGRAPHY

I n Part 1, we explained how writers wrestle with subject-matter problems. During exploration, experienced writers often redefine their problem, discover new ideas, and alter or even reverse their initial thesis. In contrast, inexperienced writers often truncate this process, closing off the period of exploratory thinking. Asserting a thesis too soon can prevent writers from acknowledging an issue's complexity, whereas dwelling with a question invites writers to contemplate multiple perspectives, entertain new ideas, and let their thinking evolve. In this chapter, we introduce two genres of writing built on exploratory thinking:

- An **exploratory essay** narrates a writer's thinking process while doing research. The essay recounts your attempt to examine your question's complexity, explore alternatives, and arrive at a solution or answer. Because an exploration often requires research, many instructors pair this project with Part 4, "A Rhetorical Guide to Research."
- An **annotated bibliography** summarizes and briefly critiques the research sources a writer used while exploring a problem. It encourages exploration and inquiry, provides a "tracing" of your work, and creates a guide for others interested in your research problem.

Even though academic readers usually expect and need thesis-driven arguments, exploratory essays are becoming more common in scholarly journals, and annotated bibliographies are a frequently encountered academic genre. Exploratory essays exist in embryo in the research or lab notebooks of scholars. For students, both the exploratory essay and the annotated bibliography serve as an intermediate stage in the research process. Student James Gardiner's exploratory paper and annotated bibliography in this chapter are products of the exploratory phase of his research about online social networking, which later resulted in a researched argument. You can compare his exploratory essay with the final thesis-driven argument in Chapter 14.

In this chapter, you will learn to:

- explore an issue and narrate your thinking process in an exploratory essay
- summarize and critique your research sources in an annotated bibliography

Exploring Exploratory Writing

Through our work in writing centers, we often encounter students disappointed with their grades on essay exams or papers. "I worked hard on this paper," they tell us, "but I still got a lousy grade. What am I doing wrong? What do college professors want?"

To help you answer this question, consider the following two essays written for a freshman placement examination in composition at the University of Pittsburgh, in response to the following assignment:

> Describe a time when you did something you felt to be creative. Then, on the basis of the incident you have described, go on to draw some general conclusions about "creativity."

How would you describe the differences in thinking exhibited by the two writers? Which essay do you think professors rated higher?

ESSAY A

I am very interested in music, and I try to be creative in my interpretation of music. While in high school, I was a member of a jazz ensemble. The members of the ensemble were given chances to improvise and be creative in various songs. I feel that this was a great experience for me, as well as the other members. I was proud to know that I could use my imagination and feelings to create music other than what was written.

Creativity to me means being free to express yourself in a way that is unique to you, not having to conform to certain rules and guidelines. Music is only one of the many areas in which people are given opportunities to show their creativity. Sculpting, carving, building, art, and acting are just a few more areas where people can show their creativity.

Through my music I conveyed feelings and thoughts which were important to me. Music was my means of showing creativity. In whatever form creativity takes, whether it be music, art, or science, it is an important aspect of our lives because it enables us to be individuals.

ESSAY B

Throughout my life, I have been interested and intrigued by music. My mother has often told me of the times, before I went to school, when I would "conduct" the orchestra on her records. I continued to listen to music and eventually started to play the guitar and the clarinet. Finally, at about the age of twelve, I started to sit down and to try to write songs. Even though my instrumental skills were far from my own high standards, I would spend much of my spare time during the day with a guitar around my neck, trying to produce a piece of music.

Each of these sessions, as I remember them, had a rather set format. I would sit in my bedroom, strumming different combinations of the five or six chords I could play, until I heard a series which sounded particularly good to me. After this, I set the music to a suitable rhythm (usually dependent on my mood at the time), and ran through the tune until I could play it fairly easily. Only after this section was complete did I go on to writing lyrics, which generally followed along the lines of the current popular songs on the radio.

At the time of the writing, I felt that my songs were, in themselves, an original creation of my own; that is, I, alone, made them. However, I now see that, in this sense of the word, I was not creative. The songs themselves seem to be an oversimplified form of the music I listened to at the time.

In a more fitting sense, however, I *was* being creative. Since I did not purposely copy my favorite songs, I was, effectively, originating my songs from my own "process of creativity." To achieve my goal, I needed what a composer would call "inspiration" for my piece. In this case the inspiration was the current hit on the radio. Perhaps, with my present point of view, I feel that I used too much "inspiration" in my songs, but, at the time, I did not.

Creativity, therefore, is a process which, in my case, involved a certain series of "small creations" if you like. As well, it is something the appreciation of which varies with one's point of view, that point of view being set by the person's experience, tastes, and his own personal view of creativity. The less experienced tend to allow for less originality, while the more experienced demand real originality to classify something a "creation." Either way, a term as abstract as this is perfectly correct, and open to interpretation.

Working as a whole class or in small groups, analyze the differences between Essay A and Essay B. What might cause college professors to rate one essay higher than the other? What would the writer of the weaker essay have to do to produce an essay more like the stronger?

Understanding Exploratory Writing

The essential move for exploratory thinking and writing is to keep a problem alive through consideration of multiple solutions or points of view. The thinker identifies a problem, considers a possible solution or point of view, explores its strengths and weaknesses, and then moves on to consider another possible solution or viewpoint. The thinker resists closure—that is, resists settling too soon on a thesis.

To show a mind at work examining multiple solutions, let's return to the two student essays you examined in the previous exploratory activity (pp. 129–130). The fundamental difference between Essay A and Essay B is that the writer of Essay B treats the concept of "creativity" as a true problem. Note that the writer of Essay A is satisfied with his or her initial definition:

> Creativity to me means being free to express yourself in a way that is unique to you, not having to conform to certain rules and guidelines.

The writer of Essay B, however, is *not* satisfied with his or her first answer and uses the essay to think through the problem. This writer remembers an early creative experience—composing songs as a twelve-year-old:

> At the time of the writing, I felt that my songs were, in themselves, an original creation of my own; that is, I, alone, made them. However, I now see that, in this sense of the word, I was not creative. The songs themselves seem to be an oversimplified form of the music I listened to at the time.

This writer distinguishes between two points of view: "On the one hand, I used to think *x*, but now, in retrospect, I think *y*." This move forces the writer to go beyond the initial answer to think of alternatives.

The key to effective exploratory writing is to create a tension between alternative views. When you start out, you might not know where your thinking process will end up; at the outset you might not have formulated an opposing, countering, or alternative view. Using a statement such as "I used to think ... , but now I think" or "Part of me thinks this ... , but another part thinks that ... " forces you to find something additional to say; writing then becomes a process of inquiry and discovery.

The second writer's dissatisfaction with the initial answer initiates a dialectic process that plays one idea against another, creating a generative tension. In contrast, the writer of Essay A offers no alternative to his or her definition of creativity. This writer presents no specific illustrations of creative activity (such as the specific details in Essay B about strumming the guitar) but presents merely space-filling abstractions ("Sculpting, carving, building, art, and acting are just a few more areas where people can show their creativity"). The writer of Essay B scores a higher grade, not because the essay creates a brilliant (or even particularly clear) explanation of creativity; rather, the writer is rewarded for thinking about the problem dialectically.

We use the term *dialectic* to mean a thinking process often associated with the German philosopher Hegel, who said that each thesis ("My act was creative") gives rise to an antithesis ("My act was not creative") and that the clash of these opposing perspectives leads thinkers to develop a synthesis that incorporates some features of both theses ("My act was a series of 'small creations'"). You initiate dialectic thinking any time you play Elbow's believing and doubting game or use other strategies to place alternative possibilities side by side.

See Chapter 2, Concept 4, for an explanation of the believing and doubting game.

Essay B's writer uses a dialectic thinking strategy that we might characterize as follows:

1. Sees the assigned question as a genuine problem worth puzzling over.
2. Considers alternative views and plays them off against each other.
3. Looks at specific examples and illustrations.
4. Continues the thinking process in search of some sort of resolution or synthesis of the alternative views.
5. Incorporates the stages of this dialectic process into the essay.

These same dialectic thinking habits can be extended to research writing where the researcher's goals are to find alternative points of view on the research question, to read sources rhetorically, to consider all the relevant evidence, to search for a resolution or synthesis of alternative views, and to use one's own critical thinking to arrive at a thesis.

Keeping a Problem Open

FOR WRITING AND DISCUSSION

1. Working individually, read each of the following questions and write out the first plausible answer that comes to your mind.
   - Why on average are males more attracted to video games than females? Are these games harmful to males?

- Have online social networks such as Facebook improved or harmed the lives of participants? Why?
- The most popular magazines sold on college campuses are women's fashion and lifestyle magazines such as *Glamour, Elle*, and *Cosmopolitan*. Why do women buy these magazines? Are these magazines harmful?

2. As a whole class, take a poll to determine the most common first-response answers for each of the questions. Then explore other possible answers and points of view. The goal of your class discussion is to postulate and explore answers that go against the grain of or beyond the common answers. Try to push deeply into each question so that it becomes more complex and interesting than it may at first seem.

See Chapters 13 and 14 for instruction on doing college-level academic research.

3. How would you use library and Internet research to deepen your exploration of these questions? Specifically, what keywords might you use in a database search? What databases would you use?

WRITING PROJECT

An Exploratory Essay

Choose a question, problem, or issue that genuinely perplexes you. At the beginning of your essay, explain why you are interested in this problem, why you think it is significant, and why you have been unable to reach a satisfactory answer. Then write a first-person, chronologically organized narrative account of your thinking process as you investigate your question through research, talking with others, and doing your own reflective thinking. Your goal is to examine your question, problem, or issue from a variety of perspectives, assessing the strengths and weaknesses of different positions and points of view. Your goal is not to answer your question but to report on the process of wrestling with it.

This assignment asks you to dwell on a problem—and not necessarily to solve that problem. Your problem may shift and evolve as your thinking progresses. What matters is that you are actively engaged with your problem and demonstrate why it is problematic.

Generating and Exploring Ideas

Your process of generating and exploring ideas is, in essence, the *subject matter* of your exploratory essay. This section will help you get started and keep going.

Posing Your Initial Problem

If your instructor hasn't assigned a specific problem to be investigated, then your first step is to choose one that currently perplexes you. Perhaps a question is problematic for you because you haven't yet had a chance to study it (Should the United States turn to nuclear power for generating electricity?). Maybe the available data seem conflicting or inconclusive (Should women younger than fifty get annual mammograms?). Or, possibly, the problem or issue draws you into an uncomfortable conflict of values (Should we legalize the sale of organs for transplant?).

The key to this assignment is to choose a question, problem, or issue *that truly perplexes you.* (Your instructor may limit the range of topics you can choose.) Here are several exercises to help you think of ideas for this essay:

- Make a list of issues or problems that both interest and perplex you within the range of subjects specified by your instructor. Then choose two or three and freewrite about them for five minutes or so. Use as your model James Gardiner's freewrite on page 29, which marked the origin of his exploratory paper for this chapter. Share your questions and your freewrites with friends and classmates because doing so often stimulates further thinking and discovery.

- A particularly valuable kind of problem to explore for this assignment is a current public controversy. Often such issues involve disagreements about facts and values that merit open-ended exploration. This assignment invites you to explore and clarify where you stand on such public issues as gay marriage, immigration, health care reform, energy policies, and so forth. Make a list of currently debated public controversies that you would like to explore. Share your list with classmates and friends.

Formulating a Starting Point

After you've chosen a problem, you are ready to write a first draft of your introduction in which you identify your chosen problem and show why you are interested in it, why you find it perplexing, and why it is significant. You might start out with a sharp, clearly focused question (Should the United States build a fence between the United States and Mexico?). Often, however, formulating a focused question will turn out to be part of the *process* of writing the paper. Instead of a single, focused question, you might start with a whole cluster of related questions swimming in your head. That's fine too because you can still explain why you are interested in this cluster of questions.

The goal of your introduction is to hook your reader's interest in your chosen problem. Often the best way to do so is to show why you yourself became interested in it. For example, James Gardiner opens his exploratory essay by noting the popularity of online social networks such as MySpace and Facebook and mentioning the shocked look of his friends when he tells them he doesn't have a Facebook profile (see p. 144). He then introduces the questions he wants to investigate—why students are attracted to Facebook or MySpace, how students use the sites, and how their communication skills are being affected. Another student, Dylan Fujitani, opened his exploratory essay by explaining his shock when seeing a newspaper photograph of mutilated corpses hanging from a bridge

Dylan Fujitani's final argument essay appears on pp. 267–271.

in Falluja, Iraq. Later, he discovered that the bodies were not American soldiers but hired contractors. This experience gave rise to a number of issues he wanted to explore about mercenary soldiers under the general question, "Is the use of private contractors in military roles a good idea?"

Taking "Double-Entry" Research Notes

After you have formulated your initial problem, you are ready to start your research. As you read, take purposeful notes. Whereas novice researchers often avoid taking notes and instead create a pile of photocopied or downloaded-and-printed articles, experienced researchers use note taking as a discipline to promote strong rhetorical reading. We recommend "double-entry" notes in which you use one column for taking notes on a source and another column for recording your own thinking about the source. When you have finished taking notes in the first column, write a "strong response" to the source in the second column, explaining how the source advanced your thinking, raised questions, or pulled you in one direction or another.

What follows is James Gardiner's double-entry research notes for one of the articles he used in his exploratory essay. When you read both his exploratory essay in this chapter and his final researched argument in Chapter 14, you'll be able to see how he used this article at a crucial place in his research.

James's Double-Entry Research Log Entry for *Financial Times* Article

Date of entry so you can reconstruct chronological order → February 24

Bibliographic citation following assigned format, in this case MLA → Bowley, Graham. "The High Priestess of Internet Friendship." *Financial Times Weekend Magazine* 27 Oct. 2006. *LexisNexis Academic*. Web. 22 Feb. 2007.

Rhetorical notation about genre, purpose, audience → Newspaper feature article in journalistic style

---

Reading Notes	**Strong Response Notes**
Reading notes in column 1 on content of the source —Begins with Danah Boyd, an expert on OSNs. Talks about how she enjoyed Internet connections when she was growing up. Says the Internet "could change the way all of us order our world, interact with each other, get information and do business." (p. 1 of printout)	*—I want to find out more about Danah Boyd.*
Include full quotations if you won't keep a copy of the full source	*—good quote*
—Two-page section on history of OSNs beginning with Friendster.	
Strong response notes in column 2 show reactions to the source —Returns to profile of Boyd. Boyd compares MySpace to an "electronic version of the local mall" (p. 2). She claims that these public spaces are no longer available so kids have gone virtual.	*—I don't think I agree with this; kids still hang out at malls.*

James's Double-Entry Research Log Entry for *Financial Times* Article

—Quote from blogger Cory Doctorow on OSN messages as "simple grooming exercises" (p. 3)—not serious talk—just saying "hi" online.	—*good quote; I should use it.*
—Paragraph on the "explosion of self-expression" on the sites—poems, songs, pictures, etc.—everyone trying to self-express creatively.	—*very interesting passage; I should try to use it.*
—Generational shift in attitudes toward privacy. Compares kids on OSNs trying to become celebrities like Paris Hilton (p. 3)—mentions Christine Dolce (AKA ForBiddeN) as example of someone who achieved celebrity status.	—*very important for my research question*
—Quotes Boyd: OSNs are about "identity production"—kids are trying to "write themselves into being." Quotes researcher Fred Stutzman about kids using OSN profiles like their bedroom walls—their private place where they can invite friends. They are "testing out identities." (p. 4)	—*I have another article by Stutzman; should read it soon.* —*great analogy*
—Has a section on online games; also has a section on how sociologists are doing interesting experiments seeing how news travels on OSNs.	—*I don't quite understand the experiments.*
—Raises some questions about dangers—stalkers—especially dangers to minors. How legislators are trying to come up with laws to make it harder for stalkers to find victims.	—*good for challenging OSNs and constructing alternative views*
—Returns to Boyd, who says these dangers are "painfully overblown." Boyd really supports OSNs as places where kids can "negotiate this new world."	—*important points; good longer quote on p. 5*
— Last part focuses on commercial aspects of OSNs; they apparently aren't yet big moneymakers. Also if there is too much advertising, kids might not like the OSN as well.	—*points make sense; might use them*

Strong response summary:
Very useful article, not scholarly but fairly deep and well-researched. I can use it to give arguments in favor of Facebook, MySpace, or other OSNs. However, Danah Boyd doesn't support OSNs in the same way that many other supporters do. Most supporters talk about how OSNs help young people enlarge their list of friends and have a feeling of connection, etc. Boyd is much more edgy and sees the dangers out there and all the role playing and phoniness. Boyd seems to like that unstable atmosphere where the rules and norms aren't really clear. She thinks that the online world is really helping students learn to find their identities and discover who they are. I still have reservations, though. I like the parts of the article where Bowley talks about students wanting to become celebrities and competing with each other for the most friends because that seems like self-enhancement rather than making connections. Also Boyd doesn't seem worried about all the time young people spend at these sites. I need to do more research into the downside of OSNs.

Shaping and Drafting

Your exploratory essay records the history of your researching and thinking process (what you read or whom you talked to, how you responded, how your thinking evolved). Along the way you can make your narrative more colorful and grounded by including your strategies for tracking down sources, your conversations with friends, your late-night trips to a coffee shop, and so forth. What you will quickly discover about this exploratory assignment is that it forces you actually to do the research. Unless you conduct your research in a timely fashion, you won't have any research process to write about.

Exploratory essays can be composed in two ways—what we might call the "real-time strategy" and the "retrospective strategy."

Strategies for Composing an Exploratory Essay	
Strategies	**Advantages**
Real-time strategy. Compose the body of the essay during the actual process of researching and thinking.	Yields genuine immediacy—like a sequence of letters or e-mails sent home during a journey.
Retrospective strategy. Look back over your completed research notes and then compose the body of the essay.	Allows for more selection and shaping of details and yields a more artistically designed essay.

In either case, the goal when writing with an exploratory aim is to reproduce the research and thinking process, taking the readers on the same intellectual and emotional journey you have just traveled. The exploratory essay has the general organizational framework shown in Figure 6.1.

There are a number of keys to writing successful exploratory papers. As you draft, pay particular attention to the following:

- *Show how you chose sources purposively and reflectively rather than randomly.* As you make a transition from one source to the next, help your reader see your thought processes. Note the following examples of bridging passages that reveal the writer's purposeful selection of sources:

   For the next stage of my research, I wanted to explore in more detail what students actually did while online in an OSN. I located my next source by searching through the Academic Search Complete database (from James Gardiner's essay, para. 6, p. 145).

   After reading Friedman's views of how globalization was changing lives in India and China, I realized that I needed to talk to some students from these countries, so I grabbed my backpack and headed to the International Student Center.

- *Give your draft both open-form and closed-form features.* Because your exploratory paper is a narrative, it follows an unfolding, open-form structure. Many of your paragraphs should open with chronological transitions such as "I *started*

FIGURE 6.1 Framework for an Exploratory Essay

Introduction (one or more paragraphs)	• Establishes that your question is complex, problematic, and significant • Shows why you are interested in it • Presents relevant background You can begin with your question or build up to it, using it to end your introductory section.
Body section 1 on first source	• Introduces your first source and shows why you started with it • Provides rhetorical context and information about the source • Summarizes the source's content and argument • Offers your strong response to this source, frequently including both with-the-grain and against-the-grain points • Talks about what this source contributes to your understanding of your question: What did you learn? What value does this source have for you? What is missing from this source that you want to consider? Where do you want to go from here?
Body section 2 on second source	• Repeats the process with a new source selected to advance the inquiry • Explains why you selected this source (to find an alternative view, pursue subquestions, find more data, and so forth) • Summarizes the source's argument • Provides a strong response • Shows how your cumulative reading of sources is shaping your thinking or leading to more questions
Body sections 3, 4, 5, etc., on additional sources	• Continues the process
Conclusion	• Wraps up your intellectual journey and explains where you are now in your thinking and how your understanding of your problem has changed • Presents your current answer to your question based on all that you have read and learned so far, or explains why you still can't answer your question, or explains what further research you might do
Works Cited or References list	• Includes a complete list of citations in MLA or APA format, depending on your assignment

by reading," "*Early the next morning,* I headed for the library to ... ," "On the *next* day, I decided," or "*After* finishing ... I *next* looked at. ... " At the same time, your summaries of your sources and your strong responses to them should be framed within closed-form structures with topic sentences and logical transitions: "This article, in raising objections to genetic screening of embryos, began changing my views about new advances in reproductive technology. Whereas before I felt ... , now I feel. ... "

• *Show yourself wrestling with ideas.* Readers want to see how your research stimulates your own thinking. Throughout, your paper should show you responding strongly to your sources. Here is a good example from James's paper on online social networks.

> After considering the views of Boyd and Stutzman, I felt I understood why they think that OSNs give young people the opportunity for self-definition and self-expression. However, I still had doubts about the beneficial effects of OSNs. They still seem to me to send superficial messages about a person's identity. I found myself wondering if it is detrimental to spend all that time in virtual space rather than actually being with one's friends. I felt I needed to start looking for articles that examine the dangers of OSNs.

Although you might feel that sentences that show your mind talking its way through your research will sound too informal, they actually work well in exploratory essays to create interest and capture your critical thinking.

Revising

Because an exploratory essay describes the writer's research and thinking in chronological order, most writers have little trouble with organization. When they revise, their major concern is to improve their essay's interest level by keeping it focused and lively. Often drafts need to be pruned to remove extraneous details and keep the pace moving. Frequently, introductions can be made sharper, clearer, and more engaging. Peer reviewers can give you valuable feedback about the pace and interest level of an exploratory piece. They can also help you achieve the right balance between summarizing sources and showing the evolution of your own thinking. As you revise, make sure you use attributive tags and follow proper stylistic conventions for quotations and citations.

Questions for Peer Review

In addition to the generic peer review questions explained in Skill 11.4, ask your peer reviewers to address these questions:

POSING THE PROBLEM:

1. In the introduction, how has the writer tried to show that the problem is interesting, significant, and problematic? How could the writer engage you more fully with the initial problem?
2. How does the writer provide cues that his/her purpose is to explore a question rather than argue a thesis? How might the opening section of the draft be improved?

NARRATING THE EXPLORATION:

3. Is the body of the paper organized chronologically so that you can see the development of the writer's thinking? Where does the writer provide chronological transitions?
4. Part of an exploratory essay involves summarizing the argument of each new research source. Where in this draft is a summary of a source particularly clear

and well developed? Where are summary passages either undeveloped or unclear or too long? How could these passages be improved?

5. Another part of an exploratory paper involves the writer's strong response to each source. Where in this draft is there evidence of the writer's own critical thinking and questioning? Where are the writer's ideas particularly strong and effective? Where are the writer's own ideas undeveloped, unclear, or weak?

6. Has the writer done enough research to explore the problem? How would you describe the range and variety of sources that the writer has consulted? Where does the writer acknowledge how the kinds of sources shape his or her perspective on the subject? What additional ideas or perspectives do you think the writer should consider?

An Annotated Bibliography

WRITING

PROJECT

Create an annotated bibliography that lists the research sources you have used for your exploratory project. Because annotated bibliographies can vary in the number, length, and kinds of entries, follow guidelines provided by your instructor. Some instructors may also require a critical preface that explains your research question and provides details about how you selected the bibliographic sources.

What Is an Annotated Bibliography?

Bibliographies are alphabetized lists of sources on a given topic, providing readers with the names of authors, titles, and publication details for each source. Unlike a plain list of sources, an **annotated bibliography** also includes the writer's "annotation" or commentary on each source. These annotations can be either *summary-only* or *evaluative.*

- A **summary-only annotation** provides a capsule of the source's contents without any additional comments from the bibliography's author.
- An **evaluative annotation** adds the author's critique or assessment of the work, including comments about the source's rhetorical context, its particular strengths or weaknesses, and its usefulness or value.

Whichever type is used, the length of the annotation is a function of its audience and purpose. Brief annotations comprise only a few sentences (one standard approach—to be described later—uses three sentences) while longer annotations can be up to 150 words. Brief annotations are most common when the annotated bibliography has numerous entries; longer annotations, which allow for fuller summaries and more detailed analyses, are often more helpful for readers but can make an annotated bibliography too long if there are many sources.

Annotated bibliographies serve several important functions. First, writing an annotated bibliography engages researchers in exploratory thinking by requiring that they read sources rhetorically like experts, entering critically into scholarly conversations. Annotated bibliographies can also be valuable time-saving tools for new researchers in a field. By providing overview information about potential sources, they help new researchers determine whether a particular source might be useful for their own purposes. Think of source annotations as analogous to short movie reviews that help you select your next film. (What's this movie about? How good is it?) Additionally, annotated bibliographies can establish the writer's *ethos* by showing the depth, breadth, and competence of the writer's research. (A good annotated bibliography proves that you have read and thought about your sources.)

Features of Annotated Bibliography Entries

Each entry has two main parts, the bibliographic citation and the annotation. The **bibliographic citation** should follow the conventions of your assigned documentation style such as the Modern Language Association (MLA) or the American Psychological Association (APA).

See Chapter 14.

An **evaluative annotation** (the most common kind) typically includes three elements. In a three-sentence evaluative annotation, each element is covered in one sentence.

- *Rhetorical information,* including the source's rhetorical context, particularly its genre and (if not implied by the genre) its purpose and audience. Is this source a scholarly article? An op-ed piece? A blog? What is the author's purpose and who is the intended audience? Are there any political biases that need to be noted?
- *A summary of the source's content.* In some cases, a writer simply lists what is covered in the source. Whenever possible, however, summarize the source's actual argument. (Note: In a *summary-only* annotation, this summary is the only element included.)
- *The writer's evaluation of the source.* What are the source's particular strengths or weaknesses? How useful is the source for specific purposes? How might the writer use the source for his or her research project? (Or, if the annotated bibliography comes at the end of the project, how did the writer use the source?)

Examples of Annotation Entries

Here are examples of different kinds of annotations based on James Gardiner's research notes for one of his sources (see pp. 134–135):

SUMMARY-ONLY ANNOTATION

Bowley, Graham. "The High Priestess of Internet Friendship." *Financial Times Weekend Magazine* 27 Oct. 2006. *LexisNexis Academic.* Web. 22 Feb. 2007.

In this feature story, Bowley explains the development of OSNs from their origins in *Friendster* to their current popularity in *MySpace* and *Facebook*. He also traces further developments of OSNs and explains their difficulties in making profits through commercial advertising. Finally, Bowley uses interviews with researchers to show how young people use OSNs to maintain social relationships and to play with different identities through self-expression.

EVALUATIVE ANNOTATION

Bowley, Graham. "The High Priestess of Internet Friendship." *Financial Times Weekend Magazine* 27 Oct. 2006. *LexisNexis Academic.* Web. 22 Feb. 2007.

This article is a feature story in the "Arts and Weekend" section of the *Financial Times Weekend Magazine.* Bowley's information comes from interviews with researchers who study online social networks (OSNs). Bowley explains the development of OSNs from their origins in *Friendster* to their current popularity in *MySpace* and *Facebook*, traces further developments of OSNs, and explains their difficulties in making profits through commercial advertising. Bowley also shows how young people use OSNs to maintain social relationships and to play with different identities through self-expression. A particularly valuable section mentions the dangers of OSNs, such as sexual predators. However, Danah Boyd, a researcher whom Bowley quotes extensively, defends OSNs as a place where young people can explore their identities and "negotiate this new world." This article gives a mostly positive view of OSNs and goes beyond other articles by showing how OSNs provide a new space for "identity production."

THREE-SENTENCE EVALUATIVE ANNOTATION

Bowley, Graham. "The High Priestess of Internet Friendship." *Financial Times Weekend Magazine* 27 Oct. 2006. *LexisNexis Academic.* Web. 22 Feb. 2007.

This article is a journalistic feature story written for readers of a major business and finance newspaper. It gives the history of online social networks (OSN) including *Friendster, MySpace,* and *Facebook*, explains their difficulties in making money through commercial advertising, and shows how young people use OSNs to maintain social relationships and to play with different identities through self-expression. This is a valuable article that gives a mostly positive view of OSNs by showing how they provide a new space for "identity production" and self-expression.

Writing a Critical Preface for Your Annotated Bibliography

Scholars who publish annotated bibliographies typically introduce them with a critical preface that explains the scope and purpose of the bibliography. When you write a critical preface for your own annotated bibliography, you have a chance to highlight your critical thinking and show the purposeful way that you conducted your research. Typically the critical preface includes the following information:

- A contextual overview that shows the purpose of the annotated bibliography and suggests its value and significance for the reader
- The research question posed by the author
- The dates during which the bibliography was compiled
- An overview of the number of items in the bibliography and the kinds of material included

A student example of an annotated bibliography with a critical preface is found in the Readings section of this chapter (pp. 149–151).

Shaping, Drafting, and Revising

The key to producing a good annotated bibliography is to take good research notes as you read. Compare the various versions of the above annotations with James Gardiner's research notes (pp. 134–135). Before composing your annotated bibliography, make sure that you understand your instructor's preferences for the number of entries required and for the length and kinds of annotations. Arrange the bibliography in alphabetical order as you would in a "Works Cited" (MLA format) or "References" (APA format) list.

The specific skills needed for an annotated bibliography are taught in various places in this text. If you are having problems with aspects of an annotated bibliography, you can find further instruction as follows.

Problems with:	Where to Find Help
Formatting the citations.	Refer to Skill 14.1 for MLA style, and Skill 14.2 for APA style.
Describing the rhetorical context and genre.	Review Chapter 1, Concept 3.
Writing a summary.	Read Chapter 5, pages 98–101, on summary writing; read also Skill 13.2.
Writing an evaluation.	Use the strategies for strong response in Chapter 5, pages 103–109, and also Skill 13.1.
Wordiness—the annotation is more than 150 words.	See Chapter 4, Concept 11, on wordy versus streamlined sentences.

Questions for Peer Review

The following questions are based on the assumption that your instructor requires evaluative annotations and a critical preface. Adjust the questions to fit a different assignment.

CRITICAL PREFACE

1. Where does the writer explain the following: The purpose and significance of the bibliography? The research question that motivated the research? The dates of the research? The kinds of sources included?
2. How could the critical preface be improved?

BIBLIOGRAPHIC CITATIONS

3. Does each citation follow MLA or APA conventions? Pay particular attention to the formatting of sources downloaded from a licensed database or from the Web.
4. Are the sources arranged alphabetically?

ANNOTATIONS

5. Where does each annotation include the following: Information about genre or rhetorical context? A capsule summary of the source's contents? An evaluative comment?

6. Identify any places where the annotations are confusing or unclear or where the writer could include more information.

7. How could one or more of the annotations be improved?

Readings   Our first reading is an exploratory essay by student writer James Gardiner on online social networks. After completing the exploratory essay, James continued his research, writing an argument on potential negative consequences of OSNs. James's final argument is our sample MLA student research paper in Chapter 14 (pp. 362–370).

James Gardiner (student)
How Do Online Social Networks Affect Communication?

1   Walk into any computer lab located at any college campus across the country and you'll see dozens of students logged onto an online social network (OSN). In the last few years, the use of these networks has sky-rocketed among Internet users, especially young adults. As a college student, I am one of the few people I know who does not have a profile on either *MySpace* or *Facebook*, and I'm constantly met with shocked looks when I inform my fellow students of this. Today, OSNs have become a staple in the life of most American young people. Although I was conscious that OSNs were impacting the way young people communicate with each other, I was largely unaware of the specific ways that people used these OSNs or how their communication skills were being affected by this new technology. For this research project, I decided to pursue the question, How are online social networks influencing the way young people communicate with each other? This question deserves to be examined because the more people move toward these new modes of communication, the more influence these networks will have on society as a whole. I suspect that these new virtual communities are changing the way people communicate with one another to an incredible degree.

2   Before I could focus on the impact of OSNs on people's communication skills, I first needed to learn more about who used these networks and for what specific purposes they joined them. I started by reading a short news article, "The Web of Social Networking," from *U.S. News & World Report* (Green), to give me a basic understanding of this phenomenon. I learned that by far the two most popular OSNs are *MySpace* and *Facebook*. *MySpace* is a general networking site that allows anybody to access it. *Facebook* is geared more toward college students, and until recently a user needed a university e-mail address to join. According to Green, in 2005, *MySpace* was one of the 20 most popular sites on the Internet while *Facebook* was the top site for 18- to 24-year-olds. Moreover, Green points out that 60% of *Facebook* members logged in daily. This high number surprised me.

3   Needing more in-depth information about how young people use OSNs, I next turned to the *Pew Internet Project* website, based on a recommendation from my composition instructor. Pew is a non-partisan, non-profit research center that examines the social impact of the Internet. On the website, I found the results of the Parents and Teens 2006 survey in which researchers conducted telephone interviews of 935 teenagers and their parents living in the United States. The key findings include the following, which I quote from this report:

- 55% of online teens have created a personal profile on OSNs.
- 66% of teens who have created a profile say that their profile is not visible to all Internet users. They limit access to their profiles.
- 48% of teens visit social networking websites daily or more often; 26% visit once a day, 22% visit several times a day.
- Older girls ages 15–17 are more likely to have used social networking sites and created online profiles; 70% of older girls have used an online social network compared with 54% of older boys, and 70% of older girls have created an online profile, while only 57% of older boys have done so. (Lenhart and Madden 2)

The survey reveals how young people were using OSNs as tools to communicate with each other. It states that 91% of users logged on to keep in touch with their regularly seen friends, while 82% used the sites to stay in touch with distant friends. The survey also indicates that 49% use the sites to make new friends (Lenhart and Madden 2).

4   The Pew survey gave me a clearer picture of how and why young people are using OSNs. Although I wasn't surprised to learn that over half of all online teens were members of OSNs, I was caught off guard by the frequency that these teens logged on to these sites. I was also unaware that almost half of all social networking teens used these sites to meet new people. These discoveries helped me to better form my understanding of OSNs as I proceeded with my investigation focusing on their effects on communication skills.

5   I was now several days into my project. Because I am kind of a private person, I would be hesitant to put much personal information on a profile. Since all online social networks are comprised of profiles created by their members, I thought it would be a good idea to next examine how extensively these people disclosed personal information. By plugging "personal information" and "Online Social Networks" into *Google*, I located a study titled, "An Evaluation of Identity-Sharing Behavior in Social Network Communities" by Frederic Stutzman, a graduate student at the School of Information and Library Science at the University of North Carolina in Chapel Hill. In this scholarly piece from a conference, Stutzman recounts how his research attempted to uncover how much and what kind of identity information young people are disclosing in OSNs. Stutzman identified a random sample of UNC students and asked them to complete a survey about their use of these social networks and their feelings about disclosure of identity information. The results showed that 90% of UNC undergraduates have a *Facebook* profile. At the heart of Stutzman's article is a graph that shows the percentage of polled students who disclose certain personal information on their *Facebook* page. For example, 75% of users post a photograph, 65% post relationship information, 55% disclose political views, and 35% disclose sexual orientation (sec. 4.3). Stutzman concludes that as the Internet grew in popularity and the tools and places for self-expression became more widely available and easier to use, many people went from wanting to be anonymous online to revealing a lot of personal information.

6   I was taken aback by the percentage of students willing to put their photographs and other personal information online. What kinds of photographs did they actually put online? How did the whole profile contribute to the way they communicated? For the next stage of my research, I wanted to explore in more detail what students actually

did while online in an OSN. I located my next source by searching through the *Academic Search Complete* database. I was fortunate to come upon a very helpful article. It was a feature article in the international business newspaper *Financial Times.* Its author, Graham Bowley, bases much of his information on an interview with OSN researcher Danah Boyd. Through a *Google* search, I found Boyd's personal website, where I learned that she is a PhD candidate at the University of California-Berkeley and a Fellow at the University of Southern California Annenberg Center for Communications. Her research focuses on "how people negotiate a presentation of self to unknown audiences in mediated contexts" (Boyd). According to Bowley, Boyd is widely known online as "the high priestess of Internet friendship" for her writings and research on the subject. His interview with Boyd confirms findings that I found in the Pew survey that while some OSN users try to find new friends on the Internet, the majority were not using OSNs for that purpose. Instead, according to Bowley, "they were using it to reinforce existing relations with the group of friends they already had from their offline lives. For them, *MySpace* had become an electronic version of the local mall or park, the place they went to with their friends when they just wanted to hang out." Besides a "virtual hang out," OSNs offer young people a way to stay in touch with friends by allowing them to view their friends' profiles and leave short messages or comments. According to Cory Doctorow, another person interviewed by Bowley, this practice can be likened to "simple grooming exercises—in the same way that other primates groom each other to reinforce their relationships" (qtd. in Bowley).

7   Throughout the article, Bowley shows why Boyd supports OSNs. Boyd believes that "online social networks have become a vital space for young people to express themselves and build their personal identities" (Bowley). What I find interesting is that she particularly seems to like some of the edgy, unstable, dangerous aspects of OSNs that cause parents to be nervous about having their children online.

> Is there porn on MySpace? Of course. And bullying, sexual teasing and harass-
> ment are rampant among teenagers. It is how you learn to make meaning, cultural
> roles, norms. These kids need to explore their life among strangers. Teach them how
> to negotiate this new world. They need these public spaces now that other public
> spaces are closed to them. They need a place that is theirs. We should not always be
> chasing them and stopping them from growing up. (qtd. in Bowley)

Danah Boyd's observations have helped me understand how OSNs provide a place for self-expression as well as for communication with friends. She says that online sites give students practice at "identity production," where they can construct an identity through the kinds of items they post in their profile while also getting feedback and recognition from their friends. I got further understanding of this aspect of OSNs from another researcher interviewed by Bowley, Fred Stutzman (a person whose article on Internet identity-sharing I had already read). Stutzman calls students' OSN profiles an online version of their bedroom wall. Just as young people place posters on bedroom walls to express their special interests, they place items (pictures, music, and so forth) in their profiles to express themselves while also searching for an identity. "They are tuning into an audience," explains Stutzman. "One of the things students do at college is they test out identities. Maybe that is one new thing we are seeing now—more rapid changes of identity. Online you get feedback and you can change at a moment's notice" (qtd. in Bowley).

8   After considering the views of Boyd and Stutzman, I felt I understood why they think that OSNs give young people the opportunity for self-definition and self-expression. However, I still had doubts about the beneficial effects of OSNs. They still seem to me to send superficial messages about a person's identity. I found myself wondering if it is detrimental to spend all that time in virtual space rather than actually being with one's friends. I felt I needed to start looking for articles that examine the dangers of OSNs.

9   Although the next two sources I found didn't focus on the dangers of OSNs, they did provide interesting information on how students use *Facebook* to gain information about people they have met offline. The first article, another proceeding from an academic conference, reports data from two surveys of 1,440 first-year students at Michigan State University who had profiles on *Facebook*. Results show that "users are largely employing *Facebook* to learn more about people they meet offline, and are less likely to use the site to initiate new connections" (Lampe, Ellison, and Steinfield 167). The study reveals that *Facebook* users primarily use *Facebook* as a tool to investigate people they've already met offline. My second article, "Click Clique: *Facebook*'s Online College Community," written by Libby Copeland and published in the reputable newspaper the *Washington Post* in December of 2004, gives specific examples of this new social practice. One student explains how she would meet someone new at a friend's party that interested her and minutes later would be in her friend's room looking at his *Facebook* profile. Another student used the site to learn about the people in his classes: "If you meet someone in class and can't remember his name, you can look him up on the class lists kept on the *Facebook*. You can also research his interests, gathering information that you keep to yourself when you talk to him so he won't ever know you looked him up." Copeland also cites another student, who went as far as to call *Facebook* a "Stalker book."

10   After learning more about how users of OSNs practice self-disclosure, how they interact with friends online, and how they used the networks to find out information about people, I wanted to address something that had caught me off guard earlier in my research: the frequency with which OSN members are logged on to the community. Copeland mentions how much time students spent logged onto *Facebook*. She uses the term "Facebook Trance," which describes a person who loses track of all time and stares at the screen for hours. Copeland quotes one student who says "You stare into it [*Facebook* profiles] FOR-EV-ER." For the next stage of my research, I wanted to learn more about this "Facebook trance" and about the concept of Internet addiction.

11   I discovered that there is a lot of material on Internet addiction, so I started with an article appearing in the *Educational Psychology Review* in 2005 (Chou, Condron, and Belland). This is a long, scholarly article, most of which doesn't talk directly about OSNs. Nevertheless, parts of the article are valuable. In contrast to most of my research so far, this article sheds light on the potential problems of OSNs—the other side of this double-edged communication sword. One section states that 13% of respondents (in one of the studies the authors reviewed) reported that Internet use

had interfered with "their academic work, professional performance, or social lives." Among them, about 2% perceived the Internet as having an "overall negative effect on their daily lives" (369). Although OSNs can help to maintain and create new relationships, the authors claim that "over-dependence on online relationships may result in significant problems with real-life interpersonal and occupational functioning" (381). Students may believe that they are "in touch" with people, when in actuality they are physically alone with their computers. Although online communication can be used to enhance relationships, this article warns that it can become a problem when it begins to replace offline interaction.

12   After learning some of the ways that online social networks affect their users' communication skills, I have concluded that these networks can improve the ability to communicate, but if overused can negatively affect these skills. Although OSNs are offering their users new tools to express themselves, stay in touch with friends, and meet new people, these networks can turn counterproductive when a person becomes addicted and thus isolated from offline interpersonal interactions.

13   As I continue with my research, I am not sure what thesis I will assert for my final project. I still want to do more research on the negative effects of OSNs. For example, I haven't found studies that explore the possible phoniness of *Facebook* relationships. I remember a passage from Copeland where one user labels *Facebook* interaction as "communication lean." According to this student, "It's all a little fake—the 'friends'; the profiles that can be tailored to what others find appealing; the 'groups' that exist only in cyberspace." I'm still thinking about that quotation. Do OSNs contribute to deeper, more meaningful relationships or do they promote a superficial phoniness? I hope to explore this issue further before writing my major paper.

Works Cited

Bowley, Graham. "The High Priestess of Internet Friendship." *Financial Times Weekend Magazine* 27 Oct. 2006. *LexisNexis Academic.* Web. 22 Feb. 2007.

Boyd, Danah. Home page. Web. 21 Feb. 2007.

Chou, Chien, Linda Condron, and John C. Belland. "A Review of the Research on Internet Addiction." *Educational Psychology Review* 17.4 (2005): 363–89. *Academic Search Complete.* Web. 22 Feb. 2007.

Copeland, Libby. "Click Clique: *Facebook*'s Online College Community." *Washingtonpost.com.* Washington Post, 28 Dec. 2004. Web. 24 Feb. 2007.

Green, Elizabeth Weiss. "The Web of Social Networking." *U.S. News & World Report* 14 Nov. 2005: 58. *Academic Search Complete.* Web. 15 Feb. 2007.

Lampe, Cliff, Nicole Ellison, and Charles Steinfield. "A Face(book) in the Crowd: Social Searching Versus Social Browsing." *Proceedings of the 2006 20th Anniversary Conference on Computer Supported Cooperative Work.* 2006: 167–70. *The ACM Digital Library.* Web. 24 Feb. 2007.

Lenhart, Amanda, and Mary Madden. "Social Networking Websites and Teens: An Overview." *Pew Internet & American Life Project.* Pew Research Center, 3 Jan. 2007. Web. 19 Feb. 2007.

Stutzman, Frederic. "An Evaluation of Identity-Sharing Behavior in Social Network Communities." *Proceedings of the 2006 iDMAa and IMS Code Conference.* Oxford, OH, 2006. Web. 20 Feb. 2007.

THINKING CRITICALLY
about "How Do Online Social Networks Affect Communication?"

1. Earlier in this chapter, we suggested ways to organize and strengthen an exploratory essay. Where do you see James including the following features: (a) A blend of open-form narrative moves with closed-form focusing sentences? (b) A purposeful selection of sources? (c) A consideration of the rhetorical context of his sources—that is, an awareness of the kinds of sources he is using and how the genre of the source influences its content? (d) Reflective/critical thinking that shows his strong response to his sources? Where might he develop these features further?

2. Trace the evolution of James's ideas in this paper. How does his thinking evolve? What subquestions does he pose? What issues connected to his main question does he pursue?

3. Read James's argument for limiting use of OSNs on pages 362–370. What new research did he do for his final argument? How do you see the exploratory paper contributing to James's argument in the final paper? How do differences in purpose (exploration versus persuasion) lead to different structures for the two papers?

4. What are the strengths and weaknesses of James's exploration of OSNs?

Our next reading is an excerpt from James's annotated bibliography based on the same research he did for his exploratory paper. We have used James's research for both examples so that you can compare an exploratory paper with an annotated bibliography. His original annotated bibliography contained six entries. We have printed three of these, along with his critical preface. Additionally, the evaluative annotated bibliography entry for Graham Bowley is shown on page 141.

James Gardiner (student)

What Is the Effect of Online Social Networks on Communication Skills?

An Annotated Bibliography

Critical Preface

1   Today, online social networks (OSNs) such as *MySpace* and *Facebook* have become staples in the lives of most American young people. Although I was conscious that OSNs were impacting the way young people communicate with each other, I was largely unaware of the specific ways that the people used these OSNs or how their communication skills were being affected by this new technology. For this research project, I set out to discover how online social networks influence the way young

people communicate with each other. I posed several specific questions that I hoped my research could help me answer: (1) Why are OSNs so popular? (2) How do young people use OSNs? (3) How do OSNs affect communication skills? And (4) To what extent might OSNs be harmful or detrimental? These questions deserve to be examined because as more people move toward these new modes of communication, these networks will increasingly influence society as a whole.

2   I conducted this research during a one-week period in late February 2007. The bibliography contains different kinds of sources: two articles from popular magazines or newspapers; three articles from scholarly journals; and one survey report from a major Internet site devoted to research on people's use of the Internet. These sources gave me preliminary answers to all my initial research questions. They show why young people are attracted to OSNs and why and how they use them. Particularly valuable for my research are the articles by Bowley and by Lampe, Ellison, and Steinfield showing the positive potential of OSNs and the article by Chou, Condron, and Belland showing the possible negative potential if persons become addicted to OSNs.

Annotated Bibliography

Chou, Chien, Linda Condron, and John C. Belland. "A Review of the Research on Internet Addiction." *Educational Psychology Review* 17.4 (2005): 363–89. *Academic Search Complete*. Web. 22 Feb. 2007.

This lengthy academic article written for scholars reviews research on Internet addiction. It has four sections: (1) explanations of how Internet addiction is defined and assessed; (2) problems created by Internet addiction and variables such as gender or psychosocial traits associated with addiction; (3) explanations for why the Internet creates addictions; and (4) ways to treat Internet addiction. For my project, section 2 on problems was most valuable. In one study 13% of respondents reported that Internet use interfered with their personal lives or academic performance. Although Internet addiction didn't seem as harmful as other addictions, the authors observed that too much dependence on online relationships can interfere with real relationships. The tables in this article show the key findings from dozens of research studies.

Lampe, Cliff, Nicole Ellison, and Charles Steinfield. "A Face(book) in the Crowd: Social Searching Versus Social Browsing." *Proceedings of the 2006 20th Anniversary Conference on Computer Supported Cooperative Work*. 2006: 167–70. *The ACM Digital Library*. Web. 24 Feb. 2007.

This scholarly research report is based on questionnaires about *Facebook* usage received from 1,440 first-year students at Michigan State University in fall 2006. The researchers investigated whether students used *Facebook* primarily to meet new people ("social browsers") or to maintain or develop friendships with persons whom they had already met ("social searchers.") The findings contradicted the popular view that *Facebook* users are social browsers. Rather, the majority of respondents used the network to keep in touch with existing friends or to find out additional information about classmates or other recent acquaintances. This article has useful data about perceived audiences for profiles (peers rather than professors or administrators) and about primary reasons for using *Facebook*. The article provided insights into why *Facebook* is popular.

Lenhart, Amanda, and Mary Madden. "Social Networking Websites and Teens: An Overview." *Pew Internet & American Life Project*. Pew Research Center, 3 Jan. 2007. Web. 19 Feb. 2007.

This source is an online memo from researchers working for the Pew Internet and American Life Project, a non-profit research organization. It reports the results of a telephone survey of a random national sample of 935 youths aged 12 to 17 in fall 2006. The document has numerous tables showing demographic data about teens' use of OSNs, the most popular sites, the frequency of use, and the reasons teens give for using the sites. Because of the scientific method of polling, this article provides reliable data for understanding how teens currently use OSNs.

THINKING CRITICALLY

about "What Is the Effect of Online Social Networks on Communication Skills? An Annotated Bibliography"

1. Explain how James includes the three common elements of an evaluative annotation (genre/rhetorical context, summary of content, evaluation) in each of his annotations.

2. Compare James's annotated bibliography with his exploratory essay (pp. 144–148), noting differences between the way each source is described in the bibliography versus the essay. What insights do you get from the exploratory essay that are missing from the bibliography? What information about the sources comes through more clearly in the bibliography than in the essay?

3. How might James use information and points in this annotated bibliography in his researched argument?

7 WRITING AN INFORMATIVE (AND SURPRISING) ESSAY

As a reader, you regularly encounter writing with an informative aim, ranging from the instruction booklet for a smart phone to a newspaper feature story on the South African AIDS crisis. Informative documents include encyclopedias, cookbooks, voters' pamphlets, and various kinds of reports, as well as informative Web sites and magazine articles. In some informative prose, visual representations of information such as diagrams, photographs, maps, tables, and graphs can be as important as the prose itself.

A useful way to begin thinking about informative writing is to classify it according to the reader's motivation for reading. From this perspective, we can place informative prose in two categories.

In the first category, readers are motivated by an immediate need for information (setting the clock on a new microwave) or by curiosity about a subject (the impressionist movement in painting or new developments in rooftop solar panels). Informative writing in this category does not necessarily contain a contestable thesis. Documents are organized effectively, of course, but they often follow a chronological, step-by-step organization (as in a set of instructions) or an "all-about" topic-by-topic organization (as in an encyclopedia article on, say, Pakistan, divided into "Geography," "Climate," "Population," "History," and so forth). The writer provides factual information about a subject without necessarily shaping the information specifically to support a thesis.

In contrast, the second category of informative writing *is* thesis-based and is therefore aligned with other kinds of thesis-based prose. The thesis brings new or surprising information to readers who may not be initially motivated by a need-to-know occasion or by their own curiosity. In fact, readers might not be initially interested in the writer's topic at all, so the writer's first task is to hook readers' interest and motivate their desire to learn something new or surprising about a topic. An excellent strategy for creating this motivation is the technique of "surprising reversal," which we explain later.

In this chapter, you will learn to:

- write an informative essay using the surprising-reversal strategy

Exploring Informative (and Surprising) Writing

Let's say that you have just watched an old James Bond movie featuring a tarantula in Bond's bathroom. Curious about tarantulas, you do a quick Web search and retrieve the following short informative pieces. Read each one, and then proceed to the questions that follow.

Our first mini-article comes from the Web site EnchantedLearning.com, a commercial site aimed at providing interesting, fact-filled learning lessons for children.

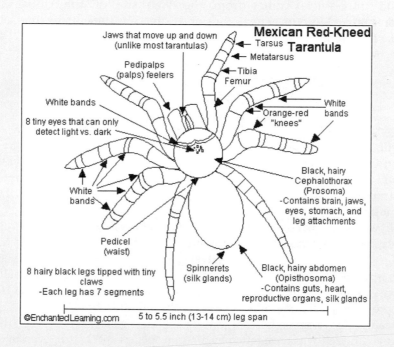

EnchantedLearning.com
Tarantulas

Jaws that move up and down (unlike most tarantulas) · Tarsus · **Mexican Red-Kneed Tarantula** · Metatarsus · Tibia · Femur · Pedipalps (palps) feelers · White bands · White bands · Orange-red "knees" · 8 tiny eyes that can only detect light vs. dark · White bands · Black, hairy Cephalothorax (Prosoma) -Contains brain, jaws, eyes, stomach, and leg attachments · Pedicel (waist) · 8 hairy black legs tipped with tiny claws -Each leg has 7 segments · Spinnerets (silk glands) · Black, hairy abdomen (Opisthosoma) -Contains guts, heart, reproductive organs, silk glands · ©EnchantedLearning.com   5 to 5.5 inch (13-14 cm) leg span

1   Tarantulas are large hairy spiders that live in warm areas around the world, including South America, southern North America, southern Europe, Africa, southern Asia, and Australia. The greatest concentration of tarantulas is in South America. There are about 300 species of tarantulas. The biggest tarantula is *Pseudotherathosa apophysis*, which has a leg span of about 13 inches (33 cm). These arachnids have a very long life span; some species can live over 30 years.

2   **Habitat:** Some tarantulas live in underground burrows; some live on the ground, and others live in trees. They live in rain forests, deserts, and other habitats.

3   **Diet:** Tarantulas are carnivores (meat-eaters). They eat insects (like grasshoppers and beetles), other arachnids, small reptiles (like lizards and snakes), amphibians (like frogs), and some even eat small birds. Tarantulas kill their prey using venomous fangs; they also inject a chemical into the prey that dissolves the flesh. Tarantulas can crush their prey using powerful mouthparts. No person has ever died of a tarantula bite.

4   **Anatomy:** Tarantulas have a hairy two-part body and very strong jaws (with venomous fangs). They have eight hairy legs; each leg has 2 tiny claws at the end and a cushioning pad behind the claws. The hairs on the body and legs are sensitive to touch, temperature, and smell. Tarantulas have a hard exoskeleton and not an internal skeleton. © Copyright EnchantedLearning.com. Used by permission.

The second mini-article comes from the Web site of the University of Washington's Burke Museum. The author of this piece is the curator of arachnids at the Burke Museum.

Rod Crawford
Myths about "Dangerous" Spiders

1   **Myth:** Tarantulas are dangerous or deadly to humans.

2   **Fact:** Outside of southern Europe (where the name is used for a wolf spider, famous in medieval superstition as the alleged cause of "tarantella" dancing), the word tarantula is most often used for the very large, furry spiders of the family Theraphosidae.

3   Hollywood is squarely to blame for these spiders' toxic-to-humans reputation. Tarantulas are large, photogenic and easily handled, and therefore have been very widely used in horror and action-adventure movies. When some "venomous" creature is needed to menace James Bond or Indiana Jones, to invade a small town in enormous numbers, or to grow to gigantic size and prowl the Arizona desert for human prey, the special-effects team calls out the tarantulas!

4   In reality, the venom of these largest-of-all-spiders generally has **very low toxicity to humans**. I myself was once bitten by a Texan species and hardly even felt it. None of the North American species or those commonly kept as pets are considered to pose even a mild bite hazard. There are some reports that a few tropical species may have venom more toxic to vertebrates, but human bite cases haven't been reported, so we can't know for sure.

5   The only health hazard posed by keeping pet tarantulas comes from the irritating chemicals on the hairs of the abdomen, which can cause skin rashes or inflammation of eyes and nasal passages. To prevent such problems, simply keep tarantulas away from your face and wash your hands after handling one.

6   Compared to common pets such as dogs, tarantulas are not dangerous at all. (For more information see the American Tarantula Society.)

European tarantula
Lycosa Tarentula
Southern Europe; body length 2–3 cm
(photo courtesy of Manuel J. Cabrero)
Click image to enlarge

Pink toe tarantula
Avicularia avicularia
Brazil to Trinidad; body length 6–7 cm
(photo courtesy of Ron Taylor)
Click image to enlarge

Both the *European wolf spiders* (**left**) originally called tarantulas, and the *theraphosid spiders* (**right**), often kept as pets and called tarantulas now, have been reputed dangerous to humans. They aren't.

THINKING CRITICALLY
about "Tarantulas" and "Myths about 'Dangerous' Spiders"

1. Why do you think the reading from EnchantedLearning.com uses a diagram of a tarantula while the Burke Museum Web site uses photographs? How is each choice connected to the piece's targeted audience and purpose?

2. How would you describe the difference in organizational strategies for each of the readings?

3. One might suppose that informational writing would be unaffected by the writer's angle of vision—that facts would simply be facts and that informational pieces on the same topic would contain the same basic information. Yet these two short pieces give somewhat different impressions of the tarantula. For example, how do these readings differ in the way they portray the bite of the tarantula? How else do they differ in overall effect?

Understanding Informative Writing

In informative writing, the writer is assumed to have more expertise than the reader on a given subject. The writer's aim is to enlarge the reader's view of the subject by bringing the reader new information. The writer's information can come from a variety of sources:

- From the writer's preexisting expertise in a subject
- From the writer's own personal experiences
- From field research such as observations, interviews, questionnaires, and so forth
- From library or Internet research

We turn now to a closer look at a commonly assigned genre with an informative aim.

Informative Essay Using the Surprising-Reversal Strategy

A commonly encountered genre is an informative article with surprising information, often found in magazines or newspapers. In this section, we focus on a specific version of this kind of essay—a thesis-based informative article aimed at general audiences. Because readers are assumed to be browsing through the pages of a magazine, the writer's rhetorical challenge is to arouse the reader's curiosity and then to keep the reader reading by providing interesting new information. The writer's first task is to hook the reader on a question and then to provide a surprising thesis that gives shape and purpose to the information. A good way to focus and sharpen the thesis, as we will show, is to use the "surprising-reversal" strategy.

"All-About" Versus "Thesis-Governed" Informative Prose Let's begin by revisiting the difference between an encyclopedic (or "all-about") informative piece and a thesis-based piece. To appreciate this distinction, consider again the difference between the EnchantedLearning.com Web site on tarantulas (pp. 153–154) and the Burke Museum piece "Myths about 'Dangerous' Spiders" (pp. 154–155). The EnchantedLearning.com piece is a short "all-about" report organized under the topic headings "Habitat," "Diet," and "Anatomy." The Web writer may simply have adapted an encyclopedia article on tarantulas into a format for children. In contrast, the Burke Museum piece by Rod Crawford is thesis-based. Crawford wishes to refute the myth that "[t]arantulas are dangerous or deadly to humans." He does so by providing information on the low toxicity of tarantula venom to humans and the relative painlessness of tarantula bites. All of Crawford's data focus on the danger potential of tarantulas. There are no data about habitat, diet, or other aspects of tarantula life—material that would be included if this were an all-about report. Because the piece also includes data about misconceptions of tarantulas, it follows the basic pattern of surprising reversal: "Many people believe that tarantulas are toxic to humans, but I will show that tarantulas are not dangerous at all."

Surprising-Reversal Pattern   Surprising reversal, as we explained in Chapter 2, Concept 5, is our term for a strategy in which the writer's thesis pushes sharply against a counterthesis. This structure automatically creates a thesis with tension focused on a question or problem. Because of its power to hook and sustain readers, surprising-reversal essays can be found in many publications, ranging from easy-reading magazines to scholarly journals. Here, for example, is an abstract of an article from *Atlantic Monthly*.

"REEFER MADNESS" BY ERIC SCHLOSSER

Marijuana has been pushed so far out of the public imagination by other drugs, and its use is so casually taken for granted in some quarters of society, that one might assume it had been effectively decriminalized. In truth, the government has never been tougher on marijuana offenders than it is today. In an era when violent criminals frequently walk free or receive modest jail terms, tens of thousands of people are serving long sentences for breaking marijuana laws.

This article asserts a surprising, new position ("the government has never been tougher on marijuana offenders than it is today") that counters a commonly held view (marijuana laws are no longer enforced). Here are additional examples of the surprising-reversal pattern:

Commonly Held, Narrow, or Inaccurate View	New, Surprising Information
Native Americans used to live in simple harmony with the earth.	Many American Indians used to "control" nature by setting fire to forests to make farming easier or to improve hunting.
Having fathers present in the delivery room helps the mother relax and have an easier birth.	Having fathers present in delivery rooms may reduce the amount of oxytocin produced by the mother and lead to more caesarian sections.

A similar pattern is often found in scholarly academic writing, which typically has the following underlying shape:

Whereas some scholars say X, I am going to argue Y.

Because the purpose of academic research is to advance knowledge, an academic article almost always shows the writer's new view against a background of prevailing views (what other scholars have said). This kind of tension is what often makes thesis-based writing memorable and provocative.

The writer's surprising information can come from personal experience, field research, or library/Internet research. If a college writer bases an informative piece on research sources and documents them according to academic conventions, the magazine genre doubles as an effective college research paper by combining academic citations with a tone and style suitable for general readers. Shannon King's article on hydrogen cars (p. 165) is an example of a student research paper written in magazine article style.

"Surprise" as a Relative Term When using the surprising-reversal strategy, keep in mind that *surprise* is a relative term based on the relationship between you and your intended audience. You don't have to surprise everyone in the world, just those who hold a mistaken or narrow view of your topic. The key is to imagine an audience less informed about your topic than you are. Suppose, as an illustration, that you have just completed an introductory economics course. You are less informed about economics than your professor, but more informed about economics than persons who have never had an econ class. You might therefore bring surprising information to the less informed audience:

> The average airplane traveler thinks that the widely varying ticket pricing for the same flight is chaotic and silly, but I can show how this pricing scheme makes perfect sense economically. [written to the "average airplane traveler," who hasn't taken an economics course]

This paper would be surprising to your intended audience, but not to the economics professor. From a different perspective, however, you could also write about economics to your professor because you might know more than your professor about, say, how students struggle with some concepts:

> Many economics professors assume that students can easily learn the concept of "elasticity of demand," but I can show why this concept was particularly confusing for me and my classmates. [written to economics professors who aren't aware of student difficulties with particular concepts]

Additionally, your surprising view doesn't necessarily have to be diametrically opposed to the common view. Perhaps you think the common view is *incomplete* or *insufficient* rather than *dead wrong*. Instead of saying, "View X is wrong, whereas my view, Y, is correct," you can say, "View X is correct and good as far as it goes, but my view, Y, adds a new perspective." In other words, you can also create surprise by going a step beyond the common view to show readers something new.

WRITING PROJECT

Informative Essay Using the Surprising-Reversal Strategy

> Using personal experience, field research, or library/Internet research, write an informative magazine article using a surprising-reversal strategy in a tone and style suitable for general readers. Your task is to arouse your readers' curiosity by posing an interesting question, summarizing a common or expected answer to the question, and then providing new, surprising information that counters or "reverses" the common view. You imagine readers who hold a mistaken or overly narrow view of your topic; your purpose is to give them a new, surprising view.

Depending on the wishes of your instructor, this assignment can draw either on personal experience or on research. Shannon King's "How Clean and Green Are Hydrogen Fuel-Cell Cars?" (pp. 165–170) is an example of a researched essay that enlarges the targeted audience's view of a subject in a surprising way. Although it is an example of a short academic research article, it is written in a relaxed style suitable for magazine publication.

For this assignment, try to avoid issues calling for persuasive rather than informative writing. With persuasive prose, you imagine a resistant reader who may argue back. With informative prose, you imagine a more trusting reader, one willing to learn from your experience or research. Although you hope to enlarge your reader's view of a topic, you aren't necessarily saying that your audience's original view is wrong, nor are you initiating a debate. For example, suppose a writer wanted to develop the following claim: "Many of my friends think that having an alcoholic mother would be the worst thing that could happen to you, but I will show that my mother's disease forced our family closer together." In this case the writer isn't arguing that alcoholic mothers are good or that everyone should have an alcoholic mother. Rather, the writer is simply offering readers a new, unexpected, and expanded view of what it might be like to have an alcoholic mother.

Generating and Exploring Ideas

If you do field research or library/Internet research for your article, start by posing a research question. As you begin doing initial research on your topic area, you will soon know more about your topic than most members of the general public. Ask yourself, "What has surprised me about my research so far? What have I learned that I didn't know before?" Your answers to these questions can suggest possible approaches to your paper. For example, Shannon King began her research believing that fuel-cell technology produced totally pollution-free energy. She didn't realize that one needs to burn fossil fuels in order to produce the hydrogen. This initial surprise shaped her paper. She decided that if this information surprised her, it should surprise others also.

What follows are two exercises you can try to generate ideas for your paper.

Individual Task to Generate Ideas

Here is a template that can help you generate ideas by asking you to think specifically about differences in knowledge levels between you and various audiences.

> I know more about X [topic area] than [specific person or persons].

For example, you might say, "I know more about [computer games/gospel music/the energy crisis] than [my roommate/my high school friends/my parents]." This exercise helps you discover subjects about which you already have expertise compared to other audiences. Likewise, you can identify a subject that interests you, do a couple of hours of research on it, and then say: "Based on just this little amount of research, I know more about X than my roommate." Thinking in this way, you might be able to create an intriguing question that you could answer through your research.

Small-Group Task to Generate Ideas

Form small groups. Assign a group recorder to make a two-column list, with the left column titled "Mistaken or Narrow View of X" and the right column titled "Groupmate's Surprising View." Using the surprising-reversal strategy, brainstorm ideas for article topics until every group member has generated at least one entry for the right-hand column. Here are several examples:

Mistaken or Narrow View of X	Groupmate's Surprising View
Being an offensive lineman in football is a no-brain, repetitive job requiring size and strength, but only enough intelligence and athletic ability to push people out of the way.	Jeff can show that being an offensive lineman is a complex job that requires mental smarts as well as size, strength, and athletic ability.
Pawnshops are disreputable places.	Samantha's uncle owns a pawnshop that is a wholesome family business that serves an important social function.
To most straight people, *Frankenstein* is a monster movie about science gone amuck.	Cody can show how to the gay community, *Frankenstein* holds a special and quite different meaning.

To help stimulate ideas, you might consider topic areas such as the following:

- *People:* computer programmers, homeless people, cheerleaders, skateboarders, gang members, priests or rabbis, reality show stars, feminists, mentally ill or developmentally disabled persons.
- *Activities:* washing dishes, climbing mountains, wrestling, modeling, gardening, living with a chronic disease or disability, owning a certain breed of dog, riding a subway at night, posting status updates on Facebook, entering a dangerous part of a city.
- *Places:* particular neighborhoods, specific buildings or parts of buildings, local attractions, junkyards, college campuses, places of entertainment, summer camps.
- *Other similar categories:* groups, events, animals and plants, gadgets, and so forth; the list is endless.

Next, go around the room, sharing with the entire class the topics you have generated. Remember that you are not yet committed to writing about any of these topics.

Shaping, Drafting, and Revising

A surprising-reversal informative essay has the features and organization shown in Figure 7.1.

To create the "surprising-reversal" feel, it's important to delay your thesis until after you have explained your audience's common, expected answer to your opening question. This delay in presenting the thesis creates an open-form feel that readers often find engaging. Shannon King's research paper on hydrogen cars (pp. 165–170) has this surprising-reversal shape.

As a way of helping you generate ideas, we offer the following five questions. Following each question, we speculate about what King might have written if she had used the same questions to help her get started on her essay.

FIGURE 7.1 Framework for an Informative Essay Using the Surprising-Reversal Strategy

Introduction (one to several paragraphs)	• Engages readers' interest in the writer's question • Provides background and context
Body section 1 (brief)	• Explains the common or popular answer to the writer's question
Body section 2 (major)	• Provides a delayed thesis—the writer's surprising answer to the question • Supports the thesis with information from personal experience or research • Displays numeric data in graphs or tables referenced in the text
Conclusion	• Suggests the significance of the writer's new perspective on the question

1. *What question does your essay address?* (King might have asked, "Will hydrogen fuel-cell automobiles solve our nation's energy and pollution crises?")
2. *What is the common, expected, or popular answer to this question held by your imagined audience?* (King might have said, "Most people believe that hydrogen fuel-cell cars will solve our country's pollution and energy crises.")
3. *What examples and details support your audience's view?* Expand on these views by developing them with supporting examples and details. (King might have noted her research examples praising fuel-cell technology such as the Bush/Cheney National Energy Report or California Governor Arnold Schwarzenegger's desire to build hydrogen fuel stations across the state.)
4. *What is your own surprising view?* (King might have said, "Although hydrogen fuel-cell cars are pollution free, getting the hydrogen in the first place requires burning fossil fuels.")
5. *What examples and details support this view? Why do you hold this view? Why should a reader believe you?* Writing rapidly, spell out the evidence that supports your point. (King would have done a freewrite about her research discoveries that hydrogen has to be recovered from carbon-based fossils or from electrolysis of water—all of which means continued use of pollution-causing fossil fuels.)

After you finish exploring your responses to these five trigger questions, you will be well on your way to composing a first draft of your article. Now finish writing your draft fairly rapidly without worrying about perfection.

Once you have your first draft on paper, the goal is to make it work better, first for yourself and then for your readers. If you discovered ideas as you wrote, you may need to do some major restructuring. Check to see that the question you are addressing is clear. If you are using the surprising-reversal strategy, make sure that you distinguish between your audience's common view and your own surprising view. Apply the strategies for global revision explained in Chapter 11.

Questions for Peer Review

In addition to the generic peer review questions explained in Skill 11.4, ask your peer reviewers to address these questions:

1. What is the question the paper addresses? How effective is the paper at hooking the reader's interest in the question?
2. Where does the writer explain the common or popular view of the topic? Do you agree that this is the common view? How does the writer develop or support this view? What additional supporting examples, illustrations, or details might make the common view more vivid or compelling?
3. What is the writer's surprising view? Were you surprised? What details does the writer use to develop the surprising view? What additional supporting examples, illustrations, or details might help make the surprising view more vivid and compelling?
4. Is the draft clear and easy to follow? Is the draft interesting? How might the writer improve the style, clarity, or interest level of the draft?
5. If the draft includes graphics, are they effective? Do the words and the visuals tell the same story? Are the visuals properly titled and labeled? How might the use of visuals be improved?

Our first reading, by student writer Kerri Ann Matsumoto (p. 164), is formatted to look like a popular magazine article.

THINKING CRITICALLY
about "How Much Does It Cost to Go Organic?"

1. In our teaching, we have discovered that students appreciate the concept of genre more fully if they occasionally "desktop-publish" a manuscript to look like a magazine article, a poster, or a brochure rather than a standard double-spaced academic paper. If Kerri Ann had been an actual freelance writer, she would have submitted this article double-spaced with attached figures, and the magazine publisher would have done the formatting. How does document design itself help signal the document's genre? To what extent has Kerri Ann made this article *sound* like a popular magazine article as well as look like one?

2. Do you think Kerri Ann used graphics effectively in her essay? How might she have revised the graphics or the wording to make the paper more effective?

3. Do you think it is worth the extra money to go organic? How would you make your case in an argument paper with a persuasive aim?

HOW MUCH DOES IT COST TO GO ORGANIC?

Kerri Ann Matsumoto

Organic foods, grown without pesticides, weed killers, or hormone additives, are gaining popularity from small privately owned organic food stores to large corporate markets. With the cost of living rising, how much can a family of four afford to pay for organically grown food before it becomes too expensive?

To find out more information about the cost of organic foods, I went to the Rainbow Market, which is a privately owned organic food store, and to a nearby Safeway. I decided to see what it would cost to create a stir-fry for a family of four. I estimated that the cost of organic vegetables for the stir-fry would cost $3.97. Non-organic vegetables for the same stir-fry, purchased at Safeway, would cost $2.37. If we imagined our family eating the same stir fry every night for a year, it would cost $1,499 for organic and $865 for non-organic for a difference of $584.

After pricing vegetables, I wanted to find out how much it would cost to add to the stir-fry free-range chicken fed only organic feeds, as opposed to non-organic factory farmed chicken. For good quality chicken breasts, the organic chicken was $6.99 per pound and the non-organic was $3.58 per pound. Projected out over a year, the organic chicken would cost $5,103 compared to $2,613 for non-organic chicken.

My research shows that over the course of one year it will cost $6,552 per year to feed our family organic stir-fry and $3,478 for non-organic for a difference of $3,074. If a family chose to eat not only organic dinner, but also all organic meals, the cost of food would sharply increase.

Before going to the Rainbow Market I knew that the price of organic foods was slightly higher than non-organic. However, I did not expect the difference to be so great. Of course, if you did comparison shopping at other stores, you might be able to find cheaper organic chicken and vegetables. But my introductory research suggests that going organic isn't cheap.

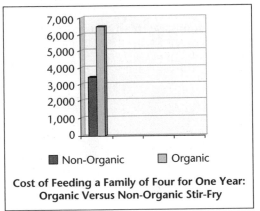

Cost of Feeding a Family of Four for One Year: Organic Versus Non-Organic Stir-Fry

Comparative Cost of Ingredients in an Organic Versus Non-Organic Stir-Fry				
	Vegetables per day	Chicken per day	Total per day	Total per year
Organic	$3.97	$13.98	$17.95	$6552
Non-Organic	$2.37	$7.16	$9.53	$3478

If we add the cost of chicken and vegetables together (see the table and the graph), we can compute how much more it would cost to feed our family of four organic versus non-organic chicken stir-fry for a year.

Is it worth it? Many people today have strong concerns for the safety of the foods that they feed to their family. If you consider that organic vegetables have no pesticides and that the organic chicken has no growth hormone additives, the extra cost may be worth it. Also if you are concerned about cruelty to animals, free-range chickens have a better life than caged chickens. But many families might want to spend the $3,074 difference in other ways. If you put that money toward a college fund, within ten years you could save over $30,000. So how much are you willing to pay for organic foods?

The next reading, by student writer Shannon King, is a short research paper using the surprising-reversal strategy. Shannon's paper uses research data to enlarge her readers' understanding of hydrogen fuel cell vehicles by showing that hydrogen fuel is not as pollution-free as the general public believes. We reproduce the paper to illustrate the manuscript form required by the American Psychological Association (APA) for scholarly papers. A brief explanation of APA documentation format and style is found in Chapter 14, Skill 14.2.

Running head: HYDROGEN FUEL-CELL CARS   1

Include shortened title and page number on each page. Include "Running head" on p. 1.

How Clean and Green Are Hydrogen Fuel-Cell Cars?

Shannon King

June 15, 2004

Center title, author, and date.

HYDROGEN FUEL-CELL CARS   2

Repeat title before body of paper.

How Clean and Green Are Hydrogen Fuel-Cell Cars?

The United States is embroiled in a controversy over energy and pollution. We are rapidly using up the earth's total supply of fossil fuels, and many experts think that children being born today will experience the end of affordable oil. One energy expert (Roberts, 2004) believes that serious oil shortages will start occurring by 2015 when the world's demand for oil will outstrip the world's capacity for further oil production. An equally serious problem is that the burning of fossil fuels spews carbon dioxide into the atmosphere, which increases the rate of global warming.

Double-space all text.

One hopeful way of addressing these problems is to develop hydrogen fuel cell cars. According to the author of the fuel cell pages on the *How Stuff Works* Web site (Nice, n.d.), a fuel cell is "an electrochemical energy conversion device that converts hydrogen and oxygen into water, producing electricity and heat in the process." A hydrogen-fueled car is therefore an electric car, powered by an electric motor. The car's electricity is generated by a stack of fuel cells that act like a battery. In the hydrogen fuel cell, the chemicals that produce the electricity are hydrogen from the car's pressurized fuel tank, oxygen from the air, and special catalysts inside the fuel cell. The fuel cell releases no pollutants or greenhouse gases. The only waste product is pure water.

To what extent will these pollution-free fuel cells be our energy salvation? Are they really clean and green?

Many people think so. The development of hydrogen fuel cells has caused much excitement. I know people who say we don't need to worry about running out of oil because cars of the future will run on water. One recent *New York Times* advertisement produced by General Motors (2004) has as its headline, "Who's driving the hydrogen economy?" The text of the ad begins by saying "The hydrogen economy isn't a pipe dream. . . . The hydrogen economy is the endgame of a multi-faceted strategy General

Use italics for titles.

Use ellipsis for omitted words in quotation.

HYDROGEN FUEL-CELL CARS   3

Motors set in motion years ago, with steps that are real, progressive, and well-underway." The Web site for the Hydrogen Fuel Cell Institute includes a picture of a crystal clear blue sky landscape with a large letter headline proclaiming "At long last, a technology too long overlooked promises to transform society." At the bottom of the picture are the words, "Offering clean & abundant power, hydrogen-based fuel cells could soon end our reliance on oil and minimize emissions of pollution and global-warming gases." According to CNN News (2004), the Bush administration has proposed devoting 1.7 billion dollars of federal funds to developing hydrogen fuel cells. The biggest nationally known proponent of hydrogen fuel cells is California Governor Arnold Schwarzenegger, who signed an Executive Order that California's "21 interstate freeways shall be designated as the 'California Hydrogen Highway Network'" (California, 2004, p. 2). In this executive order, Schwarzenegger envisions

> a network of hydrogen fueling stations along these roadways and in the urban centers that they connect, so that by 2010, every Californian will have access to hydrogen fuel, with a significant and increasing percentage produced from clean, renewable sources (p. 2).

Indent block quotations.

Schwarzenegger's optimism about the hydrogen highway sums up the common view that hydrogen is a clean alternative energy source that is abundant throughout nature. All we have to do is bottle it up, compress it, and transport it to a network of new "gas stations" where the gas being pumped is hydrogen.

But what I discovered in my research is that hydrogen is not as green as most people think. Although hydrogen fuel cells appear to be an environmentally friendly alternative to fossil fuels, the processes for producing hydrogen actually require the use of fossil fuels. The problem is that pure hydrogen doesn't occur naturally on earth. It has to be separated out from chemical compounds containing hydrogen, and that process requires other forms of energy. What I discovered is that there are only two major ways to produce hydrogen. The first is to produce it from fossil fuels by unlocking the hydrogen that is bonded to the carbon in coal, oil, or natural gas. The second is to produce it from water through electrolysis, but the power required for electrolysis would also come mainly from burning fossil fuels. These problems make hydrogen fuel cell cars look less clean and green than they first appear.

One approach to creating hydrogen from fossil fuels is to use natural gas. According to Wald (2003), natural gas is converted to hydrogen in a process called "steam reforming." Natural gas (made of hydrogen and carbon atoms) is mixed with steam (which contains hydrogen and oxygen atoms) to cause a chemical reaction that produces pure hydrogen. But it also produces carbon dioxide, which contributes to global warming. According to Wald, if fuel cell cars used hydrogen from steam reforming, they would emit 145 grams of global warming gases per mile compared to 374 grams an ordinary gas-powered car would emit. The good news is that using hydrogen power would cut carbon emissions by more than half. The bad news is that these cars would still contribute to global warming and consume natural gas. Moreover, Wald suggests that the natural gas supply is limited and that natural gas has many better, more efficient uses than converting it to hydrogen.

Another method for producing hydrogen would come from coal, which is the cheapest and most abundant source of energy. However, the current method of generating electricity by burning coal is the leading source of carbon dioxide emission. At Ohio University, engineers state we still have enough coal to last us 250 years and that we should find some better uses for coal. The engineers have received a 4 million dollar federal grant to investigate the production of hydrogen from coal. They plan on mixing coal with steam, air, and oxygen under high temperatures and pressure to produce hydrogen and carbon monoxide ("Ohio University aims," 2003). But this too would generate greenhouse gases and is a long way off from producing results.

The next likely source of hydrogen is to produce it directly from water using a device called an electrolyzer. Wald explains that the electrolyzer sends an electrical current through water to break down the water molecule into hydrogen and oxygen atoms. Creating hydrogen through electrolysis sounds like a good idea because the only waste product emitted into the atmosphere is oxygen, and there is nothing harmful about oxygen. But the hazardous environmental impact is not in the electrolysis reaction, but in the need to generate electricity to run the electrolyzer. If the electricity to run the electrolyzer came from the current electrical grid, which gets half its energy from burning coal, the carbon dioxide emissions for a fuel cell car would be 436 grams per mile—17% worse than the current emissions for gasoline powered cars (Wald). One way to avoid these emissions would be to run the electrolyzer with wind-generated or nuclear-powered electricity. But wind power would be able to produce only a small fraction of what would be needed for large-scale use of hydrogen as fuel, and nuclear power brings with it a whole new set of problems including disposal of nuclear waste.

Although there seem to be various methods of producing hydrogen, the current sources being considered do not fulfill the claim that hydrogen fuel cell technology will end the use of fossil fuels or eliminate greenhouse gases. The problem is not with the fuel cells themselves but with the processes needed to produce hydrogen fuel. I am not arguing that research and development should be abandoned, and I hope some day that the hydrogen economy will take off. But what I have discovered in my research is that hydrogen power is not as clean and green as I thought.

APA Style

HYDROGEN FUEL-CELL CARS   6

References

Start References on a new page.

California. Executive Department. (2004, April 20). Executive order S-7-04.

Retrieved from http://www.its.ucdavis.edu/hydrogenhighway

/Executive-Order.pdf

Center heading.

CNN. (2004). The issues/George Bush. *CNN.com*. Retrieved from http://www.cnn

.com/ELECTION/2004/special/president/issues/index.bush.html

Use initial cap for article titles.

General Motors. (2004, July 28). Who's driving the hydrogen economy?

[Advertisement]. *New York Times,* A19.

Italicize publication names.

Hydrogen Fuel Cell Institute. (2001). Retrieved May 27, 2004, from

http://www. h2fuelcells.org

Nice, K. (n.d.). How fuel cells work. *Howstuffworks*. Retrieved May 27, 2004,

Use initials for first names.

from http://science.howstuffworks.com

Ohio University aims to use coal to power fuel cells. (2003, November 24). *Fuel*

Cell Today. Retrieved from http://www.fuelcelltoday.com

Place date after author's name.

Roberts, P. (2004, March 6). *Los Angeles Times*. Retrieved from http://

www.commondreams.org/views04/0307-02.htm

Check that everything cited in report is in References list (except personal communications).

Wald, M. L. (2003, November 12). Will hydrogen clear the air? Maybe not,

some say. *New York Times*, p. C1.

THINKING CRITICALLY
about "How Clean and Green Are Hydrogen Fuel-Cell Cars?"

1. Explain Shannon King's use of the surprising-reversal strategy. What question does she pose? What is the common answer? What is her surprising answer? How effectively does she use research data to support her surprising answer?

2. The line between information and persuasion is often blurred. Some might argue that Shannon's essay has a persuasive aim that argues against hydrogen fuel-cell cars rather than an informative aim that simply presents surprising information about hydrogen production. To what extent do you agree with our classification of Shannon's aim as primarily informative rather than persuasive? Can it be both?

ANALYZING IMAGES

This chapter asks you to think about three major kinds of communication through images—documentary or news photos, paintings, and advertisements—to increase your visual literacy skills. By **visual literacy**, we mean your awareness of the importance of visual communication and your ability to interpret or make meaning out of images by examining their context and visual features. We focus on the ways that images influence our conceptual and emotional understanding of a phenomenon and the ways that they validate, reveal, and construct the world.

This chapter invites you to analyze images in order to understand their rhetorical and experiential effects. To **analyze** means to divide or dissolve the whole into its parts, examine these parts carefully, look at the relationships among them, and then use this understanding of the parts to better understand the whole—how it functions, what it means. As Chapter 1, Concept 2, explains, when you analyze, your goal is to raise interesting questions about the image or object being analyzed—questions that perhaps your reader hasn't thought to ask—and then to provide tentative answers, supported by points and particulars derived from your own close examination.

The ability to analyze visual texts is particularly important because we are surrounded by images from photojournalism, the Internet, billboards, newspapers, television, and magazines. These images, as one critic has stated, "have designs on us." Although glamorous and disturbing images saturate our environment, we do not necessarily have a deep understanding of how they affect us.

> **By writing in a common academic genre—a comparative analysis of two visual texts—in this chapter you will learn to:**
>
> - analyze the persuasive effects of images and how these effects are created
> - respond to visual images as a more informed citizen and perceptive cultural critic

Exploring Image Analysis

To introduce you to image analysis, we provide an exercise that asks you to interact with several news photographs on the issue of immigration reform.

Immigration reform is one of the most complex issues facing the United States today; the problem is particularly acute with respect to immigrants from Mexico and Central America. Immigrants are drawn to the United States by employment opportunities not found in their own countries. U.S. citizens benefit from immigrants' inexpensive labor, which helps keep the prices of services and goods low. In addition to a sizable Mexican-American citizenry, more than ten million illegal immigrants currently live in the United States. All these factors give rise to a number of controversial questions: Should the United States increase border security and focus on building impassable barriers? Should it deport illegal immigrants or explore easier routes to making them citizens? Should it crack down on employers of illegal immigrants or should it implement a guest worker program to legitimize immigrant labor?

Public debate about these issues is particularly susceptible to manipulation by the rhetorical appeal of images. The following exercise asks you to examine the news photos in Figures 8.1 through 8.4. Working individually or in groups, consider the rhetorical effect of these photos, first by recording your responses to

FIGURE 8.1 Wall between Tijuana, Mexico, and the United States

FIGURE 8.2 Immigrants Crossing the Border Illegally

FIGURE 8.3 Protestors Marching for Compassionate Treatment of Immigrants

FIGURE 8.4 Immigrants Saying Their Citizenship Pledge

them and then by speculating how you might use these images to increase the persuasiveness of different positions on immigration reform.

1. What objects, people, or places stand out in each photo? Does the photo look candid or staged, taken close-up or from a distance? How do the angle of the photo (taken from below or above the subject) and the use of color contribute to the effect?
2. What is the dominant impression conveyed by each photo?
3. Examine how the similarities and differences among the four photos convey different rhetorical impressions of immigrants, Latino culture, or the role of immigrants and ethnic diversity in U.S. culture.
4. Now imagine how you might use these photos to enhance the persuasiveness of particular claims. Choose one or two photos to support or attack each claim below and explain what the photo could contribute to the argument.
   • The United States should seal its border with Mexico by building a wall and increasing border patrols.
   • The United States should offer amnesty and citizenship to immigrants who are currently in the United States illegally.

Understanding Image Analysis: Documentary and News Photographs

Documentary and news photos are aimed at shaping the way we think and feel about an event or cultural/historical phenomenon. For example, consider the newspaper photos, TV news footage, or Internet videos of the billowing clouds of smoke and ash from the collapsing World Trade Center towers on September 11, 2001. Figures 8.5, 8.6, and 8.7 present three well-known documentary images of this event, taken from three different positions and at three slightly different moments as the event unfolded.

Although all three photos convey the severity of the terrorist attack, each has a different impact. Figure 8.5 records the event shortly before the north tower collapsed and just after the south tower was struck by the second plane, marked in the photo by the red flames. The sheer magnitude and horror of the moment-by-moment action unfolding before our eyes evoked shock, anger, and feelings of helplessness in Americans.

In contrast to the first image, which was taken from a distance below the towers, Figure 8.6 was taken by a police detective in a helicopter searching for survivors on the roof of the north tower before it collapsed. This photo suggests the apocalyptic explosion and implosion of a contemporary city. The destruction pictured here is too massive to be an ordinary event such as a fire in a major building, and yet the streams of ash and smoke don't reveal exactly what is happening.

Another well-publicized view of this event is that of the firefighters on the ground, seen in Figure 8.7. Here the firefighters, risking their lives while trying to rescue the people in the towers, have come to symbolize the self-sacrifice, courage, and also vulnerability of the human effort in the face of such colossal

FIGURE 8.5 Terrorist Attack on the World Trade Center

FIGURE 8.6 World Trade Center Attack Seen from the Air

FIGURE 8.7 Firefighters in the World Trade Center Wreckage

destruction. This image also suggests the terror and suspense of a science-fiction-like conflict. All three photos, while memorializing the same event, have different specific subjects, angles of vision, and emotional and mental effects.

The rest of this section introduces you to the ways that photographers think about their use of the camera and the effects they are trying to achieve.

Angle of Vision and Credibility of Photographs

Although the word "documentary" is associated with an objective, transparent, unmediated glimpse of reality, the relationship of documentary photography to its subject matter has always been complex. Historians are now reassessing early documentary photographs, exploring the class and race agendas of the photographers in the kinds of scenes chosen, the photographers' stance toward them, and the wording of the narratives accompanying the photographs. In other words, despite a photograph's appearance of capturing a moment of reality (whose reality?), its effect is always influenced by the photographer's rhetorical angle of vision conveyed through the framing and focusing power of the camera. Perhaps now more than ever, we are aware that the photographer's purpose and techniques actually shape the reality that viewers see. (Think of the multiple cameras tracking a football game and replaying a touchdown from different angles, often creating very different impressions of a particular play.)

The photographer's power to shape reality is enhanced by various strategies for making "unnatural" photographs seem "natural" or "real." For example, photographs can be manipulated or falsified in the following ways:

- staging images (scenes that appear spontaneous but are really posed)
- altering images (airbrushing, reshaping body parts)
- selecting images or parts of images (cropping photographs so that only certain parts are shown)
- mislabeling images (putting a caption on a photograph that misrepresents the image)
- constructing images (putting the head of one person on the body of another)

Research has revealed that many famous photographs were tampered with. As early as the Civil War, composite photos of generals were created by combining heads, bodies, and scenery and inserting figures into scenes. Today this manipulation is also conducted by amateur photographers using photo-editing software. The potential for altering images gives us additional reasons for considering the active role of the photographer and for investigating the credibility and purpose behind images.

How to Analyze a Documentary Photograph

Photographs are always created and interpreted within a social, political, and historical context—the original context in which the photograph was made and viewed and your own context as a current viewer and interpreter. At play are the assumptions, values, and cultural knowledge of the photographer, the original viewers, and the later viewers. Also at play are the sites in which the photograph is viewed—whether in an original news story, a museum, an upscale art exhibit, an expensive coffee-table book, a documentary film, an Internet site, or a textbook. These sites invite us to respond in different ways. For example, one site may call us to social action or deepen our understanding of an event, while another aims to elicit artistic appreciation or to underscore cultural differences.

Examining the Rhetorical Contexts of a Photo A first step in analyzing a documentary photograph is to consider its various rhetorical contexts. The following chart will help you ask illuminating questions.

Strategies for Analyzing the Rhetorical Contexts of Documentary Photographs	
Context	**Questions to Ask**
Photographer's purpose and context in making the photograph	• What was the photographer's original intention/purpose in making the image (to report an event, convey information, persuade viewers to think about the event or people a certain way)? • What was the original historical, cultural, social, and political context in which the photograph was taken?
Original context for displaying the photograph	• Where was the photograph originally viewed (news story, photo essay, scientific report, public exhibit, advocacy Web site)? • How does the original title or caption, if any, reflect the context and shape impressions of the image?
Cultural contexts for interpreting the photograph	• How does the photograph's appearance in a particular place influence your impression of it? • How does your own cultural context differ from that of original viewers? • What assumptions and values do you bring to the context?

Examining the Effects of a Photo on a Viewer In addition to considering the contexts of photographs, we can explore how photographs achieve their effects—that is, how they move us emotionally or intellectually, how they imply arguments and cause us to see the subject in a certain way. An image might soothe us or repel us; it might evoke our sympathies, trigger our fears, or call forth a web of interconnected ideas, memories, and associations.

Before you begin a detailed analysis of a photograph, you will find it helpful to explore the photograph's immediate impact.

- What words come to mind when you view this photograph?
- What is the mood or overall feeling conveyed by the photo?
- Assuming that photographs "have designs on us," what is this photograph trying to get you to feel, think, do, or "see"?

The following chart will help you examine a photograph in detail in order to analyze how it achieves its persuasive effects.*

Strategies for Analyzing the Persuasive Effects of Photographs and Other Images	
What to Examine	**Some Questions to Ask about Rhetorical Effect**
Subject matter: People in portraits Portraits can be formal or informal and can emphasize character or social role. The gaze of the human subjects can imply power through direct eye contact and deference or shyness through lack of eye contact.	Is the emphasis on identity, character, and personality, or representative status (wife of wealthy merchant, king, soldier, etc.), or symbolic (an image of wisdom, daring, etc.)? What do details of clothing and setting (a room's furnishings, for example) reveal about historical period, economic status, national or ethnic identity?
Subject matter: People in scenes Scenes can make a statement about everyday life or capture some aspect of a news event or crisis.	What is the relationship of the people to each other and the scene? Can you re-create the story behind the scene? Does the scene look natural/realistic or staged/aesthetically attractive?
Subject matter: Landscape or nature Scenes can focus on nature or the environment as the dominant subject.	If the setting is outdoors, what are the features of the landscape: urban or rural, mountain or desert? What aspects of nature are shown? If people are in the image, what is the relationship between nature and the human figures? What vision of nature is the artist constructing—majestic, threatening, hospitable, tamed, orderly, wild?

(continued)

*We are indebted to Terry Barrett, Professor Emeritus of Art Education at Ohio State University, for his formulation of questions, "Looking at Photographs, Description and Interpretation," and to Claire Garoutte, Assistant Professor of Photography at Seattle University, for informing our discussion of context in analyzing documentary photographs.

What to Examine	Some Questions to Ask about Rhetorical Effect
Distance from subject: Close-ups tend to increase the intensity of the image and suggest the importance of the subject. Long shots tend to blend the subject into the environment.	Are viewers brought close to the subject or distanced from it? How does the distance from the subject contribute to the effect of the photo or painting?
Angle and orientation: The vantage point from which the photograph was taken and the positioning of the photographer to the subject determine the effect of images. Low angle makes the subject look larger. High angle makes the subject look smaller. A level angle implies equality. Front views tend to emphasize the persons in the image. Rear views often emphasize the scene or setting.	How does the angle influence what you see? Why do you think this angle was chosen? How would the photograph have changed if it had been taken from another angle?
Framing: Framing determines what is inside the image and what is closed off to viewers; it's a device to draw the attention of viewers.	How does the framing of the image direct your attention? What is included and what is excluded from the image? How does what the photo or painting allows you to see and know contribute to its effect? Why do you think this particular frame was chosen?
Light: The direction of the light determines the shadows and affects the contrasts, which can be subtle or strong. Lighting has different effects if it is natural or artificial, bright, soft, or harsh.	How does the light reveal details? What does the direction of the light contribute to the presence of shadows? How do these shadows affect the mood or feeling of the photo?
Focus: Focus refers to what is clearly in focus or in the foreground of the photo versus what is blurry. The range between the nearest and farthest thing in focus in the photo is referred to as the depth of field.	What parts of the image are clearly in focus? Are any parts out of focus? What effect do these choices have on viewers' impression of the image? How great is the depth of field and what effect does that have?
Scale, space, and shape: Size/scale and shape affect prominence and emphasis. Size and scale can be natural, minimized, or exaggerated. Use of space can be shallow, deep, or both.	How do the scale, space, and shape of objects direct viewers' attention and affect a feeling or mood? Are shapes geometric and angular or flowing and organic?

What to Examine	Some Questions to Ask about Rhetorical Effect
Both positive shapes and voids can draw viewers' attention.	Are shapes positive such as objects, or negative such as voids?
Use of repetition, variety, and balance: Repetition of elements can create order, wholeness, and unity. Variety can create interest. Balance can create unity and harmony.	What elements are repeated in this image? What variety is present, say, in shapes? Does the visual weight of the photo seem to be distributed evenly on the sides, top, and bottom? What roles do repetition, variety, and balance play in the impression created by the photo?
Line: Lines can be curved and flowing, straight, or disjointed and angular. Lines can be balanced/symmetrical, stable, and harmonious, or disjointed and agitated.	Does the use of line create structure and convey movement/action or calm/stasis? How does the use of line control how viewers look at the photo or painting?
Color: Choice of black and white can reflect the site of publication, the date of the photo, or an artistic choice. Colors can contribute to the realism and appeal; harmonious colors can be pleasing; clashing or harsh colors can be disturbing.	How many colors are used? What is the relationship of the colors? Which colors dominate? Are the colors warm and vibrant or cool, bright, or dull? How are light and dark used? How does the use of color direct viewers' attention and affect the impression of the image? What emotional response do these colors evoke?

Sample Analysis of a Documentary Photograph

To illustrate how a documentary photograph can work on the viewer's mind and heart, we show you our own analysis of a photo titled *The Fall of the Berlin Wall* (Figure 8.8), taken by photojournalist Peter Turnley in 1989. At the time, the Berlin Wall, which separated communist East Berlin from democratic West Berlin, symbolized the oppression of communism. In 1987 President Ronald Reagan appealed to Mikhail Gorbachev, president of the Union of Soviet Socialist Republics, saying in a famous speech, "Mr. Gorbachev, tear down this wall." When the border opened in November 1989, marking the end of communist rule in Eastern Europe, East Berliners flooded into West Berlin, sparking weeks of celebration. Peter Turnley is a world-famous American photojournalist whose photos of major world events have appeared on the covers of *Newsweek* as well as international magazines. This photograph appeared in a 1996 exhibit (and later a book) entitled *In Time of War and Peace* at the International Center of Photography in New York.

This documentary photograph of a celebratory scene following the opening of the Berlin Wall in 1989 uses elements of framing, orientation, focus, balance, and color to convey the dominant impression of a life-changing explosion of energy and emotion triggered by this significant event. This distance photo is divided

FIGURE 8.8 Fall of the Berlin Wall, 1989, by Peter Turnley

into three horizontal bands—the sky, the wall, and the celebratory crowd—but the focal point is the yelling, triumphant German youth sitting astride the wall, wearing jeans, a studded belt, and a black jacket. The graffiti indicate that the photo was taken from the West Berlin side (East Berliners were not permitted to get close to the wall), and the light post between the two cranes was probably used to illuminate the no-man zone on the communist side.

Every aspect of the photograph suggests energy. In contrast with the mostly homogeneous sky, the wall and the crowd contain many diverse elements. The wall is heavily graffitied in many colors, and the crowd is composed of many people. The wall looks crowded, tattered, and dirty, something to be torn down rather than cleaned up. Most of the graffiti consist of tags, people's response to the ugly obstruction of the wall; West Berliners had no power to destroy the wall, but they could mark it up. The slightly blurred crowd of heads suggests that the people are in motion. At first it is hard to tell if they are angry protesters storming the wall or celebrators cheering on the German youth. The photograph captures this dual emotion—anger and joy—all at once.

At the center of the photograph is the German youth, whose dark jacket makes him stand out against the light blue sky. A few days earlier the wall had fenced him in (at that time, it would have been unthinkable even to approach the wall lest he be shot by border guards). Now he rides the wall like an American cowboy at a rodeo. He has conquered the wall. He has become transformed from prisoner to liberator. His cowboy gesture, reflecting European fascination with American cowboy movies, becomes the symbol of the ideological West, the land of freedom, now the wave of the future for these reunited countries. He holds in his hand a tool (a hammer or chisel?) used to chip away the wall symbolically, but the position of his arm and hand suggests a cowboy with a pistol.

What makes this photograph so powerful is the distance. Had Turnley used a telescopic lens to focus on the German youth up close, the photograph would have been about the youth himself, a personal story. But by placing the youth into a larger frame that includes the crowd, the long expanse of ugly wall, and the cranes and lamppost behind the wall, Turnley suggests both the enormous public and political nature of this event and the implications for individual lives. The youth appears to be the first of the energized crowd to demonstrate the conquering of the powerful barrier that had shaped so many German lives for almost three decades. Thus the composition of this photo packs many layers of meaning and symbolism into its depiction of this historical event.

FOR WRITING AND DISCUSSION

Exploring a Photograph's Compositional Elements and Rhetorical Effect

In the last five years, documentary photographs have played a key role in persuading audiences that climate change is a serious threat. One recurring image shows mountains with receding or disappearing glaciers. An example is Figure 8.9, a photo of the Gormer glacier near Zermatt, Switzerland, that was taken by photojournalist Jean-Christophe Bott on August 25, 2009, during the Switzerland Greenpeace Protest. The staging and showing of the photograph were intended to put pressure on national legislation to enact stricter carbon dioxide emission limits and to influence negotiators at the Copenhagen Summit on climate change in September 2009.

1. Working in groups or individually, use the strategies for analyzing the context, composition, and rhetorical effects of photos presented in the strategies charts on pages 176 and 177–179 to describe and interpret this photo. What is the dominant impression conveyed by this photograph?

FIGURE 8.9 Greenpeace Climate Change Protest in Zermatt, Switzerland

2. Then using the Internet, search for another photograph that is currently being used in the public discussion of climate change and analyze its context, composition, rhetorical effect, and possible additional uses. What does your photograph contribute to its context?
3. If you were writing to underscore to young voters the importance of climate change, would you use the Greenpeace protest photograph or the one you located? Why?

Understanding Image Analysis: Paintings

When you analyze a painting, many of the strategies used for analyzing documentary photographs still apply. You still look carefully at the subject matter of the painting (the setting, the people or objects in the setting, the arrangement in space, the clothing, the gaze of persons, the implied narrative story, and so forth). Likewise, you consider the painter's distance from the subject, the angle of orientation, the framing, and other features that paintings share with photographs. Additionally, your analysis of paintings will be enriched if you consider, as you did with documentary photographs, the context in which the painting was originally created and originally viewed as well as your own cultural context and place of viewing.

But painters—by means of their choice of paints, their brushstrokes, their artistic vision, and their methods of representation—often do something quite different from photographers. For example, they can paint mythological or imaginary subjects and can achieve nonrepresentational effects not associated with a camera such as a medieval allegorical style or the striking distortions of Cubism. Also, the long history of painting and the ways that historical periods influence painters' choices of subject matter, medium, and style affect what viewers see and feel about paintings. Background on the artist, historical period, and style of paintings (for example, Baroque, Impressionism, Expressionism, and Cubism) can be found in sources such as the Oxford Art Online database. In analyzing paintings, art critics and historians often contrast paintings that have similar subject matter (for example, two portraits of a hero, two paintings of a biblical scene, two landscapes) but that create very different dominant impressions and effects on viewers.

How to Analyze a Painting

Just as with photographs, you should ground your interpretation of a painting in close observation. Many of the elements introduced in the strategies chart on pages 177–179 for analyzing photographs can apply or be adapted to the analysis of paintings. In addition, you will want to examine the following elements of the paintings you are analyzing.

Strategies for Analyzing the Particular Elements of Paintings	
Elements to Analyze	**Questions to Ask about Rhetorical Effect**
Design and shape of the painting: The width to height, division into parts, and proportional relationship of parts influence the impression of the painting.	What is viewer's impression of the shape of the painting and the relationship of its parts? How does line organize the painting? Is the painting organized along diagonal, horizontal, or vertical lines?
Medium, technique, and brushstrokes: The material with which the painting is made (for example, pen and ink, tempura/water colors, charcoal, oil paints on paper or canvas), and the thickness and style of brushstrokes determine the artistic effect.	In what medium is the artist working? How does the medium contribute to the impression of the painting? Are brushstrokes sharp and distinct or thick, layered, fused? Are they delicate and precise or vigorous? What effect does the awareness or lack of awareness of brushstrokes have on the appearance of the painting?

Sample Analysis of a Painting

As an example of a visual analysis of a painting, we offer an interpretation of a famous painting by Pierre-Auguste Renoir (1841–1919), a French Impressionist painter of the late nineteenth century. The French Impressionists were recognized for their refusal to paint old themes; their embrace of scenes of modern society, especially the city and suburbs; and their experimentation with light and brush-strokes as a way to capture fleeting impressions. Figure 8.10 shows Renoir's oil painting *La Loge* (The Theater Box), which he painted as his main contribution to the first exhibit of Impressionist paintings in 1874. Impressionist paintings were considered too *avant garde* to be displayed at the conservative state-controlled Salon, which was the official arbiter and channel of the work of established French artists.

Renoir's *La Loge* depicts social life in nineteenth-century urban society as an occasion to act out social roles. This painting of a man and a woman elegantly dressed in a theater box at the opera, a popular social spot of the period, suggests that attending the theater/opera entailed displaying one's wealth, being seen, and inspecting others as much as it did watching a performance. This painting focuses intensely on two members of the audience and specifically on the woman, who catches and holds our gaze. While the man in the background is looking at someone in the audience through his opera glasses, the woman looks directly at viewers and invites their attention.

Renoir has compelled viewers to dwell on this woman by a number of his choices in this painting. He has chosen to paint her in a tightly framed close-up image, which the slightly off-center woman dominates. Her face and eyes convey

FIGURE 8.10 Renoir's *La Loge* (1874)

the impression that she and the viewer are staring at each other, while in the shadows the man's eyes are blocked by his opera glasses. Thus this painting combines the woman's portrait with a scene at the opera, even though most of the setting, the theater box, is excluded from the painting. (We know we are at the opera because of the painting's title and the man's and woman's accessories.) There seems to be a story behind the scene: What is the man looking at and why is he not noticing the woman as we, the viewers, are compelled to do? This depiction of a moment seems to be less a shared experience of relationship and more a site for performance: men engaged in looking, women inviting the gaze of others.

Another choice Renoir has made to focus viewers' attention on the woman is his striking use of color. In this painting, the color palette is not large—white, black, brown/gold/sepia, with her red lips and red flowers on her bodice. The white of her face and her upper body is the brightest, suggesting light shining on her. Renoir also highlights the woman with short, thick brushstrokes, which give her shimmering, elegant dress texture and the impression of silk, velvet, and lace. As additional signs of wealth, she wears earrings, a gold bracelet, a flower in her hair, and a flower at her bosom. The stark contrast of the black and white in her dress, the white of her face, and the red of her lips—and the agitated diagonal but converging lines of the stripes of her dress that, along with her arms angled out from her body, shape her into a diamond—all work to direct viewers' eyes to her bosom and most of all to her face. Although the expression of the woman is calm, smiling in mild amusement or subtle emotion, the painting captures intensity, perhaps excitement or anticipation, through the sharp contrast of the red, white, and black. The piece is fairly still and yet we are transfixed by this woman's eyes and lips. With the complex interaction of artistic elements in this painting, Renoir has invited viewers to experience an exciting scene of privileged nineteenth-century urban life.

FOR WRITING AND DISCUSSION

Contrasting the Compositional Features of Two Paintings

This exercise asks you to apply the analysis strategies presented on pages 177–179 and 183 to examine the pastel painting *Carousel* by Camille Pissarro shown in Figure 8.11 and to contrast it with Renoir's painting in Figure 8.10. Camille Pissarro (1830–1903) was also a French Impressionist who regularly exhibited his works in Impressionist exhibitions. He painted *Carousel* in 1885; the medium is pastel on paper mounted on board.

Your task: Working individually or in groups, analyze Pissarro's painting and then find some striking points of commonality or difference with the Renoir painting that you think merit discussion.

- Begin by applying the strategies for analyzing photographic images and paintings on pages 177–179 and 183.
- After you have analyzed the visual features of the paintings, consider why Pissarro titled his painting *Carousel*.

FIGURE 8.11 *Carousel* by Camille Pissarro (1885)

- Finally, what are the thematic differences between these two paintings? How do these paintings, both Impressionistic images of well-dressed women at leisure, create similar or different effects on viewers? What view or feeling about life or about the artists' worlds is conveyed in each painting? What way of seeing or thinking are these paintings persuading you to adopt?

Understanding Image Analysis: Advertisements

The images in advertisements are fascinating to analyze. Like other images, they employ the rhetorical strategies we described in the section on documentary photographs. Often, the ad's words (called the "copy") also contribute to its rhetorical effect. Moreover, ads make a more direct and constant demand on us than do documentary photographs and paintings. Advertising, a multibillion-dollar global industry whose business is communicating across a wide range of media to stimulate the purchase of products or services, comes to us in multiple forms: not just as slick, glamorous magazine ads, but also as direct mail, billboards, radio and television commercials, e-advertisements, banners, pop-ups, and spam. Figures 8.12 and 8.13, a billboard and a bus ad, illustrate

FIGURE 8.12 A Billboard Ad

FIGURE 8.13 Ad on a City Bus

the ordinary ubiquity of ads. Because of advertising's powerful role in shaping our culture and influencing our self-images, we have good reason to analyze the rhetorical strategies of advertisers.

**FOR
WRITING
AND
DISCUSSION**

Examining the Appeal of Ads

Think about the images and words in the two car insurance ads in Figures 8.12 and 8.13.

1. What do you notice most about the images and copy in these ads?
2. What is the appeal of these ads?
3. How are these ads designed to suit their contexts, a billboard and a bus panel? Why would they be less suitable for a magazine?

How Advertisers Think about Advertising

Although cultural critics frequently focus on ads as manipulative messages that need to be decoded to protect unwary consumers, we confess that we actually enjoy ads, appreciate how they hold down the consumer cost of media, and admire their often-ingenious creativity. (We suspect that others secretly enjoy ads also: Think of how the Super Bowl is popular both for its football and for its ads.) In this section, we take a look at advertising from a marketer's point of view in order to deepen your awareness of an ad's context and the many behind-the-scenes decisions and negotiations that produced it. Whether marketing professionals design an individual ad or a huge marketing campaign, they typically begin by asking questions.

Who Is Our Target Audience? At the outset, marketers identify one or more target audiences for their product or service. They often use sophisticated psychological research to identify segments of the population who share similar values, beliefs, and aspirations and then subdivide these categories according to age, gender, region, income level, ethnicity, and so forth. Think of the different way you'd pitch a product or service to, say, Wal-Mart shoppers versus Neiman Marcus shoppers, steak eaters versus vegans, or skateboarders versus geeks.

How Much Media Landscape Can We Afford? While identifying their target audience, marketers also consider how much terrain they can afford to occupy on the enormous media landscape of billboards, newspapers, magazines, mailing lists, Internet pop-ups, TV and radio commercials, posters, naming rights for sports stadiums, T-shirts, coffee mugs, product placements in films, sandwich boards, or banners carried across the sky by propeller airplanes. Each of these sites has to be rented or purchased, with the price depending on the perceived quality of the location and the timing. For example, a thirty-second TV commercial during the 2010 Super Bowl cost $2.6 million, and a one-time full-page ad in a nationally circulated popular magazine can cost up to $500,000 or more. Overall, advertisers hope to attain the best possible positioning and timing within the media landscape at a price they can afford.

What Are the Best Media for Reaching Our Target Audience? A marketer's goal is to reach the target audience efficiently and with a minimum of overflow—that is, messages sent to people who are not likely buyers. Marketers are keenly aware of both media and timing: Note, for example, how daytime TV is dominated by ads for payday loans, exercise equipment, or technical colleges, while billboards around airports advertise rental cars. Women's fashion magazines advertise lingerie and perfume but not computers or life insurance, while dating services advertise primarily through Internet ads.

Is Our Goal to Stimulate Direct Sales or to Develop Long-Term Branding and Image? Some ads are intended to stimulate retail sales directly: "Buy two, get one free." In some cases, advertisements use information and argument to show how their product or service is superior to that of their competitors. Most advertisements, however, involve parity products such as soft drinks, deodorants, breakfast cereals, or toothpaste. (*Parity products* are roughly equal in quality among competitors and so can't be promoted through any rational or scientific proof of superiority.) In such cases, advertisers' goal is to build brand loyalty based on a long-lasting relationship with consumers. Advertisers, best thought of as creative teams of writers and artists, try to convert a brand name appearing on a cereal box or a pair of jeans to a field of qualities, values, and imagery that lives inside the heads of its targeted consumers. Advertisers don't just want you to buy Nikes rather than Reeboks but also to see yourself as a Nike kind of person, who identifies with the lifestyle or values conveyed in Nike ads.

Mirrors and Windows: The Strategy of an Effective Advertisement

A final behind-the-scenes concept that will help you analyze ads is the marketers' principle of "*mirrors and windows*," a psychological and motivational strategy to associate a product with a target audience's dreams, hopes, fears, desires, and wishes (often subconscious).

- *The mirror effect* refers to the way in which the ad mirrors the target audience's self-image, promoting identification with the ad's message. The target audience has to say, "I am part of the world that this ad speaks to. I have this problem (pimples, boring hair, dandelions, cell phone service without enough bars)."
- *The window effect* provides visions of the future, promises of who we will become or what will happen if we align ourselves with this brand. The ad implies a brief narrative, taking you from your ordinary self (mirror) to your new, aspirational self (window).

For example, the acne product Proactiv Solutions uses a very common mirrors/windows strategy. Proactiv infomercials create the mirror effect by featuring regular-looking teenagers with pimples and the window effect by using a gorgeous actress as endorsing spokesperson: If I use Proactiv Solutions, ordinary "me" will look beautiful like Jessica Simpson.

FIGURE 8.14 Geico Gecko Billboard Ad

But the mirrors and windows principle can be used in much more subtle and creative ways. Consider the brilliance of the Geico insurance gecko ads promoting what advertisers call a "a resentful purchase"—that is, something you need to have but that doesn't give you material pleasure like a new pair of shoes or money in a savings account. Insurance, a hassle to buy, is also associated with fear—fear of needing it, fear of not having it, fear of not being able to get it again if you ever use it. In this light, think of the Geico campaign featuring the humorous, big-eyed gecko (friendly, cute) with the distinctive cockney voice (working-class swagger). When this chapter was being written, Geico billboards were sprouting up all over the country (see Figure 8.14), while large-print ads were appearing in popular magazines along with numerous TV and radio commercials. Here are some of the particular advantages of the gecko for Geico's layered advertising campaign across many media:

- *"Gecko" sounds like "Geico."* In fact, this sound-alike feature was the inspiration for the campaign.
- *The gecko is identifiable by both sight and sound.* If you see a print ad or a billboard, you remember what the voice sounds like; if you hear a radio ad, you remember what the gecko looks like; on TV or YouTube, you get both sight and sound.
- *The gecko is cheap.* The cost of the computer simulations that produce the gecko is minimal in comparison to the royalties paid to celebrities for an advertising endorsement.

- ***The gecko is ethnically/racially neutral.*** Marketers didn't have to decide whether to choose a white versus black versus Asian spokesperson, yet a person of any race or nationality can identify with the little lizard. (Think Kermit the Frog on *Sesame Street*.) Feminist critics, however, might rightly ask why the gecko has to be male.
- ***The gecko is scandal-proof.*** When in 2010 the Tiger Woods imbroglio ruined the golfer's public image, the huge insurance company Accenture, along with TagHauer watches and other companies, had to drop his endorsement ads, forcing them at great expense to create new advertising campaigns and to lose media visibility in the interim.

Yet we must still ask why the gecko is a good advertising device for an insurance company. How does the gecko campaign incorporate mirrors and windows? Let's start with the mirror effect. It is easy to identify with the Geico ads because everyone has to buy insurance and because everyone wants to save money. (The gecko's main sales pitch is that Geico will save you 15 percent.) Moreover, our long cultural history of identifying with animated characters (*Sesame Street, ET*) makes it easy to project our own identities onto the gecko. Additionally, the cockney voice makes the gecko a bit of an outsider, someone breaking into corporate culture through sheer bravado. (Many people think of the gecko's accent as Australian more than cockney, giving the lizard a bit of sexy, macho Crocodile Dundee appeal.)

The ads also create a window effect, which comes from the way the gecko humanizes the insurance company, removing some of the fear and anxiety of buying insurance. You don't think of the gecko as *selling* you the insurance so much as *buying* it for you as your agent, hopping right up on the corporate desk and demanding your rights. Geico becomes a fun company, and you as consumer picture yourself going away with a pile of saved money. Recent ads have added another symbolic feature to the gecko—a pair of glasses—which makes him seem intellectual and responsible, more serious and grown-up. Meanwhile, another Geico campaign, the talking-money ad (see the billboard ad in Figure 8.12), extends the concept of a humorous, friendly creature, like the gecko, that turns Geico insurance into a savings, not an expense.

FOR WRITING AND DISCUSSION

Designing Ads

This exercise asks you to apply these marketing concepts to designing your own ad. Imagine you are an advertising professional assigned to the Gloopers account. Gloopers is a seaweed (kelp)-based snack treat (a fiction, but pretend it is real) that is very popular under another name in Japan. It was introduced earlier in the American market and failed miserably—what sort of a treat is seaweed? But now, you have laboratory evidence that Gloopers provides crucial nutritional benefits for growing bodies and that it is a healthy alternative to junk food. Many food companies would kill for the endorsement of nutritious content that you now have to work with, but the product is still made out of gunky seaweed. Working in groups or individually, develop a campaign for this product by working out your answers to the following questions:

- Who is your target audience? (Will you seek to appeal to parents as well as children?)
- What is your core message or campaign concept? (Think of a visual approach, including a mirror and window appeal, and perhaps a tagline slogan.)
- What is the best positioning in the media landscape for this campaign?
- How will you build a brand image and brand loyalty?

How to Analyze an Advertisement

In addition to thinking about the decision making behind an ad, when you analyze a print ad you need to ask three overarching questions:

1. How does the ad draw in the target audience by helping them identify with the ad's problematic situation or story (mirror effect)?
2. How does the ad create a field of values, beliefs, and aspirations that serve as windows into a more fulfilled life?
3. How do the ad's images and words work together to create the desired persuasive effects?

For the images in an ad, all the strategies we have already described for documentary photographs and for paintings continue to apply—for example, angle of vision, framing, and so forth. (Review the strategies chart on pp. 177–179.) With many ads you also have to factor in the creative use of words—puns, connotations, and intertextual references to other ads or cultural artifacts. Note that in professionally created ads, every word, every punctuation mark, and every visual detail down to the props in the photograph or the placement of a model's hands are consciously chosen.

The following strategies chart focuses on questions particularly relevant to print ads.

Strategies for Analyzing the Compositional Features of Print Ads	
What to Do	**Some Questions to Ask**
Examine the settings, furnishings, and all other details.	• Is the room formal or informal; neat, lived-in, or messy? • How is the room furnished and decorated? • If the setting is outdoors, what are the features of the landscape: urban or rural, mountain or meadow? • Why are particular animals or birds included? (Think of the differences between using a crow, a hummingbird, or a parrot.)

(*continued*)

What to Do	Some Questions to Ask
Consider the social meaning of objects.	• What is the emotional effect of the objects in a den: for example, duck decoys and fishing rods versus computers and high-tech printers? • What is the social significance (class, economic status, lifestyle, values) of the objects in the ad? (Think of the meaning of a groomed poodle versus a mutt or a single rose versus a fuchsia in a pot.)
Consider the characters, roles, and actions.	• Who are these people and what are they doing? What story line could you construct behind the image? • Are the models regular-looking people, "beautiful people," or celebrities? • In product advertisements, are female models used instrumentally (depicted as mechanics working on cars or as a consumers buying cars) or are they used decoratively (bikini-clad and lounging on the hood of the latest truck)?
Observe how models are dressed, posed, and accessorized.	• What are the models' facial expressions? • What are their hairstyles and what cultural and social significance do they have? • How well are they dressed and posed?
Observe the relationships among actors and among actors and objects.	• How does the position of the models signal importance and dominance? • Who is looking at whom? • Who is above or below, in the foreground or background?
Consider what social roles are being played out and what values appealed to.	• Are the gender roles traditional or nontraditional? • Are the relationships romantic, erotic, friendly, formal, uncertain? • What are the power relationships among characters?
Consider how document design functions and how the words and images work together.	• What features of document design (variations of font style and size, placement on the page, formal or playful lettering) stand out?

What to Do	Some Questions to Ask
	• How much of the copy is devoted to product information or argument about superiority of the product or service?
	• How much of the copy helps create a field of values, beliefs, aspirations?
	• How do the words contribute to the "story" implied in the visual images?
	• What is the style of the language (for example, connotations, double entendres, puns)?

Sample Analysis of an Advertisement

With an understanding of possible photographic effects and the compositional features of ads, you now have all the background knowledge needed to begin doing your own analysis of ads. To illustrate how an analysis of an ad can reveal the ad's persuasive strategies, we show you our analysis of an ad for Coors Light (Figure 8.15) that ran in a variety of women's magazines in the mid-1990s. The marketers aimed to attract a new target audience—twenty-something or thirty-something middle-class women—and decided that print ads in magazines constituted the best medium.

This Coors Light ad uses an unusual strategy to target young adult women. Unlike typical beer ads aimed at men, which feature beach girls in bikinis or men bonding together on fishing trips or in sports bars, this Coors Light ad with its "Sam and Me" theme associates beer drinking with the warm friendship of a man and a woman.

Part of the ad's emotional appeal is the totally relaxed "story" shown in the image. The ad reveals a man and a woman, probably in their early- to mid-twenties, in relaxed conversation; they are sitting casually on a tabletop, with their legs resting on chair seats. The woman is wearing casual pants, a summery cotton top, and informal shoes. Her shoulder-length hair has a healthy, mussed appearance, and a braid comes across the front of her shoulder. She is turned away from the man, leans on her knees, and holds a bottle of Coors Light. Her sparkling eyes are looking up, and she smiles happily, as if reliving a pleasant memory. The man is wearing slacks, a cotton shirt with the sleeves rolled up, and scuffed tennis shoes with white socks. He also has a reminiscing smile on his face, and he leans on the woman's shoulder. The words "Coors Light. Just between friends." appear immediately below the picture next to a Coors Light can.

This ad creates its mirror effect by making it easy for women to identify with its story, which includes a good-looking but nonglamorous model and which is told from a woman's point of view (the "me" is the woman in the photograph). The ad's window effect is its opening onto a happy future. It appeals to women's

Sam and Me.

Me and Sam? We're just friends. Best friends, actually, since Mrs. Ainsley's first grade class when I let the hamster loose and Sam took the rap for me. I mean Sam's seen me in braces and I've seen him eat pizza. There's just way too much history here. Sam's my friend. The one I go to when I really need someone to talk to. I bring the Coors Light and Sam brings his shoulder. And sometimes it's Sam bringing the Coors Light and I'm doing the listening. Me and Sam? Together? I've never even thought about it. Okay, so I've thought about it.

Coors Light.
Just between friends.

FIGURE 8.15 Beer Ad Aimed at Women

desire for close friendships and relationships. Everything about the picture signifies long-established closeness and intimacy—old friends rather than lovers. The way the man leans on the woman shows her strength and independence. Additionally, the way they pose, with the woman slightly forward and sitting up more than the man, results in their taking up equal space in the picture. In many ads featuring male-female couples, the man appears larger and taller than the woman; this picture signifies mutuality and equality.

The words of the ad help interpret the relationship. Sam and the woman have been friends since the first grade, and they are reminiscing about old times. The relationship is thoroughly mutual. Sometimes he brings the Coors Light and sometimes she brings it; sometimes she does the listening and sometimes he does; sometimes she leans on his shoulder and sometimes he leans on hers. Sometimes the ad says, "Sam and me"; sometimes it says, "me and Sam." Even the "bad grammar" of "Sam and me" (rather than "Sam and I") suggests the lazy, relaxed absence of pretense or formality. "Sam" is a "buddy" kind of name rather than a romantic-hero name. But the last three lines of the copy give just a hint of potential romance: "Me and Sam? Together? I've never even thought about it. Okay, so I've thought about it."

Whereas beer ads targeting men portray women as sex objects, this ad appeals to many women's desire for relationships and for romance based on friendship. Its window function is mutuality and love rather than sexual acquisition.

The Coors Light ad was designed to appeal to young adult women. But cultural critics might also point out that the ad reproduces a worldview in which heterosexuality is the norm and in which women find their identities in romance and marriage. From the perspective of cultural criticism, then, advertisements are powerful cultural forces that both reflect cultural values and help construct and reproduce those values, including our sense of what is normal and not normal and our ideas about gender, race, and class. Identifying these cultural values in ads is an important part of ad analysis.

Analyzing Ads from Different Perspectives

FOR WRITING AND DISCUSSION

1. ***Credit card campaigns:*** Credit card companies have always faced a challenge: persuading consumers to buy with credit cards rather than cash and checks (with the expectation that many customers will not pay off the balance each month and thus pay substantial interest charges). Currently, banks and credit card companies must also overcome consumers' anger and distrust in this age of the banking crisis, overextended consumer debt, and high credit card interest.

   Choose one or more of the magazine ads for credit cards on pages 196–197, and analyze them using the strategies suggested in the chart on pages 191–193 as well as the ideas presented throughout this section (target audience, choice of medium, brand building, mirror and window strategy, and compositional features).

2. ***Cultural Criticism***
   a. Reexamine the same credit card ads from the perspectives of gender, class, and ethnicity. To what extent do these ads break or reinforce traditional notions of gender, race, and class?
   b. Look at the U.S. Army recruiting ad on page 273. Analyze this ad from the perspectives of gender, race, and class. Why does it pair a father and daughter rather than a mother and son?

FIGURE 8.16 MasterCharge Ad from the 1970s

    c. Locate a gallery of older ads on the Web, and choose several to analyze for perspectives on gender, race, and class. For example, you might analyze the Coppertone sunscreen ad from the 1950s, with its slogan "Don't be a Paleface" and "Tan—Don't Burn." The image of the dog tugging at the little girl's swimsuit bottoms became a national symbol of summertime fun for families. What treatment of race, class, or gender in these older ads, like the Coppertone ad, contributed to making them culturally acceptable at the time and would make them unacceptable now?

Missing the trudge to work: Free

Missing the Monday morning alarm: Free

Missing the British weather: Free

Not missing your nine favourite people: Priceless

FIGURE 8.17 Recent "Priceless: MasterCard" Ad

FIGURE 8.18 Recent American Express Card Ad

HANDY
IF YOU GET
ROBBED
IN AMERICA.

American Express® has travel offices in all corners of the globe. So should you have the misfortune to be relieved of your moneybelt we can provide emergency cash, and replace your card, usually within 24 hours. Now who would you rather have in your corner?

do more

Analysis of Two Visual Texts

Choose two documentary/news photographs, two paintings, or two print advertisements to analyze in a closed-form essay. Your two visual texts should have enough in common to facilitate meaningful comparisons. Show these images in your essay, but also describe your two visual texts in detail to highlight what you want viewers to see and to provide a foundation for your analysis. For this closed-form analysis, choose several key points of contrast as the focus. Your thesis statement should make a claim about key differences in the way that your chosen visual texts establish their purposes and achieve their persuasive effects.

Exploring and Generating Ideas for Your Analysis

For the subject of your analysis, your instructor may allow you to choose your own images or may provide them for you. If you choose your own, be sure to follow your instructor's guidelines. In choosing your visual texts, look for some important commonality that will enable you to concentrate on similarities and differences in your analysis:

- *Documentary or news photographs.* Analyze two photographs of an event from magazines with different political biases; two news photographs from articles addressing the same story from different angles of vision; or two images on Web sites presenting different perspectives on a recent controversial issue such as industrial farming or the war against terrorists.
- *Paintings.* Find two paintings with similar subject matter but different dominant impressions or emotional impacts.
- *Print ads.* Look for two ads for the same product (for example, cars, perfume, watches, shampoo) that are aimed at different target audiences or that make appeals to noticeably different value systems.

No matter what type of visual texts you are using, we suggest that you generate ideas and material for your analysis by using the question-asking strategies presented earlier in this chapter (see the strategies charts on pp. 176, 177–179, 183, and 191–193).

To help you generate more ideas, go detail by detail through your images, asking how the rhetorical effect would be different if some detail were changed:

- How would this documentary photo have a different effect if the homeless man were lying on the sidewalk instead of leaning against the doorway?
- Why did the artist blur images in the background rather than make them more distinct?
- What if the admakers had chosen a poodle rather than a black Lab? What if this model were a person of color rather than white?

FIGURE 8.19 Framework for an Analysis of Two Visuals

Introduction	• Hooks readers' interest; • Gives background on the two visual texts you are analyzing; • Sets up the similarities; • Poses the question your paper will address; • Ends with initial mapping in the form of a purpose or thesis statement.
General description of your two visual texts (ads, photographs, paintings)	• Describes each visual text in turn.
Analysis of the two visual texts	• Analyzes and contrasts each text in turn, using the ideas you generated from your observations, question asking, and close examination.
Conclusion	• Returns to the big picture for a sense of closure; • Makes final comments about the significance of your analysis.

Shaping and Drafting Your Analysis

Your closed-form essay should be fairly easy to organize at the big-picture level, but each part will require its own organic organization depending on the main points of your analysis. At the big-picture level, you can generally follow a structure like the one shown in Figure 8.19.

If you get stuck, we recommend that you write your rough draft rapidly, without worrying about gracefulness or correctness, merely trying to capture your initial ideas. Many people like to begin with the description of the two visual texts and then write the analysis before writing the introduction and conclusion. After you have written your draft, put it aside for a while before you begin revising.

Revising

Most experienced writers make global changes in their drafts when they revise, especially when they are doing analytical writing. The act of writing a rough draft generally leads to the discovery of more ideas. You may also realize that some of your original ideas aren't clearly developed or that the draft feels scattered or disorganized.

We recommend that you ask your classmates for a peer review of your draft early in the revising process to help you enhance the clarity and depth of your analysis.

Questions for Peer Review

In addition to the generic peer review questions explained in Skill 11.4, ask your peer reviewers to address these questions:

1. How well do the title, introduction, and thesis set up an academic analysis?
2. Where does the writer capture your interest and provide necessary background information? How might the writer more clearly pose the question to be addressed and map out the analysis?
3. Where could the writer describe the visual texts more clearly so that readers can "see" them?
4. How has the writer established the complexity of the texts and their commonalities and differences?
5. How well has the writer used the questions about angle of vision, artistic techniques, and compositional features presented in this chapter to achieve a detailed and insightful analysis of the texts? Where could the writer add more specific details about settings, props, furniture, posing of characters, facial expressions, manners of dress, and so forth?
6. In what ways could the writer improve this analysis by clarifying, deepening, expanding, or reorganizing the analysis? How has the writer helped you understand something new about these two texts?

Our reading is student Lydia Wheeler's analytical essay written for the writing project in this chapter. It analyzes two documentary photos focused on economic hardship and displacement. One photo, taken by photographer Stephen Crowley, accompanied a *New York Times* story about a mother and her daughters in the 2008 recession caused by the collapse of the housing bubble in the United States. The subject, Isabel Bermudez, was subsisting on food stamps at the time of the story, unable to find a job; previously she had supported her daughters with a six-figure salary. Then the market collapsed, she lost her job, and shortly afterward she lost her house. The second photo is a famous image taken in 1936 in Nipoma, California, during the Great Depression. The photo is part of the *Migrant Mother* series by photographer Dorothea Lange. Lydia decided to examine the original newspaper contexts for these photographs and to approach them as depictions of women's experiences of economic crisis.

Lydia Wheeler (student)
Two Photographs Capture Women's Economic Misery

1   During economic crises, the hardship of individuals is often presented to us as statistics and facts: number of bankruptcies, percentage of the population living below the poverty line, and foreclosures or unemployment rates. Although this numerical data can be shocking, it usually remains abstract and impersonal. In contrast, photographers such as Stephen Crowley and Dorothea Lange help us visualize the human suffering involved in the economic conditions, skillfully evoking the emotional, as well as the physical, reality of their subjects. Crowley's color photograph, first published January 2, 2010, in a *New York Times* article titled "Living on Nothing but Food Stamps," is captioned "Isabel Bermudez, who has two daughters and no cash income." Lange's black and white photograph was commissioned by the Resettlement Agency to document Americans living in the Great Depression; she originally captioned it *Destitute pea pickers in California; a 32 year old mother of seven children. February 1936.* However, in March of the same year, the *San Francisco Times* published Lange's photograph in an article demanding aid for workers like Florence Owens Thompson, the central subject of the picture. Once published, the photograph became famous and was nicknamed *Migrant Mother.* A close look at these two photos shows that through their skillful use of photographic elements such as focus, framing, orientation, and shape, Stephen Crowley and Dorothea Lange capture the unique emotional and physical realities of their subjects, eliciting compassion and admiration, respectively.

2   Stephen Crowley's photograph of a mother sitting in a room, perhaps the dining room of her house, and her young daughter standing and reaching out to comfort her sets up contrasts and tensions that underscore loss and convey grief. The accompanying article explains that Isabel Bermudez, whose income from real estate once amply supported her family, now has no income or prospect for employment and relies

entirely on food stamps. A careful examination of Crowley's photograph implies this loss by hinting that Bermudez's wealth is insecure.

3   The framing, distance, and focus of Crowley's photograph emphasize this vanished wealth and the emotional pain. The image is a medium close up with its human subjects to the side, surrounding them with empty space and hints of expensive furnishings. While part of the foreground is sharply focused, the background is blurry and unfocused. There is a suggestion that the room is spacious. Further, the high, decorative backs of the room's chairs, the repetitive design decorating the bookshelf on the frame's left, and the houseplant next to the bookshelf show that the room is well furnished, even luxurious. Bermudez and her daughter match their surroundings in being elegantly dressed. Bermudez looks across the room as if absorbed in her troubles; her daughter looks intently at her. Viewers' eyes are drawn to Bermudez's dark dress and her pearl necklace and earrings. However, the ostensible comfort of Bermudez and her surroundings starkly contrasts with her grief.

4   Crowley heightens this contrast and tension through the subjects' orientation and the space between them. The space between Bermudez and her daughter is one of the photograph's dominant features, but it contains only out-of-focus objects in the background. Neither figure is centered in the photo; neither looks at the camera. Consequently, the viewers' attention moves back and forth between them, creating a sense of uneasiness. The meaning of this photo is focused not on what Bermudez has but on what she has lost.

Isabel Bermudez, who has two daughters and no cash income, by Stephen Crowley

Destitute pea pickers in California; a 32 year old mother of seven children
[*Migrant Mother*] by Dorothea Lange

5   Crowley also evokes sympathy and compassion for his subjects with his choice of angle, scale, and detail. The photograph's slightly high angle makes viewers look down—literally—on Bermudez, making her appear vulnerable and powerless and reinforcing the pathos. The most striking bid for compassion is the tears streaming down Bermudez's well made-up face. The contrast between her tidy appearance and the tear tracks on her face suggest overwhelming sadness. The poignancy of her apparent breakdown is heightened by her somber daughter's attempt to wipe away

the tears on her mother's face. Crowley's decisions regarding *Isabel's* composition create an image that is highly disturbing.

6   In contrast to Crowley's photograph, Lange's *Migrant Mother*—through its content, focus, frame, rhythm, and angle—conveys long-standing poverty. Yet through this image of inescapable poverty pressing upon its subjects, it evokes admiration for this mother.

7   Lange's frame and focus generate much of the intensity of *Migrant Mother*. This photo is also a medium close up, but Lange's frame is tight with no open space. The lack of this openness cramps Lange's subjects and creates a claustrophobic feel intensified by the number of subjects shown—four to *Isabel's* two. There is almost no background. The subjects filling the foreground are crowded and sharply focused. The contrast between crowded foreground and empty background exaggerates the former and adds a touch of loneliness to *Migrant Mother*; this mother has no resources besides herself. Additionally, the subjects of *Migrant Mother* almost epitomize poverty: their hair is messy and uncombed, their skin dirt-stained. Even their clothes are worn—from the hem of Thompson's frayed sleeve to the smudges on her baby's blanket, Lange's photograph shows that Thompson can barely afford functional items.

8   *Migrant Mother's* circular lines also create a sense of sameness, stagnation, and hopelessness. Thompson's face draws viewers' eyes as the dominant feature, and Lange has ringed it with several arcs. The parentheses of her standing children's bodies, the angle of her baby in its blanket, and the arc of her dark hair form a ring that hems Thompson in and creates a circular path for the eyes of viewers. Seen with the obvious destitution of Lange's subjects, this repetition is threatening and grimly promises that it will be difficult, if not impossible, for this family to escape its poverty.

9   Like Crowley's *Isabel*, the impact of Lange's *Migrant Mother* derives from both the tragedy of her subjects' situation and their reactions. Lange uses angle and scale to generate sympathy and admiration for Thompson's strength. Once again we see a slightly high angle highlighting the subjects' vulnerability, which Lange reinforces with the slender necks of Thompson's children and a glimpse of her brassiere. However, Lange then contrasts this vulnerability with Thompson's strength, fostering viewers' admiration rather than compassion. *Migrant Mother's* scale, for example, exaggerates rather than diminishes Thompson's size: the photograph's frame focuses viewers' attention on the mother, who looks large, compared to her children. Additionally, Lange's subject literally supports the bodies of the children surrounding her. Unlike Bermudez, Thompson sits tall as a pillar of strength for her vulnerable children. Even her expression—worried but dry eyed—fosters admiration and respect in viewers. By juxtaposing Thompson's vulnerability with her strength, Lange creates a photograph that conveys both its subjects' poverty and their stoicism in facing the Great Depression.

10   Lange and Crowley guide viewer's reactions to their photographs through careful control of the elements that influence our emotional responses to their work. Though they both show women in economic crises, these artists are able to convey the distinct realities of their subjects' situations and consequently send viewers away in different emotional states: one of compassion, one of admiration. The fame and veneration of Lange's *Migrant Mother* is a testament to her ability to evoke desired emotions. The

photograph was exhibited at the Museum of Modern Art in 1941 and again in 1955, and was co-opted by countless movements since it was first published. Whether Crowley's *Isabel* will achieve similar fame for epitomizing this generation's economic crisis remains to be seen, but both photographs certainly succeed in delivering strong, lasting emotional statements.

THINKING CRITICALLY
about "Two Photographs Capture Women's Economic Misery"

1. What photographic elements has Lydia chosen to emphasize in her analysis of each of these photos?

2. What parts of Lydia's analysis help you see and understand these photos with greater insight? Do you agree with her choice of important elements and her analysis of their effects?

3. If you were analyzing these photos, what features would you choose to compare and stress?

WRITING A CLASSICAL ARGUMENT

The need for argument arises whenever members of a community disagree on an issue. Classical rhetoricians believed that the art of arguing is essential for good citizenship. If disputes can be resolved through exchange of perspectives, negotiation of differences, and flexible seeking of the best solutions to a problem, then nations won't have to resort to war or individuals to fisticuffs.

The writing project for this chapter introduces you to a classical way of arguing. Your goal is to persuade your audience to adopt your position or at least to regard it more openly or favorably.

In this chapter, you will learn to:

- take a stand on an issue
- offer reasons and evidence in support of your position
- summarize and respond to alternative views

What Is Argument?

The study of argumentation involves two components: truth seeking and persuasion:

- By *truth seeking,* we mean a diligent, open-minded, and responsible search for the best course of action or solution to a problem, taking into account all the available information and alternative points of view.
- By *persuasion,* we mean the art of making a claim* on an issue and justifying it convincingly so that the audience's initial resistance to your position is overcome and they are moved toward your position.

These two components of argument seem paradoxically at odds: Truth seeking asks us to relax our certainties and be willing to change our views; persuasion asks us to be certain, to be committed to our claims, and to get others to change their views. We can overcome this paradox if we dispel two common but misleading views of argument. The most common view is that argument is a fight as in "I just got into a horrible argument with my roommate." This view of argument as a fist-waving, shouting match in which you ridicule anyone who disagrees with you (popularized by radio and television talk shows and the Internet) entirely disregards argument as truth seeking, but it also misrepresents

*By long-standing tradition, the thesis statement of an argument is often called its "claim."

argument as persuasion because it polarizes people, rather than promoting understanding, new ways of seeing, and change.

Another common but misleading view is that argument is a pro/con debate modeled after high school or college debate matches. Although debating can be an excellent way to develop critical thinking skills, it misrepresents argument as a two-sided contest with winners and losers. Because controversial issues involve many different points of view, not just two, reducing an issue to pro/con positions distorts the complexity of the disagreement. Instead of thinking of *both* sides of an issue, we need to think of *all* sides. Equally troublesome, the debate image invites us to ask, "Who won the debate?" rather than "What is the best solution to the question that divides us?" The best solution might be a compromise between the two debaters or an undiscovered third position. The debate image tends to privilege the confident extremes in a controversy rather than the complex and muddled middle.

From our perspective, the best image for understanding argument is neither "fight" nor "debate" but the deliberations of a committee representing a wide spectrum of community voices charged with finding the best solution to a problem. From this perspective, argument is both a *process* and a *product.* As a process, argument is an act of inquiry characterized by fact-finding, information gathering, and consideration of alternative points of view. As a product, it is someone's contribution to the conversation at any one moment—a turn taking in a conversation, a formal speech, or a written position paper such as the one you will write for this chapter. The goal of argument as process is truth seeking; the goal of argument as product is persuasion. When members of a diverse committee are willing to argue persuasively for their respective points of view but are simultaneously willing to listen to other points of view and to change or modify their positions in light of new information or better arguments, then both components of argument are fully in play.

We cannot overemphasize the importance of both truth seeking and persuasion to your professional and civic life. Truth seeking makes you an informed and judicious employee and a citizen who delays decisions until a full range of evidence and alternative views are aired and examined. Persuasion gives you the power to influence the world around you, whether through letters to the editor or blogs on political issues or through convincing position papers for professional life. Whenever an organization needs to make a major decision, those who can think flexibly and write persuasively can wield great influence.

Exploring Classical Argument

An effective way to appreciate argument as both truth seeking and persuasion is to address an issue that is new to you and then watch how your own views evolve. Your initial position will probably reflect what social scientists sometimes call your personal *ideology*—that is, a network of basic values, beliefs, and assumptions that tend to guide your view of the world. However, if you adopt a truth-seeking attitude, your initial position may evolve as the conversation progresses. In fact, the conversation may even cause changes in some of your basic beliefs, since ideologies aren't set in stone and since many of us have unre-solved allegiance to competing ideologies that may be logically inconsistent (for example, a belief in freedom of speech combined with a belief that hate speech should be banned). In this exercise we ask you to keep track of how your views change and to note what causes the change.

The case we present for discussion involves ethical treatment of animals.

> **Situation:** A bunch of starlings build nests in the attic of a family's house, gaining access to the attic through a torn vent screen. Soon the eggs hatch, and every morning at sunrise the family is awakened by the sound of birds squawking and wings beating against rafters as the starlings fly in and out of the house to feed the hatchlings. After losing considerable early morning sleep, the family repairs the screen. Unable to get in and out, the parent birds are unable to feed their young. The birds die within a day. Is this cruelty to animals?

1. Freewrite your initial response to this question. Was the family's act an instance of cruelty to animals (that is, was their act ethically justifiable or not)?

2. Working in small groups or as a whole class, share your freewrites and then try to reach a group consensus on the issue. During this conversation (argu-ment as process), listen carefully to your classmates' views and note places where your own initial views begin to evolve.

3. So far we have framed this issue as an after-the-fact yes/no question: Is the family guilty of cruelty to animals? But we can also frame it as an open-ended, before-the-fact question: "What should the family have done about the starlings in the attic?" Suppose you are a family member discussing the starlings at dinner, prior to the decision to fix the vent screen. Make a list of your family's other options and try to reach class consensus on the two or three best alternative solutions.

4. At the end of the discussion, do another freewrite exploring how your ideas evolved during the discussion. What insights did you get about the twin components of argument, truth seeking and persuasion?

Understanding Classical Argument

Having introduced you to argument as both process and product, we now turn to the details of effective argumentation. To help orient you, we begin by describing the typical stages that mark students' growth as arguers.

Stages of Development: Your Growth as an Arguer

We have found that when we teach argument in our classes, students typically proceed through identifiable stages as their argumentative skills increase. While these stages may or may not describe your own development, they suggest the skills you should strive to acquire.

- **Stage 1: Argument as personal opinion.** At the beginning of instruction in argument, students typically express strong personal opinions but have trouble justifying their opinions with reasons and evidence and often create short, undeveloped arguments that are circular, lacking in evidence, and insulting to those who disagree. The following freewrite, written by a student first confronting the starling case, illustrates this stage:

> The family shouldn't have killed the starlings because that is really wrong! I mean that act was disgusting. It makes me sick to think how so many people are just willing to kill something for no reason at all. How are these parents going to teach their children values if they just go out and kill little birds for no good reason?!! This whole family is what's wrong with America!

This writer's opinion is passionate and heartfelt, but it provides neither reasons nor evidence why someone else should hold the same opinion.

- ***Stage 2: Argument structured as claim supported by one or more reasons.*** This stage represents a quantum leap in argumentative skill because the writer can now produce a rational plan containing point sentences (the reasons) and particulars (the evidence). The writer who produced the previous freewrite later developed a structure like this:

  The family's act constituted cruelty to animals

  - because the starlings were doing minimal harm.
  - because other options were available.
  - because the way they killed the birds caused needless suffering.

- ***Stage 3: Increased attention to truth seeking.*** In stage 3 students become increasingly engaged with the complexity of the issue as they listen to their classmates' views, conduct research, and evaluate alternative perspectives and stances. They are often willing to change their positions when they see the power of other arguments.
- ***Stage 4: Ability to articulate the unstated assumptions underlying their arguments.*** As we show later in this chapter, each reason in a writer's argument is based on an assumption, value, or belief (often unstated) that the audience must accept if the argument is to be persuasive. Often the writer needs to state these assumptions explicitly and support them. At this stage students identify and analyze their own assumptions and those of their intended audiences. Students gain increased skill at accommodating alternative views through refutation or concession.
- ***Stage 5: Ability to link an argument to the values and beliefs of the intended audience.*** In this stage students are increasingly able to link their arguments to their audience's values and beliefs and to adapt structure and tone to the resistance level of their audience. Students also appreciate how delayed-thesis arguments or other psychological strategies can be more effective than closed-form arguments when addressing hostile audiences.

The rest of this chapter helps you progress through these stages. Although you can read the remainder in one sitting, we recommend that you break your reading into sections, going over the material slowly and applying it to your own ideas in progress. Let the chapter's concepts and explanations sink in gradually, and return to them periodically for review. This section on "Understanding Classical Argument" comprises a compact but comprehensive course in argumentation.

Creating an Argument Frame: A Claim with Reasons

Somewhere in the writing process, whether early or late, you need to create a frame for your argument. This frame includes a clear question that focuses the argument, your claim, and one or more supporting reasons. Often your reasons, stated as *because* clauses, can be attached to your claim to provide a working thesis statement.

Finding an Arguable Issue At the heart of any argument is an **issue,** which we can define as a question that invites more than one reasonable answer and thus leads to perplexity or disagreement. This requirement excludes disagreements based on personal tastes, where no shared criteria can be developed ("Baseball is more fun than soccer"). It also excludes purely private questions because issues arise out of disagreements in communities.

Issue questions are often framed as yes/no choices, especially when they appear on ballots or in courtrooms: Should gay marriage be legalized? Should the federal government place a substantial tax on gasoline to elevate its price? Is this defendant guilty of armed robbery? Just as frequently, they can be framed openly, inviting many different possible answers: What should our city do about skateboarders in downtown pedestrian areas? How can we best solve the energy crisis?

It is important to remember that framing an issue as a yes/no question does not mean that all points of view fall neatly into pro/con categories. Although citizens may be forced to vote yes or no on a proposed ballot initiative, they can support or oppose the initiative for a variety of reasons. Some may vote happily for the initiative, others vote for it only by holding their noses, and still others oppose it vehemently but for entirely different reasons. To argue effectively, you need to appreciate the wide range of perspectives from which people approach the yes/no choice.

How you frame your question necessarily affects the scope and shape of your argument itself. In our exploratory exercise we framed the starling question in two ways: (1) Was the family guilty of cruelty to animals? and (2) What should the family have done about the starlings? Framed in the first way, your argument would have to develop criteria for "cruelty to animals" and then argue whether the family's actions met those criteria. Framed in the second way, you could argue for your own solution to the problem, ranging from doing nothing (waiting for the birds to grow up and leave, then fixing the screen) to climbing into the attic and drowning the birds so that their deaths are quick and painless. Or you could word the question in a broader, more philosophical way: When are humans justified in killing animals? Or you could focus on a subissue: When can an animal be labeled a "pest"?

FOR
WRITING
AND
DISCUSSION

Identifying Arguable Issues

1. Working individually, make a list of several communities that you belong to and then identify one or more questions currently being contested within those communities. (If you have trouble, check your local campus and city newspapers or an organizational newsletter; you'll quickly discover a wealth of contested issues.) Then share your list with classmates.
2. Pick two or three issues of particular interest to you, and try framing them in different ways: as broad or narrow questions, as open-ended or yes/no questions. Place several examples on the chalkboard for class discussion.

Stating a Claim Your **claim** is the position you want to take on the issue. It is your brief, one-sentence answer to your issue question:

> The family was not ethically justified in killing the starlings.
> The city should build skateboarding areas with ramps in all city parks.
> The federal government should substantially increase its taxes on gasoline.

You will appreciate argument as truth seeking if you find that your claim evolves as you think more deeply about your issue and listen to alternative views. Be willing to rephrase your claim to soften it or refocus it or even to reverse it as you progress through the writing process.

Articulating Reasons

Your claim, which is the position you take on an issue, needs to be supported by reasons and evidence. A **reason** (sometimes called a "premise") is a subclaim that supports your main claim. In speaking or writing, a reason is usually linked to the claim with such connecting words as *because, therefore, so, consequently,* and *thus.* In planning your argument, a powerful strategy for developing reasons is to harness the grammatical power of the conjunction *because;* think of your reasons as *because* clauses attached to your claim. Formulating your reasons in this way allows you to create a thesis statement that breaks your argument into smaller parts, each part devoted to one of the reasons.

For advice on how much of your supporting argument you should summarize in your thesis statement, see Skill 12.4 on effective introductions.

Suppose, for example, that you are examining the issue "Should the government legalize hard drugs such as heroin and cocaine?" Here are several different points of view on this issue, each expressed as a claim with *because* clauses:

ONE VIEW

Cocaine and heroin should be legalized

- because legalizing drugs will keep the government out of people's private lives.
- because keeping these drugs illegal has the same negative effects on our society that alcohol prohibition did in the 1920s.

ANOTHER VIEW

Cocaine and heroin should be legalized
- because taking drug sales out of the hands of drug dealers would reduce street violence.
- because decriminalization would cut down on prison overcrowding and free police to concentrate on dangerous crime rather than on finding drug dealers.
- because elimination of underworld profits would change the economic structure of the underclass and promote shifts to socially productive jobs and careers.

STILL ANOTHER VIEW

The government should not legalize heroin and cocaine
- because doing so will lead to an increase in drug users and addicts.
- because doing so will send the message that it is okay to use hard drugs.

Although the yes/no framing of this question seems to reduce the issue to a two-position debate, many different value systems are at work here. The first pro-legalization argument, libertarian in perspective, values maximum individual freedom. The second argument—although it too supports legalization—takes a community perspective valuing the social benefits of eliminating the black market drug-dealing culture. In the same way, individuals could oppose legalization for a variety of reasons.

FOR WRITING AND DISCUSSION

Generating *Because* Clauses

Working in small groups or as a whole class, generate a list of reasons for and against one or more of the following yes/no claims. State your reasons as *because* clauses. Think of as many *because* clauses as possible by imagining a wide variety of perspectives on the issue.

1. The school year for grades 1 through 12 should be lengthened to eleven months.
2. The federal government should place a substantial tax on gasoline.
3. The United States should adopt a single-payer, government-financed health system like that of Canada.
4. Playing violent video games is a harmful influence on teenage boys. [or] Women's fashion and style magazines (such as *Glamour* or *Seventeen*) are harmful influences on teenage girls.
5. The war on terror requires occasional use of "enhanced interrogation techniques" on some detainees.

Articulating Underlying Assumptions

So far, we have focused on the frame of an argument as a claim supported with one or more reasons. Shortly, we will proceed to the flesh and muscle of an argument, which is the evidence you use to support your reasons. But before turning to evidence, we need to look at another crucial part of an argument's frame: its *underlying assumptions*.

What Do We Mean by an Underlying Assumption? Every time you link a claim with a reason, you make a silent assumption that may need to be articulated and examined. Consider this argument:

> The family was justified in killing the starlings because starlings are pests.

To support this argument, the writer would first need to provide evidence that starlings are pests (examples of the damage they do and so forth). But the persuasiveness of the argument rests on the underlying assumption that it is okay to kill pests. If an audience doesn't agree with that assumption, then the argument flounders unless the writer articulates the assumption and defends it. The complete frame of the argument must therefore include the underlying assumption.

> **Claim:** The family was justified in killing the starlings.
>
> **Reason:** Because starlings are pests.
>
> **Underlying assumption:** It is ethically justifiable to kill pests.

It is important to examine the underlying assumption that connects any reason to its claim *because you must determine whether your audience will accept that assumption. If not, you need to make it explicit and support it.* Think of the underlying assumption as a general principle, rule, belief, or value that connects the reason to the claim. It answers your reader's question, "Why, if I accept your reason, should I accept your claim?"*

Here are a few more examples:

> **Claim with reason:** Women should be allowed to join combat units because the image of women as combat soldiers would help society overcome gender stereotyping.
>
> **Underlying assumption:** It is good to overcome gender stereotyping.
>
> **Claim with reason:** The government should not legalize heroin and cocaine because doing so will lead to an increase in drug users.
>
> **Underlying assumption:** It is bad to increase the number of drug users.
>
> **Claim with reason:** The family was guilty of cruelty to animals in the starling case because less drastic means of solving the problem were available.
>
> **Underlying assumption:** A person should choose the least drastic means to solve a problem.

*Our explanation of argument structure is influenced by the work of philosopher Stephen Toulmin, who viewed argument as a dynamic courtroom drama where opposing attorneys exchange arguments and cross-examinations before a judge and jury. Although we use Toulmin's strategies for analyzing an argument structure, we have chosen not to use his specialized terms, which include *warrant* (the underlying assumption connecting a reason to a claim), *grounds* (the evidence that supports the claim), *backing* (the evidence and subarguments that support the warrant), *conditions of rebuttal* (all the ways that skeptics could attack an argument or all the conditions under which the argument wouldn't hold), and finally *qualifier* (an indication of the strength of the claim). However, your instructor may prefer to use these terms and in that case may provide you with more explanation and examples.

Identifying Underlying Assumptions

Identify the underlying assumptions in each of the following claims with reasons.

1. Cocaine and heroin should be legalized because legalizing drugs will keep the government out of people's private lives.
2. The government should raise gasoline taxes because the higher price would substantially reduce gasoline consumption.
3. The government should not raise gasoline taxes because the higher price would place undo hardship on low-income people.
4. The government should not raise gasoline taxes because other means of reducing gasoline consumption would be more effective.
5. The government is justified in detaining suspected terrorists indefinitely without charging them with a crime because doing so may prevent another terrorist attack.

Using Evidence Effectively

Inside your arguments, each of your reasons (as well as any underlying assumptions that you decide to state explicitly and defend) needs to be supported either by subarguments or by evidence. By "evidence" we mean facts, examples, summaries of research articles, statistics, testimony, or other relevant data that will persuade your readers to accept your reasons. Note that evidence always exists within a rhetorical context; as a writer you select and shape the evidence that will best support your position, knowing that skeptics may point to evidence that you did not select. Evidence is thus not the same as "proof"; used ethically, evidence presents the best case for your claim without purporting to be the whole truth.

Evidence can sometimes come from personal experience, but in most cases it comes from your own field or library research. The kinds of evidence most often used in argument are the following:

Factual Data Factual data can provide persuasive support for your arguments. (Keep in mind that writers always select their facts through an angle of vision, so the use of facts doesn't preclude skeptics from bringing in counterfacts.) Here is how evolutionary biologist Olivia Judson used factual data to support her point that malaria-carrying mosquitoes cause unacceptable harm to human lives and wealth.

> Each year, malaria kills at least one million people and causes more than 300 million cases of acute illness. For children worldwide, it's one of the leading causes of death. The economic burden is significant too: malaria costs Africa more than $12 billion in lost growth each year. In the United States, hundreds of millions of dollars are spent every year on mosquito control.

Examples An example from personal experience can often be used to support a reason. Here is how student writer Ross Taylor used personal experience to argue that paintball is safe even though accidents can happen. (You can read his complete essay on pp. 234–237.)

I admit that paintball can be dangerous and that accidents do happen. I personally had a friend lose an eye after inadvertently shooting himself in the eye from a very close range. The fact of the matter is that he made a mistake by looking down the barrel of a loaded gun and the trigger malfunctioned. Had he been more careful or worn the proper equipment, he most likely would have been fine. During my first organized paintball experience I was hit in the goggles by a very powerful gun and felt no pain. The only discomfort came from having to clean all the paint off my goggles after the game. When played properly, paintball is an incredibly safe sport.

Besides specific examples like this, writers sometimes invent hypothetical examples, or *scenarios,* to illustrate an issue or hypothesize about the consequences of an event. (Of course, you must tell your reader that the example or scenario is hypothetical.)

Summaries of Research Another common way to support an argument is to summarize research articles. Here is how a student writer, investigating whether menopausal women should use hormone replacement therapy to combat menopausal symptoms, used one of several research articles in her paper. The student began by summarizing research studies showing possible dangers of hormone replacement therapy. She then made the following argument:

> Another reason not to use hormone replacement therapy is that other means are available to ease menopausal symptoms such as hot flashes, irritability, mood changes, and sleep disturbance. One possible alternative treatment is acupuncture. One study (Cohen, Rousseau, and Carey) revealed that a randomly selected group of menopausal women receiving specially designed acupuncture treatment showed substantial decreases in menopausal symptoms as compared to a control group. What was particularly persuasive about this study was that both the experimental group and the control group received acupuncture, but the needle insertion sites for the experimental group were specifically targeted to relieve menopausal symptoms whereas the control group received acupuncture at sites used to promote general well-being. The researchers concluded that "acupuncture may be recommended as a safe and effective therapy for reducing menopausal hot flushes as well as contributing to the reduction in sleep disruptions" (299).*

Statistics Another common form of evidence is statistics. Here is how one writer used statistics to argue that the federal government should raise fuel-efficiency standards placed on auto manufacturers:

> There is very little need for most Americans to drive huge SUVs. One recent survey found that 87 percent of four-wheel-drive SUV owners had never taken their SUVs off-road (Yacobucci). ... By raising fuel-efficiency standards, the government would force vehicle manufacturers to find a way to create more earth-friendly vehicles that would lower vehicle emissions and pollution. An article entitled "Update: What You Should Know Before Purchasing a New Vehicle" states that for

*The examples in this section use the MLA (Modern Language Association) style for documenting sources. See Chapter 14 for explanations of how to use both the MLA and APA (American Psychological Association) systems for citing and documenting sources. The complete bibliographic information for this article would be found in the "Works Cited" pages alphabetized under "Cohen."

every gallon of gasoline used by a vehicle, 20 to 28 pounds of carbon dioxide are released into the environment. This article further states that carbon dioxide emissions from automobiles are responsible for 20 percent of all carbon dioxide released into the atmosphere from human causes.

Just as writers select facts, examples, and research studies according to their angle of vision, so do they select and shape numerical data. In the above example, the writer focuses on the environmental harm caused by vehicles, especially SUVs. But you must always read statistics rhetorically. For example, the same statistical "fact" can be framed in different ways. There is a difference in focus and feel between these two ways of using the same data:

- "20 percent of human-caused CO_2 emissions come from automobiles" [puts automobiles in the foreground]
- "Although cars do cause some pollution, a full 80 percent of human-caused CO_2 emissions come from sources other than cars." [puts automobiles in the background]

Testimony Writers can also use expert testimony to bolster a case. The following passage from a student essay arguing in favor of therapeutic cloning uses testimony from a prominent physician and medical researcher. Part of the paragraph quotes this expert directly; another part paraphrases the expert's argument.

> As Dr. Gerald Fischbach, Executive Vice President for Health and Biomedical Sciences and Dean of Medicine at Columbia University, said in front of a United States Senate subcommittee: "New embryonic stem cell procedures could be vital in solving the persistent problem of a lack of genetically matched, qualified donors of organs and tissues that we face today." Fischbach goes on to say that this type of cloning could also lead to the discovery of cures for diseases such as ALS, Parkinson's disease, Alzheimer's disease, diabetes, heart disease, cancer, and possibly others.

Rather than provide direct research evidence that stem cell cloning might one day lead to cures for diseases, the writer draws on testimony from the dean of a prestigious medical school. Opponents of stem cell research might draw on other experts, selecting those who are skeptical of this claim.

Subarguments Sometimes writers support reasons not directly through data but through sequences of subarguments. Sometimes these subarguments develop a persuasive analogy, hypothesize about consequences, or simply advance the argument through a chain of connected points. In the following passage, taken from a philosophic article justifying torture under certain conditions, the author uses a subargument to support one of his main points—that a terrorist holding victims hostage has no "rights":

> There is an important difference between terrorists and their victims that should mute talk of the terrorist's "rights." The terrorist's victims are at risk unintentionally, not having asked to be endangered. But the terrorist knowingly initiated his actions. Unlike his victims, he volunteered for the risks of his deed. By threatening to kill for profit or idealism, he renounces civilized standards, and he can have no complaint if civilization tries to thwart him by whatever means necessary.

Rather than using direct empirical evidence, the author supports his point with a subargument showing how terrorists differ from victims and thus relinquish their claim to rights.

Evaluating Evidence: The STAR Criteria

To make your arguments as persuasive as possible, apply to your evidence what rhetorician Richard Fulkerson calls the STAR criteria (**S**ufficiency, **T**ypicality, **A**ccuracy, and **R**elevance),* as shown in the chart on this page.

It is often difficult to create arguments in which all your evidence fully meets the STAR criteria. Sometimes you need to proceed on evidence that might not be typical, verifiable, or as up-to-date as you would like. In such cases, you can often increase the effectiveness of your argument by qualifying your claim. Consider the difference between these two claims:

- **Strong claim:** Watching violent TV cartoons increases aggressive play behavior in boys.
- **Qualified claim:** Watching violent TV cartoons can increase aggressive play behavior in some boys.

To be made persuasive, the strong claim requires substantial evidence meeting the STAR criteria. In contrast, the qualified claim requires less rigorous evidence, perhaps only an example or two combined with the results of one study.

The STAR Criteria for Evaluating Evidence

STAR Criteria	Implied Question	Comments
Sufficiency	Is there enough evidence?	If you don't provide enough evidence, skeptical audiences can dismiss your claim as a "hasty generalization." To argue that marijuana is not a harmful drug, you would probably need more evidence than the results of one study or the testimony of a healthy pot smoker.
Typicality	Are the chosen data representative and typical?	If you choose extreme or rare-case examples, rather than typical and representative ones, your audience might accuse you of cherry-picking your data. Testimony from persons whose back pain was cured by yoga may not support the general claim that yoga is good for back pain.
Accuracy	Are the data accurate and up-to-date?	Providing recent, accurate data is essential for your own *ethos* as a writer. Data from 1998 on homelessness or inaccurately gathered data may be ineffective for a current policy argument.
Relevance	Are the data relevant to the claim?	Even though your evidence is accurate, up-to-date, and representative, if it's not pertinent to the claim, it will be ineffective. For example, evidence that nuclear waste is dangerous is not relevant to the issue of whether it can be stored securely in Yucca Mountain.

*Richard Fulkerson, *Teaching the Argument in Writing,* Urbana: National Council of Teachers of English, 1996, pp. 44–53. In this section we are indebted to Fulkerson's discussion.

See Skill 13.1 for advice on evaluating sources for reliability and bias.

As you gather evidence, consider also its source and the extent to which your audience will trust that source. While all data must be interpreted and hence are never completely impartial, careful readers are aware of how easily data can be skewed. Newspapers, magazines, blogs, and journals often have political biases and different levels of respectability. Generally, evidence from peer-reviewed scholarly journals is more highly regarded than evidence from secondhand sources. Particularly problematic is information gathered from Internet Web sites, which can vary widely in reliability and degree of bias.

Addressing Objections and Counterarguments

Having looked at the frame of an argument (claim, reasons, and underlying assumptions) and at the kinds of evidence used to flesh out the frame, let's turn now to the important concern of anticipating and responding to objections and counter-arguments. In this section, we show you an extended example of a student's anticipating and responding to a reader's objection. We then describe a planning schema that can help you anticipate objections and show you how to respond to counterarguments, either through refutation or concession. Finally, we show how your active imagining of alternative views can lead you to qualify your claim.

Anticipating Objections: An Extended Example   In our earlier discussions of the starling case, we saw how readers might object to the argument "The family was justified in killing the starlings because starlings are pests." What rankles these readers is the underlying assumption that it is okay to kill pests. Imagine an objecting reader saying something like this:

> It is *not* okay to get annoyed with a living creature, label it a "pest," and then kill it. This whole use of the term *pest* suggests that humans have the right to dominate nature. We need to have more reverence for nature. The ease with which the family solved their problem by killing living things sets a bad example for children. The family could have waited until fall and then fixed the screen.

Imagining such an objection might lead a writer to modify his or her claim. But if the writer remains committed to that claim, then he or she must develop a response. In the following example in which a student writer argues that it is okay to kill the starlings, note (1) how the writer uses evidence to show that starlings are pests; (2) how he summarizes a possible objection to his underlying assumption that killing pests is morally justified; and (3) how he supports his assumption with further arguments.

STUDENT ARGUMENT DEFENDING REASON AND UNDERLYING ASSUMPTION

Claim with reason

Evidence that starlings are pests

The family was justified in killing the starlings because starlings are pests. Starlings are nonindigenous birds that drive out native species and multiply rapidly. When I searched "starlings pests" on Google, I discovered thousands of Web sites dealing with starlings as pests. Starlings are hated by farmers and gardeners because huge flocks of them devour newly planted seeds in spring as well as fruits and berries at harvest. A flock of starlings can devastate a cherry orchard in a few days. As invasive nesters, starlings can also damage attics by tearing up insulation and defecating on stored items. Many of the Web site articles focused on ways to kill off starling populations. In killing the starlings, the family was protecting its own property and reducing the population of these pests.

Many readers might object to my argument, saying that humans should have a reverence for nature and not quickly try to kill off any creature they label a pest. Further, these readers might say that even if starlings are pests, the family could have waited until fall to repair the attic or found some other means of protecting their property without having to kill the baby starlings. I too would have waited until fall if the birds in the attic had been swallows or some other native species without starlings' destructiveness and propensity for unchecked population growth. But starlings should be compared to rats or mice. We set traps for rodents because we know the damage they cause when they nest in walls and attics. We don't get sentimental trying to save the orphaned rat babies. In the same way, we are justified in eliminating starlings as soon as they begin infesting our houses.

Summary of a possible objection

Response to the objection

In the preceding example, we see how the writer uses evidence to support his reason and then, anticipating readers' objection to his underlying assumption, summarizes that objection and provides a response to it. One might not be convinced by the argument, but the writer has done a good job of trying to support both his reason (starlings are pests) and his underlying assumption (it is morally justifiable to kill at least some pests).

Using a Planning Schema to Anticipate Objections In the previous example, the student's arguing strategy was triggered by his anticipation of reader objections. Note that a skeptical audience can attack an argument by attacking either a writer's reasons or a writer's underlying assumptions. This knowledge allows us to create a planning schema that can help writers develop a persuasive argument. This schema encourages writers to articulate their argument frame (claim, reason, and underlying assumption) and then to imagine what kinds of evidence or arguments could be used to support both the reason and the underlying assumption. Equally important, the schema encourages writers to anticipate counterarguments by imagining how skeptical readers might object to the writer's reason or underlying assumption or both. To create the schema, simply make a chart with slots for each of these elements. Here is how another student writer used this schema to plan an argument on the starling case:

CLAIM WITH REASON

The family showed cruelty to animals because the way they killed the birds caused needless suffering.

UNDERLYING ASSUMPTION

If it is necessary to kill an animal, then the killing should be done in the least painful way possible.

EVIDENCE TO SUPPORT REASON

First I've got to show how the way of killing the birds (starving them slowly) caused the birds to suffer. I've also got to show that this way of killing was needless since other means were available such as calling an exterminator who would remove the birds and either relocate them or kill them painlessly. If no other alternative was available, someone should have crawled into the attic and found a painless way to kill the birds.

EVIDENCE/ARGUMENTS TO SUPPORT UNDERLYING ASSUMPTIONS

I've got to convince readers it is wrong to make an animal suffer if you don't have to. Humans have a natural antipathy to needless suffering—our feeling of unease if we imagine cattle or chickens caused to suffer for our food rather than being cleanly and quickly killed. If a horse is incurably wounded, we put it to sleep rather then let it suffer. We are morally obligated to cause the least pain possible.

WAYS SKEPTICS MIGHT OBJECT

How could a reader object to my reason? A reader might say that the starlings didn't suffer much (baby birds don't feel pain). A reader might also object to my claim that other means were available: They might say there was no other way to kill the starlings. Poison may cause just as much suffering. Cost of exterminator is prohibitive.

How could a reader object to my underlying assumption? Perhaps the reader would say that my rule to cause the least pain possible does not apply to animal pests. In class, someone said that we shouldn't worry about the baby starlings any more than we would worry about killing baby rats. Laws of nature condemn millions of animals each year to death by starvation or by being eaten alive by other animals. Humans occasionally have to take their place within this tooth-and-claw natural system.

How many of the ideas from this schema would the writer use in her actual paper? That is a judgment call based on the writer's analysis of the audience. If this student's target audience includes classmates who think it is morally okay to kill pests by the most efficient means possible, then she should summarize her classmates' argument fairly and then try to convince them that humans are ethically called to rise above tooth-and-claw nature.

FOR WRITING AND DISCUSSION

Creating Argument Schemas

Working individually or in small groups, create a planning schema for the following arguments. For each claim with reason: (a) imagine the kinds of evidence needed to support the reason; (b) identify the underlying assumption; (c) imagine a strategy for supporting the assumption; and (d) anticipate possible objections to the reason and to the assumption.

1. ***Claim with reason:*** We should buy a hybrid car rather than an SUV with a HEMI engine because doing so will help the world save gasoline. (Imagine this argument aimed at your significant other, who has his or her heart set on a huge HEMI-powered SUV.)
2. ***Claim with reason:*** Gay marriage should be legalized because doing so will promote faithful, monogamous relationships among lesbians and gay men. (Aim this argument at supporters of traditional marriage.)
3. ***Claim with reason:*** The war in Iraq was justified because it rid the world of a hideous and brutal dictator. (Aim this argument at a critic of the war.)

Responding to Objections, Counterarguments, and Alternative Views

We have seen how a writer needs to anticipate alternative views that give rise to objections and counterarguments. Surprisingly, one of the best ways to approach counterarguments is to summarize them fairly. Make your imagined reader's best case against your argument. By resisting the temptation to distort a counterargument, you demonstrate a willingness to consider the issue from all sides. Moreover, summarizing a counterargument reduces your reader's tendency to say, "Yes, but have you thought of … ?" After you have summarized an objection or counterargument fairly and charitably, you must then decide how to respond to it. Your two main choices are to rebut it or concede to it.

Rebutting Opposing Views When rebutting or refuting an argument, you can question the argument's reasons and supporting evidence or the underlying assumptions or both. In the following student example, the writer summarizes her classmates' objections to abstract art and then analyzes shortcomings in their argument.

> Some of my classmates object to abstract art because it apparently takes no technical drawing talent. They feel that historically artists turned to abstract art because they lacked the technical drafting skills exhibited by Remington, Russell, and Rockwell. Therefore these abstract artists created an art form that anyone was capable of and that was less time consuming, and then they paraded it as artistic progress. But I object to the notion that these artists turned to abstraction because they could not do representative drawing. Many abstract artists, such as Picasso, were excellent draftsmen, and their early pieces show very realistic drawing skill. As his work matured, Picasso became more abstract in order to increase the expressive quality of his work. *Guernica* was meant as a protest against the bombing of that city by the Germans. To express the terror and suffering of the victims more vividly, he distorted the figures and presented them in a black and white journalistic manner. If he had used representational images and color—which he had the skill to do—much of the emotional content would have been lost and the piece probably would not have caused the demand for justice that it did.

Conceding to Opposing Views In some cases, an alternative view can be very strong. If so, don't hide that view from your readers; summarize it and concede to it.

Making concessions to opposing views is not necessarily a sign of weakness; in many cases, a concession simply acknowledges that the issue is complex and that your position is tentative. In turn, a concession can enhance a reader's respect for you and invite the reader to follow your example and weigh the strengths of your own argument charitably. Writers typically concede to opposing views with transitional expressions such as the following:

admittedly	I must admit that	I agree that	granted
even though	I concede that	while it is true that	

After conceding to an opposing view, you should shift to a different field of values where your position is strong and then argue for those new values. For example, adversaries of drug legalization argue plausibly that legalizing drugs would increase the number of users and addicts. If you support legalization, here is how you might deal with this point without fatally damaging your own argument:

> Opponents of legalization claim—and rightly so—that legalization will lead to an increase in drug users and addicts. I wish this weren't so, but it is. Nevertheless, the other benefits of legalizing drugs—eliminating the black market, reducing street crime, and freeing up thousands of police from fighting the war on drugs—more than outweigh the social costs of increased drug use and addiction, especially if tax revenues from drug sales are plowed back into drug education and rehabilitation programs.

The writer concedes that legalization will increase addiction (one reason for opposing legalization) and that drug addiction is bad (the underlying assumption for that reason). But then the writer redeems the case for legalization by shifting the argument to another field of values (the benefits of eliminating the black market, reducing crime, and so forth).

Qualifying Your Claim The need to summarize and respond to alternative views lets the writer see an issue's complexity and appreciate that no one position has a total monopoly on the truth. Consequently, writers often need to qualify their claims—that is, limit the scope or force of a claim to make it less sweeping and therefore less vulnerable. Consider the difference between the sentences "After-school jobs are bad for teenagers" and "After-school jobs are often bad for teenagers." The first claim can be refuted by one counterexample of a teenager who benefited from an after-school job. Because the second claim admits exceptions, it is much harder to refute. Unless your argument is airtight, you will want to limit your claim with qualifiers such as the following:

perhaps	maybe
in many cases	generally
tentatively	sometimes
often	usually
probably	likely
may *or* might (*rather than* is)	

You can also qualify a claim with an opening *unless* clause ("*Unless* your apartment is well soundproofed, you should not buy such a powerful stereo system").

Seeking Audience-Based Reasons

Much of the advice that we have presented so far can be consolidated into a single principle: Seek "audience-based reasons." By **audience-based reasons**, we mean reasons that depend on underlying assumptions, values, or beliefs that your targeted audience already holds. In such cases, you won't need to state and defend your underlying assumptions because the audience already accepts them. A good illustration comes from civil engineer David Rockwood's argument against wind power that we used in Chapter 1 (pp. 5–6). Rockwood's targeted readers are environmentalists who have high hopes for wind-generated electricity. Rockwood's final reason opposing wind power is that constructing thousands of wind towers will damage the pristine mountain environment. To environmentalists, this reason is powerful because its underlying assumption ("Preserving the environment is good") appeals to their values.

When you plan your argument, seek audience-based reasons whenever possible. Suppose, for example, that you are advocating the legalization of heroin and cocaine. If you know that your audience is concerned about street crime, then you can argue that legalization of drugs will make the streets safer.

We should legalize drugs *because doing so will make our streets safer:* It will cut down radically on street criminals seeking drug money, and it will free up narcotics police to focus on other kinds of crime.	Audience-based reason: Underlying assumption is that making our streets safer is a good thing—a value the audience already holds.

For another group of readers—those concerned about improving the quality of life for youths in inner cities—you might argue that legalization of drugs will lead to better lives for people in poor neighborhoods.

We should legalize drugs *because doing so will improve the lives of inner-city youth* by eliminating the lure of drug trafficking that tempts so many inner-city youth into crime.	Audience-based reason: Its underlying assumption is that it is good to improve the lives of inner-city youth.

Or if your audience is concerned about high taxes and government debt, you might say:

We should legalize drugs *because doing so will help us balance federal and state budgets:* It will decrease police and prison costs by decriminalizing narcotics; and it will eliminate the black market in drugs, allowing us to collect taxes on drug sales.	Audience-based reason: Assumes that it is a good thing to balance federal and state budgets.

In contrast, if you oppose legalizing drugs, you could appeal to those concerned about drug addiction and public health by using the following audience-based reason:

We should not legalize drugs *because doing so will increase the number of drug addicts and make drug use seem socially acceptable.*	Audience-based reason: Appeals to the underlying assumption that increasing the number of drug addicts and making drugs socially acceptable are bad things.

In each case, you move people toward your position by connecting your argument to their beliefs and values.

Appealing to *Ethos* and *Pathos*

When the classical rhetoricians examined ways that orators could persuade listeners, they focused on three kinds of proofs: *logos,* the appeal to reason; *ethos,* the appeal to the speaker's character; and *pathos,* the appeal to the emotions and the sympathetic imagination. We introduced you to these appeals in Chapter 3, Concept 9, because they are important rhetorical considerations in any kind of writing. Understanding how arguments persuade through *logos, ethos,* and *pathos* is particularly helpful when your aim is persuasion. So far in this chapter we have focused on *logos.* In this section we examine *ethos* and *pathos.*

Appeals to Ethos A powerful way to increase the persuasiveness of an argument is to gain your readers' trust. You appeal to *ethos* whenever you present yourself as credible and trustworthy. For most readers to accept your argument, they must perceive you as knowledgeable, trustworthy, and fair. In the following chart, we suggest ways to enhance your argument's *ethos:*

Strategies for Enhancing Your Argument's *Ethos*

What to Do	Explanation
Be knowledgeable by doing your homework.	Your credibility is enhanced when readers are convinced that you know your subject thoroughly.
Use evidence responsibly.	If you cherry-pick your evidence, you may be perceived as a propagandist rather than as a thoughtful arguer who recognizes complexity.
Be fair to alternative views.	If you scorn or misrepresent opposing views, you will win favor only with those who already agree with you. If you are a good listener to others, they will be more apt to listen to you.
Search for values and assumptions you can share with your audience.	You will build bridges toward skeptical readers, rather than alienate them, if you can highlight shared assumptions or values. Use audience-based reasons where possible.
Show that you care about your issue; show also why your readers should care about it.	By showing why the issue matters both to you and your readers, you portray yourself as a person of integrity rather than as someone playing an argumentative game.

Appeals to Pathos Besides appealing to *logos* and *ethos,* you might also appeal to what the Greeks called *pathos.* Sometimes *pathos* is interpreted narrowly as an appeal to the emotions and is therefore devalued on the grounds that arguments should be rational rather than emotional. Although appeals to *pathos* can sometimes be irrational and irrelevant ("If you don't give me at least a B in this course, I will lose my scholarship and break my ill grandmother's heart"), they can also arouse audience interest and deepen understanding of an argument's human dimensions. The following chart suggests ways to increase *pathos* in your arguments:

Strategies for Enhancing Your Argument's *Pathos*

What to Do	Explanation	Example
Include storylike anecdotes.	Specific stories often create more emotional appeal than abstract statistics or generalizations.	In promoting health care reform, President Obama often told stories of persons made bankrupt by an illness or deprived of care because of a pre-existing condition. On many occasions, he spoke of his own mother's fight with insurance companies as she lay dying of cancer.
Choose words with emotional or values-laden connotations.	Connotations of words often carry heavy emotional impact.	Opponents of health care reform talked about the Democrats' bill as "being jammed down people's throats"; supporters used words like "safety net," "compassion," or "care for children in poverty."
Where appropriate, use vivid language low on the ladder of abstraction.	Specific words paint pictures that have emotional appeal.	"The homeless man is huddled over the sewer grate, his feet wrapped in newspapers. He blows on his hands, then tucks them under his armpits and lies down on the sidewalk with his shoulders over the grate, his bed for the night." *[creates sympathy for the homeless]* "Several ratty derelicts drinking wine from a shared sack caused shoppers to avoid going into the store." *[creates sympathy for shoppers rather than the homeless]*
If the genre permits, include visuals with emotional impact.	Photographs or other visuals, including dramatic graphs or charts, can have a strong emotional appeal.	Articles promoting the environment often include photographs of smoke-belching factories or of endangered animals (often emphasizing their beauty or cuteness); often charts can have emotional appeals—such as a graph portraying dramatic increases in coal-fired electricity plants.

A Brief Primer on Informal Fallacies

We'll conclude our explanation of classical argument with a brief overview of the most common informal fallacies. Informal fallacies are instances of murky reasoning that can cloud an argument and lead to unsound conclusions. Because they can crop up unintentionally in anyone's writing, and because advertisers and hucksters often use them intentionally to deceive, it is a good idea to learn to recognize the more common fallacies.

Post Hoc, Ergo Propter Hoc *("After This, Therefore Because of This")* This fallacy involves mistaking sequence for cause. Just because one event happens before another event doesn't mean the first event caused the second. The connection may be coincidental, or some unknown third event may have caused both of these events.

> **Example**   When the New York police department changed its policing tactics in the early 1990s, the crime rate plummeted. But did the new police tactics cause the decline in crime? (Many experts attributed the decline to other causes.) Persons lauding the police tactics ("Crime declined because the NYPD adopted new tactics") were accused of the *post hoc* fallacy.

Hasty Generalization   Closely related to the *post hoc* fallacy is the hasty generalization, which refers to claims based on insufficient or unrepresentative data. Generally, persuasive evidence should meet the STAR criteria that we explained on page 217. Because the amount of evidence needed in a given case can vary with the audience's degree of skepticism, it is difficult to draw an exact line between hasty and justified generalizations.

> **Example**   The news frequently carries stories about vicious pit bulls. Therefore all pit bulls must be vicious. [or] This experimental drug has been demonstrated safe in numerous clinical trials [based on tests using adult subjects]. Therefore this drug is safe for children.

False Analogy   Arguers often use analogies to support a claim. (We shouldn't go to war in Iraq because doing so will lead us into a Vietnam-like quagmire.) However, analogical arguments are tricky because there are usually significant differences between the two things being compared as well as similarities. (Supporters of the war in Iraq argued that the situation in Iraq in 2002 was very different from that in Vietnam in 1964.) Although it is hard to draw an exact line between a false analogy and an acceptable one, charges of false analogy are frequent when skeptical opponents try to refute arguments based on analogies.

> **Example**   Gun control will work in the United States because it works in England. [or] It's a mistake to force little Johnnie to take piano lessons because you can't turn a reluctant child into a musician any more than you can turn a tulip into a rose.

Either/Or Reasoning This fallacy occurs when a complex, multisided issue is reduced to two positions without acknowledging the possibility of other alternatives.

> **Example**   Either you are pro-choice on abortion or you are against the advancement of women in our culture.

Ad Hominem *("Against the Person")* When people can't find fault with an argument, they sometimes attack the arguer, substituting irrelevant assertions about that person's character for an analysis of the argument itself.

> **Example**   We should discount Senator Jones's argument against nuclear power because she has huge holdings in oil stock.

Appeals to False Authority and Bandwagon Appeals These fallacies offer as support the fact that a famous person or "many people" already support it. Unless the supporters are themselves authorities in the field, their support is irrelevant.

> **Example**   Buy Freeble oil because Joe Quarterback always uses it in his fleet of cars. [or] How can abortion be wrong if millions of people support a woman's right to choose?

Non Sequitur *("It Does Not Follow")* This fallacy occurs when there is no evident connection between a claim and its reason. Sometimes a *non sequitur* can be repaired by filling in gaps in the reasoning; at other times, the reasoning is simply fallacious.

> **Example**   I don't deserve a B for this course because I am a straight-A student.

Circular Reasoning This fallacy occurs when you state your claim and then, usually after rewording it, you state it again as your reason.

> **Example**   Marijuana is injurious to your health because it harms your body.

Red Herring This fallacy refers to the practice of raising an unrelated or irrelevant point deliberately to throw an audience offtrack. Politicians often employ this fallacy when they field questions from the public or press.

> **Example**   You raise a good question about my support of companies' outsourcing jobs to find cheaper labor. Let me tell you about my admiration for the productivity of the American worker.

Slippery Slope The slippery slope fallacy is based on the fear that one step in a direction we don't like inevitably leads to the next step with no stopping place.

> **Example**   If we allow embryonic stem cells to be used for medical research, we will open the door for full-scale reproductive cloning.

A Classical Argument

Write a position paper that takes a stand on a controversial issue. Your introduction should present your issue, provide background, and state the claim you intend to support. In constructing your claim, strive to develop audience-based reasons. The body of your argument should summarize and respond to opposing views as well as present reasons and evidence in support of your own position. You will need to choose whether to summarize and refute opposing views before or after you have made your own case. Try to end your essay with your strongest arguments. Try also to include appeals to *pathos* and to create a positive, credible *ethos*.

We call this assignment a "classical" argument because it is patterned after the persuasive speeches of ancient Greek and Roman orators. A framework chart showing the generic structure of a classical argument is shown in Figure 9.1. Although there are many other ways to persuade audiences, the classical approach is a particularly effective introduction to persuasive writing.

FIGURE 9.1 Framework for a Classical Argument

INTRODUCTION	• Attention-grabber (often a memorable scene) • Explanation of issue and needed background • Writer's thesis (claim) • Forecasting passage
PRESENTATION OF WRITER'S POSITION	• Main body of essay • Presents and supports each reason in turn • Each reason is tied to a value or belief held by the audience
SUMMARY OF OPPOSING VIEWS	• Summary of views differing from writer's (should be fair and complete)
RESPONSE TO OPPOSING VIEWS	• Refutes or concedes to opposing views • Shows weaknesses in opposing views • May concede to some strengths
CONCLUSION	• Brings essay to closure • Often sums up argument • Leaves strong, lasting impression • Often calls for action or relates topic to a larger context of issues

Generating and Exploring Ideas

The tasks that follow are intended to help you generate ideas for your argument. Our goal is to help you build up a storehouse of possible issues, explore several of these possibilities, and then choose one for deeper exploration before you write your initial draft.

Finding an Issue

If you are having trouble finding an arguable issue for this writing project, consider the following strategies:

Strategies for Finding an Arguable Issue	
What to Do	**Explanation**
Make an inventory of various communities you belong to.	See the exercise on page 230. Communities can range from the local (family, dorm, campus) to the state, nation, and world.
Brainstorm contested issues in these communities.	Start off with a fairly large list and then narrow it down according to your personal interest, current knowledge level, and degree of engagement.
On a few of these issues, explore the causes of disagreement.	Ask questions like these: What is at the heart of the disagreement? Disagreement about facts? About beliefs and values? About benefits versus costs?
Then explore your own point of view.	Ask: What is my position on the issue and why? What are alternative points of view? What is at stake?
Determine how much research you'll need to do.	If your issue requires research (check with your instructor), do a bibliographic search and enough skim reading to determine the kinds of arguments surrounding your issue, the kinds of evidence available, and the alternative views that people have taken.
Choose your issue and begin your research.	Your goal is to "wallow in complexity" in order to earn your thesis and create a knowledgeable *ethos*. Note: Some issues allow you to argue from personal experience (see Ross Taylor's argument on paintball, pp. 234–236). Again, check with your instructor.
Brainstorm claims and reasons on various sides of the issue.	State your own claim and possible *because* clause reasons in support of your claim. Do the same thing for one or more opposing or alternative claims.

Conduct an In-Depth Exploration Prior to Drafting

The following set of tasks is designed to help you explore your issue in depth. Most students take one or two hours to complete these tasks; the time will pay off, however, because most of the ideas that you need for your rough draft will be on paper.

See the discussion of issue questions on p. 210.

1. Write out the issue your argument will address. Try phrasing your issue in several different ways, perhaps as a yes/no question and as an open-ended question. Try making the question broader, then narrower. Finally, frame the question in the way that most appeals to you.
2. Now write out your tentative answer to the question. This will be your beginning thesis statement or claim. Put a box around this answer. Next, write out one or more different answers to your question. These will be alternative claims that a neutral audience might consider.
3. Why is this a controversial issue? Is there insufficient evidence to resolve the issue, or is the evidence ambiguous or contradictory? Are definitions in dispute? Do the parties disagree about basic values, assumptions, or beliefs?
4. What personal interest do you have in this issue? How does the issue affect you? Why do you care about it? (Knowing why you care about it might help you get your audience to care about it.)
5. What reasons and evidence support your position on this issue? Freewrite everything that comes to mind that might help you support your case. This freewrite will eventually provide the bulk of your argument. For now, freewrite rapidly without worrying whether your argument makes sense. Just get ideas on paper.
6. Imagine all the counterarguments your audience might make. Summarize the main arguments against your position and then freewrite your response to each of the counterarguments. What are the flaws in the alternative points of view?
7. What kinds of appeals to *ethos* and *pathos* might you use to support your argument? How can you increase your audience's perception of your credibility and trustworthiness? How can you tie your argument to your audience's beliefs and values?
8. Why is this an important issue? What are the broader implications and consequences? What other issues does it relate to? Thinking of possible answers to these questions may prove useful when you write your introduction or conclusion.

Shaping and Drafting

Once you have explored your ideas, create a plan. Here is a suggested procedure:

Begin your planning by analyzing your intended audience. You could imagine an audience deeply resistant to your views or a more neutral, undecided audience acting like a jury. In some cases, your audience might be a single person, as when you petition your department chair to waive a requirement in your major. At other times, your audience might be the general readership of a newspaper, church bulletin, or magazine. When the audience is a general readership, you need to imagine from the start the kinds of readers you particularly want to sway. Here are some questions you can ask:

- *How much does your audience know or care about your issue?* Will you need to provide background? Will you need to convince them that your issue is important? Do you need to hook their interest? Your answers to these questions will particularly influence your introduction and conclusion.
- *What is your audience's current attitude toward your issue?* Are they deeply opposed to your position? If so, why? Are they neutral and undecided? If so, what other views will they be listening to?
- *How do your audience's values, assumptions, and beliefs differ from your own?* What aspects of your position will be threatening to your audience? Why? How does your position on the issue challenge your imagined reader's worldview or identity? What objections will your audience raise toward your argument? Your answers to these questions will help determine the content of your argument and alert you to the extra research you may have to do to respond to audience objections.
- *What values, beliefs, or assumptions about the world do you and your audience share?* Despite your differences with your audience, where can you find common links? How might you use these links to build bridges to your audience?

Your next step is to plan an audience-based argument by seeking audience-based reasons or reasons whose underlying assumptions you can defend. Here is a process you can use:

1. Create a skeleton, tree diagram, outline, or flowchart for your argument by stating your reasons as one or more *because* clauses attached to your claim. Each *because* clause will become the head of a main section or *line of reasoning* in your argument.
2. Use the planning schema on pages 219–220 to plan each line of reasoning. If your audience accepts your underlying assumption, you can concentrate on supporting your reason with evidence. However, if your audience is apt to reject the underlying assumption for one of your lines of reasoning, then you'll need to state it directly and argue for it. Try to anticipate audience objections by exploring ways that an audience might question either your reasons or your underlying assumptions.
3. Using the skeleton you created, finish developing an outline or tree diagram for your argument. Although the organization of each part of your argument will grow organically from its content, the main parts of your classical argument should match the framework chart shown on page 228 (Figure 9.1).

This classical model can be modified in numerous ways. A question that often arises is where to summarize and respond to objections and counterarguments. Writers generally have three choices: One option is to handle opposing positions before you present your own argument. The rationale for this approach is that skeptical audiences may be more inclined to listen attentively to your argument if they have been assured that you understand their point of view. A second option is to place this material after you have presented your argument. This approach is effective for neutral audiences who don't start off with strong opposing views. A final option is to intersperse opposing views throughout your argument at appropriate moments. Any of these possibilities, or a combination of all of them, can be effective.

Another question often asked is, "What is the best way to order one's reasons?" A general rule of thumb when ordering your own argument is to put your strongest reason last and your second-strongest reason first. The idea here is to start and end with your most powerful arguments. If you imagine a quite skeptical audience, build bridges to your audience by summarizing alternative views early in the paper and concede to those that are especially strong. If your audience is neutral or undecided, you can summarize and respond to possible objections after you have presented your own case.

Revising

As you revise your argument, you need to attend both to the clarity of your writing (all the principles of closed-form prose described in Chapter 12) and also to the persuasiveness of your argument. As always, peer reviews are valuable, and especially so in argumentation if you ask your peer reviewers to role-play an opposing audience.

Questions for Peer Review

In addition to the generic peer review questions explained in Skill 11.4, ask your peer reviewers to address these questions:

INTRODUCTION

1. How could the title be improved so that it announces the issue, reveals the writer's claim, or otherwise focuses your expectations and piques interest?
2. What strategies does the writer use to introduce the issue, engage your interest, and convince you that the issue is significant and problematic? What would add clarity and appeal?
3. How could the introduction more effectively forecast the argument and present the writer's claim? What would make the statement of the claim more focused, clear, or risky?

ARGUING FOR THE CLAIM

1. Consider the overall structure: What strategies does the writer use to make the structure of the paper clear and easy to follow? How could the structure of the argument be improved?
2. Consider the support for the reasons: Where could the writer provide better evidence or support for each line of reasoning? Look for the kinds of evidence for each line of reasoning by noting the writer's use of facts, examples,

statistics, testimony, or other evidence. Where could the writer supply more evidence or use existing evidence more effectively?

3. Consider the support for the underlying assumptions: For each line of reasoning, determine the assumptions that the audience needs to grant for the argument to be effective. Are there places where these assumptions need to be stated directly and supported with arguments? How could support for the assumptions be improved?

4. Consider the writer's summary of and response to alternative viewpoints: Where does the writer treat alternative views? Are there additional alternative views that the writer should consider? What strategies does the writer use to respond to alternative views? How could the writer's treatment of alternative views be improved?

CONCLUSION

1. How might the conclusion more effectively bring completeness or closure to the argument?

Our first reading, by student writer Ross Taylor, aims to increase appreciation of paintball as a healthy sport. An avid paintballer, Ross was frustrated by how many of his friends and acquaintances didn't appreciate paintball and had numerous misconceptions about it. The following argument is aimed at those who don't understand the sport or those who condemn it for being dangerous and violent.

Ross Taylor (student)
Paintball:
Promoter of Violence or Healthy Fun?

1   Glancing out from behind some cover, I see an enemy soldier on the move. I level my gun and start pinching off rounds. Hearing the incoming fire, he turns and starts to fire, but it is far too late. His entire body flinches when I land two torso shots, and he falls when I hit his leg. I duck back satisfied with another good kill on my record. I pop up again, this time to scan for more enemy forces. Out of the corner of my eye I see some movement and turn to see two soldiers peeking out from behind a sewer pipe. I move to take cover again, but it's futile. I feel the hits come one by one hitting me three times in the chest and once on the right bicep before I fall behind the cover. I'm hit. It's all over—for me at least. The paintball battle rages on as I carefully leave the field to nurse my welts, which are already showing. Luckily, I watch my three remaining teammates trample the two enemy soldiers who shot me to win the game. This is paintball in all its splendor and glory.

2   Paintball is one of the most misunderstood and generally looked down upon recreational activities. People see it as rewarding violence and lacking the true characteristics of a healthy team sport like ultimate Frisbee, soccer, or pickup basketball. Largely the accusations directed at paintball are false because it is a positive recreational activity. Paintball is a fun, athletic, mentally challenging recreational activity that builds teamwork and releases tension.

3   Paintball was invented in the early 1980s as a casual activity for survival enthusiasts, but it has grown into a several hundred million dollar industry. It is, quite simply, an expanded version of tag. Players use a range of CO_2 powered guns that fire small biodegradable marbles of paint at approximately 250–300 feet per second. The result of a hit is a small splatter of oily paint and a nice dark bruise. Paintball is now played nationwide in indoor and outdoor arenas. Quite often variants are played such as "Capture the Flag" or "Assassination." In "Capture the Flag" the point is to retrieve the heavily guarded flag from the other team and return it to your base. The game of "Assassination" pits one team of "assassins" against the "secret service." The secret service men guard an unarmed player dubbed the "president." Their goal is get from point A to point B without the president's getting tagged. Contrary to popular belief, the games are highly officiated and organized. There is always a referee present. Barrel plugs are required until just before a game begins and must be reinserted as soon as the game ends. No hostages may be taken. A player catching another off guard at close range must first give the player the opportunity to surrender. Most importantly there is no physical contact between players. Punching, pushing, or butt-ending with the gun

is strictly prohibited. The result is an intense game that is relatively safe for all involved.

4   The activity of paintball is athletically challenging. There are numerous sprint and dives to avoid being hit. At the end of a game, typically lasting around 20 minutes, all the players are winded, sweaty, and ultimately exhilarated. The beginning of the game includes a mad dash for cover by both teams with heavy amounts of fire being exchanged. During the game, players execute numerous strategic moves to gain a tactical advantage, often including quick jumps, dives, rolls, and runs. While undercover, players crawl across broad stretches of playing field often still feeling their bruises from previous games. These physical feats culminate in an invigorating and physically challenging activity good for building muscles and coordination.

5   In addition to the athletic challenge, paintball provides strong mental challenge, mainly the need for constant strategizing. There are many strategic positioning methods. For example, the classic pincer move involves your team's outflanking an opponent from each side to eliminate his or her mobility and shelter. In the more sophisticated ladder technique, teammates take turns covering each other as the others move onward from cover to cover. Throughout the game, players' minds are constantly reeling as they calculate their positions and cover, their teammates' positions and cover, and their opponents' positions and strength. Finally, there is the strong competitive pull of the individual. It never fails to amaze me how much thought goes into one game.

6   Teamwork is also involved. Paintball takes a lot of cooperation. You need special hand signals to communicate with your teammates, and you have to coordinate, under rapidly changing situations, who is going to flank left or right, who is going to charge, and who is going to stay back to guard the flag station. The importance of teamwork in paintball explains why more and more businesses are taking their employees for a day of action with the intent of creating a closer knit and smooth-functioning workplace. The value of teamwork is highlighted on the Web site of a British Columbia facility, Action and Adventure Paintball, Ltd, which says that in paintball,

> as in any team sport, the team that communicates best usually wins. It's about thinking, not shooting. This is why Fortune 500 companies around the world take their employees to play paintball together.

An advantage of paintball for building company team spirit is that paintball teams, unlike teams in many other recreational sports, can blend very skilled and totally unskilled players. Women like paintball as much as men, and the game is open to people of any size, body type, and strength level. Since a game usually takes no more than seven to ten minutes, teams can run a series of different games with different players to have lots of different match-ups. Also families like to play paintball together.

7   People who object to paintball criticize its danger and violence. The game's supposed danger gets mentioned a lot. The public seems to have received the impression that paintball guns are simply eye-removing hardware. It is true that paintball can lead to eye injuries. An article by medical writer Cheryl Guttman in a trade magazine for ophthalmologists warns that eye injuries from paintball are on the rise. But the fact is that Guttman's article says that only 102 cases of eye injuries from paintballs were

reported from 1985 to 2000 and that 85 percent of those injured were not wearing the required safety goggles. This is not to say that accidents don't happen. I personally had a friend lose an eye after inadvertently shooting himself in the eye from a very close range. The fact of the matter is that he made a mistake by looking down the barrel of a loaded gun and the trigger malfunctioned. Had he been more careful or worn the proper equipment, he most likely would have been fine. During my first organized paintball experience I was hit in the goggles by a very powerful gun and felt no pain. The only discomfort came from having to clean all the paint off my goggles after the game. When played properly, paintball is an incredibly safe sport.

8   The most powerful argument against paintball is that it is inherently violent and thus unhealthy. Critics claim paintball is simply an accepted form of promoting violence against other people. I have anti-war friends who think that paintball glorifies war. Many new parents today try to keep their kids from playing cops and robbers and won't buy them toy guns. These people see paintball as an upgraded and more violent version of the same antisocial games they don't want their children to play. Some people also point to the connections between paintball and violent video games where participants get their fun from "killing" other people. They link paintball to all the other violent activities that they think lead to such things as gangs or school shootings. But there is no connection between school shootings and paintball. As seen in Michael Moore's *Bowling for Columbine*, the killers involved there went bowling before the massacre; they didn't practice their aim by playing paintball.

9   What I am trying to say is that, yes, paintball is violent to a degree. After all, its whole point is to "kill" each other with guns. But I object to paintball's being considered a promotion of violence. Rather, I feel that it is a healthy release of tension. From my own personal experience, when playing the game, the players aren't focused on hurting the other players; they are focused on winning the game. At the end of the day, players are not full of violent urges, but just the opposite. They want to celebrate together as a team, just as do softball or soccer teams after a game. Therefore I don't think paintball is an unhealthy activity for adults. (The only reason I wouldn't include children is because I believe the pain is too intense for them. I have seen some younger players cry after being shot.) Paintball is simply a game, a sport, that produces intense exhilaration and fun. Admittedly, paintball guns can be used in irresponsible manners. Recently there have been some drive-by paintballings, suggesting that paintball players are irresponsible and violent. However, the percentage of people who do this sort of prank is very small and those are the bad apples of the group. There will always be those who misuse equipment. For example, baseball bats have been used in atrocious beatings, but that doesn't make baseball a violent sport. So despite the bad apples, paintball is still a worthwhile activity when properly practiced.

10   Athletic and mentally challenging, team-building and fun—the game of paintball seems perfectly legitimate to me. It is admittedly violent, but it is not the evil activity that critics portray. Injuries can occur, but usually only when the proper safety equipment is not being used and proper precautions are ignored. As a great recreational activity, paintball deserves the same respect as other sports. It is a great way to get physical exercise, make friends, and have fun.

Thinking Critically
about "Paintball: Promoter of Violence or Healthy Fun?"

1. Before reading this essay, what was your own view of paintball? To what extent did this argument create for you a more positive view of paintball? What aspects of the argument did you find particularly effective or ineffective?

2. How effective are Ross's appeals to *ethos* in this argument? Does he create a persona that you find trustworthy and compelling? How does he do so or fail to do so?

3. How effective are Ross's appeals to *pathos*? How does he appeal to his readers' values, interests, and emotions in trying to make paintball seem like an exhilarating team sport? To what extent does he show empathy with readers when he summarizes objections to paintball?

4. How effective are Ross's appeals to *logos*? How effective are Ross's reasons and evidence in support of his claim? How effective are Ross's responses to opposing views?

5. What are the main strengths and weaknesses of Ross's argument?

Our next two readings focus on the issue of nuclear power—specifically, whether the United States should increase its production of electricity by building more nuclear power plants. The first of these readings, by electrical engineer and science writer William Sweet, appeared in the "Better Planet" section of the science magazine *Discover* in August 2007. Under the title "Why Uranium Is the New Green," it presents arguments in favor of greatly expanding our nuclear-generating capacity. William Sweet, a graduate of the University of Chicago and Princeton University, is the author of *Kicking the Carbon Habit: Global Warming and the Case for Nuclear and Renewable Energy* (Columbia University Press, 2006).

William Sweet
Why Uranium Is the New Green

1   ExxonMobil has thrown in the towel, terminating its campaign to convince the public that global warming is a hoax concocted by some pointy-headed intellectuals. All three major Democratic candidates for president, and some of the top Republican contenders as well, have promised serious action. Leading members of Congress have introduced a half dozen bills that would impose some kind of carbon regulation, and even the president now concedes that climate change is important.

2   Using coal to make electricity accounts for about a third of America's carbon emissions. As a result, tackling emissions from coal-fired power plants represents our best opportunity to make sharp reductions in greenhouse gases.

3   Fortunately, we already have the technology to do that. Unfortunately, right now the United States is addicted to coal, a cheap, abundant power source. Burning coal

produces more than half the country's electricity, despite its immense human and environmental costs. Particulates and other air pollutants from coal-fired power plants cause somewhere between 20,000 and 30,000 premature deaths in the United States *each year.* Fifty tons of mercury—one-third of all domestic mercury emissions—are pumped into the atmosphere annually from coal plants. In addition, the extraction of coal, from West Virginia to Wyoming, devastates the physical environment, and its processing and combustion produce gigantic volumes of waste.

4   For the last decade, coal-burning utilities have been fighting a rearguard action, resisting costly antipollution measures required by environmental legislation. At the same time, they have been holding out the prospect of "clean coal"—in which carbon is captured and stored as coal is burned. But clean-coal technologies have yet to be demonstrated on a large scale commercially, and by the admission of even the president's own climate-technology task force, clean coal doesn't have any prospect of making a big dent in the climate problem in the next 15 to 20 years.

5   By comparison, nuclear and wind power are proven technologies whose environmental risks and costs are thoroughly understood and which can make an immediate difference for the better.

6   The first thing to be appreciated about reactors in the United States is that they are essentially immune to the type of accident that occurred at Chernobyl in April 1986. Put simply, because of fundamental design differences, U.S. reactors cannot experience a sudden and drastic power surge, as happened at Chernobyl's Unit Number 4, causing it to explode and catch fire. In addition, the reliability of U.S. nuclear plants has been constantly improving. In 1980, American nuclear power plants were generating electricity only 56 percent of the time because they frequently needed special maintenance or repair. By 2004, reactor performance had improved to the point of generating electricity over 90 percent of the time.

7   Our regulatory regime, which was enormously strengthened in the wake of the 1979 Three Mile Island accident (during which no one was hurt, by the way), is indisputably much better than the Soviet system, which bred endemic incompetence. Management of U.S. nuclear power plants has improved dramatically since Three Mile Island, and security has been tightened significantly since 9/11 (though more remains to be done). By comparison with other tempting terrorist targets like petrochemical complexes, reactors are well fortified.

8   What about the problem of storing radioactive waste? It is overrated from an engineering standpoint and pales in comparison with the challenges associated with the permanent sequestration of immense quantities of carbon, as required by clean-coal systems. Though the wastes from nuclear power plants are highly toxic, their physical quantity is surprisingly small—barely more than 2,000 tons a year in the United States. The amount of carbon dioxide emitted by our coal plants? Nearly 2 *billion* tons.

9   Let us say it plainly: Today coal-fired power plants routinely kill tens of thousands of people in the United States each year by way of lung cancer, bronchitis, and other ailments; the U.S. nuclear economy kills virtually no one in a normal year.

10   Perhaps the most serious concern about increasing our reliance on nuclear power is whether it might lead to an international proliferation of atomic bombs. Contrary to a stubborn myth, however, countries do not decide to build nuclear weapons because

they happen to get nuclear reactors first; they acquire nuclear reactors because they want to build nuclear weapons. This was true of France and China in the 1950s, of Israel and India in the '60s and '70s, and it's true of Korea and Iran today. Does anybody honestly think that whether Tehran or Pyongyang produces atomic bombs depends on how many reactors the United States decides to build in the next 10 to 20 years?

11   Ultimately, the replacement of old, highly polluting coal-fired power plants by nuclear reactors is essentially no different from deciding, after putting sentimental considerations aside, to replace your inexpensive and reliable—but obsolete—1983 Olds Omega with a 2007 Toyota Camry or BMW 3 Series sedan.

12   All that said, it's important to be clear about nuclear energy's limits. It's likely that the construction of at least one new nuclear power plant will be initiated by the end of this year, ending a two-decade drought in new nuclear plant construction. But by its own estimates, the U.S. nuclear industry can handle only about two new nuclear reactor projects annually at its present-day capacity.

13   Obviously, given these limits, a lot of new wind generation, conservation, and improvements in energy use will also be needed. Wind is especially important because, despite the hopes of many, solar power just isn't going to cut it on a large scale in the foreseeable future. Right now, on a dollar per megawatt basis, solar installations are six or seven times as expensive as wind.

14   Wind turbines already generate electricity almost as inexpensively as fossil fuels. Thanks to a two cents per kiolwatt-hour production incentive from the U.S. government, they are being built at a rate that will increase the amount of wind-generated electricity by nearly three gigawatts a year. Taking into account that wind turbines produce electricity only about a third of the time, that's roughly the equivalent of building one standard one-gigawatt nuclear power plant a year.

15   Currently, nuclear and wind energy (as well as clean coal) are between 25 and 75 percent more expensive than old-fashioned coal at current prices (not including all the hidden health and environmental costs of coal), so it will take a stiff charge on coal to induce rapid replacement of obsolete plants. A tax or equivalent trading scheme that increases the cost of coal-generated electricity by, say, 50 percent would stimulate conservation and adoption of more efficient technologies throughout the economy and prompt replacement of coal by some combination of wind, nuclear, and natural gas. Proceeds from the tax or auctioned credits could (and should) be used to compensate regions and individuals most adversely affected by the higher costs, like the poor.

16   For the last six years, the U.S. government, with well-orchestrated support from industry, has told the American people that we can't afford to attack global warming aggressively. That's nonsense. We're the world's richest country, and we use energy about twice as extravagantly as Europe and Japan. It's no surprise that we account for a quarter of the globe's greenhouse-gas emissions.

17   What the United States needs to do is get in step with the Kyoto Protocol, both to establish its bona fides with the other advanced industrial countries and to give countries like India and China an incentive to accept mandatory carbon limits. That implies cutting U.S. carbon emissions by 25 percent as soon as possible.

18   The United States could do that by simply making the dirtiest and most inefficient coal plants prohibitively expensive by means of the carbon tax or trading systems mentioned above.

19   All we need to move decisively on carbon reduction is a different kind of political leadership at the very top. Surprisingly, it's the muscle-bound action-movie star who runs California who has best captured the spirit of what's needed. Last September, the day Arnold Schwarzenegger signed a bill committing his state to a program of sharp greenhouse-gas reductions, he told an ABC interviewer that climate change kind of "creeps up on you. And then all of a sudden it is too late to do something about it. We don't want to go there."

Thinking Critically
about "Why Uranium Is the New Green"

1. This article includes most of the features typically associated with classical argument—a claim with supporting reasons, a summary of alternative or opposing views, and responses to those views.
   a. What are the chief reasons that Sweet supports nuclear-generated electricity?
   b. What arguments against nuclear-generated electricity does Sweet mention or summarize?
   c. Where and how does he respond to those alternative views or opposing arguments?

2. From the perspective of *logos,* what reasons and evidence in favor of nuclear-generated power do you find most effective in Sweet's argument? Are there weaknesses in his argument? Where and how?

3. How, and to what effect, does Sweet appeal to *pathos* and *ethos*?

4. One of the chief arguments against nuclear power is the problem of storing nuclear waste. How would you analyze rhetorically Sweet's method of responding to that objection? How effective is his response?

Our second nuclear power reading is an editorial appearing in the *Los Angeles Times* on July 23, 2007. It responds to a growing public reassessment of nuclear power as a possible solution to global warming. Its immediate context is the July 2007 earthquake in Japan that damaged a nuclear power plant, causing leakage of a small amount of contaminated water.

Editorial from the *Los Angeles Times*
No to Nukes

1   Japan sees nuclear power as a solution to global warming, but it's paying a price. Last week, a magnitude 6.8 earthquake caused dozens of problems at the world's biggest nuclear plant, leading to releases of radioactive elements into the air and ocean and an indefinite shutdown. Government and company officials initially downplayed the incident and stuck to the official line that the country's nuclear plants are earthquake-proof, but they gave way in the face of overwhelming evidence to the contrary. Japan has a sordid history of serious nuclear accidents or spills followed by cover-ups.

2   It isn't alone. The U.S. government allows nuclear plants to operate under a level of secrecy usually reserved for the national security apparatus. Last year, for example, about nine gallons of highly enriched uranium spilled at a processing plant in Tennessee, forming a puddle a few feet from an elevator shaft. Had it dripped into the shaft, it might have formed a critical mass sufficient for a chain reaction, releasing enough radiation to kill or burn workers nearby. A report on the accident from the Nuclear Regulatory Commission was hidden from the public, and only came to light because one of the commissioners wrote a memo on it that became part of the public record.

3   The dream that nuclear power would turn atomic fission into a force for good rather than destruction unraveled with the Three Mile Island disaster in 1979 and the Chernobyl meltdown in 1986. No U.S. utility has ordered a new nuclear plant since 1978 (that order was later canceled), and until recently it seemed none ever would. But rising natural gas prices and worries about global warming have put the nuclear industry back on track. Many respected academics and environmentalists argue that nuclear power must be part of any solution to climate change because nuclear power plants don't release greenhouse gases.

4   They make a weak case. The enormous cost of building nuclear plants, the reluctance of investors to fund them, community opposition and an endless controversy over what to do with the waste ensure that ramping up the nuclear infrastructure will be a slow process—far too slow to make a difference on global warming. That's just as well, because nuclear power is extremely risky. What's more, there are cleaner, cheaper, faster alternatives that come with none of the risks.

Glowing Pains

5   Modern nuclear plants are much safer than the Soviet-era monstrosity at Chernobyl. But accidents can and frequently do happen. The Union of Concerned Scientists cites 51 cases at 41 U.S. nuclear plants in which reactors have been shut down for more than a year as evidence of serious and widespread safety problems.

6   Nuclear plants are also considered attractive terrorist targets, though that risk too has been reduced. Provisions in the 2005 energy bill required threat assessments at nuclear plants and background checks on workers. What hasn't improved much is the

risk of spills or even meltdowns in the event of natural disasters such as earthquakes, making it mystifying why anyone would consider building reactors in seismically unstable places like Japan (or California, which has two, one at San Onofre and the other in Morro Bay).

7   Weapons proliferation is an even more serious concern. The uranium used in nuclear reactors isn't concentrated enough for anything but a dirty bomb, but the same labs that enrich uranium for nuclear fuel can be used to create weapons-grade uranium. Thus any country, such as Iran, that pursues uranium enrichment for nuclear power might also be building a bomb factory. It would be more than a little hypocritical for the U.S. to expand its own nuclear power capacity while forbidding countries it doesn't like from doing the same.

8   The risks increase when spent fuel is recycled. Five countries reprocess their spent nuclear fuel, and the Bush administration is pushing strongly to do the same in the U.S. Reprocessing involves separating plutonium from other materials to create new fuel. Plutonium is an excellent bomb material, and it's much easier to steal than enriched uranium. Spent fuel is so radioactive that it would burn a prospective thief to death, while plutonium could be carried out of a processing center in one's pocket. In Japan, 200 kilograms of plutonium from a waste recycling plant have gone missing; in Britain, 30 kilograms can't be accounted for. These have been officially dismissed as clerical errors, but the nuclear industry has never been noted for its truthfulness or transparency. The bomb dropped on Nagasaki contained six kilograms.

9   Technology might be able to solve the recycling problem, but the question of what to do with the waste defies answers. Even the recycling process leaves behind highly radioactive waste that has to be disposed of. This isn't a temporary issue: Nuclear waste remains hazardous for tens of thousands of years. The only way to get rid of it is to put it in containers and bury it deep underground—and pray that geological shifts or excavations by future generations that have forgotten where it's buried don't unleash it on the surface.

10   No country in the world has yet built a permanent underground waste repository, though Finland has come the closest. In the U.S., Congress has been struggling for decades to build a dump at Yucca Mountain in Nevada but has been unable to overcome fierce local opposition. One can hardly blame the Nevadans. Not many people would want 70,000 metric tons of nuclear waste buried in their neighborhood or transported through it on the way to the dump.

11   The result is that nuclear waste is stored on-site at the power plants, increasing the risk of leaks and the danger to plant workers. Eventually, we'll run out of space for it.

Goin' Fission?

12   Given the drawbacks, it's surprising that anybody would seriously consider a nuclear renaissance. But interest is surging; the NRC expects applications for up to 28 new reactors in the next two years. Even California, which has a 31-year-old ban on construction of nuclear plants, is looking into it. Last month, the state Energy Commission held a hearing on nuclear power, and a group of Fresno businessmen plans a ballot measure to assess voter interest in rescinding the state's ban.

13   Behind all this is a perception that nuclear power is needed to help fight climate change. But there's little chance that nuclear plants could be built quickly enough to make much difference. The existing 104 nuclear plants in the U.S., which supply roughly 20% of the nation's electricity, are old and nearing the end of their useful lives. Just to replace them would require building a new reactor every four or five months for the next 40 years. To significantly increase the nation's nuclear capacity would require far more.

14   The average nuclear plant is estimated to cost about $4 billion. Because of the risks involved, there is scarce interest among investors in putting up the needed capital. Nor have tax incentives and subsidies been enough to lure them. In part, that's because the regulatory process for new plants is glacially slow. The newest nuclear plant in the U.S. opened in 1996, after having been ordered in 1970—a 26-year gap. Though a carbon tax or carbon trading might someday make the economics of nuclear power more attractive, and the NRC has taken steps to speed its assessments, community opposition remains high, and it could still take more than a decade to get a plant built.

15   Meanwhile, a 2006 study by the Institute for Energy and Environmental Research found that for nuclear power to play a meaningful role in cutting greenhouse gas emissions, the world would need to build a new plant every one to two weeks until mid-century. Even if that were feasible, it would overwhelm the handful of companies that make specialized parts for nuclear plants, sending costs through the roof.

16   The accelerating threat of global warming requires innovation and may demand risk-taking, but there are better options than nuclear power. A combination of energy-efficiency measures, renewable power like wind and solar, and decentralized power generators are already producing more energy worldwide than nuclear power plants. Their use is expanding more quickly, and the decentralized approach they represent is more attractive on several levels. One fast-growing technology allows commercial buildings or complexes, such as schools, hospitals, hotels or offices, to generate their own electricity and hot water with micro-turbines fueled by natural gas or even biofuel, much more efficiently than utilities can do it and with far lower emissions.

17   The potential for wind power alone is nearly limitless and, according to a May report by research firm Standard & Poor's, it's cheaper to produce than nuclear power. Further, the amount of electricity that could be generated simply by making existing non-nuclear power plants more efficient is staggering. On average, coal plants operate at 30% efficiency worldwide, but newer plants operate at 46%. If the world average could be raised to 42%, it would save the same amount of carbon as building 800 nuclear plants.

18   Nevertheless, the U.S. government spends more on nuclear power than it does on renewables and efficiency. Taxpayer subsidies to the nuclear industry amounted to $9 billion in 2006, according to Doug Koplow, a researcher based in Cambridge, Mass., whose Earth Track consultancy monitors energy spending. Renewable power sources, including hydropower but not ethanol, got $6 billion, and $2 billion went toward conservation.

19   That's out of whack. Some countries—notably France, which gets nearly 80% of its power from nuclear plants and has never had a major accident—have made nuclear energy work, but at a high cost. The state-owned French power monopoly is severely indebted, and although France recycles its waste, it is no closer than the U.S. to approving a permanent repository. Tax dollars are better spent on windmills than on cooling towers.

Thinking Critically
about "No to Nukes"

1. This article, like William Sweet's, includes the typical elements associated with classical argument.
   a. What are the editorial writer's chief arguments against nuclear power?
   b. What arguments in favor of nuclear power does this editorial mention or summarize?
   c. How and where does the editorial writer respond to these alternative views?

2. From the perspective of *logos,* what reasons and evidence opposing nuclear-generated power do you find most effective in this editorial? Are there weaknesses in the editorial's arguments? Where and how?

3. In what ways, and with what effectiveness, does the editorial appeal to *pathos* and *ethos*?

4. Both Sweet and the editorial writer have high hopes for wind energy. In fact, the editorial writer concludes by saying, "Tax dollars are better spent on windmills than on cooling towers." How would David Rockwood (see Rockwood's letter to the editor in Chapter 1, pp. 5–6) respond to both writers?

5. Where do you place yourself on the spectrum from "strong support of nuclear power" to "strong opposition to nuclear power"? What new research evidence would be required to persuade you to move in one direction or the other along this spectrum?

PROPOSING A SOLUTION

10

Proposal arguments call an audience to action. They make a claim that some action should or ought to be taken. Sometimes referred to informally as *should arguments,* proposals are among the most common kinds of arguments that you will write or read.

Practical proposals focus on local, practical problems and generally target a specific audience (usually the person with the power to act on the proposal). For example, Lucy Morsen's proposal in this chapter (pages 263–266) advocates banning laptops and cell phones in classrooms. In the work world, many individuals and businesses generate new revenues by writing competitive proposals to solve a prospective client's practical problem.

Another kind of proposal, a **policy proposal,** addresses public policy issues with the aim of swaying public support toward the writer's proposed solution. Student writer Dylan Fujitani's proposal against using civilian contractors in military roles (pages 267–271) illustrates a researched policy proposal.

The power of proposal arguments is often enhanced with images, which can appeal to both *logos* and *pathos*. In fact, proposal arguments sometimes take the form of striking visual-verbal texts such as posters or advocacy advertisements calling an audience to action. Additionally, proposal arguments can be delivered as **oral presentations** when, for example, a citizen presents a proposal at an open-mike public hearing.

The writing projects for this chapter consist of a written proposal, and a speech with visual aids. No matter what genre you choose, you must make the problem vivid to your audience before proposing and justifying a course of action.

In this chapter, by writing a proposal argument, you will learn to:

- convince your audience that a serious problem exists
- persuade them that some action should be taken to resolve it

---

Exploring Proposal Writing

The following activity introduces you to the thinking processes involved in writing a proposal argument.

1. In small groups, identify and list several major problems facing students in your college or university.

2. Decide among yourselves which problems are most important and rank them in order of importance.
3. Choose your group's number-one problem and explore answers to the following questions. Group recorders should be prepared to present answers to the class as a whole.
   a. Why is the problem a problem?
   b. For whom is the problem a problem?
   c. How will these people suffer if the problem is not solved? Give specific examples.
   d. Who has the power to solve the problem?
   e. Why hasn't the problem been solved up to this point?
   f. How can the problem be solved? Create a proposal for a solution.
   g. What are the probable benefits of acting on your proposal?
   h. What costs are associated with your proposal?
   i. Who will bear these costs?
   j. Why should this proposal be enacted?
   k. What makes this proposal better than alternative proposals?
4. As a group, draft an outline for a proposal argument in which you:
   a. Describe the problem and its significance.
   b. Propose your solution to the problem.
   c. Justify your proposal by showing how the benefits outweigh the costs.
5. Recorders for each group should write the group's outline on the board and be prepared to present the group's argument orally to the class.

Understanding Proposal Writing

All proposals have one feature in common—they offer a solution to a problem. For every proposed solution, there are always alternative solutions, including doing nothing. Your task therefore is to convince readers that the problem is worth solving, that your proposed solution will actually work, and that the benefits outweigh the costs. Accordingly, a proposal argument typically has three main parts:

1. ***Description of the problem.*** You must first demonstrate that a significant problem exists. Your goal is to make the problem vivid and real for your readers. Who is affected by the problem? What are its causes? Why hasn't it been solved before? What are the negative consequences of not solving the problem?
2. ***Proposal for a solution.*** This section describes your solution with enough detail to show how it would work and what it would cost. If you don't have a solution, you may choose to generate a planning proposal calling for a committee to propose solutions at a later date.
3. ***Justification.*** Here you persuade your audience that your proposal should be enacted. Typically you show that the benefits of your proposal outweigh the costs. You also need to show why your proposed solution is better than alternative solutions. Point out why other possible approaches would not solve the problem, would provide fewer benefits, or would cost significantly more than your proposed solution.

In the following sections, we examine the special challenges of proposal arguments and then show you a powerful strategy for developing the justification section of a proposal.

Special Challenges of Proposal Arguments

To get your readers to take action—the ultimate purpose of a proposal—you must overcome some difficult challenges. In the following chart, we examine the special difficulties people encounter when writing proposal arguments and offer strategies for overcoming them.

Strategies for Overcoming the Special Challenges of Proposal Arguments		
Challenge	**Explanation**	**What to Do**
Giving the problem presence	To convince readers that a problem exists, you must make them *see* and *feel* the problem—give the problem *presence*.	• Use anecdotes or examples of people suffering from the problem. • Provide startling facts or statistics to dramatize the problem. • Include a photograph or other image that conveys the problem. • Use other appeals to *pathos*.
Appealing to the interests and values of decision makers	A proposal that benefits one group often creates costs for others. Decision makers may not share the sufferers' perspective on a problem. Solving your problem may simply cause more problems for the decision maker.	• Show decision makers how acting on your proposal will benefit *them* directly. • Use audience-based reasons. • If appropriate, appeal to idealism and principle (do the right thing, even if it will cause temporary grief). • Show how benefits to the sufferers outweigh costs to others.
Overcoming inherent conservatism	People are inherently resistant to change, often willing to live with a flawed but bearable situation rather than risk change that could make the situation worse. "Better the devil you know than the one you don't know."	• Emphasize the seriousness of the problem (give it *presence*). • Stress the benefits of solving the problem. • Emphasize the lost potential in not acting. • Show that the risks are minimal. • Show that negative consequences are unlikely.

(continued)

Challenge	Explanation	What to Do
Predicting consequences	Often readers distrust the proposal writer's rosy scenario. They doubt that the predicted benefits will occur, or they fear negative consequences.	• Take care not to overpromise benefits. • Persuade readers that your predictions are realistic—show how the links in the chain lead directly from the solution to the benefits. • Cite cases where a similar proposal led to real benefits.
Evaluating consequences	Any solution that benefits one group may bring costs to another group. It is difficult to establish a common principle of measurement for weighing costs against benefits.	• In some cases, you can use money as measurement—the savings from this proposal will be more than the initial costs. • In other cases, emphasize that the benefits of increased happiness, less suffering, or saved time outweigh the initial dollar costs. • Emphasize the greatest good for the greatest number (more people will have benefits; fewer will bear costs). • Emphasize idealism and principle (this is the right thing to do despite the cost).

With these particular challenges in mind, we now set forth some strategies for making proposals as effective as possible.

Developing an Effective Justification Section

The distinctions between proposals and other kinds of arguments invite particular kinds of support for proposals. Writers often develop support for their proposals by using the three-strategy approach, which focuses sequentially on principles, consequences, and precedents or analogies, as explained here.

Strategies for Developing a Justification Section			
Strategies	**What to Do**	**Templates and Comments**	**Examples**
Argument from principle	Argue that an action should (should not) be taken because it is right (wrong) according to some value, assumption, principle, or belief you share with your audience.	We should (should not) do (this action) because (this action) is _____. Fill in the blank with a belief or value that the audience holds: *good, honest, fair,* and so on.	"We should create publicly financed jobs for poor people because doing so is both charitable and just."

Strategies	What to Do	Templates and Comments	Examples
Argument from consequence	Argue that an action should (should not) be taken because doing so will lead to consequences that you and your audience think are good (bad).	We should (should not) do (this action) because (this action) will lead to these good (bad) consequences: _____, _____, and . _____. Use consequences that your audience will agree are good or bad, as needed.	"We should create publicly financed jobs for poor people because doing so will provide them with money for food and housing, promote a work ethic, and produce needed goods and services."
Argument from precedent or analogy	Argue that an action should (should not) be taken because doing so is similar to what was done in another case, which turned out well (badly).	We should (should not) do (this action) because doing (this action) is like _____, which turned out to be good (bad). Use precedents or analogies that are similar to your proposed action and that will have good (bad) associations for your audience.	*Precedent:* "We should create publicly financed jobs for poor people because doing so will alleviate poverty just as a similar program has helped the poor in Upper Magnesia." *Analogy:* " … because doing so is like teaching the poor how to fish rather than giving them fish."

Each of these argumentation strategies was clearly evident in a public debate in Seattle, Washington, over a proposal to raise county sales taxes to build a new baseball stadium. Those favoring the stadium put forth arguments such as these:

We should build the new stadium because preserving our national pastime for our children is important (*argument from principle*), because building the stadium will create new jobs and revitalize the adjacent Pioneer Square district (*argument from consequence*), and because building the stadium will have the same beneficial effects on the city that building Camden Yards had in Baltimore (*argument from precedent*).

Those opposing the stadium created arguments using the same strategies:

We should not build the stadium because it is wrong to subsidize rich owners and players with tax dollars (*argument from principle*), because building a stadium diverts tax money from more important concerns such as low-income housing (*argument from consequence*), and because Toronto's experience with Skydome shows that once the novelty of a new stadium wears off, attendance declines dramatically (*argument from precedent*).

Using Different Strategies to Develop Support

Working individually or in small groups, use the strategies of principle, conse-quence, and precedent/analogy to create *because* clauses that support (or oppose) the following proposals. Try to have at least one *because* clause from each of the strategies, but generate as many reasons as possible.

Example:

Claim	Spanking children should be made illegal.
Principle	Because it is wrong to cause bodily pain to children.
Consequence	Because it teaches children that it is okay to hit someone out of anger; because it causes children to obey rules out of fear rather than respect; because it can lead children to be abusive parents.
Precedent/analogy	Because spanking a child is like throwing dishes or banging your fists against a wall—it relieves your anger but turns the child into an object.

1. The school year for grades K–12 should/should not be extended to eleven months.
2. "Enhanced interrogation techniques" (such as sleep deprivation, stressful positions, or water boarding) should/should not be used on suspected terrorists.
3. An impenetrable fence should/should not be built between the United States and Mexico.
4. Marijuana should/should not be legalized.
5. The federal government should/should not enact a substantially increased tax on gasoline.

Proposals as Visual Arguments and PowerPoint Presentations

Proposal arguments are often enhanced by photographs, drawings, graphs, or other images. Frequently we encounter proposal arguments as condensed, attention-grabbing verbal-visual texts such as posters or flyers, paid advertisements in news-papers or magazines, brochures, or Web pages in advocacy Web sites. Their creators know the arguments must work fast to capture our attention, give presence to a problem, advocate a solution, and enlist our support. These advocacy ads fre-quently use photographs, images, or icons that are arresting or in some way memo-rable and that appeal to a reader's emotions and imagination.

Since proposal arguments are often delivered orally rather than visually as ads, speakers frequently create visual aids with presentation software like PowerPoint.*

---

*PowerPoint, which is a registered trademark of Microsoft, has become the common name for all kinds of computer-created and -projected slides. However, other companies also make presentation software. We use the term "PowerPoint presentation" because its use has become ubiquitous in business and industry. We intend the term to include any kind of oral presentation supported by visual aids developed on presentation software. Most businesses and professions now expect new management-level hires to be adept at using presentation software in oral presentations.

Although effectively designed slides can enhance the impact of a speech, PowerPoint presentations are controversial among communication experts. Used poorly, PowerPoint can detract from an argument rather than enhance it. A Web search reveals wonderfully satirical diatribes against PowerPoint—including Lincoln's Gettysburg address imagined as a PowerPoint presentation, complete with Lincoln's mumbling, grumbling, off-the-cuff remarks as he tries to connect his laptop to the projector. Despite all the ways that PowerPoint can go wrong, using it to produce effective visual aids can enhance an argument's appeals to *logos, pathos,* and *ethos.* In the second writing project for this chapter, we offer advice on powerful ways to use PowerPoint in support of a proposal speech.

A Proposal Argument

Call your audience's attention to a problem, propose a solution to that problem, and present a justification for your solution. You have two choices (or your instructor may limit you to just one): (a) create a practical proposal, with a letter of transmittal, proposing a nuts-and-bolts solution to a local problem; or (b) write a more general policy proposal, addressing a public issue, in the form of a feature editorial for a particular (state, local, or college) newspaper. If you choose (b), your instructor might ask you to do research and model your proposal after a magazine or journal article.

Generating and Exploring Ideas

If you have trouble thinking of a proposal topic, try making an idea map of local problems you would like to see solved. Consider some of the following starting points:

Finding a Proposal Issue

Problems at your university: parking, registration system, absence of recycling options, hours of cafeterias and eating facilities, too many activities on campus during the week, poor school spirit, problems with residence halls, availability of internships

Problems in your city or town: lack of bike paths, inadequate lighting, unattractive public parks or lack of public parks, zoning problems, inadequate support for public education, need for public transportation, conservation of water

Problems at your place of work: flow of customer traffic, inadequate staffing during peak times, unclear division of responsibilities, no policies for raises or training new employees, health care coverage, safety issues

Social problems and problems related to other aspects of your life: problems with credit card debt, need for financial literacy, physical fitness in the public schools, aid for victims of disasters, employment opportunities for college students, media consumption and awareness of current events

Another approach is to freewrite your response to these trigger statements:

I would really like to solve the problem of _____.
I believe that X should _____. (Substitute for X words such as *my instructor, the president, the school administration, Congress, my boss,* and so forth.)

Note that the problem you pose for this paper can be personal, but shouldn't be private; that is, others should be able to benefit from a solution to your personal problem. For example, your inability to find child care for your daughter is a private problem. But if you focus your proposal on how zoning laws discourage development of in-home day care—and propose a change in those zoning laws to permit more in-home day care centers—then your proposal will benefit others.

Using Stock Issues to Explore Your Problem

Once you have decided on a proposal issue, explore it by freewriting your responses to the following questions. These questions are often called *stock issues,* since they represent generic, or stock, questions that apply to almost any kind of proposal.

1. Is there a problem here that has to be solved?
2. Will the proposed solution really solve this problem?
3. Can the problem be solved in a simpler way without disturbing the status quo?
4. Is the proposed solution practical enough that it really stands a chance of being implemented?
5. What will be the positive and negative consequences of the proposal?

You might also try freewriting your responses to the questions in the exploratory exercise on page 245. Although these questions cover much the same territory as the stock issues, their different presentation might stimulate additional thought.

Finally, try thinking of justifications for your solution by using the three-strategy approach described on pages 248–249.

Avoiding Presupposing Your Solution in Your Problem Statement

A common mistake of inexperienced proposal writers is to write problem statements that presuppose their solutions. As a restaurant server, suppose you notice that customers want coffee refills faster than servers can provide them. To solve this problem, you propose placing carafes of hot coffee at each table. When describing your problem, don't presuppose your solution: "The problem is that we don't have carafes of hot coffee at the tables." Rather, describe the problematic situation itself: annoyed customers clamoring for coffee and harassed servers trying to bring around refills. Only by giving presence to the original problem can you interest readers in your proposed solution, which readers will compare to other possible approaches (including doing nothing).

Here is another example:

Weak: The problem is that the Student Union doesn't stay open late enough at night.

Better: The problem is that students who study late at night don't have an attractive, convenient place to socialize or study; off-campus coffee houses are too far to walk to at night; dorm lounges aren't attractive or conducive to studying; late-nighters make noise in the dorms instead of going to a convenient place.

Shaping and Drafting

In Figure 10.1, we show a typical organizational plan for a proposal argument that you might use if you get stuck while composing the first draft of your essay.

Revising

After you have completed your first draft and begun to clarify your argument for yourself, you are ready to start making your argument clear and persuasive for your readers. Use the strategies for clear closed-form prose outlined in Chapter 12. At this stage, feedback from peer readers can be very helpful.

Questions for Peer Review

In addition to the generic peer review questions explained in Skill 11.4, ask your peer reviewers to address these questions:

1. How could the title more effectively focus the paper and pique your interest?
2. Where does the writer convince you that a problem exists and that it is significant (worth solving) and solvable? Where does the writer give the problem presence? How could the writer improve the presentation of the problem?
3. Does the writer's thesis clearly propose a solution to the problem? Could the thesis be made more precise?

FIGURE 10.1 Framework of a Proposal Argument

Introduction	• Presents and describes a problem that needs solving, giving it presence • Gives background including previous attempts to solve the problem • Argues that the problem is solvable (optional)
Presentation of the proposed solution	• States the solution succinctly • Explains the specifics of the solution
Justification	• Persuades readers that the proposal should be implemented • Presents and develops Reasons 1, 2, and so forth • Reasons to support the proposed solution may be arguments from principle, consequence, and precedent or analogy
Summary and rebuttal of opposing views	*Policy proposal:* • Presents opposing view(s) • Rebuts opposing view(s) *Practical proposal:* • Presents alternative solution(s) • Explains why alternative solution(s) are inferior
Conclusion	• Asks readers to act (sometimes incorporated into the last sentences of the final supporting reason)

4. Could the writer give you more details about the solution so that you can understand it and see how it works? How could the writer make the solution clearer?

5. In the justification section, how could the writer provide stronger reasons for acting on the proposal? Where could the reasons be better supported with more details and evidence? How could the reasons appeal more to the values and beliefs of the audience?

6. Can you help the writer think of additional justifying arguments (arguments from principle, from consequences, from precedent or analogy)? How else could the writer improve support for the proposal?

7. Where does the writer anticipate and address opposing views or alternative solutions? How does the writer convince you that the proposed solution is superior to alternative solutions?

8. Has the writer persuaded you that the benefits of this proposal will outweigh the costs? Who will pay the costs and who will get the benefits? What do you think the gut reaction of a typical decision maker would be to the writer's proposal?

9. Can you think of other, unforeseen costs that the writer should acknowledge and address? What unforeseen benefits could the writer mention?

10. How might the writer improve the structure and clarity of the argument? Where might the writer better apply the principles of clarity from Chapter 12?

WRITING PROJECT

Proposal Speech with Visual Aids

Deliver a proposal argument as a prepared but extemporaneous speech of approximately five to eight minutes supported with visual aids created on presentation software such as PowerPoint or through other means. Your speech should present a problem, propose a solution, justify the solution with reasons and evidence, and defend it against objections or alternative solutions. As you deliver your speech, use appropriate visual aids to give presence to the problem, highlight points, provide memorable data or evidence, or otherwise enhance appeals to *logos, ethos,* and *pathos.* Although the following explanations focus on PowerPoint (or equivalent presentation software), low-tech means of using visual aids (for example, overhead transparencies or flip charts) can also be effective. Follow the guidelines provided by your instructor.

As you contemplate this project, consider its three different components: creating the speech itself, designing the visuals, and delivering the speech. As you create your proposal argument, think *aurally* by imagining your audience listening to a speech rather than reading a written text and think *visually* by considering how visual aids can increase the clarity and persuasive power of your argument.

Developing, Shaping, and Outlining Your Proposal Speech

This project asks you to deliver your proposal speech extemporaneously. To speak extemporaneously means to spend ample time preparing the speech, but not to read it from a script or to recite it from memory. Instead, the speaker talks directly to the audience with the aid of an outline or note cards.

Long before the delivery of the speech, the speaker should have engaged in the same sort of composing process that precedes a finished essay, including giving attention to both subject-matter and rhetorical problems. Effective speakers typically spend an hour of preparation time per minute of speaking time. Much of this work focuses on creating a well-developed sentence outline for the speech. Finding the balance between a speech that is too impromptu and one that is too "scripted," and therefore begs for an audience of readers, is a main consideration in creating a speech.

One way to accommodate the needs of listeners is to make your speech even more closed form than are closed-form essays. To help an audience grasp an argument aurally, speakers need to forecast their points and provide aural signals. The most common formula for a speech is sometimes called the "tell 'em rule." It says: Tell 'em what you are about to say, say it, and then tell 'em what you just said. This redundancy greatly enhances an audience's ability to follow a spoken argument without a text. This "tell 'em rule" serves audience-based needs for unity and coherence, for receiving old information before new information, and for forecasting and fulfillment. Another important way to help your audience follow your speech is to use attributive tags to indicate who and when you are quoting: "According to Pat Miller, a clinical psychologist at Children's Hospital, … " These attributive tags signal a quotation and also indicate why the quoted material is important.

In developing the content for your speech, follow the suggestions for idea generation and development covered in the first writing project for this chapter, pages 251–252. Also try the following strategies:

Strategies for Creating Effective Speech Outlines	
Strategies	**Rationales and Explanations of How They Work**
Plan the structure and content of your speech with the needs of your audience in mind.	How can you make the problem come alive for your audience and make your solution understandable and persuasive? What background information or defined terms does your audience need? What kinds of evidence will you need to show the seriousness of the problem and to support your reasons for enacting the proposal? What objections will your listeners be apt to raise? How can you motivate action?

(continued)

Strategies	Rationales and Explanations of How They Work
Create a complete-sentence outline of your argument; use parallel structures, coordination, and subordination to clarify relationships among ideas.	See Skill 12.3 for advice about different kinds of outlines, particularly the advantage of complete-sentence outlines, which state meanings rather than topics. Since you won't be writing out the complete argument in prose, this outline will be the written frame for your speech.
Build into your outline places for explicit signposting to help the audience follow your speech.	Indicate where you are in your speech: "My second reason is that. … " "As I stated earlier. … "
Early on, practice saying your speech in a normally paced speaking voice to determine its length.	Often speeches can cover much less ground than a written argument. By timing the speech when it is still in its rough draft stage, you will know whether you must cut or add material.

Designing Your Visual Aids

If you use presentation software such as PowerPoint to design your visual aids, focus on making your argument clear and persuasive rather than on demonstrating your technical wizardry.* A common mistake with PowerPoint presentations—in addition to producing boring or jumbled slides—is to make too many slides, to overdesign them, or to become enamored with special effects rather than with the ideas in the speech.

Using Points, Not Topics, as Slide Titles

Many communication researchers object to Microsoft's default PowerPoint template, which encourages short topic phrases for the title of a slide. The "title" box uses a large (for example, Arial 44-point bold) font that limits the number of words at the top of the slide. Dissatisfied with this approach, many researchers argue that points (stated in complete sentences) are more effective than topic phrases for conveying meanings, and they recommend writing complete-sentence assertions at the top of the slide. To do so, however, one has to override the PowerPoint default to use a smaller font. Professor Michael Alley recommends using an Arial 28-point bold font for slide headlines. This font is large enough to be seen throughout the room, but small enough to allow a two-line complete sentence for the headline.

*Our discussion of visual aids designed on PowerPoint is indebted to advice from our rhetorician colleague, Professor Jeffrey Philpott in the Department of Communication at Seattle University. We are also indebted to the work of Professor Michael Alley of Virginia Technical University. Alley's Web site at http://writing.eng.vt.edu/slides.html provides an overview of rhetorical objections to PowerPoint and shows the value of an assertion-evidence design for slides rather than a topic-subtopic design.

Here are some examples of the differences between a topic and a point for a slide:

Topics Versus Points for Slide Title

Slide Title as Topic	Slide Title as Point
Gender Stereotypes in Children's Birthday Cards	95 percent of children's birthday cards revealed gender stereotyping.
Wage Comparison: CEO Versus Worker	In 2008, the average CEO of a large corporation earned 300 times more than the average worker.

We recommend the point approach wherever possible. When the title of a slide makes a point, the body of the slide can then either provide evidence supporting the point (through a graph or bullet points) or reinforce the point with a photograph, drawing, or diagram.

Given this background, we offer the following strategies for creating your visual aids.

Strategies for Creating Effective Visual Aids	
Strategies	**Rationales and Explanations of How They Work**
Make sure each visual aid (slide) is graphically interesting, relevant, functional, and directly connected to the points of your speech.	Visual aids (slides) should be visual and integral to your presentation. Create your speech first and then create visuals.
Use meaningful features as visual aids; don't use cutesy bells and whistles.	PowerPoint has special effects like exploding figures, words circling into position, and little buses wheeling across the screen. Using these special effects can distract the audience from the content of your speech, creating the *ethos* of a technical whiz rather than a serious presenter of a proposal.
Use slides as a way to visually enhance meaning or impact. Do not use them as index cards of talking points.	If you convert your outline into slides, you simply replicate rather than enhance the speech. Use images (rather than words) wherever possible. Think visually.
Make slides simple, neat, and big enough for everyone to see.	PowerPoint wisely limits the number of words in a line. Include no more than eight to ten lines of text per slide. Don't create slides that need to be read as text.

(*continued*)

Strategies	Rationales and Explanations of How They Work
Where appropriate, follow a point-evidence design, rather than a topic-subtopic design. Titles (headlines) should be complete sentences that state a point.	The point-evidence design promotes audience understanding by emphasizing meanings. (See examples on p. 260.) Note: You'll need to change the PowerPoint title font to 28-point Arial bold.
Use different font sizes and spacing to indicate hierarchy.	The title font should be the largest font on the slide. Subordinate points should be in a smaller font size.
Limit the number of visual aids you use.	Communication experts advise speakers to use no more than one visual aid per minute of presentation. In many parts of the speech, the screen can be blank.

Student Example of a Speech Outline and Slides

To illustrate how slides can be effectively integrated into a speech, we offer the example of student Sam Rothchild, who created a speech (5–8 minutes) proposing an increase in income tax rates on the nation's wealthiest households. Here is Sam's sentence outline for his speech.

SAM'S SPEECH OUTLINE

Reward Work Not Wealth:
A Proposal to Increase Income Tax Rates for the Richest 1 Percent of Americans

PROBLEM

1. Since 1980 the gap between rich and poor has increased enormously.
   a. Statistical evidence demonstrates the gap.
      (i) The rich have gotten richer.
      (ii) The poor have gotten poorer.
      (iii) The middle class are treading water.
   b. A primary cause of the income gap is the Bush-era tax cuts that benefited the rich more than the poor.
   c. Income gap leads to an unhealthy middle class and increased poverty, hurting all Americans.

SOLUTION

2. The solution is to raise the income tax rates on the ultra-rich back to 1980 levels.

REASONS TO SUPPORT THIS PROPOSAL

3. A more progressive income tax structure promotes a more just society.
   a. Sales taxes and payroll taxes (Social Security, Medicare) take a high percentage chunk out of low income salaries and a tiny percentage out of high income salaries.
   b. Progressive income tax balances the regressive effect of sales taxes and payroll taxes.
4. Reducing the gap between rich and poor creates a stronger middle class and reduces poverty.

5. Increasing tax rates on the very rich will not hurt the incentive to work or the entrepreneurial spirit.

6. The ultra rich will still be ultra rich.

CONCLUSION

After Sam had completed his argument outline, he began designing PowerPoint slides aimed at enhancing the impact of his proposal. He limited himself to eight slides and turned off the screen during part of his speech. He displayed a slide only when he felt it increased the impact of his speech. His slides can be placed into three design categories:

- Slides using images to enhance *pathos*
- Slides using a graph for evidence
- Slides using bulleted subpoints for evidence (all text)

In all cases, Sam used "points" for the slide titles (making an assertion) rather than a topic phrase. Six of Sam's slides, illustrating the first two of the above categories, are shown in Figures 10.2–10.7.

In a reflection paper accompanying his speech, Sam explained his thinking process in designing the slides. At the start of his speech, Sam wanted to give "presence" to the income gap problem—to have the audience feel the huge gap between ultra-rich Americans and the poor or middle class. For his title slide (Figure 10.2), he selected a stock photo of a construction worker in order to emphasize the social contribution of blue-collar laborers, who undertake difficult, often dangerous, yet important jobs. The upward angle of the camera suggested to Sam the dignity and value of the hard hat worker dangerously walking on a high beam. Likewise, in Figure 10.3 Sam chose the image of an out-of-work-American in an unemployment line, a photograph that highlights the man's humanity and courage and invites empathy. Sam thought that both these images made strong appeals to *pathos*.

Figures 10.4 and 10.5 represent a different thought process. Sam wanted to emphasize the gap between ordinary Americans' conception of wealth and the unimaginably larger actual wealth of the ultra-rich. Most Americans, Sam felt, would consider a person "really wealthy" if he or she could afford a Ferrari (Figure 10.4). But Sam made his own back-of-the-envelope calculations and found that the ultra-rich could afford five Ferraris a day every day of the week. He photoshopped the image in Figure 10.5 to make this point humorously.

Finally, Figures 10.6 and 10.7 show two slides using graphs for evidence. The title of each slide is a complete-sentence "point." During his speech, Sam spent several minutes on the slide shown in Figure 10.6. He pointed out that for the very rich, the vertical axis (annual income) starts at $5,000,000 and then goes skyward. For the "median earner," however, the vertical axis starts at $24,000. He also explained the meaning of "median"—half of all American workers have incomes above the median line and half have incomes below it. The half below the line are the ones most suffering from the declining wealth of the middle class.

Our takeaway message in this section is that Sam first placed emphasis on the content of his speech and then designed PowerPoint slides to enhance the impact of the speech. He did not employ any of the bells and whistles of PowerPoint software, nor did he use the slides simply to display the section-by-section outline of his speech.

FIGURE 10.2 Sam's Title Slide Using an Image for *Pathos*

FIGURE 10.3 Slide Using an Image for Pathos

FIGURE 10.4 First of a Two-Slide Sequence Using Images to Illustrate Income Gap

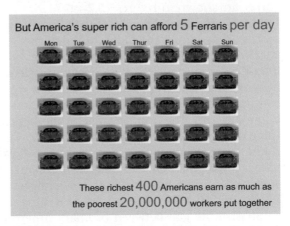

FIGURE 10.5 Second Slide in Sequence, Designed by Sam to Dramatize Wealth

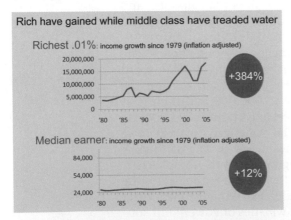

FIGURE 10.6 Slide with Point Title and Graphics for Evidence

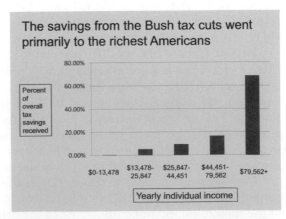

FIGURE 10.7 Another Slide with Point Title and Graphics for Evidence

Delivering Your Speech

Adapting your argument to be delivered orally as a speech requires some special considerations. First, it is important that you allow plenty of time to practice delivering your speech. You can practice before a mirror, with a recorder, or in front of friends until you are confident about the length of your speech and your ability to deliver it with minimal prompting from your notes. In addition, you should think about these important strategies for successful speechmaking.

Strategies for Successfully Delivering Speeches	
Strategies	**What to Do**
Control your volume and pace.	• Speak loudly enough to be heard and add emphasis by speaking louder or softer. • Speed up to get through details quickly and slow down for points you want to stress.
Use posture and gestures to your advantage.	• Stand straight and tall to help your breathing and projection. • Use natural gestures or a few carefully planned ones. • Avoid distracting or nervous gestures.
Maintain eye contact with your audience and look at every member of your audience.	• Know your speech well enough that you can look at your audience, not read your note cards. • Make steady and even eye contact with your audience.
Show enthusiasm and passion for the issue of your speech.	• Make your audience care about your issue through your own enthusiasm. • Show your audience that your issue is important by the energy you put into your delivery. • Also, use your enthusiasm to help you control nervousness.
Use note cards, PowerPoint slides, visual aids, and handouts effectively.	• Control the flow of ideas and information that comes through your slides and visual aids. • Keep your audience listening to you rather than reading handouts or the projector screen.
Overcome nervousness by controlling your hands, your breathing, and the volume of your voice.	• Take deep breaths and speak slightly louder than usual to help your body relax. • Use a podium if one is available.

Revising

After practicing your speech on your own or in front of an informal audience, think about ways you can improve the clarity of your message, your use of visual aids, and your delivery. After you make these improvements, practice the final outline of your speech a number of times to develop familiarity and confidence.

Questions for Peer Review

In addition to the generic peer review questions explained in Skill 11.4, many of which will pertain to your outlined speech, ask your informal audience/reviewers to address these questions:

CONTENT OF THE SPEECH:

1. How well does this speech follow the problem-solution-justification-opposing views-rebuttal structure? How could the speaker improve the clarity of these parts of the speech?
2. How has the speaker tailored the speech to the audience? What could make the speech more lively and easier to follow?
3. Does this speech fit the time limit specified by the assignment? If not, what changes could develop or condense the speech?

USE OF VISUAL AIDS:

4. How functional, simple, clear, and illustrative are the visual aids? Which visual aids enhance the impact of the speech? If any are unclear or distracting, what could improve them?
5. How well do the visual aids support the message of the speech? Where could the speaker more effectively employ the strategies for using PowerPoint or other visual aids?

DELIVERY:

6. Where could the speaker improve his/her volume, enunciation, eye contact, posture, and gestures?
7. How well does the speaker maintain control of his/her material, visual aids, and manner? What suggestions do you have for the speaker to improve his or her enthusiasm and composure?

Our first reading, by student writer Lucy Morsen, is a practical proposal entitled "A Proposal to Improve the Campus Learning Environment by Banning Laptops and Cell Phones from Class." Because practical proposals are aimed at a specific audience, they are often accompanied by a letter of transmittal that introduces the writer, sets the context, and summarizes the proposal. We reproduce here Lucy's transmittal letter followed by her proposal. We also show you the appearance of her title page.

April 26, 2010

Professor Ralph Sorento
Chair, Faculty Senate
_____ University
Street
City, State, Zip

Dear Professor Sorento:

1   Enclosed is a proposal that I hope you will present to the Faculty Senate. It asks the university to ban all laptops and cell phones from classes in consideration of those many students like myself whose educational experience is diminished by classmates who surf the Web or send text messages during lectures or class discussion. As I try to show in this proposal, the effect of laptops and cell phones in class is distracting to many students and may hurt the academic performance of students who think they can multitask without any negative effects. I use both personal experience and recent research reports on multitasking as support for my argument.

2   Banning laptops and cell phones from class would deepen students' engagement with course material and make for more lively and energetic class discussions. I argue that an outright campus ban would be more effective than leaving the decision up to individual instructors.

3   Thank you for considering my proposal. I am happy that this university has a Faculty Senate that welcomes ideas from students on how to make teaching and learning more effective.

Sincerely,
Lucy Morsen,
First-Year Student

A PROPOSAL TO IMPROVE THE CAMPUS LEARNING ENVIRONMENT
BY BANNING LAPTOPS AND CELL PHONES FROM CLASS

Submitted to Professor Ralph Sorento
Chair of the Faculty Senate

Lucy Morsen
First-Year Student, Williamson Hall

If this were the actual proposal, it would begin on a new page following the cover page.

1   Although I am generally happy as a first-year student at this university, I wish to call the Faculty Senate's attention to a distracting problem: classmates' frequent use of laptops and cell phones during class. In many classes more than half the students have open laptops on their desks or are openly text-messaging on cell phones. Inevitably, laptop users multitask between taking notes and checking email, perusing Facebook, surfing the Web, looking at YouTube videos, playing a game, or working on an assignment for another class. (I have yet to see a student use his or her laptop solely for note-taking.) Even though I try to focus on class lectures and discussion, I find myself missing key points and ideas as my eyes are drawn to the animations and flashing colors on neighboring laptop screens. Other distractions come from the clicking of cell phone keypads—or the momentary vibration of a phone on a desktop—which can seem surprisingly loud in an otherwise quiet environment. When the person next to me continually picks up and sets down her phone to send and receive text messages, she not only distracts me from the lecture but also lets me know that she is not engaged in class, and seemingly has no interest in being so. My annoyance at my classmates and my frustration at not being able to focus undercut my enjoyment of class.

2   Given the extensive use of laptops and cell phones in class, I question the academic motivation of my classmates. As a student, I most enjoy classes when I and my classmates are actively interested and engaged in class lecture and discussion. Collective interest has a way of feeding on itself. I mean, we as students do not operate in isolation from one another, but instead we affect and influence one another in gross and subtle ways. Together with our professor we create a collective environment in the classroom, and just as we as individuals affect this collective environment, this collective environment influences us as individuals. The broad effects and consequences of this dynamic interplay should not be underestimated. Humans are highly social beings; we have the power to influence each other in both positive and negative ways. I believe that the distracting nature of laptops and cell phones is negatively affecting classroom environments. Any steps we can take collectively to help each other learn and succeed should be considered.

3   To address this problem, I propose a campus-wide ban on laptops and cell phones during class. I believe a campus-wide ban would be more effective than more limited measures some institutions have adopted, such as blocking wireless access from classrooms or allowing each professor to choose whether or not to ban laptops in his or her classroom. Blocking wireless access does not address the problem of cell phones or non-Web-based laptop distractions (such as computer games or other class work). Leaving the decision up to professors creates an added difficulty for them. I can imagine that professors, fearing resentment and poor evaluations from their students, would be reluctant to enforce a ban in their classrooms, even if they feel it would improve the classroom experience.

4   A campus-wide ban, on the other hand, would be easy to enforce, and students would more easily establish new habits—namely, not using laptops and cell phones during class. Over time, this could become the new campus norm.

5   Although many students might at first object to a ban, the decision to ban all laptops and cell phones in class would bring benefits not only to distracted students like me but also to current users of laptops and cell phones as well as to professors.

6   For one thing, the banning of laptops and cell phones would improve the learning atmosphere of a classroom. These technologies simply create too many distractions for students, and the negative consequences of these distractions are significant enough to call for institutional intervention. While some of my classmates may begrudge the ban, I believe they would quickly get used to it and notice improvements in their own classroom interest and performance. Many of my classmates may actually welcome the ban because they—like myself—are aware of the negative distractions laptops and cell phones create. In fact, an informal survey by a Georgetown University law professor who bans laptops in his classroom indicated that 70% of his students welcomed the ban (Cole, 2008).

7   Second, a ban might directly improve academic performance of current users of laptops and cell phones. A recent study at the University of Winona (Fried, 2008) found that laptop use in the classroom had a significant negative effect on class performance. In Fried's study, students who brought laptops to class received lower grades than their classmates who did not bring laptops to class. Moreover, those who brought laptops to class reported using their laptops for non-class purposes for nearly a quarter of class time.

8   Many of my classmates will likely argue that this study doesn't apply to them. They believe that they are skilled multitaskers who can continue to pay attention to a lecture while also engaging in these other activities. There is empirical evidence that they are in fact mistaken about their ability to multitask. A study by three Stanford University researchers found that persons who self-reported being heavy multitaskers were *more* easily distracted from a primary task than those who reported themselves as light multitaskers (Ophir, Nass, & Wagner, 2009). The researchers conducted this study in a lab by giving multitasking tasks to a group of self-identified heavy multitaskers and then to a group of light multitaskers. This study suggests that a person's own perception of how well he or she multitasks may not be reliable. Moreover it suggests that large amounts of daily multitasking may actually decrease a person's ability to concentrate on a single task and suppress irrelevant information.

9   A handful of students will likely argue that they only use their laptops for class-related purposes, and that an outright ban on laptops in the classroom would be unfair because they would be prohibited from using them for note-taking. However, I am skeptical of any claims that students make of only using laptops for class-related purposes. I personally have never seen any evidence of this, and research is indicating that multitasking is overwhelmingly the common norm among laptop users in the classroom. In a study by Benbunan-Fich and Truman (2009), student laptop use was monitored for 28 classroom sessions of 80 minutes (with students' permission). The researchers analyzed how often the students toggled between screens, and whether the screens were class-related or non-class-related. They found that 76% of the time students toggled between screens that were non-class-related. On average, students toggled between computer-based activities 37.5 times per 80-minute session. This research suggests that the temptations of non-class-related activities are simply too

great for students *not* to engage in multitasking in class—it is just too easy to do a brief check of email or a quick Facebook scan with a swift click of a mouse.

10   University institutions may feel reluctant to propose a campus-wide ban on laptops and cell phones in the classroom for fear of seeming overly authoritative and unnecessarily limiting student freedom. After all, students might rightly claim that they have a right to do whatever they want in the classroom as long as they aren't harming anyone else. (I have already shown they actually are harming others.) While I believe that individual rights are an important concern—in general I believe university institutions should allow for a great amount of autonomy for their students—I think that laptop use has too many negative consequences to be allowed simply in the name of student freedom. (Of course, a professor can always allow laptop use for students with special needs.)

11   For these reasons, I propose that a campus-wide ban on laptops and cell phones in the classroom should be considered. A campus-wide ban would help to create more positive, cohesive classroom experiences, and it would provide a reprieve for students from the myriad of distractions this modern technological age presents us. A campus-wide ban would be easier on professors to enforce, and it would help to establish a new (and improved) norm.

References

Benbunan-Fich, R., & Truman, G. E. (2009). Multitasking with laptops during meetings. *Communications of the ACM, 52*(2), 139–141. doi:10.1145/1461928.1461963

Cole, D. (2008, October 23). Why I ban laptops in my classroom [Web log post]. Retrieved from http://www.britannica.com/blogs/2008/10/why-i-ban-laptops-in-my-classroom

Fried, C. B. (2008). In-class laptop use and its effects on student learning. *Computers and Education, 50*, 906–914. Retrieved from www.elsevier.com

Ophir, E., Nass, C., & Wagner, A. D. (2009). Cognitive control in media multitaskers. *Proceedings of the National Academy of Sciences.* PNAS Early Edition. Retrieved from www.pnas.org

THINKING CRITICALLY
about "A Proposal to Improve the Campus Learning Environment by Banning Laptops and Cell Phones from Class."

1. What strategies does Lucy Morsen use to convince the Faculty Senate that a problem exists?

2. What strategies does Lucy employ to persuade the Faculty Senate that her proposal is worth enacting and that it is more effective than alternative solutions?

3. How does Lucy tie her proposal to the values and beliefs of her audience—college professors who are members of the Faculty Senate?

4. How effective is Lucy's use of research evidence to support her proposal?

5. If you were a faculty member, how effective would you find Lucy's proposal? How effective do you find it as a student? What are its chief strengths and weaknesses?

Our second reading, by student writer Dylan Fujitani, is a researched policy argument that addresses the problem of civilian contractors taking military roles in Iraq.

Dylan Fujitani (student)
"The Hardest of the Hardcore":
Let's Outlaw Hired Guns in Contemporary American Warfare

1   On March 31, 2004, America was shocked by the news that four civilians had been brutally killed, mutilated, and hung up on a bridge in Falluja, Iraq. This horrific event publicized the little-known role of civilian "contractors" in the Iraq war. The public's unawareness that some of these contractors are armed to the teeth is hardly surprising, however, because the language used to refer to non-military personnel in Iraq is often so vague that one can scarcely tell whether a reference to a contractor means a truck driver working for Halliburton or a South African mercenary with a history of killing blacks under the apartheid government working for a private security company. These personnel are often referred to using such broad and mundane terms as "security consultants" or simply "civilian contractors." But in reality, the jobs involved and the kinds of people doing them vary so greatly that these catchall labels are inaccurate. Persons referred to as "civilian contractors" are often well-armed ex-military personnel who took an early retirement to double their pay by working for one of many private security firms hired by the Pentagon. With their obvious training and heavy weaponry, these contractors bear a striking resemblance to soldiers, but one enormous difference sets them apart from the regular troops of the U.S. military: They are actually civilians who can be hired without even the symbolic approval of Congress. Without the need for approval, contractors give the Pentagon the flexibility of outsourcing certain military jobs to private security companies. Despite being paid much more than regular troops, contractors may actually cost less when military benefits and retirement are taken into account.

2   Soldiers for hire have historically been called mercenaries. A case could be made that this term is inapplicable in Iraq because contractors in Iraq are being hired to *support* the military's operations, not to fight the war itself. It is true that many of these civilians are support personnel who should not be called mercenaries—for example, highly specialized technicians or drivers of supply trucks—even though these persons may carry a weapon in case of an attack. But some of these personnel replace soldiers in combat roles historically filled by the military. According to Joshua Hammer of the *New Republic*, these jobs include guarding the Baghdad airport, protecting oil fields, escorting convoys, training local police, and serving as prison interrogators (18). The use of these mercenaries circumvents public and congressional scrutiny of some aspects of war. Their non-military status gives virtual legal immunity to heavily armed individuals who often have questionable backgrounds, who profit from violent conflict, and who ultimately have responsibility to no one but their employers. In light of these dangerous developments, the use of mercenary soldiers must be halted or brought under intense congressional scrutiny.

3   Using mercenaries in war is problematic for six major reasons. First, the deployment of mercenaries disguises the true cost of war to the American public. According to *New York Times* reporter David Barstow, there are roughly 20,000 mercenaries on the ground in Iraq supporting U.S. military operations, and these numbers are not included in reports of the number of American soldiers in Iraq. These 20,000 private contractors make up the second largest contingent in Iraq, surpassing even the British deployment ("Privatizing Warfare"), yet they have received relatively little media attention even as their numbers continue to increase. The use of contractors enables the Pentagon to get by with a smaller number of actual troops through outsourcing to private military companies. Only the deployments of actual troops are reported, so the Pentagon appears to have done more with less. According to a Baghdad-based security consultant, "If you're going to keep the number of troops down, this is the way to do it. ... The expense is the same or more. But politically it's much less expensive" (qtd. in Daragahi). The use of mercenaries in Iraq blurs the high cost of war in the public eye, both in terms of dollars and in terms of human lives. Contractors have suffered casualties, yet the public scarcely hears of their death toll unless they are mutilated and publicly exhibited. Furthermore, with the service of a civilian mercenary in Iraq costing as much as $1,500 a day ("Privatizing Warfare"), contractor use is consuming an enormous portion of the funding allocated for reconstruction. *New York Times* reporter David Barstow asserts that "security costs could claim up to 25 percent of the $18 billion budgeted for reconstruction," diverting capital from important reconstruction projects like school and road construction. Thus, the use of mercenaries in Iraq makes it more difficult for the American public to determine the true cost of war.

4   The second major problem with use of mercenaries is that as a group they have no national loyalties and ultimately answer to their employers, not the armed forces. According to the Brookings Institution's P. W. Singer, "during the Persian Gulf War, a 'very small number' of private contractors working at an air base in Saudi Arabia fled from fear that chemical weapons might be used" (qtd. in Bredemeier). In using mercenaries, the Pentagon is outsourcing what the *New York Times* calls its "core responsibilities" ("Privatizing Warfare"), and despite the importance of these tasks, the jobs are being assigned to people who can basically leave whenever they want to. As P. W. Singer has pointed out, a soldier faces a court-martial for refusing to face battle, whereas a contractor merely loses his job (Bredemeier). In addition, the mercenaries and regular military personnel sometimes have poor working relationships. Since contractors are not required to abide by normal military procedures, mercenaries can pretty much operate any way they want, sometimes to the armed forces' disliking. Writing in the *New Republic*, Joshua Hammer explains the attitudes of the Marines who had been with the four contractors killed in Falluja the day before their deaths. Quoting a Marine officer, Hammer writes, "We would have told them not to do it [take an unauthorized shortcut through Baghdad]." According to Hammer, the officer "angrily called the contractors 'cowboys' and said they had failed to inform anyone on the base of their plans, a direct violation of military policy" (19). Relying on such a large number of poorly supervised and unaccountable

mercenaries to fill crucial roles leaves the United States dangerously vulnerable to the future uncertainties of war.

5   Another problem with the use of mercenaries is their civilian status, creating legal ambiguity and making discipline extremely difficult if not impossible. Phillip Carter, a former U.S. Army officer, writing for the e-magazine *Slate*, commented that the involvement of private contractors in the Abu Ghraib prison abuse scandal brought the issue of discipline to the forefront ("How to Discipline"). According to Carter, mercenaries don't fit the Geneva convention definition of "non-combatants" (since they are armed), or of "lawful combatants" (since they don't wear uniforms or fit within a military chain of command). Rather, "they fall into an international legal gray zone" ("Hired Guns"). This problem is highlighted in an editorial from the *Economist*, which pointed out that the "great sanction on wrongdoing—the law—does not really operate. Regular soldiers are subject to courts-martial or international law. But it is not clear what law applies to private security firms" ("Dangerous Work"). Borzou Daragahi, in a piece for the *Post-gazette.com*, wrote that contractors are not subject to the Uniform Code of Military Justice and that there are military personnel who are very uncomfortable with their seemingly untouchable status. Contractors' fuzzy legal status with regard to military justice and international law is highly problematic.

6   Some have argued against these claims of virtual immunity, saying that in reality a lot can be done to discipline law-breaking private contractors. Carter says that possible disciplinary measures include termination of contracts, prohibition from bidding for future contracts, criminal prosecution, and civil suits ("How to Discipline"). All of these penalties, however, are at "the discretion of the agency that issued the original contract," or in this case, presumably the Pentagon. Although Carter effectively makes the point that contractors are not entirely immune from discipline, many of these forms of punishment ultimately amount to nothing more than loss of the job. Carter admits that government contractors are "shielded" from civil suits by a legal doctrine called the "government contractor" defense. Under the current circumstances in Iraq where offensive and defensive roles are becoming increasingly muddied, the only form of punishment contractors are concerned with is financial. This virtual legal immunity is striking considering the strict rules that govern the actions of military personnel. The threat of mere financial punishment cannot be expected to deter mercenaries from possible abusive and criminal behavior. Their legal status must be clarified as soon as possible in both domestic and international law.

7   The fourth major problem with mercenaries is that private military companies frequently hire employees with questionable backgrounds. Inadequate governmental oversight has allowed private companies to hire known war criminals who have been or continue to be paid with American taxpayer dollars. According to journalist Louis Nevaer, writing for the *National Catholic Reporter*, roughly 1,500 South African mercenaries are now in Iraq, many of them former Apartheid-era mercenaries, some of whom have even confessed to killing blacks. Nevaer states that there are "terrorists … and war criminals on the payrolls of companies contracted by the Pentagon." He gives the example of a former South African police officer who was "a member of the Vlakplass death squad that terrorized blacks under apartheid." Not only are the

personal histories of the mercenaries questionable, but their motivations are also dubious. Joshua Hammer in his *New Republic* article "Cowboy Up" describes what he observed of these private contractors in Baghdad:

> [M]ost of the contractors are the hardest of the hard core—veterans of such elite outfits as the U.S. Special Forces; the Rhodesian Selous Scouts, the former special forces of the Rhodesian white regime; and Executive Outcomes, the now-disbanded South African mercenary army that fought in Sierra Leone and Angola. These men thrive on the danger of working in war zones. (19)

Given the current uncertainly about the legal status of private contractors, and given the fact that actual American military personnel could be targeted in retaliation for the behavior of mercenaries, Congress must quickly act to regulate hiring practices of private military companies to screen against the hiring of terrorists, war criminals, or anyone who would potentially misrepresent the United States.

8   The fifth problem with the use of mercenaries is that the growth of the private security industry entices many of America's most experienced soldiers to leave the military for higher paying contractor jobs. Eric Schmitt and Tom Shanker, writing in the *New York Times*, explain the lure of contractors' salaries:

> Senior enlisted members of the Army Green Berets or Navy Seals with 20 years or more experience now earn about $50,000 in base pay, and can retire with a $23,000 pension. But private security companies ... are offering salaries of $100,000 to nearly $200,000 a year to the most experienced of them.

The military is losing some of its finest soldiers to the private sector where their expertise goes to the highest bidder. The use of mercenaries must be swiftly restrained and eventually halted lest the military be gradually stripped of its edge and become further reliant upon the expertise of private military companies.

9   Finally, the sixth major problem regarding the use of mercenaries is that the rapid increase in their numbers is creating large international interest groups who will *want war* in the long run. For mercenaries, war means fortune and excitement, and peace means a boring period of unemployment. The creation of such groups who thrive off violent conflict is dangerous on a very fundamental level. In the interests of peace, mercenaries and any other war profiteers must not be encouraged through governmental employment. The business of war has proven lucrative, and the free market must not be allowed to encourage war any more than it already does.

10   The expanded use of mercenaries in American warfare has given rise to numerous problems that must be addressed immediately. Among the obvious, their use hides the true cost of war from the American people; contractors' backgrounds and loyalties are questionable; and they have been given a great reason to hope for war in the world. These problems must be addressed swiftly and immediately, particularly by Congress. Mercenaries are used because they are cheaper, both economically and politically, but they also serve the critical purpose of circumventing the scrutiny of Congress and the people of the United States. Action must be taken now to disable this circumvention of democracy and to protect legitimate uses of war from market forces, lawlessness, and the abuse of power.

Works Cited

Barstow, David. "Security Companies: Shadow Soldiers in Iraq." *New York Times* 19 Apr. 2004: A1+. *LexisNexis*. Web. 19 May 2004.

Bredemeier, Kenneth. "Thousands of Private Contractors Support U.S. Forces in Persian Gulf." *Washington Post*. Washington Post, 3 Mar. 2003: E01. Web. 19 May 2004.

Carter, Phillip. "Hired Guns: What to Do about Military Contractors Run Amok." *Slate* 9 Apr. 2004. Web. 12 June 2004.

—. "How to Discipline Private Contractors." *Slate* 4 May 2004. Web. 19 May 2004.

"Dangerous Work." *Economist* 10 Apr. 2004: 22–23. *Academic Search Premier*. Web. 23 May 2004.

Daragahi, Borzou. "In Iraq, Private Contractors Lighten Load on U.S. Troops." *Post-gazette.com*. PG Publishing, 28 Sept. 2003. Web. 19 May 2004.

Hammer, Joshua. "Cowboy Up." *New Republic* 24 May 2004: 18–19. *Academic Search Premier*. Web. 23 May 2004.

Nevaer, Louis. "Many Hired Guns in Iraq Have War Crimes Pasts." *National Catholic Reporter* 14 May 2004: 10. Print.

"Privatizing Warfare." Editorial. *New York Times* 21 Apr. 2004: A22. *LexisNexis*. Web. 19 May 2004.

Schmitt, Eric, and Tom Shanker. "Big Pay Luring Military's Elite to Private Jobs." *New York Times* 30 Mar. 2004: A1+. *LexisNexis*. Web. 19 May 2004.

THINKING CRITICALLY
about "'The Hardest of the Hardcore': Let's Outlaw Hired Guns in Contemporary American Warfare"

1. Many people are unaware that a problem might exist with civilian contractors in Iraq. Dylan's major rhetorical task, therefore, is to persuade readers that a problem exists. To what extent do you think he convinces readers that the use of civilian contractors to fulfill military roles constitutes a problem? Point to passages that you think are or are not persuasive in building his case.

2. The structure of Dylan's paper is almost entirely devoted to showing that a problem exists. However, his proposed solution is vague: either to eliminate the use of contractors in military roles entirely or to demand more congressional oversight. Dylan's strategy is typical for "planning proposals" (see p. 246) where the writer points out a problem but is unable to propose a clear plan for solving it. Does this strategy work for you? Do you think Dylan needs to propose a more specific solution, or is it enough that he identifies a problem?

3. Overall, how would you evaluate the *logos* of this argument? How effective is Dylan's use of reasons and evidence to convince you that the continued use of civilian contractors in military roles is a problem that requires some action?

4. How effective are Dylan's appeals to *ethos* and *pathos*? To what extent does Dylan project a credible and trustworthy persona? To what extent does he connect his argument to the values and beliefs of his audience, appealing to readers' emotions and sympathies as well as to their minds?

PART 3

A GUIDE TO COMPOSING AND REVISING

This ad for the United States Army, which first appeared in a general news commentary magazine, highlights qualities traditionally associated with patriotic military service to the country: respect, honor, and courage. Note that this poster does not depict soldiers in uniform on a battlefield or in the midst of a drill. Consider the way the images of the father and daughter and the words in this ad connect character-building, family relationships, the Army, and success. Think about how gender functions in this ad by focusing on the young woman's long hair, tasteful makeup, and earnest manner. This advertisement is part of a For Writing and Discussion exercise in Chapter 8.

**YOU TAUGHT HER ABOUT RESPECT, HONOR AND COURAGE.
IS IT ANY SURPRISE THAT NOW SHE WANTS TO USE THEM?**

She'll experience the most challenging training, use the latest technology and get the strongest support. Every drill and every mission will reinforce in her that character always leads to success. Encourage her to consider becoming a Soldier — AN ARMY OF ONE.®

 AN ARMY OF ONE

GOARMY.COM U.S.ARMY

11 WRITING AS A PROBLEM-SOLVING PROCESS

> I rewrite as I write. It is hard to tell what is a first draft because it is not determined by time. In one draft, I might cross out three pages, write two, cross out a fourth, rewrite it, and call it a draft. I am constantly writing and rewriting. I can only conceptualize so much in my first draft—only so much information can be held in my head at one time; my rewriting efforts are a reflection of how much information I can encompass at one time. There are levels and agenda which I have to attend to in each draft.*
>
> —*Description of Revision by an Experienced Writer*

> I read what I have written and I cross out a word and put another word in; a more decent word or a better word. Then if there is somewhere to use a sentence that I have crossed out, I will put it there.*
>
> —*Description of Revision by an Inexperienced Writer*

> Blot out, correct, insert, refine,
> Enlarge, diminish, interline;
> Be mindful, when invention fails,
> To scratch your head, and bite your nails.
>
> —*Jonathan Swift*

Throughout this text, we have emphasized writing as a critical thinking process requiring writers to "wallow in complexity." This opening chapter of Part 3 explains how experienced writers use multiple drafts to manage the complexities of writing.

In this chapter, you will learn to improve your own writing processes:

- SKILL 11.1 Follow the experts' practice of using multiple drafts.
- SKILL 11.2 Revise globally as well as locally.
- SKILL 11.3 Develop ten expert habits to improve your writing processes.
- SKILL 11.4 Use peer reviews to help you think like an expert.

*From Nancy Sommers, "Revision Strategies of Student Writers and Experienced Adult Writers," *College Composition and Communication* 31 (October 1980): 291–300.

SKILL 11.1 **Follow the experts' practice of using multiple drafts.**

We begin this chapter with a close look at why expert writers use multiple drafts to move from an initial exploration of ideas to a finished product. As composition theorist Peter Elbow has asserted about the writing process, "meaning is not what you start out with" but "what you end up with." In the early stages of writing, experienced writers typically discover, deepen, and complicate their ideas before they can clarify them and arrange them effectively. Only in the last drafts will expert writers be in sufficient control of their ideas to shape them elegantly for readers.

What most distinguishes expert from novice writers is the experts' willingness to keep revising their work until they feel it is ready to go public. They typically work much harder at drafting and revising than do novice writers, taking more runs at their subject. Expert writers also make more substantial alterations in their drafts during revision—what we call "global" rather than "local" revision. This difference between expert and novice writers might seem counterintuitive. One might think that novices would need to revise more than experts. But decades of research on the writing process of experts reveals how extensively experts revise. Compare the first two quotations that open this chapter—one from an experienced and one from an inexperienced writer. The experienced writer crosses out pages and starts over while the inexperienced writer crosses out a word or two. The experienced writer feels cognitive overload while drafting, having to attend to many different "levels and agendas" at once. In contrast, the inexperienced writer seems to think only of replacing words or adding an occasional transition. Learning to revise extensively is thus a hallmark of a maturing writer.

Figure 11.1 shows how a first-year college student demonstrates expert writing behavior when she makes a substantial revision of an early draft. Note that she crosses out several sentences at the end of one paragraph, creates a new topic sentence for the next paragraph, and moves a detail sentence so that it follows the topic sentence.

Why Expert Writers Revise So Extensively

Our emphasis on experts' substantial revision might have surprised you. If the experts are such good writers, why do they need multiple drafts? Why don't they get it right the first time? Our answer is simply this: Expert writers use multiple drafts to break a complex task into manageable subtasks. Let's look more closely at some of the functions that drafting and revising can perform for writers.

- ***Multiple drafts help writers overcome the limits of short-term memory.***
  Cognitive psychologists have shown that working memory—often called short-term memory—has remarkably little storage space. You can picture short-term memory as a small tabletop surrounded by filing cabinets (long-term memory). As you write, you can place on your tabletop (working memory) only a few chunks of material at any given moment—a few sentences of a draft or several ideas in an outline. The remaining portions of your draft-in-progress

First Draft with Revisions

sticks of our favorite flavors in the bottom of the bag. ~~That discovery was, by far, the best discovery that could ever be made, week after week. So, as you can probably guess, my opinion of farmer's markets has always been very high as they were what fulfilled my sugar fix.~~

~~However, another important point can come out of that story. That point being about~~ the man who sold us our precious honey sticks. He was kind, patient, and genuinely happy to have our business. ^{In contrast to} ~~Not quite the same vibe that one would expect to get from~~ the supermarket employee who ^often^ doesn't ~~even really~~ know what isle you need in order to find the peanut butter. ^Another^ A~~ huge selling point of farmer's markets, for me, is that you can go and talk to people who know about the food they are selling. It is so refreshing to go

Revised Draft

sticks of our favorite flavors in the bottom of the bag.

Another huge selling point of farmer's markets, for me, is that you can go and talk to people who know about the food they are selling. The man who sold us our ^precious^ honey sticks was kind, patient, and genuinely happy to have our business, in contrast to the supermarket employee who ^often^ doesn't ~~even really~~ know what aisle you need in order to find the peanut butter.

FIGURE 11.1 A First-Year Student's Substantial Revisions

fall off the table without getting stored in long-term memory. (Think of your horror when your computer eats your draft—proof that you can't rely on long-term memory to restore what you wrote.) Writing a draft captures and stores your ideas as your working memory develops them. When you reread these stored ideas, you can then see your evolving ideas whole, note problem areas, develop more ideas, see material that doesn't fit, recall additional information, and begin extending or improving the draft.

- *Multiple drafts help accommodate shifts and changes in the writer's ideas.* Early in the writing process, expert writers often are unsure of where their ideas are leading; they find that their ideas shift and evolve as their drafts progress. An expert writer's finished product often is radically different from the first draft—not simply in form and style but also in actual content.
- *Multiple drafts help writers clarify audience and purpose.* While thinking about their subject matter, experienced writers also ask questions

about audience and purpose: What do my readers already know and believe about my subject? How am I trying to change their views? In the process of drafting and revising, the answers to these questions may evolve so that each new draft reflects a deeper or clearer understanding of audience and purpose.

- ***Multiple drafts help writers improve structure and coherence for readers.*** Whereas the ideas in early drafts often follow the order in which writers conceived them, later drafts are often restructured—sometimes radically—to meet readers' needs. Writing teachers sometimes call this transformation a movement from writer-based to reader-based prose.* The composing and revising skills taught in Chapter 12 will help you learn how to revise your drafts from a reader's perspective.
- ***Multiple drafts let writers postpone worrying about correctness.*** Late in the revision process, experienced writers turn their energy toward fixing errors and revising sentences for increased cohesion, conciseness, and clarity. Focusing on correctness too soon can shut down the creative process.

An Expert's Writing Processes Are Recursive

Given this background on why expert writers revise, we can see that for experts, the writing process is recursive rather than linear. Writers continually cycle back to earlier stages as their thinking evolves. Sometimes writers develop a thesis statement early in the writing process. But just as frequently, they formulate a thesis during an "aha!" moment of discovery later in the process, perhaps after several drafts. ("So *this* is my point! Here is my argument in a nutshell!") Even very late in the process, while checking usage and punctuation, experienced writers are apt to think of new ideas, thus triggering more revision.

SKILL 11.2 **Revise globally as well as locally.**

To think like an expert writer, you need to appreciate the difference between "global" and "local" revision. You revise **locally** whenever you make changes to a text that affect only the one or two sentences that you are currently working on. In contrast, you revise **globally** when a change in one part of your draft drives changes in other parts of the draft. Global revision focuses on the big-picture concerns of ideas, structure, purpose, audience, and genre. It often involves substantial rewriting, even starting over in places with a newly conceived plan. For example, your revising part of the middle of your essay might cause you to rewrite the whole introduction or to change the tone or point of view throughout the essay.

*The terms "writer-based" and "reader-based" prose come from Linda Flower, "Writer-Based Prose: A Cognitive Basis for Problems in Writing." College English, 1979, 41.1, 19–37.

What follows are some on-the-page strategies that you can adopt to practice the global and local revision strategies of experts:*

On-the-Page Strategies for Doing Global and Local Revision	
Strategies to Use on the Page	**Reasons**
Throw out the whole draft and start again.	• Original draft helped writer discover ideas and see the whole territory. • New draft needs to be substantially refocused and restructured.
Cross out large chunks and rewrite from scratch.	• Original passage was unfocused; ideas have changed. • New sense of purpose or point meant that the whole passage needed reshaping. • Original passage was too confused or jumbled for mere editing.
Cut and paste; move parts around; (then write new transitions, mapping statements, and topic sentences).	• Parts didn't follow in logical order. • Parts occurred in the order writer thought of them rather than the order needed by readers. • Conclusion was clearer than introduction; part of conclusion had to be moved to introduction. • Revised thesis statement required different order for parts.
Add/revise topic sentences of paragraphs; insert transitions.	• Reader needs signposts to see how parts connect to previous parts and to whole. • Revision of topic sentences often requires global revision of paragraph.
Make insertions; add new material.	• Supporting particulars needed to be added: examples, facts, illustrations, statistics, other evidence (usually added to bodies of paragraphs). • New section was needed or more explanation was needed for a point. • Gaps in argument needed to be filled in.
Delete material.	• Material is no longer needed or is irrelevant. • Deleted material may have been good but went off on a tangent.

(continued)

*We have chosen to say "on the page" rather than "on the screen" because global revision is often facilitated by a writer's working off double-spaced hard copy rather than a computer screen. See page 280 for our advice on using hard copy for revision.

Strategies to Use on the Page	Reasons
Recast sentences (cross out and rewrite portions; combine sentences; rephrase sentences; start sentences with a different grammatical structure).	• Passage violated old/new contract (see Skill 12.7). • Passage was wordy/choppy or lacked rhythm or voice. • Grammar was tangled, diction odd, or meaning confused. • Passage lost focus of topic sentence of paragraph.
Edit sentences to correct mistakes.	• Writer found comma splices, fragments, dangling modifiers, nonparallel constructions, or other problems of grammar and usage. • Writer found spelling errors, typos, repeated or omitted words.

Revising a Paragraph Globally

FOR WRITING AND DISCUSSION

Choose an important paragraph in the body of a draft you are currently working on. Then write your answers to these questions about that paragraph.

1. Why is this an important paragraph?
2. What is its main point?
3. Where is that main point stated?

Now—as an exercise only—write the main point at the top of a blank sheet of paper, put away your original draft, and, without looking at the original, write a new paragraph with the sole purpose of developing the point you wrote at the top of the page.

When you are finished, compare your new paragraph to the original. What have you learned that might help you revise your original?

Here are some typical responses of writers who have tried this exercise:

> I recognized that my original paragraph was unfocused. I couldn't find a main point.
> I recognized that my original paragraph was underdeveloped. I had a main point but not enough particulars supporting it.
> I began to see that my draft was scattered and that I had too many short paragraphs.
> I recognized that I was making a couple of different points in my original paragraph and that I needed to break it into separate paragraphs.
> I recognized that I hadn't stated my main point (or that I had buried it in the middle of the paragraph).
> I recognized that there was a big difference in style between my two versions and that I had to choose which version I liked best. (It's not always the "new" version!)

SKILL 11.3 Develop ten expert habits to improve your writing processes.

Now that you understand why experts revise more extensively than novices and what they do on the page, we describe in Skill 11.3 the habitual ways of thinking and acting that experts use when they write. Our hope is that this description will help you develop these same habits for yourself. Because one of the best ways to improve your writing process is to do what the experts do, we offer you the following ten habits of experienced writers, expressed as advice:

1. ***Use exploratory writing and talking to discover and clarify ideas.*** Don't let your first draft be the first occasion when you put your ideas into writing. Use exploratory strategies such as freewriting and idea mapping to generate ideas (see Chapter 2, Concept 4). Also seek out opportunities to talk about your ideas with classmates or friends in order to clarify your own thinking and appreciate alternative points of view.

2. ***Schedule your time.*** Don't begin your paper the night before it is due. Plan sufficient time for exploration, drafting, revision, and editing. Recognize that your ideas will shift, branch out, and even turn around as you write. Allow some time off between writing the first draft and beginning revision. For many writers, revision takes considerably longer than writing the first draft. If your institution has a writing center, consider scheduling a visit.

3. ***Discover what methods of drafting work best for you.*** Some people compose rough drafts directly on the computer; others write longhand. Some make outlines first; others plunge directly into drafting and make outlines later. Some revise extensively on the computer as they are drafting; others plough ahead until they have a complete draft before they start revising. Some people sit at their desk for hours at a time; others need to get up and walk around every couple of minutes. Some people need a quiet room; others work best in a coffee shop. Discover the methods that work best for you.

4. ***Think about audience and purpose from the start.*** Early on, think about the effect you want your writing to have on readers. In formulating a thesis, look to change your readers' view of your subject. ("Before reading my paper, my readers will think X. But after reading my paper, my readers will think Y.")

5. ***For the first draft, reduce your expectations.*** Many novice writers get blocked by trying to make their first draft perfect. In contrast, expert writers expect the first draft to be an unreadable mess. (They often call it a "zero draft" or a "garbage draft" because they don't expect it to be good.) They use the first draft merely to get their ideas flowing, knowing they will revise later. If you get blocked, just keep writing. Get some ideas on paper.

6. ***Revise on double- or triple-spaced hard copy.*** Although many experienced writers revise on the screen without going through paper drafts, there are powerful advantages in printing occasional paper drafts. Research suggests that writers are more apt to make global changes in a draft if they work from hard copy because they can see more easily how the parts connect to the whole. They can refer quickly to page two while revising page six without having to scroll back and forth. We suggest that you occasionally print out a double- or triple-spaced hard copy of your draft and then mark it up aggressively. (See again Figure 11.1, which shows how a first-year student learned the benefits of revising off hard copy.) When your draft gets too messy, keyboard your changes into your computer and begin another round of revision.

7. ***As you revise, think increasingly about the needs of your readers.*** Experts use first drafts to help them clarify their ideas for themselves but not necessarily for readers. In many respects, writers of first drafts are talking to

themselves. Through global revision, however, writers gradually convert "writer-based prose" to "reader-based prose." Writers begin to employ consciously the skills of reader-expectation theory that we explain in detail in Chapter 12.

8. ***Exchange drafts with others.*** Get other people's reactions to your work in exchange for your reactions to theirs. Experienced writers regularly seek critiques of their drafts from trusted readers. Later in this chapter we explain procedures for peer review of drafts.

9. ***Save correctness for last.*** To revise productively, concentrate first on the big questions: Do I have good ideas in this draft? Am I responding appropriately to the assignment? Are my ideas adequately organized and developed? Save questions about exact wording, grammar, mechanics, and documentation style for later. These concerns are important, but they cannot be efficiently attended to until after higher-order concerns are met. Your first goal is to create a thoughtful, richly developed draft.

10. ***To meet deadlines and bring the process to a close, learn how to satisfice.*** Our description of the writing process may seem formidable. Technically, it seems, you could go on revising forever. How can you ever know when to stop? There is no ready answer to that question, which is more a psychological than a technical problem. Expert writers have generally learned how to **satisfice**, a term coined by influential social scientist Herbert Simon from two root words, *suffice* and *satisfy*. It means to do the best job you can under the circumstances considering your time constraints, the pressures of other demands on you, and the difficulty of the task. Expert writers begin the writing process early and get as far as they can before their deadline looms. Then they let the deadline give them the energy for intensive revision. From lawyers preparing briefs for court to engineers developing design proposals, writers have used deadlines to help them put aside doubts and anxieties and to conclude their work, as every writer must. "Okay, it's not perfect, but it's the best I can do for now."

Analyzing Your Own Writing Process

FOR WRITING AND DISCUSSION

When you write, do you follow a process resembling the one we just described? Have you ever

- had a writing project grow out of your engagement with a problem or question?
- explored ideas by talking with others or by doing exploratory writing?
- made major changes to a draft because you changed your mind or otherwise discovered new ideas?
- revised a draft from a reader's perspective by consciously trying to imagine and respond to a reader's questions, confusions, and other reactions?
- road tested a draft by trying it out on readers and then revising it as a result of what they told you?

Working in groups or as a whole class, share stories about previous writing experiences that match or do not match the description of experienced writers' processes. To the extent that your present process differs, what strategies of experienced writers might you like to try?

SKILL 11.4 Use peer reviews to help you think like an expert.

One of the best ways to become a better reviser is to see your draft from a *reader*'s rather than a *writer*'s perspective. As a writer, you know what you mean; you are already inside your own head. But you need to see what your draft looks like to readers—that is, to people who are not inside your head.

A good way to learn this skill is to practice reading your classmates' drafts and have them read yours. In this section we offer advice on how to respond candidly to your classmates' drafts and how to participate in peer reviews.

Becoming a Helpful Reader of Classmates' Drafts

When you respond to a writer's draft, learn to make *readerly* rather than *writerly* comments. For example, instead of saying, "Your draft is disorganized," say, "I got lost when .... " Instead of saying, "This paragraph needs a topic sentence," say, "I had trouble seeing the point of this paragraph." In other words, describe your mental experience in trying to understand the draft rather than use technical terms to point out problem areas or to identify errors.

When you help a writer with a draft, your goal is both to point out where the draft needs more work and to brainstorm with the writer possible ways to improve the draft. Begin by reading the draft all the way through at a normal reading speed. As you read, make mental notes to help focus your feedback. We recommend that you also mark passages that you find confusing. Write "G!" for "Good" next to parts that you like. Write "?" next to places where you want to ask questions.

After you have read the draft, use the following strategies for making helpful responses, either in writing or in direct conversation with the writer.

Strategies for Responding Helpfully to a Classmate's Draft	
Kinds of Problems Noted	**Helpful Responses**
If the ideas in the draft seem thin or undeveloped, or if the draft is too short	• Help the writer brainstorm for more ideas. • Help the writer add more examples, better details, more supporting data or arguments.
If you get confused or lost in some parts of the draft	• Show the writer where you got confused or miscued in reading the draft ("I started getting lost here because I couldn't see why you were giving me this information" or "I thought you were going to say X, but then you said Y"). • Have the writer talk through ideas to clear up confusing spots.

(continued)

Kinds of Problems Noted	Helpful Responses

If you get confused or lost at the "big-picture" level	• Help the writer sharpen the thesis: suggest that the writer view the thesis as the answer to a controversial or problematic question; ask the writer to articulate the question that the thesis answers.
	• Help the writer create an outline, tree diagram, or flowchart (see Skill 12.3).
	• Help the writer clarify the focus by asking him or her to complete these statements about purpose:
	  • The purpose of this paper is _____.
	  • The purpose of this section (paragraph) is _____.
	  • Before reading my paper, my reader will think X. But after reading my paper, my reader will think Y.

If you can understand the sentences but can't see the point	• Help the writer articulate the meaning by asking "So what?" questions, making the writer bring the point to the surface. ("I can understand what you are saying here but I don't quite understand why you are saying it. What do these details have to do with the topic sentence of the paragraph? Or what does this paragraph have to do with your thesis?") • Help the writer create transitions, new topic sentences, or other means of making points clear.
If you disagree with the ideas or think the writer has avoided alternative points of view	• Play devil's advocate to help the writer deepen and complicate ideas. • Show the writer specific places where you had queries or doubts.

Using a Generic Peer Review Guide

When participating in peer reviews, writers and reviewers often appreciate a list of guiding questions or checkpoints. What follows is a list of generic questions that can be used for peer-reviewing many different kinds of drafts. In each assignment chapter for Part 2 of this text, we have created additional peer review questions tailored specifically to that chapter's rhetorical aim and genres. For any given peer review session, your instructor may specify which generic or assignment-specific questions you are to use for the peer review.

Generic Peer Review Guide

For the writer
Prepare two or three questions you would like your peer reviewer to address while responding to your draft. The questions can focus on some aspect of your draft that you are uncertain about, on one or more sections where you particularly seek help or advice, on some feature that you particularly like about your draft, or on some part you especially wrestled with. Write out your questions and give them to your peer reviewer along with your draft.

For the reviewer
Basic overview: Read the draft at a normal reading speed from beginning to end. As you read do the following:

- Mark a "?" next to any passages that you find confusing, that somehow slow down your reading, or that raise questions in your mind.
- Mark a "G" next to any passages where you think the writing is particularly good, strong, or interesting.

Going into more depth: Prior to discussion with the writer, complete the following tasks:

- Identify at least one specific place in the draft where you got confused. Make notes for why you got confused, using readerly rather than writerly comments.
- Identify one place in the draft where you think the ideas are thin or need more development. Make discussion notes.
- Identify one place where you might write "So what?" after the passage. These are places where you don't understand the significance or importance of the writer's points. These are also places where you can't see how certain sentences connect to a topic sentence or how certain paragraphs or sections connect to the thesis statement.
- Identify at least one place where you could play devil's advocate or otherwise object to the writer's ideas. Make notes on the objections or alternative views that you will raise with the writer.

Evaluating the writer's argument: Look at the draft's effectiveness from the perspective of the classical rhetorical appeals:

- *Logos:* How effectively does the writer use reasons and evidence to support his or her claim? How effectively does the writer use details, particulars, examples, and other means as evidence to support points? How logical are the points and how clearly are they connected?
- *Ethos:* What kind of image does the writer project? How effective is the tone? How trustworthy, reliable, knowledgeable, and fair does this writer seem?
- *Pathos:* How effectively does the writer engage the audience's interest? How effectively does the writer tie into the audience's beliefs and values? To what extent does the writer make the reader care about the topic?

Noting problems of grammar and editing: Mark the draft wherever you notice problems in grammar, spelling, punctuation, documentation form, or other issues of mechanics.

Summing up: Create a consolidated summary of your review:

- Sum up the strengths of the draft.
- Identify two or three main weaknesses or problem areas.
- Make two or three suggestions for revision.

Practicing a Peer Review

Background: In the following exercise, we invite you to practice a peer review by responding to a student's draft ("Should the University Carpet the Dorm Rooms?" below) or to another draft provided by your instructor. The "Carpets" assignment asked students to take a stand on a local campus issue. Imagine that you have exchanged drafts with this student and that your task is to help this student improve the draft through both global and local revision.

Individual task: Read the draft carefully following the instructions in the "Generic Peer Review Guide." Write out your responses to the bulleted items under "Going into more depth," "Evaluating the writer's argument," and "Summing up."

Small group or whole class: Share your responses. Then turn to the following additional tasks:

1. With the instructor serving as a guide, practice explaining to the writer where or how you got confused while reading the draft. Readers often have difficulty explaining their reading experience to a writer. Let several class members role-play being the reader. Practice using language such as "I like the way this draft started because . . . ." "I got confused when . . . ." "I had to back up and reread when . . . ." "I saw your point here, but then I got lost again because . . . ." Writing theorist Peter Elbow calls such language a "movie of your mind."

2. Have several class members role-play being devil's advocates by arguing against the writer's thesis. Where are the ideas thin or weak?

SHOULD THE UNIVERSITY CARPET THE DORM ROOMS?

Tricia, a university student, came home exhausted from her work-study job. She took a blueberry pie from the refrigerator to satisfy her hunger and a tall glass of milk to quench her thirst. While trying to get comfortable on her bed, she tipped her snack over onto the floor. She cleaned the mess, but the blueberry and milk stains on her brand-new carpet could not be removed.

Tricia didn't realize how hard it was to clean up stains on a carpet. Luckily this was her own carpet.

A lot of students don't want carpets. Students constantly change rooms. The next person may not want carpet.

Some students say that since they pay to live on campus, the rooms should reflect a comfortable home atmosphere. Carpets will make the dorm more comfortable. The carpet will act as insulation and as a soundproofing system.

Paint stains cannot be removed from carpets. If the university carpets the rooms, the students will lose the privilege they have of painting their rooms any color. This would limit students' self-expression.

The carpets would be an institutional brown or gray. This would be ugly. With tile floors, the students can choose and purchase their own carpets to match their taste. You can't be an individual if you can't decorate your room to fit your personality.

According to Rachel Jones, Assistant Director of Housing Services, the cost will be $300 per room for the carpet and installation. Also the university will have to buy more vacuum cleaners. But will vacuum cleaners be all that is necessary to keep the carpets clean? We'll need shampoo machines too.

What about those stains that won't come off even with a shampoo machine? That's where the student will have to pay damage deposit costs.

There will be many stains on the carpet due to shaving cream fights, food fights, beverage parties, and smoking, all of which can damage the carpets.

Students don't take care of the dorms now. They don't follow the rules of maintaining their rooms. They drill holes into the walls, break mirrors, beds, and closet doors, and leave their food trays all over the floor.

If the university buys carpets our room rates will skyrocket. In conclusion, it is a bad idea for the university to buy carpets.

Participating in Peer Review Workshops

If you are willing to respond candidly to a classmate's draft—in a readerly rather than a writerly way—you will be a valuable participant in peer review workshops. In a typical workshop, classmates work in groups of two to six to respond to each other's rough drafts and offer suggestions for revisions. These workshops are most helpful when group members have developed sufficient levels of professionalism and trust to exchange candid responses. A frequent problem in peer review workshops is that classmates try so hard to avoid hurting each other's feelings that they provide vague, meaningless feedback. Saying, "Your paper's great. I really liked it. Maybe you could make it flow a little better" is much less helpful than saying, "Your issue about environmental pollution in the Antarctic is well defined in the first paragraph, but I got lost in the second paragraph when you began discussing penguin coloration."

Responsibilities of Peer Reviewers and Writers Learning to respond conscientiously and carefully to others' work may be the single most important thing you can do to improve your own writing. When you review a classmate's draft, you are not acting as a teacher, but simply as a fresh reader. You can help the writer appreciate what it's like to encounter his or her text for the first time. Your primary responsibility is to articulate your understanding of what the writer's words say to you and to identify places where you get confused, where you need more details, where you have doubts or queries, and so on.

When you play the role of writer during a workshop session, your responsibilities parallel those of your peer reviewers. You need to provide a legible rough draft, preferably typed and double-spaced, that doesn't baffle the reader with hard-to-follow corrections and confusing pagination. Your instructor may ask you to bring copies of your draft for all group members. During the workshop, your primary responsibility is to *listen,* taking in how others respond to your draft without becoming defensive. Many instructors also ask writers to formulate two or three specific questions about their drafts—questions they particularly want their reviewers to address. These questions might focus on something writers particularly like about their drafts or on specific problem areas or concerns.

Responding to Peer Reviews

After you and your classmates have gone over each other's papers and walked each other through the responses, everyone should identify two or three things about his or her draft that particularly need work. Before you leave the session, you should have some notion about how you want to revise your paper.

You may get mixed or contradictory responses from different reviewers. One reviewer may praise a passage that another finds confusing or illogical. Conflicting advice is a frustrating fact of life for all writers, whether students or professionals. Such disagreements reveal how readers cocreate a text with a writer: Each brings to the text a different background, set of values, and way of reading.

It is important to remember that you are in charge of your own writing. If several readers offer the same critique of a passage, then no matter how much you love that passage, you probably need to follow their advice. But when readers disagree, you have to make your own best judgment about whom to heed.

Once you have received advice from others, reread your draft again slowly and then develop a revision plan, allowing yourself time to make sweeping, global changes if needed. You also need to remember that you can never make your draft perfect. Plan when you will bring the process to a close so that you can turn in a finished product on time and get on with your other classes and your life.

12 COMPOSING AND REVISING CLOSED-FORM PROSE

Form is an arousing and fulfillment of desires. A work has form insofar as one part of it leads a reader to anticipate another part, to be gratified by the sequence.

—*Kenneth Burke, Rhetorician*

Chapter 11 presents strategies for improving your revising process. In Chapter 12 we focus specifically on strategies for composing and revising closed-form prose. To help you avoid information overload, we recommend that you don't try to read this whole chapter in one sitting. The skills taught in this chapter are presented in ten self-contained lessons that can be read comfortably in half an hour or less. You will benefit most from these lessons if you focus on one skill at a time and then return to the lessons periodically as you progress through the term. Each lesson's advice will become increasingly meaningful and relevant as you gain experience as a writer. The first lesson (Skill 12.1) is intended as a theoretical overview to the rest of the chapter. The remaining lessons can then be assigned and read in any order your instructor desires.

In this chapter, you will learn how these skills can improve your writing:

- **SKILL 12.1**   Understand reader expectations.
- **SKILL 12.2**   Convert loose structures into thesis/support structures.
- **SKILL 12.3**   Plan and visualize your structure.
- **SKILL 12.4**   Set up reader expectations through effective titles and introductions.
- **SKILLS 12.5–12.7**   Keep readers on track through the use of topic sentences, transitions, and the old/new contract.
- **SKILL 12.8**   Learn four expert moves for organizing and developing ideas.
- **SKILL 12.9**   Use effective tables, graphs, and charts to present numeric data.
- **SKILL 12.10**   Write effective conclusions.

Together these lessons will teach you strategies for making your closed-form prose reader-friendly, well structured, clear, and persuasive.

SKILL 12.1 **Understand reader expectations.**

In this opening lesson, we show you how to think like a reader. Imagine for a moment that your readers have only so much *reader energy*, which they can use either to follow your ideas or to puzzle over confusing passages.* In order to follow your ideas, skilled readers continually make predictions about where a text is heading based on cues provided by the writer. When readers get lost, the writer has often either failed to provide cues or has given misleading cues. "Whoa, you lost me on the turn," a reader might say. "How does this passage relate to what you just said?" In this lesson we explain what readers of closed-form prose expect from writers in order to predict where a text is heading. Specifically we show you that readers expect three things in a closed-form text:

- They expect unity and coherence.
- They expect old information before new information.
- They expect forecasting and fulfillment.

    Let's look at each in turn.

Unity and Coherence

Together the terms *unity* and *coherence* are defining characteristics of closed-form prose:

- **Unity** refers to the relationship between each part of an essay and the larger whole.
- **Coherence** refers to the relationship between adjacent sentences, paragraphs, and parts.

    The following thought exercise will explore your own expectations for unity and coherence:

THOUGHT EXERCISE 1

    Read the following two passages and try to explain why each fails to satisfy your expectations as a reader:

    A. Recent research has given us much deeper—and more surprising—insights into the father's role in childrearing. My family is typical of the east side in that we never had much money. Their tongues became black and hung out of their mouths. The back-to-basics movement got a lot of press, fueled as it was by fears of growing illiteracy and cultural demise.

    B. Recent research has given us much deeper—and more surprising—insights into the father's role in childrearing. Childrearing is a complex process that is frequently investigated by psychologists. Psychologists have also investigated sleep patterns and dreams. When we are dreaming, psychologists have shown, we are often reviewing recent events in our lives.

---

*For the useful term *reader energy*, we are indebted to George Gopen and Judith Swan, "The Science of Scientific Writing," *American Scientist* 78 (1990): 550–559. In addition, much of our discussion of writing in this chapter is indebted to the work of Joseph Williams, George Gopen, and Gregory Colomb. See especially Gregory G. Colomb and Joseph M. Williams, "Perceiving Structure in Professional Prose: A Multiply Determined Experience," in Lee Odell and Dixie Goswamie (eds.), *Writing in Nonacademic Settings* (New York: The Guilford Press, 1985), pp. 87–128.

If you are like most readers, Passage A comically frustrates your expectations because it is a string of random sentences. Because the sentences don't relate to each other or to a larger point, Passage A is neither unified nor coherent.

Passage B frustrates expectations in a subtler way. If you aren't paying attention, Passage B may seem to make sense because each sentence is linked to the one before it. But the individual sentences don't develop a larger whole: The topics switch from a father's role in childrearing to psychology to sleep patterns to the function of dreams. This passage has coherence without unity.

To fulfill a reader's expectations, then, a closed-form passage must be both unified and coherent:

> C. (*Unified and coherent*) Recent research has given us much deeper—and more surprising—insights into the father's role in childrearing. It shows that in almost all of their interactions with children, fathers do things a little differently from mothers. What fathers do—their special parenting style—is not only highly complementary to what mothers do but is by all indications important in its own right. [The passage continues by showing the special ways that fathers contribute to childrearing.]

This passage makes a unified point—that fathers have an important role in childrearing. Because all the parts relate to that whole (unity) and because the connections from sentence to sentence are clear (coherence), the passage satisfies our expectations: It makes sense.

Because achieving unity and coherence is a major goal in revising closed-form prose, we'll refer frequently to these concepts in later lessons.

Old before New

One dominant way that readers process information and register ideas is by moving from already known (old) information to new information. In a nutshell, this concept means that new material is meaningful to a reader only if it is linked to old material that is already meaningful. To illustrate this concept, consider the arrangement of names and numbers in a telephone directory. Because we read from left to right, we want people's names in the left column and the telephone numbers in the right column. A person's name is the old, familiar information we already know and the number is the new, unknown information that we seek. If the numbers were in the left column and the names in the right, we would have to read backward.

You can see the same old-before-new principle at work in the following thought exercise:

THOUGHT EXERCISE 2

You are a passenger on an airplane flight into Chicago and need to transfer to Flight 16 to Memphis. As you descend into Chicago, the flight attendant announces transfer gates. Which of the following formats is easier for you to process? Why?

Option A		Option B	
To Atlanta on Flight 29	Gate C12	Gate C12	Flight 29 to Atlanta
To Dallas on Flight 35	Gate C25	Gate C25	Flight 35 to Dallas
To Memphis on Flight 16	Gate B20	Gate B20	Flight 16 to Memphis

If you are like most readers, you prefer Option A, which puts old information before new. In this case, the old/known information is our destination (cities arranged alphabetically) and perhaps our flight number (To Memphis on Flight 16). The new/unknown information is Gate B20. Option B causes us to expend more energy than does Option A because it forces us to hold the number of each gate in memory until we hear its corresponding city and flight number. Whereas Option A allows us to relax until we hear the word "Memphis," Option B forces us to concentrate intensely on each gate number until we find the meaningful one.

Old before New at the Essay Level The principle of old before new has great explanatory power for writers. At the level of the whole essay, this principle helps writers establish the main structural frame and ordering principle of their argument. An argument's frame derives from the writer's purpose to change some aspect of the reader's view of the topic. The reader's original view of the topic—what we might call the common, expected, or ordinary view—constitutes old/known/familiar material. The writer's surprising view constitutes the new/unknown/unfamiliar material. The writer's hope is to move readers from their original view to the writer's new and different view. By understanding what constitutes old/familiar information to readers, the writer can determine how much background to provide, how to anticipate readers' objections, and how to structure material by moving from the old to the new. We treat these matters in more depth in Skill 12.4, on writing effective titles and introductions.

Old before New at the Sentence Level At the sentence level, the principle of old before new also helps writers create coherence between adjacent parts and sentences. Most sentences in an essay should contain both an old element and a new element. To create coherence, the writer begins with the old material, which links back to something earlier, and then puts the new material at the end of the sentence. (See the discussion of the old/new contract in Skill 12.7.)

Forecasting and Fulfillment

Finally, readers of closed-form prose expect writers to forecast what is coming and then to fulfill those forecasts. To appreciate what we mean by forecasting and fulfillment, try one more thought exercise:

THOUGHT EXERCISE 3

Although the following paragraph describes a simple procedure in easy-to-follow sentences, most readers still scratch their heads in bewilderment. Why? What makes the passage difficult to understand?

The procedure is actually quite simple. First, you arrange things into different groups. Of course, one pile may be sufficient depending on how much there is to do. If you have to go somewhere else due to lack of facilities, that is the next step; otherwise, you are pretty well set. Next you operate the machines according to the instructions. After the procedure is completed, one arranges the materials into different groups again. Then they can be put in their appropriate places. Eventually, they will be used once more and the whole cycle will have to be repeated. However, that is part of life.

Most readers report being puzzled about the paragraph's topic. Because the opening sentence doesn't provide enough context to tell them what to expect, the paragraph makes no forecast that can be fulfilled. Now try rereading the paragraph, but this time substitute the following opening sentence:

> The procedure for washing clothes is actually quite simple.

With the addition of "for washing clothes," the sentence provides a context that allows you to predict and understand what's coming. In the language of cognitive psychologists, this new opening sentence provides a schema for interpretation. A *schema* is the reader's mental picture of a structure for upcoming material. The new opening sentence allows you as reader to say mentally, "This paragraph will describe a procedure for washing clothes and argue that it is simple." When the schema proves accurate, you experience the pleasure of prediction and fulfillment. In the language of rhetorician Kenneth Burke, the reader's experience of form is "an arousing and fulfillment of desires."

What readers expect from a closed-form text, then, is an ability to predict what is coming as well as regular fulfillment of those predictions. Writers forecast what is coming in a variety of ways:

- by writing effective titles
- by writing effective introductions with forecasting cues
- by placing topic sentences near the beginning of paragraphs
- by creating effective transitions and mapping statements
- by using effective headings and subheadings if appropriate for the genre.

To meet their readers' needs for predictions and fulfillment, closed-form writers start and end with the big picture. They tell readers where they are going before they start the journey, they refer to this big picture at key transition points, and they refocus on the big picture in their conclusion.

SKILL 12.2 **Convert loose structures into thesis/support structures.**

In Skill 12.1 we described readers' expectations for unity and coherence, old information before new, and forecasting and fulfillment. In academic contexts, readers also expect closed-form prose to have a thesis/support structure. As we explained in Chapter 2, most closed-form academic writing—especially writing with the aim of analysis or persuasion—is governed by a contestable or risky thesis statement. Because developing and supporting a thesis is complex work requiring much critical thought, writers sometimes retreat into loose structures that are easier to compose than a thesis-based argument with points and particulars.

In this lesson we help you better understand thesis-based writing by contrasting it with prose that looks like thesis-based writing but isn't. We show you three common ways in which inexperienced writers give the appearance of writing thesis-based prose while actually retreating from the rigors of making and developing an argument. Avoiding the pitfalls of these loose structures can go a long way toward improving your performance on most college writing assignments.

Avoiding *And Then* Writing, or Chronological Structure

Chronological structure, often called "narrative," is the most common organizing principle of open-form prose. It may also be used selectively in closed-form prose to support a point. But sometimes the writer begins recounting the details of a story and chronological order takes over, driving out the thesis-based structure of points and particulars.

To a large degree, chronological order is the default mode we fall into when we aren't sure how to organize material. For example, if you were asked to analyze a fictional character, you might slip into a plot summary instead. In much the same way, you might substitute historical chronology ("First A happened, then B happened ...") for historical analysis ("B happened because A happened ..."); or you might give a chronological recounting of your research ("First I discovered A, then I discovered B ...") instead of organizing your material into an argument ("I question A's account of this phenomenon on the grounds of my recent discovery of B ...").

The tendency toward loose chronological structure is revealed in the following example from a student's essay on Shakespeare's *The Tempest*. This excerpt is from the introduction of the student's first draft:

PLOT SUMMARY— *AND THEN* WRITING

Prospero cares deeply for his daughter. In the middle of the play Prospero acts like a gruff father and makes Ferdinand carry logs in order to test his love for Miranda and Miranda's love for him. In the end, though, Prospero is a loving father who rejoices in his daughter's marriage to a good man.

Here the student seems simply to retell the play's plot without any apparent thesis. (The body of her rough draft primarily retold the same story in more detail.) However, during an office conference, the instructor discovered that the student regarded her sentence about Prospero's being a loving father as her thesis. In fact, the student had gotten in an argument with a classmate over whether Prospero was a good person or an evil one. The instructor helped her convert her draft into a thesis/support structure:

REVISED INTRODUCTION—THESIS/SUPPORT STRUCTURE

Many persons believe that Prospero is an evil person in the play. They claim that Prospero exhibits a harsh, destructive control over Miranda and also, like Faust, seeks superhuman knowledge through his magic. However, I contend that Prospero is a kind and loving father.

This revised version implies a problem (What kind of father is Prospero?), presents a view that the writer wishes to change (Prospero is harsh and hateful), and asserts a contestable thesis (Prospero is a loving father). The body of her paper can now be converted from plot summary to an argument with reasons and evidence supporting her claim that Prospero is loving.

This student's revision from an *and then* to a thesis/support structure is typical of many writers' experience. Because recounting events chronologically is a natural

Chapter 2, Concept 5, discusses this principle in depth: "A strong thesis statement surprises readers with something new or challenging."

way to organize, many writers—even very experienced ones—lapse into long stretches of *and then* writing in their rough drafts. However, experienced writers have learned to recognize these *and then* sections in their drafts and to rework this material into a closed-form, thesis-based structure.

Avoiding *All About* Writing, or Encyclopedic Structure

Whereas *and then* writing turns essays into stories by organizing details chronologically, *all about* writing turns essays into encyclopedia articles by piling up details in heaps. When *all about* writing organizes these heaps into categories, it can appear to be well organized: "Having told you everything I learned about educational opportunities in Cleveland, I will now tell you everything I learned about the Rock and Roll Hall of Fame." But the categories do not function as points and particulars in support of a thesis. Rather, like the shelving system in a library, they are simply ways of arranging information for convenient retrieval, not a means of building a hierarchical structure.

An Example of "All About" Structure To illustrate the differences between *all about* writing and thesis-based writing, consider the case of two students choosing to write term papers on the subject of female police officers. One student is asked simply to write "all about" the topic; the other is asked to pose and investigate some problem related to female police officers and to support a thesis addressing that problem. In all likelihood, the first student would produce an initial outline with headings such as the following:

>   I. History of women in police roles
>   A. Female police or soldiers in ancient times
>   B. 19th century (Calamity Jane)
>   C. 1900s–1960
>   D. 1960–present
>   II. How female police officers are selected and trained
>   III. A typical day in the life of a female police officer
>   IV. Achievements and acts of heroism of female police officers
>   V. What the future holds for female police officers

Such a paper is a data dump that places into categories all the information the writer has uncovered. It is riskless, and, except for occasional new information, surpriseless. In contrast, when a student focuses on a significant question—one that grows out of the writer's own interests and demands engagement—the writing can be quite compelling.

Conversion to Problem-Thesis Structure Consider the case of a student, Lynnea, who wrote a research paper entitled "Women Police Officers: Should Size and Strength Be Criteria for Patrol Duty?" Her essay begins with a group of male police officers complaining about being assigned to patrol duty with a new female officer, Connie Jones (not her real name), who is four feet ten inches tall and weighs ninety pounds. Here is the rest of the introduction to Lynnea's essay.

FROM LYNNEA'S INTRODUCTION

Connie Jones has just completed police academy training and has been assigned to patrol duty in _____. Because she is so small, she has to have a booster seat in her patrol car and has been given a special gun, since she can barely manage to pull the trigger of a standard police-issue .38 revolver. Although she passed the physical requirements at the academy, which involved speed and endurance running, situps, and monkey bar tests, most of the officers in her department doubt her ability to perform competently as a patrol officer. But nevertheless she is on patrol because men and women receive equal assignments in most of today's police forces. But is this a good policy? Can a person who is significantly smaller and weaker than her peers make an effective patrol officer?

Lynnea examined all the evidence she could find—through library and field research (interviewing police officers)—and arrived at the following thesis: "Because concern for public safety overrides all other concerns, police departments should set stringent size and strength requirements for patrol officers, even if these criteria exclude many women." This thesis has plenty of tension because it sets limits on equal rights for women. Because Lynnea considers herself a feminist, it caused her considerable distress to advocate setting these limits and placing public safety ahead of gender equity. The resulting essay was engaging precisely because of the tension it creates and the controversy it engenders.

Avoiding *Engfish* Writing, or Structure without Surprise

Unlike the chronological story and the *all about* paper, the **engfish** essay has a thesis.* But the thesis is a riskless truism supported with predictable reasons—often structured as the three body paragraphs in a traditional five-paragraph theme. It is fill-in-the-blank writing: "The food service is bad for three reasons. First, it is bad because the food is not tasty. Blah, blah, blah about tasteless food. Second, it is bad because it is too expensive. Blah, blah, blah about the expense." And so on. The writer is on autopilot and is not contributing to a real conversation about a real question. In some situations, writers use *engfish* intentionally: bureaucrats and politicians may want to avoid saying something risky; students may want to avoid writing about complex matters that they fear they do not fully understand. In the end, using *engfish* is bad not because what you say is *wrong*, but because what you say couldn't *possibly be* wrong. To avoid *engfish*, stay focused on the need to surprise your reader.

---

*The term *engfish* was coined by the textbook writer Ken Macrorie to describe a fishy kind of canned prose that bright but bored students mechanically produce to please their teachers. See Ken Macrorie, *Telling Writing* (Rochelle Park, NJ: Hayden Press, 1970).

FOR WRITING AND DISCUSSION

Developing a Thesis/Support Structure

As a class, choose a topic from popular culture such as reality TV shows, Twitter, rap, fad diets, legalizing marijuana, or a topic similar to these.

1. Working as a whole class or in small groups, give examples of how you might write about this topic in an *and then* way, an *all about* way, and an *engfish* way.
2. Then develop one or more questions about the topic that could lead to thesis/support writing. What contestable theses can your class create?

SKILL 12.3 **Plan and visualize your structure.**

As we explained in Skill 12.2, closed-form writing supports a contestable thesis through a hierarchical network of points and particulars. One way to visualize this structure is to outline its skeleton, an exercise that makes visually clear that not all points are on equal levels. The highest-level point is an essay's thesis statement, which is usually supported by several main points that are in turn supported by subpoints and sub-subpoints, all of which are supported by their own particulars. In this lesson we show you how to create such a hierarchical structure for your own papers and how to visualize this structure through an outline, tree diagram, or flowchart.

At the outset, we want to emphasize that structural diagrams are not rigid molds, but flexible planning devices that evolve as your thinking shifts and changes. The structure of your final draft may be substantially different from your initial scratch outline. In fact, we want to show you how your evolving outlines or diagrams can help you generate more ideas and reshape your structure.

With this background, we now proceed to a sequence of steps you can take to plan and visualize a structure.

Making Lists of "Chunks" and a Scratch Outline Early in the Writing Process

We first introduced James's research problem in Chapter 2, p. 29; James's final paper is shown in Chapter 14, pp. 362–370.

Early in the writing process, before you know how to organize your material, you know that you have certain ideas, sections, parts, or "chunks" that you want to include somewhere. Just making a list of these chunks will help you get started. Here is a list of chunks by student writer James Gardiner early in his process of writing a researched argument on online social networks:

CHUNKS THAT I WANT TO INCLUDE SOMEWHERE IN MY PAPER

- Section on the popularity of online social networks (OSNs)
- Tamyra Pierce article that OSNs can lead to bad grades
- Examples of athletes embarrassing team by putting drinking pictures on Facebook
- One of my research article's argument about OSNs and narcissism
- Danah Boyd's argument that OSNs are positive and provide a place to experiment with identity

- Story of college student who posted a revealing picture of herself as Catwoman and was later embarrassed
- The term "Facebook trance"

Once you make a list of chunks, you can begin thinking about which of them are high-level points and which are details in support of a point. Before writing a rough draft, many writers like to make a brief scratch outline to help with planning. Here is James's initial scratch outline.

JAMES'S INITIAL SCRATCH OUTLINE

- Attention-grabber (maybe story of my watching friends use Facebook or some kind of statistic)
- Evidence of popularity of OSNs
- Show the good side of OSNs (Boyd's argument, statements from my friends)
- Then move to bad side (use term "Facebook trance")
  - Narcissism
  - Embarrassing cases (Catwoman, athletes)
  - Lower grades

"Nutshelling" Your Argument as an Aid to Finding a Structure

As you begin drafting, you will find your ideas gradually becoming clearer and more structured. You can accelerate this process through the following short exercise that will help you "nutshell" your argument. The six prompts in this exercise invite you to look at your argument from different perspectives. We recommend that you write your responses to each prompt as a preliminary step in helping you visualize your structure.

EXERCISE FOR NUTSHELLING YOUR ARGUMENT

1. What puzzle or problem initiated your thinking about X?
2. *Template: Many people think X, but I am going to argue Y.*

   Before reading my paper, my readers will think X: [specify what you imagine your readers initially think about your topic] _____.

   But after reading my paper, my readers will think Y: [specify the new or different way readers will think after finishing your paper] _____.

3. The purpose of my paper is _____.
4. My paper addresses the following question: _____.
5. My one-sentence summary answer to this question is this: _____.
6. A tentative title for my paper is this: _____.

Here are James Gardiner's responses to these prompts:

1. I was initially puzzled why so many students used online social networks. I didn't have a profile on Facebook or MySpace and wondered what the advantages and disadvantages of OSNs might be.
2. Before reading my paper, my readers will believe that OSNs have few detrimental consequences. After reading my paper, my readers will appreciate the potential dangers of OSNs.

3. The purpose of this paper is to point out potential negative consequences of OSNs.
4. What are the possible negative consequences of OSNs?
5. Overuse of OSNs can contribute to a decline in grades, to a superficial view of relationships, to an increase in narcissism, and to possible future embarrassment.
6. Some Dangers of Online Social Networks

Articulating a Working Thesis with Main Points

Once you have nutshelled your argument, you are ready to create a working thesis statement that includes main supporting points. These supporting points help you visualize an emerging structure. Here is James Gardiner's working thesis statement.

> Despite the benefits of online social networks such as MySpace or Facebook, these networks can have negative consequences such as a decline in grades, a superficial view of relationships, an increase in narcissism, and possible future embarrassment.

Chapter 2, Concept 5, explains in detail how a thesis statement needs to surprise readers with something new or challenging.

Using Complete Sentences in Outlines to Convey Meanings

An effective working outline helps you organize *meanings*, not topics. Note that in the outline, tree diagram, and flowchart that follow, James Gardiner uses *complete sentences* rather than phrases in the high-level slots. Because sentences have both subjects and verbs, they can make a point, which asserts a meaning, unlike a phrase, which identifies a topic but doesn't make an assertion about it. Here are examples:

Phrase: Lower grades
Sentence: OSNs can have a negative effect on grades.

Phrase: OSNs and narcissism
Sentence: OSNs may contribute to a rise in narcissism among today's young people.

Any point—whether a thesis, a main point, or a subpoint—is a contestable assertion that requires its own particulars for support. By using complete sentences rather than phrases in an outline, the writer is forced to articulate the point of each section of the emerging argument.

Sketching Your Structure Using an Outline, Tree Diagram, or Flowchart

Once you have created a working thesis statement, you can sketch your structure to show how points, subpoints, and particulars can be arranged to support your thesis. We offer you three different ways to visualize your argument: outlines, tree diagrams, and flowcharts. Use whichever strategy best fits your way of thinking and perceiving.

Outlines The most common way of visualizing structure is the traditional outline, which uses letters and numerals to indicate levels of points, subpoints, and particulars. If you prefer outlines, we recommend that you use the outlining feature of your word processing program, which allows you to move and insert material and change heading levels with great flexibility.

Figure 12.1 shows the first half of James Gardiner's detailed outline for his argument. Note that, except in the introduction, James uses complete sentences rather than phrases for each level.

FIGURE 12.1 James Gardiner's Outline for First Half of Paper

Thesis: Despite the benefits of online social networks like MySpace or Facebook, these networks can have negative consequences such as a decline in grades, a superficial view of relationships, an increase in narcissism, and possible future embarrassment.

I   Introduction
  A   Attenion-grabber about walking into any computer lab
  B   Media evidence shows a large increase in the popularity of OSNs among young people.
  C   The term "Facebook Trance" indicates possible harms of OSNs.
  D   Thesis paragraph

II Admittedly, OSNs have positive benefits.
  A   They provide a way to stay in close contact with friends and family.
  B   Researcher Danah Boyd says that OSNs give young people a place to experiment with identities and voices.
  C   They provide a way to get quick additional information about someone you've met in class or at a party.

III Despite these benefits, OSNs have potential negative consequences.
  A   They can have a negative effect on grades.
    1 Researcher Tamyra Pierce found that high school students with MySpace accounts were more likely to report a decline in grades than those without accounts.
    2 Her data show heavy use of OSNs among as many as 59 percent of students, taking time away from school, work, and sleep.
    3 Other writers apply the high school study to college.
  B   OSNs have a tendency to promote superficial relationships.
    1 A study by Chou, Condron, and Belland shows that for some users, online relationships can result in problems with real-life interpersonal relationships.
    2 Another researcher, Matsuba, found that online relationships might hinder some people from developing an adult identity.
    3 A possible contributing factor to the superficiality of online relationships might be the absence of nonverbal communication.
  C   OSNs might also contribute to a rise in narci...

Tree Diagrams A tree diagram displays a hierarchical structure visually, using horizontal and vertical space instead of letters and numbers. Figure 12.2 shows James's argument as a tree diagram. His thesis is at the top of the tree. His main reasons, written as point sentences, appear as branches beneath his claim. Supporting evidence and arguments are subbranches beneath each reason.

Unlike outlines, tree diagrams allow us to *see* the hierarchical relationship of points and particulars. When you develop a point with subpoints or particulars, you move down the tree. When you switch to a new point, you move across the tree to make a new branch. Our own teaching experience suggests that for many writers, this visual/spatial technique produces fuller, more detailed, and more logical arguments than does a traditional outline.

Flowcharts A flowchart presents the sequence of sections as separate boxes, inside which (or next to which) the writer notes the material needed to fill each box. A flowchart of James's essay is shown in Figure 12.3.

FIGURE 12.2 James's Tree Diagram

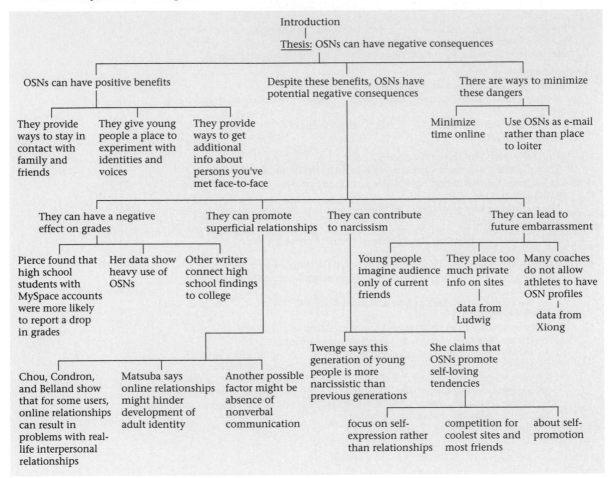

Letting the Structure Evolve

Once you have sketched out an initial structural diagram, use it to generate ideas. Tree diagrams are particularly helpful because they invite you to place question marks on branches to "hold open" spots for new points or supporting particulars. If you have only two main points, for example, you could draw a third main branch and place a question mark under it to encourage you to think of another supporting idea. Likewise, if a branch has few supporting particulars, add question marks beneath it. The trick is to think of your structural diagrams as evolving sketches rather than rigid blueprints. As your ideas grow and change, revise your structural diagram, adding or removing points, consolidating and refocusing sections, moving parts around, or filling in details.

FIGURE 12.3 James's Flowchart

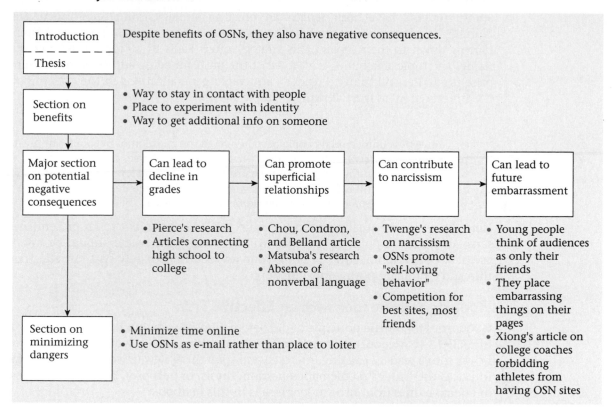

Making Outlines, Tree Diagrams, or Flowcharts

Working individually, complete the outline or the tree diagram for James Gardiner's researched argument (pp. 362–370). Use complete sentences in the outline. Then convene in small groups to compare your outlines. Finally, share points of view on which method of representing structure—outlines, tree diagrams, or flowcharts—works best for different members of the class.

**FOR
WRITING
AND
DISCUSSION**

SKILL 12.4 **Set up reader expectations through effective titles and introductions.**

Because effective titles and introductions give readers a big-picture overview of a paper's argument, writers often can't compose them until they have finished one or more drafts. But as soon as you know your essay's big picture, you'll find that writing titles and introductions follows some general principles that are easy to learn.

Avoiding the "Topic Title" and the "Funnel Introduction"

Some students have been taught an opening strategy, sometimes called the "funnel," that encourages students to start with broad generalizations and then narrow down to their topics. This strategy often leads to a "topic title" (which names the topic area but doesn't forecast the problem being addressed or the surprise the writer will bring to readers) and vapid generalizations in the opening of the introduction, as the following example shows:

B. F. SKINNER

Since time immemorial people have pondered the question of freedom. The great philosophers of Greece and Rome asked what it means to be free, and the question has echoed through the ages up until the present day. One modern psychologist who asked this question was B. F. Skinner, who wanted to study whether humans had free will or were programmed by their environment to act the way they did. ...

Here the writer eventually gets to his subject, B. F. Skinner, but so far presents no sense of what the point of the essay will be or why the reader should be interested. A better approach is to hook your readers immediately with an effective title and a problem-posing introduction.

Hooking Your Reader with an Effective Title

Good titles follow the principle of old before new information that we introduced in Skill 12.1. A good title needs to have something old (a word or phrase that hooks into a reader's existing interests) and something new (a word or phrase that forecasts the writer's problematic question, thesis, or purpose). Here are examples of effective titles from two student essays in this textbook:

> "Why Facebook Might Not Be Good for You"
> "Paintball: Promoter of Violence or Healthy Fun?"

The old information in these titles ("Facebook" and "Paintball") ties into readers' preexisting knowledge or interests. But the titles also indicate each essay's direction or purpose—the new information that promises to expand or challenge the readers' views. The first writer will argue that Facebook might be harmful in some way; the second writer will explore the problem of violence versus fun in paintball.

As these examples show, your title should provide a brief overview of what your paper is about. Academic titles are typically longer and more detailed than are titles in popular magazines. There are three basic approaches that academic writers take, as shown in the following strategies chart.

Strategies for Writing Titles of Academic Papers

What to Do	Examples
State or imply the question that your essay addresses.	Will Patriarchal Management Survive Beyond the Decade?
	The Impact of Cell Phones on Motor Vehicle Fatalities [Implied question: What is the impact ... ?]

What to Do	Examples
State or imply, often in abbreviated form, your essay's thesis.	The Writer's Audience Is Always a Fiction How Foreign Aid Can Foster Democratization in Authoritarian Regimes
Use a two-part title separated by a colon: • On the left, present key words from your essay's issue or problem or a "mystery phrase" that arouses interest. • On the right, place the essay's question, thesis, or summary of purpose.	Deep Play: Notes on a Balinese Cockfight Coping with Hurricane Katrina: Psychological Stress and Resilience among African-American Evacuees

Such titles might seem overly formal to you, but they indicate how much an academic writer wishes to preview an article's big picture. Although the titles in popular magazines may be more informal, they often use these same strategies. Here are some titles from popular magazines such as *Redbook* and *Forbes*:

> "Is the Coffee Bar Trend About to Peak?" (question)
> "A Man *Can* Take Maternity Leave—And Love It" (abbreviated thesis)
> "Feed Your Face: Why Your Complexion Needs Vitamins" (two parts linked by colon)

Composing a title for your essay can help you find your focus when you get bogged down in the middle of a draft. Thinking about your title forces you to *nutshell* your ideas by seeing your project's big picture. It causes you to reconsider your purpose and to think about what's old and what's new for your audience.

From Old to New: The General Principle of Closed-Form Introductions

Just as effective titles present something old and something new, so do dynamic and powerful introductions. Old information is something your readers already know and find interesting before they start reading your essay. New information is the surprise of your argument, the unfamiliar material that you add to your readers' understanding.

Because the writer's thesis statement forecasts the new information the paper will present, a thesis statement for a closed-form essay typically comes *at the end of the introduction*. What precedes the thesis is typically the problem or question that the thesis addresses—the old information that the reader needs in order to understand the conversation that the thesis joins. A typical closed-form introduction has the following shape:

In this section, we elaborate on the rhetorical concept introduced in Chapter 2, Concept 6: "In closed-form prose, an introduction starts with the problem, not the thesis."

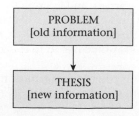

The length and complexity of your introduction is a function of how much your reader already knows and cares about the question or problem your paper addresses. The function of an introduction is to capture the reader's interest in the first few sentences, to identify and explain the question or problem that the essay addresses, to provide any needed background information, and to present the thesis. You can leave out any of the first three elements if the reader is already hooked on your topic and already knows the question you are addressing. For example, in an essay exam you can usually start with your thesis statement because you can assume the instructor already knows the question and finds it interesting.

To illustrate how an effective closed-form introduction takes the reader from the question to the thesis, consider how the following student writer revised his introduction to a paper on Napster.com:

ORIGINAL INTRODUCTION (CONFUSING)

Thesis statement

Background on Napster

Napster is all about sharing, not stealing, as record companies and some musicians would like us to think. Napster is an online program that was released in October of '99. Napster lets users easily search for and trade mp3s—compressed, high-quality music files that can be produced from a CD. Napster is the leading file sharing community; it allows users to locate and share music. It also provides instant messaging, chat rooms, an outlet for fans to identify new artists, and a forum to communicate their interests.

Most readers find this introduction confusing. The writer begins with his thesis statement before the reader is introduced to the question that the thesis addresses. He seems to assume that his reader is already a part of the Napster conversation, and yet in the next sentences, he gives background on Napster. If the reader needs background on Napster, then the reader also needs background on the Napster controversy. In rethinking his assumptions about old-versus-new information for his audience, this writer decided he wants to reach general newspaper readers who may have heard about a lawsuit against Napster and are interested in the issue but aren't sure of what Napster is or how it works. Here is his revised introduction:

REVISED INTRODUCTION (CLEARER)

Triggers readers' memory of lawsuit

Background on Napster

Clarification of problem (Implied question: Should Napster be shut down?)

Thesis

Several months ago the rock band Metallica filed a lawsuit against Napster.com, an online program that lets users easily search for and trade mp3s—compressed, high-quality music files that can be produced from a CD. Napster.com has been wildly popular among music lovers because it creates a virtual community where users can locate and share music. It also provides instant messaging, chat rooms, an outlet for fans to identify new artists, and a forum to communicate their interests. But big-name bands like Metallica, alarmed at what they see as lost revenues, claim that Napster.com is stealing their royalties. However, Napster is all about sharing, not stealing, as some musicians would like us to think.

This revised introduction fills in the old information the reader needs in order to recall and understand the problem; then it presents the thesis.

Typical Elements of a Closed-Form Introduction

Now that you understand the general principle of closed-form introductions, let's look more closely at its four typical features or elements:

1. ***An opening attention-grabber.*** If you aren't sure that your reader is already interested in your problem, you can begin with an attention-grabber (what journalists call the "hook" or "lead"), which is typically a dramatic vignette, a startling fact or statistic, an arresting quotation, an interesting scene, or something else that taps into your reader's interests. Attention-grabbers are uncommon in academic prose (where you assume your reader will be initially engaged by the problem itself) but frequently used in popular prose.

2. ***Explanation of the question to be investigated.*** If your reader already knows about the problem and cares about it, then you need merely to summarize it. This problem or question is the starting point of your argument. If you aren't sure whether your audience fully understands the question or fully cares about it, then you need to explain it in more detail, showing why it is both problematic and significant.

3. ***Background information.*** In order to understand the conversation you are joining, readers sometimes need background information such as a definition of key terms, a summary of events leading up to the problem, factual details needed for explaining the context of the problem, and so forth. In academic papers, this background often includes a review of what other scholars have said about the problem.

4. ***A preview of where your paper is heading.*** The final element of a closed-form introduction sketches the big picture of your essay by previewing the kind of surprise or challenge readers can expect and giving them a sense of the whole. This preview is initially new information for your readers (this is why it comes at the end of the introduction). Once stated, however, it becomes old information that readers will use to locate their position in their journey through your argument. By predicting what's coming, this preview initiates the pleasurable process of forecasting/fulfillment that we discussed in Skill 12.1. Writers typically forecast the whole by stating their thesis, but they can also use a purpose statement or a blueprint statement to accomplish the same end. These strategies are the subject of the next section.

Forecasting the Whole with a Thesis Statement, Purpose Statement, or Blueprint Statement

The most succinct way to forecast the whole is to state your thesis directly. Student writers often ask how detailed their thesis statements should be and whether it is permissible, sometimes, to delay revealing the thesis until the conclusion—an open-form move that gives papers a more exploratory, mystery-novel feel. It is useful, then, to outline briefly some of your choices as a writer. To illustrate a writer's options for forecasting the whole, we use James Gardiner's research paper on online social networks.

To see the choices James Gardiner actually made, see his complete essay on pp. 362–370.

Strategies for Forecasting the Whole Paper

Options	What to Do	Examples
Short thesis	State claim without summarizing your supporting argument or forecasting your structure.	Online social networks can have negative consequences.
Detailed thesis	Summarize whole argument; may begin with an *although* clause that summarizes the view you are trying to change.	Despite the benefits of online social networks like MySpace or Facebook, these networks can have negative consequences such as a decline in grades, a superficial view of relationships, an increase in narcissism, and possible future embarrassment.
Purpose statement	State your purpose or intention without summarizing the argument. A purpose statement typically begins with a phrase such as "My purpose is to …" or "In the following paragraphs I wish to …"	My purpose in this essay is to show the potential negative consequences of online social networks.
Blueprint or mapping statement	Describe the structure of your essay by announcing the number of main parts and describing the function or purpose of each one.	After discussing briefly the positive benefits of online social networks, I will describe four potential negative consequences. Finally I will suggest ways to avoid these consequences by using OSNs wisely.
Combination of elements	Include two or more of these elements. In long essays, academic writers sometimes have a purpose statement followed by a detailed thesis and blueprint statement.	[James's essay is not long enough nor complex enough to need an extensive multisentence overview.]
Thesis question only *[Implies a reflective or exploratory paper rather than an argument]*	State the question only, without initially implying your answer. This open-form strategy invites the reader to join the writer in a mutual search.	Although online social networks are widely popular, something about them makes me feel uncomfortable. I am wondering if there are unappreciated risks as well as benefits associated with OSNs.

Which of these options should a writer choose? There are no firm rules to help you answer this question. How much you forecast in the introduction and where you reveal your thesis is a function of your purpose, audience, and genre. The more you forecast, the clearer your argument is and the easier it is to read quickly. You minimize the demands on readers' time by giving them the gist of your argument in the introduction, making it easier to skim your essay if they don't have time for a thorough reading. The less you forecast, the more demands you make on readers' time: You invite them, in effect, to accompany you through the twists and turns of your own thinking process, and you risk losing them if they become confused, lost, or bored. For these reasons, academic writing is generally closed form and aims at maximum clarity. In many rhetorical contexts, however, more open forms are appropriate.

If you choose a closed-form structure, we can offer some advice on how much to forecast. Readers sometimes feel insulted by too much forecasting, so include only what is needed for clarity. For short papers, readers usually don't need to have the complete supporting argument forecast in the introduction. In longer papers, however, or in especially complex ones, readers appreciate having the whole argument forecast at the outset. Academic writing in particular tends to favor explicit and often detailed forecasting.

Chapter 1, Concept 1, gives more advice on when to choose closed or open forms.

FOR WRITING AND DISCUSSION

Revising a Title and Introduction

Individual task: Choose an essay you are currently working on or have recently completed and examine your title and introduction. Ask yourself these questions:

- What audience am I imagining? What do I assume are my readers' initial interests that will lead them to read my essay (the old information I must hook into)? What is new in my essay?
- Do I have an attention-grabber? Why or why not?
- Where do I state or imply the question or problem that my essay addresses?
- Do I explain why the question is problematic and significant? Why or why not?
- For my audience to understand the problem, do I provide too much background information, not enough, or just the right amount?
- What strategies do I use to forecast the whole?

Based on your analysis of your present title and introduction, revise as appropriate.

Group task: Working with a partner or in small groups, share the changes you made in your title or introduction and explain why you made the changes.

SKILL 12.5 **Create effective topic sentences for paragraphs.**

In our lesson on outlining (Skill 12.3) we suggested that you write complete sentences rather than phrases for the high-level slots of the outline in order to articulate the *meaning* or *point* of each section of your argument. In this lesson we show you how to place these points where readers expect them: near the beginning of the sections or paragraphs they govern.

When you place points before particulars, you follow the same principle illustrated in our old-before-new exercise (Skill 12.1) with the flight attendant announcing the name of the city before the departure gate (the city is the old information, the departure gate the new information). When you first state the point, it is the new information that the next paragraph or section will develop. Once you have stated it, it becomes old information that helps readers understand the meaning of the particulars that follow. If you withhold the point until later, the reader has to keep all the particulars in short-term memory until you finally reveal the point that the particulars are supposed to support or develop.

Placing Topic Sentences at the Beginning of Paragraphs

Readers of closed-form prose need to have point sentences (usually called "topic sentences") at the beginnings of paragraphs. However, writers of rough drafts often don't fulfill this need because, as we explained in Chapter 11, drafting is an exploratory process in which writers are often still searching for their points as they compose. Consequently, in their rough drafts writers often omit topic sentences entirely or place them at the ends of paragraphs, or they write topic sentences that misrepresent what the paragraphs actually say. During revision, then, you should check your body paragraphs carefully to be sure you have placed accurate topic sentences near the beginning.

What follow are examples of the kinds of revisions writers typically make. We have annotated the examples to explain the changes the writer has made to make the paragraphs unified and clear to readers. The first example is from a later draft of the essay on the dorm room carpets from Chapter 11 (pp. 285–286).

Revision–Topic Sentence First

Topic sentence placed first

Another reason for the university not to buy carpets is the cost.
ₐAccording to Rachel Jones, Assistant Director of Housing Services, the

initial purchase and installation of carpeting would cost $300 per room.

Considering the number of rooms in the three residence halls, carpeting amounts

to a substantial investment. Additionally, once the carpets are installed, the

university would need to maintain them through the purchase of more vacuum

cleaners and shampoo machines. This money would be better spent on other

dorm improvements that would benefit more residents, such as expanded kitchen

facilities and improved recreational space. ~~Thus carpets would be too expensive.~~

In the original draft, the writer states the point at the end of the paragraph. In his revision he states the point in an opening topic sentence that links back to the thesis statement, which promises "several reasons" that the university should not buy carpets for the dorms. The words "Another reason" thus link the topic sentence to the argument's big picture.

Revising Paragraphs for Unity

In addition to placing topic sentences at the heads of paragraphs, writers often need to revise topic sentences to better match what the paragraph actually says, or revise the paragraph to better match the topic sentence. Paragraphs have unity when all their sentences develop the point stated in the topic sentence. Paragraphs in rough drafts are often not unified because they reflect the writer's shifting, evolving, thinking-while-writing process. Consider the following paragraph from an early draft of an argument against euthanasia by student writer Dao Do. Her peer reviewer labeled it "confusing." What makes it confusing?

We look at more examples from Dao's essay later in this chapter.

Early Draft–Confusing

First, euthanasia is wrong because no one has the right to take the life of another person. Some people say that euthanasia or suicide will end suffering and pain. But what proofs do they have for such a claim? Death is still mysterious to us; therefore, we do not know whether death will end suffering and pain or not. What seems to be the real claim is that death to those with illnesses will end *our* pain. Such pain involves worrying over them, paying their medical bills, and giving up so much of our time. Their deaths end our pain rather than theirs. And for that reason, euthanasia is a selfish act, for the outcome of euthanasia benefits us, the nonsufferers, more. Once the sufferers pass away, we can go back to our normal lives.

The paragraph opens with an apparent topic sentence: "Euthanasia is wrong because no one has the right to take the life of another person." But the rest of the paragraph doesn't focus on that point. Instead, it focuses on how euthanasia benefits the survivors more than the sick person. Dao had two choices: to revise the paragraph to fit the topic sentence or to revise the topic sentence to fit the paragraph. Here is her revision, which includes a different topic sentence and an additional sentence midparagraph to keep particulars focused on the opening point. Dao unifies this paragraph by keeping all its parts focused on her main point: "Euthanasia ... benefits the survivors more than the sick person."

Revision for Unity

First, euthanasia is wrong because it benefits the survivors more than the sick person.
~~First, euthanasia is wrong because no one has the right to take the life of another person.~~ Some people say that euthanasia or suicide will end‚suffering and pain. But what proofs do they have for such a claim? Death is still

Revised topic sentence better forecasts focus of paragraph

Keeps focus on "sick person"

*Concludes
subpoint about
sick person*

*Supports
subpoint about
how euthanasia
benefits survivors*

mysterious to us; therefore, we do not know whether death will end suffering and
Moreover, modern pain killers can relieve most of the pain a sick person has to endure.
pain or not. What seems to be the real claim is that death to those with illnesses

will end *our* pain. Such pain involves worrying over them, paying their medical

bills, and giving up so much of our time. Their deaths end our pain rather than

theirs. And for that reason, euthanasia is a selfish act, for the outcome of

euthanasia benefits us, the nonsufferers, more. Once the sufferers pass away,

we can go back to our normal lives.

A paragraph may lack unity for a variety of reasons. It may shift to a new direction in the middle, or one or two sentences may simply be irrelevant to the point.
The key is to make sure that all the sentences in the paragraph fulfill the reader's
expectations based on the topic sentence.

Adding Particulars to Support Points

Just as writers of rough drafts often omit point sentences from paragraphs, they
also sometimes leave out the particulars needed to support a point. In such cases,
the writer needs to add particulars such as facts, statistics, quotations, research
summaries, examples, or further subpoints. Consider how adding additional particulars to the following draft paragraph strengthens a student writer's argument
opposing the logging of old-growth forests.

DRAFT PARAGRAPH: PARTICULARS MISSING

One reason that it is not necessary to log old-growth forests is that the timber
industry can supply the world's lumber needs without doing so. For example, we have
plenty of new-growth forest from which timber can be taken (Sagoff 89). We could
also reduce the amount of trees used for paper products by using other materials
besides wood for paper pulp. In light of the fact that we have plenty of trees and ways
of reducing our wood demands, there is no need to harvest old-growth forests.

REVISED PARAGRAPH: PARTICULARS ADDED

*Added
particulars
support subpoint
that we have
plenty of new-
growth forest*

*Added
particulars
support second
subpoint that
wood
alternatives are
available*

One reason that it is not necessary to log old-growth forests is that the timber
industry can supply the world's lumber needs without doing so. For example, we
have plenty of new-growth forest from which timber can be taken as a result of
major reforestation efforts all over the United States (Sagoff 89). In the Northwest,
for instance, Oregon law requires every acre of timber harvested to be replanted.
According to Robert Sedjo, a forestry expert, the world's demand for industrial wood
could be met by a widely implemented tree farming system (Sagoff 90). We could
also reduce the amount of trees used for paper products by using a promising new
innovation called Kenaf, a fast-growing annual herb which is fifteen feet tall and is
native to Africa. It has been used for making rope for many years, but recently it was
found to work just as well for paper pulp. In light of the fact that we have plenty
of trees and ways of reducing our wood demands, there is no need to harvest
old-growth forests.

Revising Paragraphs for Points-First Structure

Individual task: Bring to class a draft-in-progress for a closed-form essay. Pick out several paragraphs in the body of your essay and analyze them for "points-first" structure. For each paragraph, ask the following questions:

- Does my paragraph have a topic sentence near the beginning?
- If so, does my topic sentence accurately forecast what the paragraph says?
- Does my topic sentence link to my thesis statement or to a higher-order point that my paragraph develops?
- Does my paragraph have enough particulars to develop and support my topic sentence?

Group task: Then exchange your draft with a partner and do a similar analysis of your partner's selected paragraphs. Discuss your analyses of each other's paragraphs and then help each other plan appropriate revision strategies. If time permits, revise your paragraphs and show your results to your partner. [Note: Sometimes you can revise simply by adding a topic sentence to a paragraph, rewording a topic sentence, or making other kinds of local revisions. At other times, you may need to cross out whole paragraphs and start over, rewriting from scratch after you rethink your ideas.]

SKILL 12.6 Guide your reader with transitions and other signposts.

As we have explained, when readers read closed-form prose, they expect each new sentence, paragraph, and section to link clearly to what they have already read. They need a well-marked trail with signposts signaling the twists and turns along the way. They also need resting spots at major junctions where they can review where they've been and survey what's coming. In this lesson, we show you how transition words as well as summary and forecasting passages can keep your readers securely on the trail.

Using Common Transition Words to Signal Relationships

Transitions are like signposts that signal where the road is turning and limit the possible directions that an unfolding argument might take. Consider how the use of "therefore" and "nevertheless" limits the range of possibilities in the following examples:

> While on vacation, Suzie caught the chicken pox. Therefore, _____.
> While on vacation, Suzie caught the chicken pox. Nevertheless, _____.

"Therefore" signals to the reader that what follows is a consequence. Most readers will imagine a sentence similar to this one:

> Therefore, she spent her vacation lying in bed itchy, feverish, and miserable.

In contrast, "nevertheless" signals an unexpected or denied consequence, so the reader might anticipate a sentence such as this:

> Nevertheless, she enjoyed her two weeks off, thanks to a couple of bottles of calamine lotion, some good books, and a big easy chair overlooking the ocean.

Here is a list of the most common transition words and phrases and what they signal to the reader:*

Words or Phrases	What They Signal
first, second, third, next, finally, earlier, later, meanwhile, afterward	*sequence*—First we went to dinner; then we went to the movies.
that is, in other words, to put it another way, — (dash), : (colon)	*restatement*—He's so hypocritical that you can't trust a word he says. To put it another way, he's a complete phony.
rather, instead	*replacement*—We shouldn't use the money to buy opera tickets; rather, we should use it for a nice gift.
for example, for instance, a case in point	*example*—Mr. Carlyle is very generous. For example, he gave the janitors a special holiday gift.
because, since, for	*reason*—Taxes on cigarettes are unfair because they place a higher tax burden on the working class.
therefore, hence, so, consequently, thus, then, as a result, accordingly, as a consequence	*consequence*—I failed to turn in the essay; therefore I flunked the course.
still, nevertheless	*denied consequence*—The teacher always seemed grumpy in class; nevertheless, I really enjoyed the course.
although, even though, granted that (*with* still)	*concession*—Even though the teacher was always grumpy, I still enjoyed the course.
in comparison, likewise, similarly	*similarity*—Teaching engineering takes a lot of patience. Likewise, so does teaching accounting.
however, in contrast, conversely, on the other hand, but	*contrast*—I disliked my old backpack immensely; however, I really like this new one.
in addition, also, too, moreover, furthermore	*addition*—Today's cars are much safer than those of ten years ago. In addition, they get better gas mileage.
in brief, in sum, in conclusion, finally, to sum up, to conclude	*conclusion or summary*—In sum, the plan presented by Mary is the best choice.

FOR WRITING AND DISCUSSION

Using Transitions

This exercise is designed to show you how transition words govern relationships between ideas. Working in groups or on your own, finish each of the following statements using ideas of your own invention. Make sure what you add fits the logic of the transition word.

1. Writing is difficult; therefore _____.
2. Writing is difficult; however, _____.

*Although all the words on the list serve as transitions or connectives, grammatically they are not all equivalent, nor are they all punctuated the same way.

3. Writing is difficult because _____.

4. Writing is difficult. For example, _____.

5. Writing is difficult. To put it another way, _____.

6. Writing is difficult. Likewise, _____.

7. Although writing is difficult, _____.

In the following paragraph, various kinds of linking devices have been omitted. Fill in the blanks with words or phrases that would make the paragraph coherent. Clues are provided in brackets.

Writing an essay is a difficult process for most people. _____ [contrast] the process can be made easier if you learn to practice three simple techniques. _____ [sequence] learn the technique of nonstop writing. When you are first trying to think of ideas for an essay, put your pen to your paper and write nonstop for ten or fifteen minutes without letting your pen leave the paper. Stay loose and free. Let your pen follow the waves of thought. Don't worry about grammar or spelling. _____ [concession] this technique won't work for everyone, it helps many people get a good cache of ideas to draw on. A _____ [sequence] technique is to write your rough draft rapidly without worrying about being perfect. Too many writers try to get their drafts right the first time. _____ [contrast] by learning to live with imperfection, you will save yourself headaches and a wastepaper basket full of crumpled paper. Think of your first rough draft as a path hacked out of the jungle—as part of an exploration, not as a completed highway. As a _____ [sequence] technique, try printing out a triple-spaced copy to allow space for revision. Many beginning writers don't leave enough space to revise. _____ [consequence] these writers never get in the habit of crossing out chunks of their rough draft and writing revisions in the blank spaces. After you have revised your rough draft until it is too messy to work from anymore, you can _____ [sequence] enter your changes into your word processor and print out a fresh draft, again setting your text on triple-space. The resulting blank space invites you to revise.

Writing Major Transitions between Parts

In long closed-form pieces, writers often put *resting places* between major parts—transitional passages that allow readers to shift their attention momentarily away from the matter at hand to get a sense of where they've been and where they're going. Often such passages sum up the preceding major section, refer back to the essay's thesis statement or opening blueprint plan, and then preview the next major section. Here are three typical examples:

So far I have looked at a number of techniques that can help people identify debilitating assumptions that block their self-growth. In the next section, I examine ways to question and overcome these assumptions.

Now that the difficulty of the problem is fully apparent, our next step is to examine some of the solutions that have been proposed.

These, then, are the major theories explaining why Hamlet delays. But let's see what happens to Hamlet if we ask the question in a slightly different way. In this next section, we shift our critical focus, looking not at Hamlet's actions, but at his language.

Signaling Major Transitions with Headings

In many genres, particularly scientific and technical reports, government documents, business proposals, textbooks, and long articles in magazines or scholarly journals, writers conventionally break up long stretches of text with headings and subheadings. Headings are often set in different type sizes and fonts and mark transition points between major parts and subparts of the argument.

SKILL 12.7 **Bind sentences together by placing old information before new information.**

The previous skill focused on marking the reader's trail with transitions. This skill will enable you to build a smooth trail without potholes or washed-out bridges.

The Old/New Contract in Sentences

A powerful way to prevent gaps is to follow the old/new contract—a writing strategy derived from the principle of old before new that we explained and illustrated in Skill 12.1. Simply put, the old/new contract asks writers to begin sentences with something old—something that links to what has gone before—and then to end sentences with new information.

To understand the old/new contract more fully, try the following thought exercise. We'll show you two passages, both of which explain the old/new contract. One of them, however, follows the principle it describes; the other violates it.

THOUGHT EXERCISE

Which of these passages follows the old/new contract?

VERSION 1

The old/new contract is another principle for writing clear closed-form prose. Beginning your sentences with something old—something that links to what has gone before—and then ending your sentences with new information that advances the argument is what the old/new contract asks writers to do. An effect called *coherence*, which is closely related to *unity*, is created by following this principle. Whereas the clear relationship between the topic sentence and the body of the paragraph and between the parts and the whole is what *unity* refers to, the clear relationship between one sentence and the next is what *coherence* relates to.

VERSION 2

Another principle for writing clear closed-form prose is the old/new contract. The old/new contract asks writers to begin sentences with something old—something that links to what has gone before—and then to end sentences with new information that advances the argument. Following this principle creates an effect called *coherence*, which is closely related to unity. Whereas *unity* refers to the clear relationship between the body of a paragraph and its topic sentence and between the parts and the whole, *coherence* refers to the clear relationship between one sentence and the next, between part and part.

If you are like most readers, you have to concentrate much harder to understand Version 1 than Version 2 because Version 1 violates the old-before-new way that our minds normally process information. When a writer doesn't begin a sentence with old material, readers have to hold the new material in suspension until they have figured out how it connects to what has gone before. They can stay on the trail, but they have to keep jumping over the potholes between sentences.

To follow the old/new contract, place old information near the beginning of sentences in what we call the **topic position** and place new information that advances the argument in the predicate or **stress position** at the end of the sentence. We associate topics with the beginnings of sentences simply because in the standard English sentence, the topic (or subject) comes before the predicate—hence the notion of a "contract" by which we agree not to fool or frustrate our readers by breaking with the "normal" order of things. The contract says that the old, backward-linking material comes at the beginning of the sentence and that the new, argument-advancing material comes at the end.

Practicing the Old/New Contract

FOR
WRITING
AND
DISCUSSION

Here are two more passages, one of which obeys the old/new contract while the other violates it. Working in small groups or as a whole class, reach consensus on which of these passages follows the old/new contract. Explain your reasoning by showing how the beginning of each sentence links to something old.

PASSAGE A

Play is an often-overlooked dimension of fathering. From the time a child is born until its adolescence, fathers emphasize caretaking less than play. Egalitarian feminists may be troubled by this, and spending more time in caretaking may be wise for fathers. There seems to be unusual significance in the father's style of play. Physical excitement and stimulation are likely to be part of it. With older children more physical games and teamwork that require the competitive testing of physical and mental skills are also what it involves. Resemblance to an apprenticeship or teaching relationship is also a characteristic of fathers' play: Come on, let me show you how.

PASSAGE B

An often-overlooked dimension of fathering is play. From their children's birth through adolescence, fathers tend to emphasize play more than caretaking. This emphasis may be troubling to egalitarian feminists, and it would indeed be wise for most fathers to spend more time in caretaking. Yet the fathers' style of play seems to have unusual significance. It is likely to be both physically stimulating and exciting. With older children it involves more physical games and teamwork that require the competitive testing of physical and mental skills. It frequently resembles an apprenticeship or teaching relationship: Come on, let me show you how.

How to Make Links to the "Old"

To understand how to link to "old information," you need to understand more fully what we mean by "old" or "familiar." In the context of sentence-level coherence, we mean everything in the text that the reader has read so far. Any upcoming sentence is new information, but once the reader has read it, it becomes old information. For example, when a reader is halfway through a text, everything previously read—the title, the introduction, half the body—is old information to which you can link to meet your readers' expectations for unity and coherence.

In making these backward links, writers have three targets:

1. They can link to a key word or concept in the immediately preceding sentence (creating coherence).
2. They can link to a key word or concept in a preceding point sentence (creating unity).
3. They can link to a preceding forecasting statement about structure (helping readers map their location in the text).

Writers have a number of textual strategies for making these links. In Figure 12.4 our annotations show how a professional writer links to old information within the first five or six words of each sentence. What follows is a compendium of these strategies on page 317.

FIGURE 12.4 How a Professional Writer Follows the Old/New Contract

Recent research has given us much deeper—and more surprising—insights into the father's role in childrearing. It shows that in almost all of their interactions with children, fathers do things a little differently from mothers. What fathers do—their special parenting style—is not only highly complementary to what mothers do but is by all indications important in its own right.

For example, an often-overlooked dimension of fathering is play. From their children's birth through adolescence, fathers tend to emphasize play more than caretaking. This may be troubling to egalitarian feminists, and it would indeed be wise for most fathers to spend more time in caretaking.

Yet the fathers' style of play seems to have unusual significance. It is likely to be both physically stimulating and exciting. With older children it involves more physical games and teamwork that require the competitive testing of physical and mental skills. It frequently resembles an apprenticeship or teaching relationship: Come on, let me show you how.

Annotations (left side):
- *Refers to "fathers" in previous sentence*
- *Transition tells us new paragraph will be an example of previous concept*
- *Refers to "fathers"*
- *New information that becomes topic of this paragraph*
- *Repeats words "father" and "play" from the topic sentence of the preceding paragraph*

Annotations (right side):
- *Refers to "research" in previous sentence*
- *Rephrases idea of "childrearing"*
- *Repeats "fathers" from previous sentence*
- *Rephrases concept in previous paragraph*
- *Pronoun sums up previous concept*
- *"It" refers to fathers' style of play*

David Popenoe, "Where's Papa?" from *Life Without Father: Compelling New Evidence that Fatherhood and Marriage Are Indispensable for the Good of Children and Society.*

Strategies for Linking to the "Old"

What to Do	Example Shown in Figure 12.4
Repeat a key word from the preceding sentence or an earlier point sentence.	Note the number of sentences that open with "father," "father's," or "fathering." Note also the frequent repetitions of "play."
Use a pronoun to substitute for a key word.	In our example, the second sentence opens with the pronouns "It," referring to "research," and "their," referring to "fathers." The last three sentences open with the pronoun "It," referring to "father's style of play."
Summarize, rephrase, or restate earlier concepts.	In the second sentence, "interactions with children" restates the concept of childrearing. Similarly, the phrase "an often-overlooked dimension" sums up a concept implied in the preceding paragraph—that recent research reveals something significant and not widely known about a father's role in childrearing. Finally, note that the pronoun "This" in the second paragraph sums up the main concept of the previous two sentences. (But see our warning on p. 319 about the overuse of "this" as a pronoun.)
Use a transition word such as *first ...* , *second ...* , *third ...* , or *therefore* or *however* to cue the reader about the logical relationship between an upcoming sentence and the preceding ones.	Note how the second paragraph opens with "For example," indicating that the upcoming paragraph will illustrate the concept identified in the preceding paragraph.

These strategies give you a powerful way to check and revise your prose. Comb your drafts for gaps between sentences where you have violated the old/new contract. If the opening of a new sentence doesn't refer back to an earlier word, phrase, or concept, your readers could derail, so use what you have learned to repair the tracks.

Applying the Old/New Contract to Your Own Draft

FOR WRITING AND DISCUSSION

Individual task: Bring to class a draft-in-progress for a closed-form essay. On a selected page, examine the opening of each sentence. Place a vertical slash in front of any sentence that doesn't contain near the beginning some backward-looking element that links to old, familiar material. Then revise these sentences to follow the old/new contract.

> **Group task:** Working with a partner, share the changes you each made on your drafts. Then on each other's pages, work together to identify the kinds of links made at the beginning of each sentence. (For example, does the opening of a sentence repeat a key word, use a pronoun to substitute for a key word, rephrase or restate an earlier concept, or use a transition word?)

As we discussed in Skill 12.1, the principle of old before new has great explanatory power in helping writers understand their choices when they compose. In this last section, we give you some further insights into the old/new contract.

Avoiding Ambiguous Use of "This" to Fulfill the Old/New Contract

Some writers try to fulfill the old/new contract by frequent use of the pronoun *this* to sum up a preceding concept. Occasionally such usage is effective, as in our example passage on fathers' style of play when the writer says: "*This* may be troubling to egalitarian feminists." But frequent use of *this* as a pronoun creates lazy and often ambiguous prose. Consider how our example passage might read if many of the explicit links were replaced by *this*:

LAZY USE OF *THIS* AS PRONOUN

Recent research has given us much deeper—and more surprising—insights into **this.** It shows that in doing **this,** fathers do things a little differently from mothers. **This** is not only highly complementary to what mothers do but is by all indications important in its own right.

For example, an often-overlooked dimension of **this** is play.

Perhaps this passage helps you see why we refer to *this* (used by itself as a pronoun) as "the lazy person's all-purpose noun-slot filler."*

SKILL 12.8 Learn four expert moves for organizing and developing ideas.

Writers of closed-form prose often employ a conventional set of moves to organize parts of an essay. In using the term *moves*, we are making an analogy with the "set moves" or "set plays" in such sports as basketball, volleyball, and soccer. For example, a common set move in basketball is the "pick," in which an offensive player without the ball stands motionless in order to block the path of a defensive player who is guarding the dribbler. Similarly, certain organizational patterns in writing occur frequently enough to act as set plays for

---

*It's acceptable to use *this* as an adjective, as in "this usage"; we refer here only to *this* used by itself as a pronoun.

writers. These patterns set up expectations in the reader's mind about the shape of an upcoming stretch of prose, anything from a few sentences to a paragraph to a large block of paragraphs. As you will see, these moves also stimulate the invention of ideas. Next, we describe four of the most powerful set plays.*

The *For Example* Move

Perhaps the most common set play occurs when a writer makes an assertion and then illustrates it with one or more examples, often signaling the move explicitly with transitions such as *for example, for instance*, or *a case in point is* ... . Here is how student writer Dao Do used the *for example* move to support her third reason for opposing euthanasia:

FOR EXAMPLE MOVE

My third objection to euthanasia is that it fails to see the value in suffering. ← *Topic sentence* Suffering is a part of life. We see the value of suffering only if we look deeply within our suffering. For example, I never thought my crippled uncle from Vietnam was a *Transition signaling the move* blessing to my grandmother until I talked to her. My mother's little brother was born prematurely. As a result of oxygen and nutrition deficiency, he was born crippled. His tiny arms and legs were twisted around his body, preventing him from any normal movements such as walking, picking up things, and lying down. He could only sit. Therefore, his world was very limited, for it consisted of his own room and the garden viewed through his window. Because of his disabilities, my grandmother had to wash him, feed him, and watch him constantly. It was hard, but she managed to care for him for forty-three years. He passed away after the death of my *Extended example supporting point* grandfather in 1982. Bringing this situation out of Vietnam and into Western society shows the difference between Vietnamese and Western views. In the West, my uncle might have been euthanized as a baby. Supporters of euthanasia would have said he wouldn't have any quality of life and that he would have been a great burden. But he was not a burden on my grandmother. She enjoyed taking care of him, and he was always her company after her other children got married and moved away. Neither one of them saw his defect as meaningless suffering because it brought them closer together.

This passage uses a single, extended example to support a point. You could also use several shorter examples or other kinds of illustrating evidence such as facts or statistics. In all cases the *for example* move creates a pattern of expectation and fulfillment. This pattern drives the invention of ideas in one of two ways: It urges the writer either to find examples to develop a generalization or to formulate a generalization that shows the point of an example.

---

*You might find it helpful to follow the set plays we used to write this section. This last sentence is the opening move of a play we call "division into parallel parts." It sets up the expectation that we will develop four set plays in order. Watch for the way we chunk them and signal transitions between them.

FOR
WRITING
AND
DISCUSSION

Practicing the *For Example* Move

Working individually or in groups, develop a plan for supporting one or more of the following generalizations using the *for example* move:

1. Another objection to state sales taxes is that they are so annoying.
2. Although assertiveness training has definite benefits, it can sometimes get you into real trouble.
3. Sometimes effective leaders are indecisive.

The *Summary/However* Move

This move occurs whenever a writer sums up another person's viewpoint in order to qualify or contradict it or to introduce an opposing view. Typically, writers use transition words such as *but, however, in contrast*, or *on the other hand* between the parts of this move. This move is particularly common in academic writing, which often contrasts the writer's new view with prevailing views. Here is how Dao uses a *summary/however* move in the introduction of her essay opposing euthanasia:

SUMMARY/HOWEVER MOVE

Issue over which there is disagreement

Summary of opposing viewpoint

Transition to writer's viewpoint

Statement of writer's view

Should euthanasia be legalized? My classmate Martha and her family think it should be. Martha's aunt was blind from diabetes. For three years she was constantly in and out of the hospital, but then her kidneys shut down and she became a victim of life support. After three months of suffering, she finally gave up. Martha believes this three-month period was unnecessary, for her aunt didn't have to go through all of that suffering. If euthanasia were legalized, her family would have put her to sleep the minute her condition worsened. Then, she wouldn't have had to feel pain, and she would have died in peace and with dignity. However, despite Martha's strong argument for legalizing euthanasia, I find it wrong.

The first sentence of this introduction poses the question that the essay addresses. The main body of the paragraph summarizes Martha's opposing view on euthanasia, and the final sentence, introduced by the transition "However," presents Dao's thesis.

FOR
WRITING
AND
DISCUSSION

Practicing the *Summary/However* Move

For this exercise, assume that you favor development of wind-generated electricity. Use the *summary/however* move to acknowledge the view of civil engineer David Rockwood, whose letter opposing wind-generated electricity you read in Chapter 1 (p. 5). Assume that you are writing the opening paragraph of your own essay. Follow the pattern of Dao's introduction: (a) begin with a one-sentence issue or question; (b) summarize Rockwood's view in approximately one hundred words; and (c) state your own view, using *however* or *in contrast* as a transition. Write out your paragraph on your own, or work in groups to write a consensus paragraph. Then share and critique your paragraphs.

The *Division-into-Parallel-Parts* Move

Among the most frequently encountered and powerful of the set plays is the *division-into-parallel-parts* move. To initiate the move, a writer begins with an umbrella sentence that forecasts the structure and creates a framework. (For example, "Freud's theory differs from Jung's in three essential ways" or "The decline of the U.S. space program can be attributed to several factors.") Typical overview sentences either specify the number of parts that follow by using phrases such as "two ways," "three differences," or "five kinds," or they leave the number unspecified, using words such as *several, a few,* or *many.* Alternatively, the writer may ask a rhetorical question that implies the framework: "What are some main differences, then, between Freud's theory and Jung's? One difference is. ... "

To signal transitions from one part to the next, writers use two kinds of signposts in tandem. The first is a series of transition words or bullets to introduce each of the parallel parts. Here are typical series of transition words:

> First ... Second ... Third ... Finally ...
> First ... Another ... Still another ... Finally ...
> One ... In addition ... Furthermore ... Also ...

The second kind of signpost, usually used in conjunction with transitions, is an echolike repetition of the same grammatical structure to begin each parallel part.

> I learned several things from this course. First, *I learned that* [development]. Second, *I learned that* [development]. Finally, *I learned that* [development].

The *division-into-parallel-parts* move can be used within a single paragraph, or it can control larger stretches of text in which a dozen or more paragraphs may work together to complete a parallel series of parts. (For example, you are currently in the third part of a parallel series introduced by the mapping sentence on p. 319: "Next, we describe four of the most powerful set plays.") Here is an example of a student paragraph organized by the *division-into-parallel-parts* move.

DIVISION-INTO-PARALLEL-PARTS MOVE

In this paper I will argue that political solutions to homelessness must take into account four categories of homeless people. A first category is persons who are out of work and seek new jobs. Persons in this category may have been recently laid off, unable to meet their rental payments, and forced temporarily to live out of a car or van. They might quickly leave the ranks of the homeless if they can find new jobs. A second category includes the physically disabled or mentally ill. Providing housing addresses only part of their problems since they also need medical care and medication. For many, finding or keeping a job might be impossible. A third category is the street alcoholic or drug addict. These persons need addiction treatment as well as clothing and shelter and will not become productive citizens until they become sober or drug free. The final category includes those who, like the old railroad "hobo," choose homelessness as a way of life.

Mapping statement forecasts "move"

Transition to first parallel part

Transition to second parallel part

Transition to third parallel part

Final transition completes "move"

Instead of transition words, writers can also use bullets followed by indented text:

USE OF BULLETS TO SIGNAL PARALLEL PARTS

The Wolf Recovery Program is rigidly opposed by a vociferous group of ranchers who pose three main objections to increasing wolf populations:

- They perceive wolves as a threat to livestock. [development]
- They fear the wolves will attack humans. [development]
- They believe ranchers will not be compensated by the government for their loss of profits. [development]

FOR WRITING AND DISCUSSION

Practicing the *Division-into-Parallel-Parts* Move

Working individually or in small groups, use the *division-into-parallel-parts* move to create, organize, and develop ideas to support one or more of the following point sentences.

1. To study for an exam effectively, a student should follow these [specify a number] steps.
2. Why do U.S. schoolchildren lag so far behind European and Asian children on standardized tests of mathematics and science? One possible cause is . . . [continue].
3. Constant dieting is unhealthy for several reasons.

The *Comparison/Contrast* Move

A common variation on the *division-into-parallel-parts* move is the *comparison/ contrast* move. To compare or contrast two items, you must first decide on the points of comparison (or contrast). If you are contrasting the political views of two presidential candidates, you might choose to focus on four points of comparison: differences in their foreign policy, differences in economic policy, differences in social policy, and differences in judicial philosophy. You then have two choices for organizing the parts: the *side-by-side pattern,* in which you discuss all of candidate A's views and then all of candidate B's views; or the *back-and-forth pattern,* in which you discuss foreign policy, contrasting A's views with B's views, then move on to economic policy, then social policy, and then judicial philosophy. Figure 12.5 shows how these two patterns would appear on a tree diagram.

There are no cut-and-dried rules that dictate when to use the *side-by-side pattern* or the *back-and-forth pattern.* However, for lengthy comparisons, the *back-and-forth pattern* is often more effective because the reader doesn't have to store great amounts of information in memory. The *side-by-side pattern* requires readers to remember all the material about A when they get to B, and it is sometimes difficult to keep all the points of comparison clearly in mind.

FIGURE 12.5 Two Ways to Structure a Comparison or Contrast

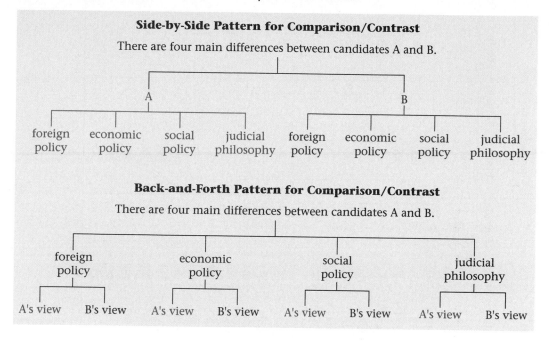

Practicing the *Comparison/Contrast* Move

Working individually or in groups, create tree diagrams for stretches of text based on one or more of the following point sentences, all of which call for the *comparison/contrast* move. Make at least one diagram follow the *back-and-forth pattern* and at least one diagram follow the *side-by-side pattern*.

1. To understand U.S. politics, an outsider needs to appreciate some basic differences between Republicans and Democrats.
2. Although they are obviously different on the surface, there are many similarities between the Boy Scouts and a street gang.
3. There are several important differences between closed-form and open-form writing.

SKILL 12.9 **Use effective tables, graphs, and charts to present numeric data.**

In contemporary analyses and arguments, writers often draw on quantitative data to support their points. Writers can make numbers speak powerfully by means of reader-effective graphics including tables, graphs, and charts. Generally, quantitative data displayed in tables invite the reader to tease out many different stories that the numbers might tell. In contrast, line graphs, bar graphs, or pie charts focus vividly on one story.

TABLE 12.1 Earned Degrees Conferred by Level and Sex: 1960 to 2007

[In thousands (477 represents 477,000), except percent. Based on survey; see Appendix III]

Year ending	All degrees		Associate's		Bachelor's		Master's		First professional		Doctoral	
	Total	Percent male	Male	Female	Male	Female	Male	Female	Male	Female	Male	Female
1960[1]	477	65.8	(NA)	(NA)	254	138	51	24	(NA)	(NA)	9	1
1970	1,271	59.2	117	89	451	341	126	83	33	2	26	4
1975	1,666	56.0	191	169	505	418	162	131	49	7	27	7
1980	1,731	51.1	184	217	474	456	151	147	53	17	23	10
1985	1,828	49.3	203	252	483	497	143	143	50	25	22	11
1990	1,940	46.6	191	264	492	560	154	171	44	27	24	14
1991	2,025	45.8	199	283	504	590	156	181	44	28	25	15
1992	2,108	45.6	207	297	521	616	162	191	45	29	26	15
1993	2,167	45.5	212	303	533	632	169	200	45	30	26	16
1994	2,206	45.1	215	315	532	637	176	211	45	31	27	17
1995	2,218	44.9	218	321	526	634	179	219	45	31	27	18
1996[2]	2,248	44.2	220	336	522	642	179	227	45	32	27	18
1997[2]	2,288	43.6	224	347	521	652	181	238	46	33	27	19
1998[2]	2,298	43.2	218	341	520	664	184	246	45	34	27	19
1999[2]	2,323	42.7	218	342	519	682	186	254	44	34	25	19
2000[2]	2,385	42.6	225	340	530	708	192	265	44	36	25	20
2001[2]	2,416	42.4	232	347	532	712	194	274	43	37	25	20
2002[2]	2,494	42.2	238	357	550	742	199	283	43	38	24	20
2003[2]	2,621	42.1	253	380	573	775	211	301	42	39	24	22
2004[2]	2,755	41.8	260	405	595	804	230	329	42	41	25	23
2005[2]	2,850	41.6	268	429	613	826	234	341	44	43	27	26
2006[2]	2,936	41.3	270	443	631	855	238	356	44	44	29	27
2007[2]	3,007	41.2	275	453	650	875	238	366	45	45	30	30

NA Not available.

[1] First-professional degrees are included with bachelor's degrees.

[2] Beginning 1996, data reflect the new classification of institutions.

Source: U.S. National Center for Education Statistics, *Digest of Education Statistics*, annual.

How Tables Tell Many Stories

Data displayed in tables usually have their origins in raw numbers collected from surveys, questionnaires, observational studies, scientific experiments, and so forth. These numbers are then consolidated and arranged in tables where they can be analyzed for potentially meaningful patterns. Consider, for example, Table 12.1, produced by the National Center for Education Statistics. It shows the number of postsecondary degrees earned by men and women from 1960 to 2007.

Reading a Table Tables are read in two directions: from top to bottom and from left to right. To read a table efficiently, begin with the title, *which always includes elements from both the vertical and horizontal dimensions of the table.* Note how this rule applies to Table 12.1.

- The table's horizontal dimension is indicated in the first part of the title: "Earned Degrees Conferred by Level and Sex." Reading horizontally, we see the names of the degrees (associate's, bachelor's, and so forth) with subcategories indicating male and female.
- The table's vertical dimension is indicated in the second part of the title: "1960 to 2007." Reading vertically, we see selected years between 1960 and 2007.

Beneath the title are further instructions: Numbers represent thousands except for one column labeled "percent."

We are now prepared to read specific information from the table. In 1994, for example, colleges and universities in the United States conferred 2,206,000 degrees, of which 45.1 percent were earned by men. In that same year, 532,000 men and 637,000 women earned bachelors's degrees while 27,000 men and 17,000 women earned doctoral degrees.

Discovering Stories in the Data You need to peruse the table carefully before interesting patterns begin to emerge. Among the stories the table tells are these:

- The percent of women receiving postsecondary degrees rose substantially between 1960 and 2007 (with a corresponding fall for men).
- This increased percentage of degrees given to women is more dramatic for associate's and bachelor's degrees than it is for master's, first professional, or doctoral degrees.

As we show in the next section, these two stories, which must be teased out of this table, can be told more dramatically with graphs.

Using a Graphic to Tell a Story

Whereas tables can embed many stories and invite detailed examination of the numbers, a graph or chart makes one selected story immediately visible.

Line Graph A line graph converts numerical data to a series of points on a grid and connects them to create flat, rising, or falling lines. The result gives us a picture of the relationship between the variables represented on the horizontal and vertical axes.

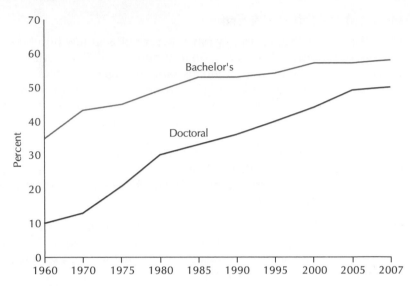

FIGURE 12.6 Percentage of Bachelor's and Doctoral Degrees Conferred on Females: 1960–2007

Suppose you wanted to tell the story of the increasing percentage of women receiving bachelor's and doctoral degrees from 1960 to 2007. Using Table 12.1 you can calculate these percentages yourself and display them in a line graph as shown in Figure 12.6. To determine what a graph tells you, you need to clarify what's represented on the two axes. By convention, the horizontal axis of a graph contains the predictable, known variable that has no surprises, such as time or some other sequence—in this case, the years 1960 to 2007 in predictable chronological order. The vertical axis contains the unpredictable variable that tells the graph's story—in this case, the percent of degrees conferred on women in each year on the graph. The ascending lines tell the stories at a glance.

Bar Graph Bar graphs use bars of varying lengths, extending either horizontally or vertically, to contrast two or more quantities. To make the story of women's progress in earning doctoral degrees particularly vivid (the same story told in the "doctoral" line in Figure 12.6), you could use a bar graph as shown in Figure 12.7. To read a bar graph, note carefully the title and the axes to see what is compared to what. Bars are typically distinguished from each other by use of different colors, shades, or patterns of cross-hatching. The special power of bar graphs is that they can help you make quick comparisons. Figure 12.7 tells you at a glance that in 1960, women received far fewer doctoral degrees than men but that in 2007 they received an equal percentage.

Pie Chart A pie chart, also called a circle graph, depicts the different percentages of a total (the pie) represented by variously sized slices. Suppose you wanted to know the most popular undergraduate majors in American colleges and universities. These statistics, which are available in table format from the National Center for Education Statistics, can be quickly converted into a pie chart as

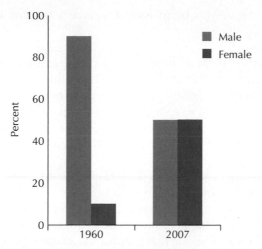

FIGURE 12.7 Percentage of Doctoral Degrees Conferred on Males and Females: 1960 and 2007

shown in Figure 12.8. As you can see, a pie chart shows at a glance how the whole of something is divided into segments. In 2007, for example, 7 percent of graduating seniors majored in education while 22 percent majored in business. The effectiveness of pie charts diminishes as you add more slices. In most cases, you begin to confuse readers if you include more than five or six slices.

Incorporating a Graphic into Your Essay

Today, most word processing programs, often integrated with a spreadsheet, easily allow you to create a graphic and insert it into your document. In some cases,

FIGURE 12.8 Distribution of Bachelor's Degrees by Majors, 2007

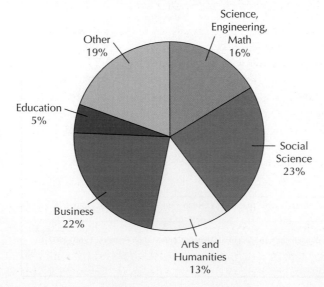

your instructor may give you permission to make a graphic with pen or pencil and paste it into your document.

Designing Your Graphic In academic manuscripts, graphics are designed conservatively without bells and whistles such as three-dimensional effects or special fonts and patterns. Keep the graphic as simple and uncluttered as possible. Also in academic manuscripts, do not wrap text around the graphic. In contrast, in popular published work, writers often use flashy fonts, three dimensions, text wrapping, and other effects that would undermine your *ethos* in an academic setting.

Numbering, Labeling, and Titling the Graphic In newspapers and popular magazines, writers often include graphics in boxes or sidebars without specifically referring to them in the text. However, in academic manuscripts or scholarly works, graphics are always labeled, numbered, titled, and referred to in the text. Tables are listed as "Tables," while line graphs, bar graphs, pie charts, or any other kinds of drawings or photographs are labeled as "Figures." By convention, the title for tables goes above the table, while the title for figures goes below.

Referencing the Graphic in Your Text Academic and professional writers follow a referencing convention called independent redundancy. The graphic should be understandable without the text; the text should be understandable without the graphic. In other words, the text should tell in words the same story that the graphic displays visually. An example is shown in Figure 12.9.

FIGURE 12.9 Example of a Student Text with a Referenced Graph

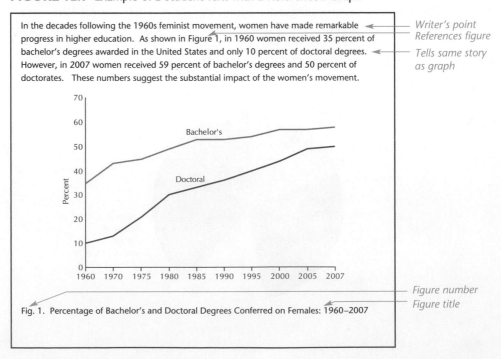

In the decades following the 1960s feminist movement, women have made remarkable progress in higher education. As shown in Figure 1, in 1960 women received 35 percent of bachelor's degrees awarded in the United States and only 10 percent of doctoral degrees. However, in 2007 women received 59 percent of bachelor's degrees and 50 percent of doctorates. These numbers suggest the substantial impact of the women's movement.

Writer's point
References figure
Tells same story as graph

Fig. 1. Percentage of Bachelor's and Doctoral Degrees Conferred on Females: 1960–2007

Figure number
Figure title

SKILL 12.10 **Write effective conclusions.**

Conclusions can best be understood as complements to introductions. In both the introduction and the conclusion, writers are concerned with the essay as a whole more than with any given part. In a conclusion, the writer attempts to bring a sense of completeness and closure to the profusion of points and particulars laid out in the body of the essay. The writer is particularly concerned with helping the reader move from the parts back to the big picture and to understand the importance or significance of the essay.

Because many writers find conclusions challenging to write, we offer six possible strategies for ending an essay.

Strategies for Concluding an Essay		
Strategies	**What to Do**	**Comments**
Simple summary conclusion	Recap what you have said.	This approach is useful in a long or complex essay or in an instructional text that focuses on concepts. However, in a short, easy-to-follow essay, a summary conclusion can be dull and even annoying to readers. A brief summary followed by a more artful concluding strategy can sometimes be effective.
Larger significance conclusion	Draw the reader's attention to the importance or the applications of your argument.	The conclusion is a good place to elaborate on the significance of your problem by showing how your proposed solution to a question leads to understanding a larger, more significant question or brings practical benefits to individuals or society. If you posed a question about values or about the interpretation of a confusing text or phenomenon, you might show how your argument could be applied to related questions, texts, or phenomena.
Proposal conclusion	Call for action.	Often used in analyses and arguments, a *proposal* conclusion states the action that needs to be taken and briefly

(continued)

Strategies	What to Do	Comments
		explains its advantages over alternative actions or describes its beneficial consequences. If your paper analyzes the negative consequences of shifting from a graduated to a flat-rate income tax, your conclusion may recommend an action such as modifying or opposing the flat tax.
	Call for future study.	A *call-for-future-study* conclusion indicates what else needs to be known or resolved before a proposal can be offered. Such conclusions are especially common in scientific writing.
Scenic or *anecdotal* conclusion	Use a scene or brief story to illustrate the theme without stating it explicitly.	Often used in popular writing, a scene or anecdote can help the reader experience the emotional significance of the topic. For example, a paper favoring public housing for the homeless may end by describing an itinerant homeless person collecting bottles in a park.
Hook and return conclusion	Return to something mentioned at the beginning of the essay.	If the essay begins with a vivid illustration of a problem, the conclusion can return to the same scene or story but with some variation to indicate the significance of the essay.
Delayed-thesis conclusion	State the thesis for the first time at the end of the essay.	This strategy is effective when you are writing about complex or divisive issues and you don't want to take a stand until you have presented all sides. The introduction of the essay merely states the problem, giving the essay an exploratory feel.

Writing Conclusions

Choose a paper you have just written and write an alternative conclusion using one of the strategies discussed in this lesson. Then share your original and revised conclusions in groups. Have group members discuss which one they consider most effective and why.

A RHETORICAL GUIDE TO RESEARCH

This screen capture shows the home page of Women Against Gun Control (www.wagc.com), a grassroots organization dedicated to supporting women's right to defend themselves. This organization participates in pro-gun political activism, legislative research, media awareness, distribution of print resources, and gun-related education. The Web site itself uses color, images, other design features, and bold text to stake out its position in the complex controversy over women's role in the hotly contested, larger issue of gun control. This Web site home page is featured in a class discussion exercise in Chapter 13.

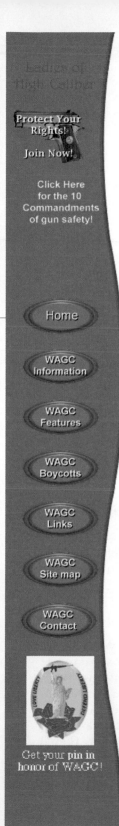

Women Against Gun Control

"The Second Amendment IS the Equal

Click here to sign and read our new forum board!

WAGC sends amicus brief to the U. S. Supreme Court!

Click Here (Opens New Window)

Click here to read a press release regarding this hearing.

Click here for a special message from WAGC President, Janalee Tobias

Contact Us

Postal Address

- WAGC

  PO Box 95357
  South Jordan, UT
  84095

Telephone

- 801-328-9660

E-Mail

- info@wagc.com
- State and Local Chapters
- webmaster

It's a Fact:

RECENT RESEARCH INDICATES THAT GUNS ARE USED DEFENSIVELY 2.5 MILLION TIMES PER YEAR.

It's not surprising then, that more women than ever want to keep their rights to own and carry a gun.
The reason is simple: Women **are** concerned about becoming victims of crime. Guns give women a fighting chance against crime.

Join Women Against Gun Control. Take the Women Against Gun Control Pledge and you qualify for a membership in Women Against Gun Control, a grass roots volunteer organization dedicated to preserving our gun rights.

Join thousands of women (and men) in sending a powerful message throughout the world.

"Guns **SAVE** Lives. We do **NOT** support gun control. Gun Control does **NOT** control crime!"

2nd Amendment
A well regulated Militia being necessary to the security of a free State, the right of the people to keep and bear Arms shall not be infringed.

"The Second Amendment IS Homeland Security."

Special Article
Have gun, will not fear it anymore

USING SOURCES

13

Our goal in Part 4 is to explain the skills you'll need for successful college research papers. We'll show you how to apply your growing knowledge of rhetoric and composition to research tasks by explaining how to evaluate research sources and use them properly in your own writing.

In this chapter, you will learn these research skills:

- **SKILL 13.1** Evaluate sources for reliability, credibility, angle of vision, and degree of advocacy.
- **SKILL 13.2** Know when and how to use summary, paraphrase, and quotation.
- **SKILL 13.3** Use attributive tags to distinguish your ideas from a source's.
- **SKILL 13.4** Avoid plagiarism by following academic conventions for ethical use of sources.

SKILL 13.1 Evaluate sources for reliability, credibility, angle of vision, and degree of advocacy.

When you read sources for your research project, you need to evaluate them as you go along. As you read each potential source, ask yourself questions about the author's reliability, credibility, angle of vision, and degree of advocacy.

Reliability

"Reliability" refers to the accuracy of factual data in a source. If you check a writer's "facts" against other sources, do you find that the facts are correct? Does the writer distort facts, take them out of context, or otherwise use them unreasonably? In some controversies, key data are highly disputed—for example, the frequency of date rape or the risk factors for many diseases. A reliable writer acknowledges these controversies and doesn't treat disputed data as fact. Furthermore, if you check out the sources used by a reliable writer, they'll reveal accurate and careful research—respected primary sources rather than hearsay or secondhand reports. Journalists of reputable newspapers (not tabloids) pride themselves on meticulously checking out their facts, as do editors of serious popular magazines. Editing is often minimal for Web sources, however, and they can be notoriously unreliable. As you gain knowledge of your research question, you'll develop a good ear for writers who play fast and loose with data.

Credibility

"Credibility" is similar to "reliability" but is based on internal rather than external factors. It refers to the reader's trust in the writer's honesty, goodwill, and trustworthiness and is apparent in the writer's tone, reasonableness, fairness in summarizing opposing views, and respect for different perspectives. Audiences differ in how much credibility they will grant to certain authors. Nevertheless, a writer can achieve a reputation for credibility, even among bitter political opponents, by applying to issues a sense of moral courage, integrity, and consistency of principle.

"Credibility" is synonymous with the classical term ethos. *See pp. 57–58.*

Angle of Vision and Political Stance

By "angle of vision," we mean the way that a piece of writing is shaped by the underlying values, assumptions, and beliefs of its author, resulting in a text that reflects a certain perspective, worldview, or belief system. Of paramount importance are the underlying values or beliefs that the writer assumes his or her readers will share. You can get useful clues about a writer's angle of vision and intended audience by doing some quick research into the politics and reputation of the author on the Internet or by analyzing the genre, market niche, and political reputation of the publication in which the material appears.

Angle of vision is discussed in detail in Chapter 3, Concept 8. See also Chapter 5, pp. 97–98, which shows how analyzing angle of vision helps you read a text with and against the grain.

Determining Political Stance Your awareness of angle of vision and political stance is especially important if you are doing research on contemporary cultural or political issues. In Table 13.1, we have categorized some well-known political commentators, publications, policy research institutes (commonly known as *think tanks*), and blogs across the political spectrum from left/liberal to right/conservative.

Although the terms *liberal* and *conservative* or *left* and *right* often have fuzzy meanings, they provide convenient shorthand for signaling a person's overall views about the proper role of government in relation to the economy and social values. Liberals, tending to sympathize with those potentially harmed by unfettered free markets (workers, consumers, plaintiffs, endangered species), are typically comfortable with government regulation of economic matters while conservatives, who tend to sympathize with business interests, typically assert faith in free markets and favor a limited regulatory role for government. On social issues, conservatives tend to espouse traditional family values and advocate laws that would maintain these values (for example, promoting a Constitutional amendment limiting marriage to a bond

TABLE 13.1   Angles of Vision in U.S. Media and Think Tanks: A Sampling Across the Political Spectrum[1]

Commentators

Left	Left Center	Center	Right Center	Right
Barbara Ehrenreich	E. J. Dionne	David Ignatius	David Brooks	Charles Krauthammer
Bob Herbert	Leonard Pitts	Thomas Friedman	Peggy Noonan	Cal Thomas
Michael Moore (film-maker)	Eugene Robinson	Kathleen Hall Jamieson	Jonah Goldberg	Glenn Beck (radio/TV)
Bill Moyers (television)	Nicholas Kristof	Kevin Phillips	Andrew Sullivan	Rush Limbaugh (radio/TV)
Paul Krugman	Maureen Dowd	David Broder	George Will	Bill O'Reilly (radio/TV)
Thom Hartman (radio)	Mark Shields	William Saletan	Ruben Navarrette, Jr.	Kathleen Parker
Rachel Maddow (radio)	Frank Rich	Mary Sanchez		Thomas Sowell

Newspapers and Magazines[2]

Left/Liberal	Center	Right/Conservative
The American Prospect	Atlantic Monthly	American Spectator
Harper's	Business Week	Fortune
Los Angeles Times	Commentary	National Review
Mother Jones	Commonweal	Reader's Digest
The Nation	Foreign Affairs	Reason
New York Times	New Republic	Wall Street Journal
New Yorker	Slate	Washington Times
Salon	Washington Post	Weekly Standard
Sojourners		

Blogs

Liberal/Left	Center	Right/Conservative
americablog.com	donklephant.com	conservativeblogger.com
atrios.blogspot.com	newmoderate.blogspot.com	drudgereport.com
crooksandliars.com	politics-central.blogspot.com	instapundit.com
dailykos.com	rantingbaldhippie.com	littlegreenfootballs.com
digbysblog.blogspot.com	stevesilver.net	michellemalkin.com
firedoglake.com	themoderatevoice.com	polipundit.com
huffingtonpost.com	washingtonindependent.com	powerlineblog.com
mediamatters.com	watchingwashington.blogspot.com	sistertoldjah.com
talkingpointsmemo.com		redstate.com
wonkette.com		townhall.com

Think Tanks

Left/Liberal	Center	Right/Conservative
Center for American Progress	The Brookings Institution	American Enterprise Institute
Center for Media and Democracy (sponsors Disinfopedia.org)	Carnegie Endowment for International Peace	Cato Institute (Libertarian)
Institute for Policy Studies	Council on Foreign Relations	Center for Strategic and International Studies
Open Society Institute (Soros Foundation)	Jamestown Foundation	Heritage Foundation (sponsors Townhall.com)
Progressive Policy Institute	National Bureau of Economic Research	Project for the New American Century
Urban Institute		

[1] For further information about the political leanings of publications or think tanks, ask your librarian about Gale Directory of Publications and Broadcast Media or NIRA World Directory of Think Tanks.

[2] Newspapers are categorized according to positions they take on their editorial page; any reputable newspaper strives for objectivity in news reporting and includes a variety of views on its op-ed pages. Magazines do not claim and are not expected to present similar breadth and objectivity.

between a man and a woman). Liberals, on the other hand, tend to espouse individual choice regarding marital partnerships and a wide range of other issues. Some persons identify themselves as economic conservatives but social liberals; others side with workers' interests on economic issues but are conservative on social issues.

Finally, many persons regard themselves as "centrists." In Table 13.1 the column labeled "Center" includes commentators who seek out common ground between the left and the right and who often believe that the best civic decisions are compromises between opposing views. Likewise, centrist publications and institutes often approach issues from multiple points of view, looking for the most workable solutions.

Degree of Advocacy

By "degree of advocacy" we mean the extent to which an author unabashedly takes a persuasive stance on a contested position as opposed to adopting a more neutral, objective, or exploratory stance. For example, publications affiliated with advocacy organizations (the Sierra Club, the National Rifle Association) will have a clear editorial bias. When a writer has an ax to grind, you need to weigh carefully the writer's selection of evidence, interpretation of data, and fairness to opposing views. Although no one can be completely neutral, it is always useful to seek out authors who offer a balanced assessment of the evidence. Evidence from a more detached and neutral writer may be more trusted by your readers than the arguments of a committed advocate. For example, if you want to persuade corporate executives on the dangers of global warming, evidence from scholarly journals may be more persuasive than evidence from an environmentalist Web site or from a freelance writer for a leftist popular magazine such as *Mother Jones*.

Criteria for Evaluating a Web Source

When you evaluate a Web source, we suggest that you ask five different kinds of questions about the site in which the source appeared, as shown in Table 13.2. These questions, developed by scholars and librarians as points to consider when you are evaluating Web sites, will help you determine the usefulness of a site or source for your own purposes.

As a researcher, the first question you should ask about a potentially useful Web source should be, Who placed this piece on the Web and why? You can begin answering this question by analyzing the site's home page, where you will often find navigational buttons linking to "Mission," "About Us," or other

TABLE 13.2 Criteria for Evaluating Web Sites	
Criteria	**Questions to Ask**
1. Authority	• Is the document author or site sponsor clearly identified?
	• Does the site identify the occupation, position, education, experience, or other credentials of the author?
	• Does the home page or a clear link from the home page reveal the author's or sponsor's motivation for establishing the site?
	• Does the site provide contact information for the author or sponsor such as an e-mail or organization address?
2. Objectivity or Clear Disclosure of Advocacy	• Is the site's purpose clear (for example, to inform, entertain, or persuade)?
	• Is the site explicit about declaring its point of view?
	• Does the site indicate whether the author is affiliated with a specific organization, institution, or association?
	• Does the site indicate whether it is directed toward a specific audience?
3. Coverage	• Are the topics covered by the site clear?
	• Does the site exhibit a suitable depth and comprehensiveness for its purpose?
	• Is sufficient evidence provided to support the ideas and opinions presented?
4. Accuracy	• Are the sources of information stated?
	• Do the facts appear to be accurate?
	• Can you verify this information by comparing this source with other sources in the field?
5. Currency	• Are dates included in the Web site?
	• Do the dates apply to the material itself, to its placement on the Web, or to the time the site was last revised and updated?
	• Is the information current, or at least still relevant, for the site's purpose? For your purpose?

identifying information about the site's sponsors. You can also get hints about the site's purpose by asking, What kind of Web site is it? Different kinds of Web sites have different purposes, often revealed by the domain identifier following the server name:

- *.com sites:* These are commercial sites designed to promote a business's image, attract customers, market products and services, and provide customer service. Their angle of vision is to promote the view of the corporation or business. Often material has no identified author. (The sponsoring company is often cited as the author.)
- *.org sites:* These are sites for nonprofit organizations or advocacy groups. Some sites provide accurate, balanced information related to the organization's mission work (Red Cross, World Vision), while others promote political views (Heritage Foundation) or advocate a cause (Persons for the Ethical Treatment of Animals).
- *.edu sites:* These sites are associated with a college or university. Home pages aim to attract prospective students and donors and provide a portal into the site. Numerous subsites are devoted to research, pedagogy, libraries, and so forth. The angle of vision can vary from strong advocacy on issues (a student paper, an on-campus advocacy group) to the objective and scholarly (a university research site).
- *.gov or .mil sites:* These sites are sponsored by a government agency or military units. They can provide a range of basic data about government policy, bills in Congress, economic forecasts, census data, and so forth. Their angle of vision varies from objective informational sites to sites that promote the agency's agenda.

Analyzing the Rhetorical Elements of Two Home Pages

FOR WRITING AND DISCUSSION

Working in small groups or as a whole class, try to reach consensus answers to the following questions about how Web sites seek to draw in readers. Use the illustration on page 333 and a pro-gun control site such as Million Mom March (Figure 13.1).

1. How are the images of women in the Women Against Gun Control site different from those on the Million Mom March page? How do pieces of text (such as "Ladies of High-Caliber" on the Women Against Gun Control site or one of the "facts" on the Million Mom March site) contribute to the visual-verbal effects of the home pages?
2. In the Women Against Gun Control (WAGC) page, what seems to be the Web designer's intention in the use of color, curved background lines, and images?
3. How does the home page for each site use *logos, ethos*, and *pathos* to sway readers toward its point of view?

What started as one of the largest marches on Washington is now a national network of 75 Million Mom March Chapters that work locally in the fight against gun violence and the devastation it causes.

contact your local chapter

why i march

I march for my son, Chad, who was an innocent victim of gun violence.

- *Rita*

Read Rita's story.
Read stories from other moms.

Other anecdotes cycle through this box

fact file

Other "facts" that cycle into "Fact File" every five seconds

15,000 kids were killed by firearms in the last five years

- One child or a teen is killed by firearms every 3 hours
- A person is killed by a gun every 17 minutes in America
- More than 176 Americans go to an ER with a firearm injury every day
- 34 percent of America's children live in a home with at least one firearm
- On average, more than a thousand kids commit suicide with a firearm every year

FIGURE 13.1 Images, Anecdotes, and Fact Statements from the Million Mom March Home Page (www.millionmommarch.org)

SKILL 13.2 Know when and how to use summary, paraphrase, and quotation.

As a research writer, you need to incorporate sources gracefully into your own prose so that you stay focused on your own argument. Depending on your purpose, you might (1) summarize all or part of a source author's argument, (2) paraphrase a relevant portion of a source, or (3) quote small passages from the source directly. Whenever you use a source, you need to avoid plagiarism by referencing the source with an in-text citation, by putting paraphrases and summaries entirely in your own words, and by placing quotation marks around quoted passages. The following strategies chart gives you an overview of summary, paraphrase, and quotation as ways of incorporating sources into your own prose.

For an explanation of plagiarism in academic writing and a summary of how to avoid plagiarism, see Skill 13.4. For making in-text citations, see Chapter 14.

Strategies for Incorporating Sources into Your Own Prose

Strategies	What to Do	When to Use These Strategies
Summarize the source.	Condense a source writer's argument by keeping main ideas and omitting details (see Chapter 5, pp. 98–103).	• When the source writer's whole argument is relevant to your purpose • When the source writer presents an alternative or opposing view that you want to push against • When the source writer's argument can be used in support of your own
Paraphrase the source.	Reproduce an idea from a source writer but translate the idea entirely into your own words; a paraphrase should be approximately the same length as the original.	• When you want to incorporate factual information from a source or to use one specific idea from a source • When the source passage is overly complex or technical for your targeted audience • When you want to incorporate a source's point in your own voice without interrupting the flow of your argument

(continued)

Strategies	What to Do	When to Use These Strategies
Quote short passages from the source using quotation marks.	Work brief quotations from the source smoothly into the grammar of your own sentences.	• When you need testimony from an authority (state the authority's credentials in an attributive tag—see Skill 13.3) • In summaries, when you want to reproduce a source's voice, particularly if the language is striking or memorable • In lieu of paraphrase when the source language is memorable
Quote long passages from the source using the block method.	Results in a page with noticeably lengthy block quotations.	• When you intend to analyze or critique the quotation—the quotation is followed by your detailed analysis of its ideas or rhetorical features • When the flavor and language of testimonial evidence is important

With practice, you'll be able to use all these strategies smoothly and effectively.

Summarizing

Detailed instructions on how to write a summary of an article and incorporate it into your own prose are provided in Chapter 5, "Reading Rhetorically" (pp. 98–103). Summaries can be as short as a single sentence or as long as a paragraph. Make the summary as concise as possible so that you don't distract the reader from your own argument.

Paraphrasing

Unlike a summary, which is a condensation of a source's whole argument, a **paraphrase** translates a short passage from a source's words into the writer's own words. Writers often choose to paraphrase when the details of a source passage are particularly important or when the source is overly technical and needs to be simplified for the intended audience. When you paraphrase, be careful to avoid reproducing the original writer's grammatical structure and syntax. If you mirror the original sentence structure while replacing occasional words with synonyms or small structural changes, you will be doing what composition specialists call **"patchwriting"**—that is, patching some of your language into someone else's writing.* Patchwriting is a form of academic dishonesty because you aren't fully composing your own sentences and thus misrepresent both your own work and that of the source writer. An acceptable paraphrase needs to be entirely in your own words. To understand patchwriting more fully, track the differences between unacceptable patchwriting and acceptable paraphrase in the following example.

McGRATH ORIGINAL, PAGE 554

There is considerable evidence that women in Bodie were rarely the victims of crime. Between 1878 and 1882 only one woman, a prostitute, was robbed, and there were no reported cases of rape. (There is no evidence that rapes occurred but were not reported.)

Finally, juvenile crime, which accounts for a significant portion of the violent crime in the United States today, was limited in Bodie to pranks and malicious mischief.

UNACCEPTABLE PATCHWRITING

According to McGrath, much evidence exists that women in Bodie were rarely the victims of crime. Between 1878 and 1882 only one woman was robbed, and she was a prostitute. There were no reported cases of rape and no evidence that unreported rapes occurred. Also juvenile crime, which occurs frequently in the United States today, was limited in Bodie to pranks and mischief.

Note phrases taken word for word from original.

ACCEPTABLE PARAPHRASE

Violence in Bodie was different from violence today. According to McGrath, women in Bodie seldom suffered at the hands of criminals. No reported rapes occurred in Bodie between 1878 and 1882, and the only female robbery victim was a prostitute. Another difference, as McGrath points out, is that juvenile crime was rare except for occasional "pranks and malicious mischief" (554).

Only one word-for-word phrase

Quotation marks around exact phrase

Page number of original

Both the patchwriting example and the acceptable paraphrase reproduce the same ideas as the original in approximately the same number of words. But the writer of the paraphrase has been more careful to change the sentence structure substantially and to focus more clearly on his own argument (differences between Bodie and the present). In the acceptable paraphrase, one unquoted phrase still mirrors the original: "between 1878 and 1882." But this phrase is short and carries little of the passage's meaning. The longer mirrored phrase is quoted exactly. In contrast, the patchwritten version contains longer strings of borrowed language without quotation marks.

Among novice writers, the use of Web sources can particularly lead to patchwriting. It is all too easy to copy and paste a Web-based passage into your own draft and then attempt to revise it by changing some of the words. In contrast, patchwriting almost never occurs if you are generating your own language—that

---

*We are indebted to the work of Rebecca Moore Howard and others who have led composition researchers to reexamine the use of sources and plagiarism from a cultural and rhetorical perspective. See especially Rebecca Moore Howard, *Standing in the Shadow of Giants: Plagiarists, Authors, Collaborators*. Stamford, CT: Ablex Pub., 1999.

is, if you are converting information from a source into your own words in order to make your own argument.

When you first practice paraphrasing, you might try paraphrasing a passage twice to avoid patchwriting and achieve an acceptable paraphrase.

- The first time, read the passage carefully and put it into your own words, looking at the source as little as possible.
- The second time, paraphrase your own paraphrase. Then recheck your final version against the original to make sure you have eliminated similar sentence structure and word-for-word strings.

We'll return to the problem of patchwriting in our discussion of plagiarism (Skill 13.4).

Quoting

Besides summary and paraphrase, writers often choose to quote directly in order to give the reader the flavor and style of the source author's prose or to make a memorable point in the source author's own voice. Our previous example of an acceptable paraphrase includes such a quotation in the last sentence. Be careful not to quote a passage that you don't fully understand. (Sometimes novice writers quote a passage because it sounds impressive.) When you quote, you must reproduce the source author's original words exactly, without any changes, unless you indicate changes with ellipses or brackets. Also be careful to represent the author's intentions and meaning fairly; don't change the author's meaning by taking quotations out of context.

SKILL 13.3 Use attributive tags to distinguish your ideas from a source's.

Whenever you use sources in your writing, you need to signal to your reader which words and ideas come from your source and which are your own. There are generally two ways of doing so:

- ***State source author's name in an attributive tag.*** You can identify the source by using a short phrase (called an **attributive tag** or sometimes a **signal phrase** or **signal tag**) such as "according to McGrath," "McGrath says," "in McGrath's view," and so on. In the humanities, the source author's full name is commonly used the first time the author is mentioned. If the tag refers to a specific passage or quotation in the source, then a page number is placed in parentheses at the end of the quotation.

Attributive tag   According to Roger D. McGrath, violence was not as common in the Wild West as most people think.

McGrath explains that "frontier violence was very different from violence today" (553).

Attributive tag

Page number of quotation.

- *State source author's name in a parenthetical citation.* You can identify a source by placing the author's name in parentheses at the end of the material taken from the source (called a **parenthetical citation**).

Violence was not as common in the Wild West as most people think (McGrath).

"Frontier violence was very different from violence today" (McGrath 553).

Source identified in parentheses

Page number of quotation.

Of these two methods, attributive tags are generally preferred, especially when you are writing for general rather than specialist audiences. The attributive tag method has three advantages:

- It signals where borrowed material starts and ends.
- It avoids ambiguities about what is "fact" and what is filtered through a source's angle of vision.
- It allows the writer to frame the borrowed material rhetorically.

Let's look at each of these in turn.

Attributive Tags Mark Where Source Material Starts and Ends

The parenthetical method requires readers to wait until the end of the writer's use of source material before the source is identified. Attributive tags, in contrast, identify the source from the moment it is first used. Here are excerpts from a writer's summary of McGrath, in which we have highlighted the attributive tags. Note the frequency with which the writer informs the reader that this material comes from McGrath.

USE OF ATTRIBUTIVE TAGS IN WRITER 1'S SUMMARY

Many people believe that our Wild West heritage is one of the causes of contemporary violence. But Roger McGrath, in his article "The Myth of Violence in the Old West," shows that today's violence is much different from frontier violence. He explains that. . . . On the other hand, McGrath explains, killings were fueled. . . . Thus, according to McGrath, there is little resemblance between violence on the frontier and violence in today's cities. . . .

Here the attributive tags signal the use of McGrath's ideas throughout the summary. The reader is never confused about which words and ideas come from McGrath.

Attributive Tags Avoid Ambiguities that Can Arise with the Parenthetical Citations

Not only does the parenthetical method fail to mark where the source material begins, it also tends to imply that the source material is a "fact" rather than the view of the source author. In contrast, attributive tags always call attention to the source's angle of vision. Note this ambiguity in the following passage, where parenthetical citations are used without attributive tags:

AMBIGUOUS ATTRIBUTION

There are many arguments in favor of preserving old-growth forests. First, it is simply unnecessary to log these forests to supply the world's lumber. We have plenty of new-growth forest from which lumber can be taken (Sagoff 89–90). Recently there have been major reforestation efforts all over the United States, and it is common practice now for loggers to replant every tree that is harvested. These new-growth forests, combined with extensive planting of tree farms, provide more than enough wood for the world's needs. Tree farms alone can supply the world's demand for industrial lumber (Sedjo 90).

When confronted with this passage, skeptical readers might ask, "Who are Sagoff and Sedjo? I've never heard of them." It is also difficult to tell how much of the passage is the writer's own argument and how much is borrowed from Sagoff and Sedjo. Is this whole passage a paraphrase? Finally, the writer tends to treat Sagoff's and Sedjo's assertions as uncontested facts rather than as professional opinions. Compare the preceding version with this one, in which attributive tags are added:

CLEAR ATTRIBUTION

There are many arguments in favor of preserving old-growth forests. First, it is simply unnecessary to log these forests to supply the world's lumber. According to environmentalist Carl Sagoff, we have plenty of new-growth forest from which lumber can be taken (89–90). Recently there have been major reforestation efforts all over the United States, and it is common practice now for loggers to replant every tree that is harvested. These new-growth forests, combined with extensive planting of tree farms, provide more than enough wood for the world's needs. According to forestry expert Robert Sedjo, tree farms alone can supply the world's demand for industrial lumber (90).

We can now see that most of the paragraph is the writer's own argument, into which she has inserted the expert testimony of Sagoff and Sedjo, whose views are treated not as indisputable facts but as the opinions of authorities in this field.

Attributive Tags Frame the Source Material Rhetorically

When you introduce a source for the first time, you can use the attributive tag not only to introduce the source but also to shape your readers' attitudes toward the source. In the previous example, the writer wants readers to respect Sagoff and Sedjo, so she identifies Sagoff as an "environmentalist" and Sedjo as a "forestry expert." If the writer favored logging old-growth forests and supported the logging industry's desire to create more jobs, she might have used different tags: "Carl Sagoff, an outspoken advocate for spotted owls over people," or "Robert Sedjo, a forester with limited knowledge of world lumber markets."

When you compose an initial tag, you can add to it any combination of the following kinds of information, depending on your purpose, your audience's values, and your sense of what the audience already knows or doesn't know about the source:

Strategies for Modifying Attributive Tags to Shape Reader Response	
Add to Attributive Tags	**Examples**
Author's credentials or relevant specialty (enhances credibility)	Civil engineer David Rockwood, a noted authority on stream flow in rivers
Author's lack of credentials (decreases credibility)	City Council member Dilbert Weasel, a local politician with no expertise in international affairs
Author's political or social views	Left-wing columnist Alexander Cockburn [has negative feeling]; Alexander Cockburn, a longtime champion of labor [has positive feeling]
Title of source if it provides context	In her book *Fasting Girls: The History of Anorexia Nervosa,* Joan Jacobs Brumberg shows that [establishes credentials for comments on eating disorders]
Publisher of source if it adds prestige or otherwise shapes audience response	Dr. Carl Patrona, in an article published in the prestigious *New England Journal of Medicine*
Historical or cultural information about a source that provides context or background	In his 1960s book popularizing the hippie movement, Charles Reich claims that
Indication of source's purpose or angle of vision	Feminist author Naomi Wolfe, writing a blistering attack on the beauty industry, argues that

Our point here is that you can use attributive tags rhetorically to help your readers understand the significance and context of a source when you first introduce it and to guide your readers' attitudes toward the source.

Evaluating Different Ways to Use and Cite a Source

What follow are four different ways that a writer can use the same passage from a source to support a point about the greenhouse effect. Working in groups or as a whole class, rank the four methods from "most effective" to "least effective." Assume that you are writing a researched argument addressed to your college classmates.

1. *Quotation with parenthetical citation*
   The greenhouse effect will have a devastating effect on the earth's environment: "Potential impacts include increased mortality and illness due to heat stress and worsened air pollution, as in the 1995 Chicago heat wave that killed hundreds of people. ... Infants, children and other vulnerable populations—especially in already-stressed regions of the world—would likely suffer disproportionately from these impacts" (Hall 19).

2. *Quotation with attributive tag*
   The greenhouse effect will have a devastating effect on the earth's environment. David C. Hall, president of Physicians for Social Responsibility, claims the following: "Potential impacts include increased mortality and illness due to heat stress and worsened air pollution, as in the 1995 Chicago heat wave that killed hundreds of people. ... Infants, children and other vulnerable populations—especially in already-stressed regions of the world—would likely suffer disproportionately from these impacts" (19).

3. *Paraphrase with parenthetical citation*
   The greenhouse effect will have a devastating effect on the earth's environment. One of the most frightening effects is the threat of diseases stemming from increased air pollution and heat stress. Infants and children would be most at risk (Hall 19).

4. *Paraphrase with attributive tag*
   The greenhouse effect will have a devastating effect on the earth's environment. One of the most frightening effects, according to David C. Hall, president of Physicians for Social Responsibility, is the threat of diseases stemming from increased air pollution and heat stress. Infants and children would be most at risk (19).

SKILL 13.4 Avoid plagiarism by following academic conventions for ethical use of sources.

In the next chapter, we proceed to the nuts and bolts of citing and documenting sources—a skill that will enhance your *ethos* as a skilled researcher and as a person of integrity. Unethical use of sources—called **plagiarism**—is a major concern not only for writing teachers but for teachers in all disciplines. To combat plagiarism, many instructors across the curriculum use plagiarism-detection software like turnitin.com. Their purpose, of course, is to discourage students from cheating. But sometimes students who have no intention of cheating can fall into producing papers that look like cheating. That is, they produce papers that might be accused of plagiarism even though the students had no intention of deceiving their readers.* Our goal in this section is to explain the concept of plagiarism more fully and to sum up the strategies needed to avoid it.

Why Some Kinds of Plagiarism May Occur Unwittingly

To understand how unwitting plagiarism might occur, consider Table 13.2, where the middle column—"Misuse of Sources"—shows common mistakes of novice writers. Everyone agrees that the behaviors in the "Fraud" column constitute deliberate cheating and deserve appropriate punishment. Everyone also agrees that good scholarly work meets the criteria in the "Ethical Use of Sources" column. Novice researchers, however, may find themselves unwittingly in the

TABLE 13.2   Plagiarism and the Ethical Use of Sources

Plagiarism		Ethical Use of Sources
Fraud	**Misuse of Sources** *(Common Mistakes Made by New Researchers)*	
The writer	The writer	The writer
• buys paper from a paper mill	• copies passages directly from a source, references the source with an in-text citation, but fails to use quotation marks or block indentation	• writes paper entirely in her own words or uses exact quotations from sources
• submits someone else's work as his own		
• copies chunks of text from sources with obvious intention of not being detected	• in attempting to paraphrase a source, makes some changes, but follows too closely the wording of the original ("patchwriting")	• indicates all quotations with quotation marks or block indentation
• fabricates data or makes up evidence	• fails to indicate the sources of some ideas or data (often is unsure what needs to be cited or has lost track of sources through poor note taking)	• indicates her use of all sources through attribution, in-text citation, and an end-of-paper list of works cited
• intends to deceive		
	• in general, misunderstands the conventions for using sources in academic writing	

*See Rebecca Moore Howard, *Standing in the Shadow of Giants: Plagiarists, Authors, Collaborators*. Stamford, CT: Ablex Pub., 1999.

middle column until they learn the academic community's conventions for using research sources.

You might appreciate these conventions more fully if you recognize how they have evolved from Western notions of intellectual property and patent law associated with the rise of modern science in the seventeenth and eighteenth centuries. A person not only could own a house or a horse, but also could own an idea and the words used to express that idea. You can see these cultural conventions at work—in the form of laws or professional codes of ethics—whenever a book author is disgraced for lifting words or ideas from another author or whenever an artist or entrepreneur is sued for stealing song lyrics, publishing another person's photographs without permission, or infringing on some inventor's patent.

This understanding of plagiarism may seem odd in some non-Western cultures where collectivism is valued more than individualism. In these cultures, words written or spoken by ancestors, elders, or other authority figures may be regarded with reverence and shared with others without attribution. Also in these cultures, it might be disrespectful to paraphrase certain passages or to document them in a way that would suggest the audience didn't recognize the ancient wisdom.

However, such collectivist conventions won't work in research communities committed to building new knowledge. In the academic world, the conventions separating ethical from unethical use of sources are essential if research findings are to win the community's confidence. Effective research can occur only within ethical and responsible research communities where people do not fabricate data and where current researchers respect and acknowledge the work of those who have gone before them.

Strategies for Avoiding Plagiarism

The following chart will help you review strategies for using source material ethically and avoiding plagiarism.

Strategies for Avoiding Plagiarism or the Appearance of Plagiarism		
What to Do	**Why to Do It**	**Where to Find More Information**
At the beginning		
Read your college's policy on plagiarism as well as statements from your teachers in class or on course syllabi.	Understanding policies on plagiarism and academic integrity will help you research and write ethically.	Chapter 2
Pose a research question rather than a topic area.	Arguing your own thesis gives you a voice, establishes your *ethos,* and urges you to write ethically.	Chapter 1, concept 2

What to Do	Why to Do It	Where to Find More Information
At the note-taking stage		
Create a bibliographic entry for each source.	This action makes it easy to create an end-of-paper bibliography and encourages rhetorical reading	Chapter 6, page 139
When you copy a passage into your notes, copy word for word and enclose it within quotation marks.	It is important to distinguish a source's words from your own words.	Chapter 6, page 134
When you enter summaries or paraphrases into your notes, avoid patchwriting.	If your notes contain any strings of a source's original wording, you might later assume that these words are your own.	Skill 13.2
Distinguish your informational notes from your personal exploratory notes	Keeping these kinds of notes separate will help you identify borrowed ideas when it's time to incorporate the source material into your paper.	Chapter 6, page 134
When writing your draft		
Except for exact quotations, write the paper entirely in your own words.	This strategy keeps you from patchwriting when you summarize or paraphrase.	Skill 13.2
Indicate all quotations with quotation marks or block indentation. Use ellipses or brackets to make changes to fit your own grammar.	Be careful to represent the author fairly; don't change meaning by taking quotations out of context.	Skill 13.2
When you summarize or paraphrase, avoid patchwriting.	Word-for-word strings from a source must either be avoided or placed in quotation marks. Also avoid mirroring the source's grammatical structure.	Skill 13.2
Never cut and paste a Web passage directly into your draft. Paste it into a separate note file and put quotation marks around it.	Pasted passages are direct invitations to patchwrite.	Skill 13.2

(*continued*)

What to Do	Why to Do It	Where to Find More Information
Inside your text, use attributive tags or parenthetical citations to identify all sources. List all sources alphabetically in a concluding works cited or references list.	This strategy makes it easy for readers to know when you are using a source and where to find it.	Skills 13.3 14.1, and 14.2
Cite with attributive tags or parenthetical citations all quotations, paraphrases, summaries, and any other references to specific sources.	These are the most common in-text citations in a research paper.	Skills 14.1, and 14.2
Use in-text citations to indicate sources for all visuals and media such as graphs, maps, photographs, films, videos, broadcasts, and recordings.	The rules for citing words and ideas apply equally to visuals and media cited in your paper.	Skill 14.1
Use in-text citations for all ideas and facts that are not common knowledge.	Although you don't need to cite widely accepted and noncontroversial facts and information, it is better to cite them if you are unsure.	Skill 14.1

FOR WRITING AND DISCUSSION

Avoiding Plagiarism

Read the two passages below, an ethical summary of an article and a summary that would likely be accused of plagiarism.

SUMMARY 1 (AN ETHICAL SUMMARY)

Many people believe that our Wild West heritage is one of the causes of contemporary violence. But Roger McGrath, in his article "The Myth of Violence in the Old West," shows that today's violence is much different from frontier violence. He explains that in a typical frontier town, violence involved gunslingers who were "willing combatants," whereas today's typical victims— "the old, the young, the weak, and the female"—were unaffected by crime (554). Because the presence of an armed populace deterred robbery and burglary, theft was much less common in the Old West than today. On the other hand, McGrath explains, killings were fueled by guns, alcohol, and a code of conduct that invited fighting, so murders were much more frequent than in any U.S. city today (555). Thus, according to McGrath, there is little resemblance between violence on the frontier and violence in today's cities, so we cannot blame current violence on a tumultuous frontier past.

SUMMARY 2 OF McGRATH'S ARTICLE (AN EXAMPLE OF PLAGIARISM)

It is commonly assumed that violence is part of our Wild West heritage. But Roger McGrath, in his article "The Myth of Violence in the Old West," shows that frontier violence was very different from violence today. He explains that in a typical frontier town, violence involved gunslingers who were "willing combatants," whereas today's typical victims—the old, the young, the weak, and the female—were unaffected by crime (554). The greatest deterrent to crime in Bodie was the fact that so many people were armed. Armed guards prevented bank robberies and stagecoach holdups, and armed citizens stopped burglary. On the other hand, McGrath explains, Bodie had a high homicide rate. Most of the town's residents were young single males who adhered to a code of conduct that frequently required them to fight. Alcohol also played a major role. Therefore murders were much more frequent than in any U.S. city today (554). Thus, according to McGrath, there is little resemblance between violence on the frontier and violence in today's cities, so we cannot blame current violence on our tumultuous frontier past.

Working in small groups or as a whole class, respond to the following questions.

1. How does summary 2 cross the line into plagiarism? (You'll need to compare the passage to summary 1.)
2. The writer of summary 2 might say, "How can this be plagiarism? I cited my source and gave page numbers." How would you explain the problem to this writer?
3. Psychologically or cognitively, what may have caused this writer to misuse the source? How might this writer's note-taking process or composing process have differed from that of the writer of summary1? In other words, what happened that got this writer into trouble?

14 | CITING AND DOCUMENTING SOURCES

I n the previous chapter we explained how to evaluate sources and incorporate them into your writing; in this chapter we focus on the nuts and bolts of documenting those sources in a way appropriate to your purpose, audience, and genre, using the systems of the Modern Language Association (MLA) and the American Psychological Association (APA).* Accurate documentation not only helps other researchers locate your sources but also contributes substantially to your own *ethos* as a writer.

Specifically, in this chapter you will learn the following skills:

- **SKILL 14.1** Cite and document sources using MLA style.
- **SKILL 14.2** Cite and document sources using APA style.

SKILL 14.1 **Cite and document sources using MLA style.**

An in-text citation and its corresponding Works Cited entry are linked in a chicken-and-egg system: You can't cite a source in the text without first knowing how the source's entry will be alphabetized in the Works Cited list. However, since most Works Cited entries are alphabetized by the first author's last name, for convenience we start with in-text citations.

In-Text Citations in MLA Style

A typical in-text citation contains two elements: (1) the last name of the author and (2) the page number of the quoted or paraphrased passage. However, in some cases a work is identified by something other than an author's last name, and sometimes no page number is required. Let's begin with the most common cases.

Typically, an in-text citation uses one of these two methods:

- ***Parenthetical method.*** Place the author's last name and the page number in parentheses immediately after the material being cited.

---

*Our discussion of MLA style is based on the *MLA Handbook for Writers of Research Papers*, 7th ed. (2009). Our discussion of APA style is based on the *Publication Manual of the American Psychological Association*, 6th ed. (2010).

> The Spanish tried to reduce the status of Filipina, women who had been able to do business, get divorced, and sometimes become village chiefs (Karnow 41).

- ***Attributive tag method.*** Place the author's name in an attributive tag at the beginning of the source material and the page number in parentheses at the end.

> According to Karnow, the Spanish tried to reduce the status of Filipina women, who had been able to do business, get divorced, and sometimes become village chiefs (41).

Once you have cited an author and it is clear that the same author's material is being used, you need cite only the page numbers in parentheses in subsequent citations. A reader who wishes to look up the source will find the bibliographic information in the Works Cited section by looking for the entry under "Karnow."

Let's now turn to the variations. Table 14.1 identifies the typical variations and shows again the one-to-one connection between the in-text citation and the Works Cited list.

When to Use Page Numbers in In-Text Citations When the materials you are citing are available in print or in .pdf format, you can provide accurate page numbers for parenthetical citations. If you are working with Web sources or

---

TABLE 14.1   In-Text Citations in MLA Style

Type of Source	Works Cited Entry at End of Paper (Construct the entry while taking notes on each source.)	In-Text Citation in Body of Paper (Use the first word of the Works Cited entry in parentheses or an attributive tag; add page number at end of quoted or paraphrased passage.)
One author	Pollan, Michael. *The Omnivore's Dilemma: A Natural History of Four Meals.* New York: Penguin, 2006. Print.	…(Pollan 256). OR According to Pollan,…(256).
More than one author	Pollay, Richard W., Jung S. Lee, and David Carter-Whitney. "Separate, but Not Equal: Racial Segmentation in Cigarette Advertising." *Journal of Advertising* 21.1 (1992): 45–57. Print.	…race" (Pollay, Lee, and Carter-Whitney 52). OR Pollay, Lee, and Carter-Whitney have argued that "advertisers…race" (52). *For the in-text citation, cite the specific page number rather than the whole range of pages given in the Works Cited entry.*

(continued)

MLA Style

TABLE 14.1 *continued*

Type of Source	Works Cited Entry at End of Paper	In-Text Citation in Body of Paper (*Use the first word of the Works Cited entry in parentheses or an attributive tag; add page number at end of quoted or paraphrased passage.*)
Author has more than one work in Works Cited list	Dombrowski, Daniel A. *Babies and Beasts: The Argument from Marginal Cases.* Urbana: U of Illinois P, 1997. Print. ---. *The Philosophy of Vegetarianism.* Amherst: U of Massachusetts P, 1984. Print.	…(Dombrowski, *Babies* 207). …(Dombrowski, *Philosophy* 328). OR According to Dombrowski,…(*Babies* 207). Dombrowski claims that… (*Philosophy* 328). *Because author has more than one work in Works Cited, include a short version of title to distinguish between entries.*
Corporate author	American Red Cross. *Standard First Aid.* St. Louis: Mosby Lifeline, 1993. Print.	…(American Red Cross 102). OR Snake bite instructions from the American Red Cross show that…(102).
No named author (Work is therefore alphabetized by title.)	"Ouch! Body Piercing." *Menstuff.* National Men's Resource Center, 1 Feb. 2001. Web. 17 July 2004.	…("Ouch!"). According to the National Men's Resource Center,…("Ouch!"). • *Add "Ouch!" in parentheses to show that work is alphabetized under "Ouch!" not "National."* • *No page numbers are shown because Web site pages aren't stable.*
Indirect citation of a source that you found in another source *Suppose you want to use a quotation from Peter Singer that you found in a book by Daniel Dombrowski. Include Dombrowski but not Singer in Works Cited.*	Dombrowski, Daniel A. *Babies and Beasts: The Argument from Marginal Cases.* Urbana: U of Illinois P, 1997. Print.	Animal rights activist Peter Singer argues that…(qtd. in Dombrowski 429). • *Singer is used for the attributive tag, but the in-text citation is to Dombrowski.* • *"qtd. in" stands for "quoted in."*

HTML files, however, do not use the page numbers obtained from a printout because they will not be consistent from printer to printer. If the item has numbered paragraphs, cite them with the abbreviation *par.* or *pars.*—for example, "(Jones, pars. 22–24)." In the absence of reliable page numbers for the original material, MLA says to omit page references from the parenthetical citation.

Works Cited List in MLA Style

In the MLA system, you place a complete Works Cited list at the end of the paper. The list includes all the sources that you mention in your paper. However, it does *not* include works you read but did not use. Entries in the Works Cited list follow these general guidelines:

- Entries are arranged alphabetically by author, or by title if there is no author.
- Each entry includes the medium of publication of the source you consulted—for example, *Print, Web, DVD, Performance, Oil on canvas,* and so on.
- If there is more than one entry per author, the works are arranged alphabetically by title. For the second and all additional entries, type three hyphens and a period in place of the author's name.

> Dombrowski, Daniel A. *Babies and Beasts: The Argument from Marginal Cases.*
>   Urbana: U of Illinois P, 1997. Print.
>
> ---. *The Philosophy of Vegetarianism.* Amherst: U of Massachusetts P, 1984. Print.

MLA Citation Models

Print Articles in Scholarly Journals

General Format for Print Article in Scholarly Journal

Author. "Article Title." *Journal Title* volume number.issue number (year): page
    numbers. Print.

To see what citations look like when typed in a research paper, see James Gardiner's Works Cited list on pp. 362–370.

Note that all scholarly journal entries include both volume number and issue number, regardless of how the journal is paginated. For articles published in a scholarly Web journal, see page 360. For scholarly journal articles retrieved from an online database, see page 359.

One author

Herrera-Sobek, Maria. "Border Aesthetics: The Politics of Mexican Immigration in Film
    and Art." *Western Humanities Review* 60.2 (2006): 60–71. Print.

Two or three authors

Pollay, Richard W., Jung S. Lee, and David Carter-Whitney. "Separate, but Not Equal:
    Racial Segmentation in Cigarette Advertising." *Journal of Advertising* 21.1 (1992):
    45–57. Print.

Four or more authors

Either list all the authors in the order in which they appear, or use "et al." (meaning "and others") to replace all but the first author.

Buck, Gayle A., et al. "Examining the Cognitive Processes Used by Adolescent Girls and
    Women Scientists in Identifying Science Role Models: A Feminist Approach."
    Science Education 92.4 (2008): 688–707. Print.

Print Articles in Magazines and Newspapers

General Format for Magazines and Newspapers

Author. "Article Title." *Magazine Title* day Month year: page numbers. Print.

Magazine article with named author

Snyder, Rachel L. "A Daughter of Cambodia Remembers: Loung Ung's Journey." *Ms.*
    Aug.–Sept. 2001: 62–67. Print.

Magazine article without named author

"Daddy, Daddy." *New Republic* 30 July 2001: 2–13. Print.

Newspaper article

Henriques, Diana B. "Hero's Fall Teaches Wall Street a Lesson." *Seattle Times* 27 Sept. 1998:
    A1+. Print.

Page numbers in newspapers are typically indicated by a section letter or number as well as a page number. The "+" indicates that the article continues on one or more pages later in the newspaper.

Newspaper editorial

"Dr. Frankenstein on the Hill." Editorial. *New York Times* 18 May 2002, natl. ed.: A22. Print.

Print Books

General Format for Print Books

Author. *Title.* City of publication: Publisher, year of publication. Print.

Pollan, Michael. *The Omnivore's Dilemma: A Natural History of Four Meals*. New York:
    Penguin, 2006. Print.

Second, later, or revised edition

Montagu, Ashley. *Touching: The Human Significance of the Skin*. 3rd ed. New York:
    Perennial, 1986. Print.

Anthology article

Royer, Ann. "The Role of the Transcendental Meditation Technique in Promoting
    Smoking Cessation: A Longitudinal Study." *Self Recovery: Treating Addictions
    Using Transcendental Meditation and Maharishi Ayur-Veda*. Ed. David F.
    O'Connell and Charles N. Alexander. New York: Haworth, 1994.
    221–39. Print.

Articles or Books from an Online Database

General Format for Material from Online Databases

Author. "Title." *Periodical Name* Print publication data including date and volume/
    issue numbers: pagination. *Database*. Web. Date of access.

Journal article from online database

Matsuba, M. Kyle. "Searching for Self and Relationships Online." *CyberPsychology and Behavior* 9.3 (2006): 275–84. *Academic Search Complete.* Web. 14 Apr. 2007.

E-book from online database

Hanley, Wayne. *The Genesis of Napoleonic Propaganda, 1796–1799.* New York: Columbia UP, 2002. *Gutenberg-e.* Web. 31 July 2010.

Machiavelli, Niccolo. *Prince.* 1513. *Bibliomania.* Web. 31 July 2009.

Other Internet Sources

General Format for Web Sources Since Web sources are often unstable, MLA recommends that you download or printout your Web sources. The goal in citing these sources is to enable readers to locate the material. To that end, use the basic citation model and adapt it as necessary.

Author, editor, director, narrator, performer, compiler, or producer of the work, if available. *Title of a long work, italicized.* OR "Title of page or document that is part of a larger work, in quotation marks." *Title of the overall site, usually taken from the home page, if this is different from the title of the work.* Publisher or sponsor of the site (if none, use N.p.), day Month year of publication online or last update of the site (if not available, use n.d.). Web. day Month year you accessed the site.

Saucedo, Robert. "A Bad Idea for a Movie." *theeagle.com.* Bryan College Station Eagle, 1 July 2010. Web. 7 July 2010.

MLA assumes that readers will use a search engine to locate a Web source, so do not include a URL *unless* the item would be hard to locate without it. If you do include a URL, it goes at the end of the citation, after the access date. Enclose it in angle brackets <> followed by a period. If you need to break the URL from one line to the next, divide it only after a slash. Do not hyphenate a URL.

Entire Web site

BlogPulse. Intelliseek, n.d. Web. 24 July 2010.

Padgett, John B., ed. *William Faulkner on the Web.* U of Mississippi, 26 Mar. 2007. Web. 25 June 2009.

Document within a Web site

Marks, John. "Overview: Letter from the President." *Search for Common Ground.* Search for Common Ground, n.d. Web. 25 June 2007.

Article from a newspaper or newswire site

Bounds, Amy. "Thinking Like Scientists." *Daily Camera* [Boulder]. Scripps Interactive Newspaper Group, 26 June 2007. Web. 26 June 2007.

"Great Lakes: Rwanda Backed Dissident Troops in DRC-UN Panel." *IRIN*. UN Office for the Coordination of Humanitarian Affairs, 21 July 2004. Web. 31 July 2004.

Article from a scholarly e-journal

Welch, John R., and Ramon Riley. "Reclaiming Land and Spirit in the Western Apache Homeland." *American Indian Quarterly* 25.4 (2001): 5–14. Web. 19 Dec. 2001.

Blog posting

Dyer, Bob, and Ella Barnes. "The 'Greening' of the Arctic." *Greenversations*. U.S. Environmental Protection Agency, 7 Oct. 2008. Web. 11 Oct. 2010. <http://blog.epa.gov/blog/2008/10/07/the-greening-of-the-artic/>.

Web video

Beck, Roy. "Immigration Gumballs." *YouTube*. YouTube, 2 Nov. 2006. Web. 23 July 2009.

Home Page

Agatucci, Cora. *Culture and Literature of Africa*. Course home page. Humanities Dept., Central Oregon Community College, Jan. 2007–May 2007. Web. 31 July 2007. <http://web.cocc.edu/cagatucci/classes/hum211/>.

E-mail

Daffinrud, Sue. "Scoring Guide for Class Participation." Message to the author. 12 Dec. 2001. E-mail.

Miscellaneous Sources

Television or radio program

"Lie Like a Rug." *NYPD Blue*. Dir. Steven Bochco and David Milch. ABC. KOMO, Seattle. 6 Nov. 2001. Television.

Ashbrook, Tom. "Turf Wars and the American Lawn." *On Point*. Natl. Public Radio, 22 July 2008. Web. 23 July 2009.

Film or video recording

Shakespeare in Love. Dir. John Madden. Perf. Joseph Fiennes and Gwyneth Paltrow. Screenplay by Marc Norman and Tom Stoppard. Universal Miramax, 1998. Film.

Use "DVD" or "Videocassette" rather than "Film" as the medium of publication if that is the medium you consulted. If you accessed a film or video on the Web, omit the original medium of publication, include the Web site or database name (italicized), the sponsor and posting date, "Web" as medium of publication, and the date of access.

Shakespeare in Love. Dir. John Madden. Perf. Joseph Fiennes and Gwyneth Paltrow. Screenplay by Marc Norman and Tom Stoppard. Universal Miramax, 1998. *Netflix*. Netflix, n.d. Web. 9 Mar. 2010.

Interview

Castellucci, Marion. Personal interview. 7 Oct. 2010.

Lecture, speech, or conference presentation

Sharples, Mike. "Authors of the Future." Conference of European Teachers of Academic
    Writing. U of Groningen. Groningen, Neth. 20 June 2001. Lecture.

James Gardiner (student), "Why *Facebook* Might Not Be Good for You" (MLA-Style Research Paper)

As an illustration of a student research paper written in MLA style, we present James Gardiner's paper on online social networks. James's process in producing this paper has been discussed in various places throughout the text.

Gardiner 1

James Gardiner

Professor Johnson

Writing Seminar: Inquiry and Argument

15 May 2007

Why *Facebook* Might Not Be Good for You:

Some Dangers of Online Social Networks

Walk into any computer lab located at any college campus across the country and you'll see dozens of students logged onto an online social network (OSN). In the last few years, the use of these networks has skyrocketed among Internet users, especially young adults. These new virtual communities are significantly influencing the way young people communicate and interact with one another. A report titled "E-Expectations: The Class of 2007" went so far as to label upcoming college freshmen "the Social-Networking Generation" (qtd. in Joly).

In late 2006, the Pew Internet Project, a nonpartisan, nonprofit research group that examines the social impact of the Internet, reported that 55 percent of online teens have created a personal profile on OSNs and that 48 percent of teens visit social networking Web sites daily, with 22 percent visiting several times a day (Lenhart and Madden 2). The two most popular OSNs are *MySpace* and *Facebook*. *MySpace* is a general networking site that allows anyone to join, develop a profile, and display personal information. In less than four years of existence, *MySpace* has exploded to become the third most visited Web site on the Internet behind only *Google* and *Yahoo* ("Top Sites") with more than 100 million members (Joly). *Facebook* is geared more toward college students (until recently it required that a person attend a university to join the network) and is the number-one site accessed by 18- to 24-year-olds. According to research studies cited in an article in the *Toronto Star*, 90 percent of all undergraduates log on to *Facebook* and

Gardiner 2

60 percent log on daily (George-Cosh W1). *Facebook* has also experienced

unprecedented growth in its relatively short existence and now ranks as the seventh

most visited site on the Internet ("Top Sites") and has a member base of more than

19 million (Joly).

 With the use of OSNs increasing among young people, the term

"Facebook trance" has emerged to describe a person who loses all track of time

and stares at the screen for hours (Copeland). While "Facebook trance" might

describe only an occasional and therefore harmless phenomenon, it gives rise to

important questions: What are the possible negative consequences of OSNs?

What should youthful users be watchful for and guard against? The purpose of

this paper is to identify the possible harms of OSNs. I will suggest that overuse

of OSNs can be a contributing factor to a decline in grades as well as to other

problems such as a superficial view of relationships, an increase in narcissism,

and possible future embarrassment.

 I don't mean to deny that OSNs have positive consequences for young

people. For one thing, they provide a "virtual hangout" that acts as a convenient

and cost-effective way to stay in close contact with friends and family.

According to the Pew survey, 91 percent of users use OSNs to keep in touch

with their regularly seen friends, while 82 percent use the sites to stay in touch

with distant friends (Lenhart and Madden). OSNs let young people regularly

view their friends' profiles, leave short messages or comments, and share

personal information. OSN researcher Danah Boyd also claims that these sites

give young people a platform on which to experiment with identities, voice their

opinions, and practice how they present themselves through personal data,

pictures, and music placed in their profiles (Bowley). OSNs also assist them in

learning more about people they've met offline. Used as an investigative tool,

OSNs offer quick ways to get additional background information on someone.

For example, a student could use an OSN to decide whom to partner with for

Gardiner 3

a class project, to learn more about a new roommate, or to find out more about someone he or she just met at a party, all by browsing classmates' profiles.

Despite these benefits, OSNs have a downside. One potential harm is that OSNs could have a negative effect on grades. One study shows a direct connection between the amount of time spent on the networks and declining grades in school. A college newspaper article entitled "Research Links *MySpace* Use to Drop in Grades" reports a survey of high school students conducted by Fresno State University professor Tamyra Pierce. Pierce found that students with *MySpace* accounts were significantly more likely than students without *MySpace* accounts to report a decline in grades since the previous year. According to Pierce, "We can't know for sure that *MySpace* caused the lower grades, but when compared to other after-school activities (work, sports, video games, etc.), only *MySpace* showed significance" (qtd. in "Research Links"). Pierce's research also revealed that 42 percent of polled students said they often had *MySpace* open while doing homework, and 34 percent stated that they would delay homework to spend time on social networking sites. Pierce adds that 59 percent of students reported spending "between 30 minutes and six hours daily on *MySpace*." Such heavy usage significantly takes time away from school work, extracurricular activities, and sleep. Although this specific study focused on high school students, it would be safe to assume that the results would be generally similar for college students. In fact, the results of the Fresno State study were reported in other college newspapers (Scrabis; Jimenez); the writers for these college newspapers usually included anecdotes from their own campuses about college students obsessed with OSNs. One Penn State student said of *MySpace*, "I keep getting rid of it and then getting it back again because I'm addicted. It's like cocaine" (qtd. in Scrabis).

Another potential problem with OSNs is their tendency to promote superficial or unsatisfying relationships. According to Chou, Condron, and

Use quotation marks for article titles.

Use "qtd. in" for a source quoted in another source.

Gardiner 4

Belland, for some users "over-dependence on online relationships may result in significant problems with real-life interpersonal and occupational functioning" (381). When logged on to the network, students may believe that they are "in touch" with people, when actually they are physically alone with their computers. In a controversial 1998 article cited by Matsuba, Kraut and his colleagues suggested that extensive Internet use "was associated with declines in participants' communication with family members in the household, declines in the size of their social circle, and increases in their depression and loneliness" (qtd. in Matsuba 275). Matsuba conducted an extensive study to test Kraut's conclusions. Matsuba found that persons who scored high on measures of loneliness spent more time on the Internet than persons who scored low on the loneliness measures. In another facet of his study, Matsuba found that for persons who established online friendships, these friendships did not seem "as rich and diverse in quality compared to face-to-face friendships" (283). Matsuba concludes that while online communication can be used to enhance relationships, it can become a problem when it begins to replace offline interaction. He found that face-to-face friendships scored higher for both positive and negative aspects of relationships than did online friendships. He then speculates, "While it is possible that the internet is helping [lonely] people in their search, the possibility remains that the internet is hindering them in facing life in the 'real' world and thus preventing them from developing an adult identity" (283).

Matsuba's finding that face-to-face friendships are more "rich and diverse in quality" than online friendships has led me to speculate that a possible problem with OSNs is the complete lack of nonverbal communication exchanged between users. According to communications professor Julia T. Woods, "Scholars estimate that nonverbal behaviors account for 65 percent to 93 percent of the total meaning of communication" (132). Since the people

Gardiner 5

interacting on OSNs are unable to view each other, they are unable to gauge the other's subtle body language, facial expressions, and voice tones that are such vital ingredients of effective communication. Part of achieving the "adult identity" called for by Matsuba is learning to communicate nonverbally as well as verbally in an environment requiring real contact.

For me, a particularly interesting yet subtle danger of OSNs is their contribution to a rise in narcissism. In an article with the subtitle "Study Says Many Students Are Narcissists," journalist E. Hoover reports on the unpublished research of Jean M. Twenge, a psychology professor at San Diego State University, who says that new technologies such as OSNs have "stoked the self-loving tendencies of modern students" (qtd. in Hoover). Twenge's recent research shows that college kids today are more narcissistic than college kids were in the 1980s; she labels the current generation of youth as "the most narcissistic in recent history" (Hoover). According to Hoover, Twenge defines narcissism as "excessive vanity and a sense of entitlement." Narcissists, Hoover reports, "tend to lack empathy for others, behave aggressively when insulted, and ignore the needs of those around them."

According to Twenge, narcissism finds expression on OSNs in the way that young people on *MySpace* and *Facebook* compete with each other to be heard. In another article reporting Twenge's research, Melissa Ludwig states that OSNs have "gone beyond touching base with friends to an arena where people vie for the most digital friends, the best videos, the coolest sites, and the biggest audience" (A15). She then quotes Twenge: "Now it all becomes a competition, seeking attention and seeking status rather than a true connection between people, or a meaningful connection." The work of Twenge and others suggests that the popularity of OSNs is partly the result of young people's finding an online way to express their narcissistic tendencies. The sites may contribute to self-expression more than to connection and friendship.

Gardiner 6

A final danger of OSNs is that persons will place on their sites material that they will later regret. Young people tend to think that their audiences are only their like-minded friends and classmates. They often don't imagine their professors, their potential employers, or even their parents reading their sites. One journalist describes a *MySpace* profile in which a college student has posted photos of herself in "a skin-tight black leather Catwoman costume, two triangles of vinyl struggling to cover her silicone-enhanced breasts" (Ludwig A15). Ludwig continues:

> Much of the stuff floating around in cyberspace is tame, mundane even. But there also is plenty that's racy, embarrassing or squeamishly intimate. Bad or good, Generation Next is living out loud and doing it online, before a global audience, in a medium where digital archives may linger for a long, long time.... [Generation Nexters] still are too young to fully grasp the permanence of their online actions, and the possible consequences down the road. (A15)

Indent longer quotations 10 spaces or 1 inch.

Use ellipsis to show omitted words.

Use brackets when inserting explanatory words in quotation.

Cite page number after period.

One indication of this danger has already surfaced in the case of some sports teams. The University of Minnesota Duluth recently barred all athletes from creating profiles on *MySpace*, *Facebook*, and similar sites, a policy that, according to journalist Chao Xiong, aims to shield students and the school from bad press that might occur from the posting of inappropriate material. Xiong reports that athletic departments across the country are considering similar bans. One coach at the UM-Duluth campus said, "It was amazing to me how revealing people are with their lives on the Internet" (qtd. in Xiong 1A). (This coach had established her own *Facebook* profile in order to police the activities of her team members.) Xiong reports that across the country athletes have embarrassed their programs by posting pictures of themselves drinking blindfolded at parties or making disparaging comments about coaches or teammates. It is unclear whether coaches have the legal right to forbid their team members to place profiles on OSNs (some students are claiming violation of free speech rights). However, the fact that athletic programs are concerned about the impact of these social networks shows the potential negative consequence of posting embarrassing material on OSNs.

Although I don't support the banning of *Facebook* or *MySpace* profiles for athletes or other students, I do think that young people should be aware of some of the problems associated with them. Two of the problems I have noted here—decline in grades and narcissistic competition for the coolest sites—could be avoided by students' simply limiting their time online. Knowing that OSNs can promote a superficial view of friendships might encourage people to use OSNs to stay in touch face-to-face with friends rather than try to find online substitutes for real friendships. Finally, young people should be aware that the materials they post on their profiles might one day come back to haunt them. To gain the maximum benefits of online social networks and avoid the pitfalls associated with them, my advice to today's students would be to use them as an advanced e-mail-type communication tool rather than as a place to loiter and waste valuable hours that they will never get back.

Gardiner 8

Works Cited

Bowley, Graham. "The High Priestess of Internet Friendship." *Financial Times Weekend Magazine* 27 Oct. 2006. *LexisNexis Academic*. Web. 22 Feb. 2007.

Chou, Chien, Linda Condron, and John C. Belland. "A Review of the Research on Internet Addiction." *Educational Psychology Review* 17.4 (2005): 363–89. *Academic Search Complete*. Web. 22 Feb. 2007.

Copeland, Libby. "Click Clique: *Facebook's* Online College Community." *Washingtonpost.com*. Washington Post, 28 Dec. 2004. Web. 24 Feb. 2007.

George-Cosh, David. "Social Net: Thousands of Local Students Build Friendships on *Facebook*." *TheStar.com*. Toronto Star, 20 Jan. 2007. Web. 15 Apr. 2007.

Hoover, E. "Here's You Looking at You, Kid: Study Says Many Students Are Narcissists." *Chronicle of Higher Education* 53.29 (9 Mar. 2007): A41. *Academic Search Complete*. Web. 14 Apr. 2007.

Jimenez, Eddie. "*MySpace* Adds to Overload for Teens." *Fresno Bee* 9 Mar. 2007. *Newspaper Source*. Web. 14 Apr. 2007.

Joly, Karine. "*Facebook, MySpace*, and Co." *University Business*. Professional Media Group, Apr. 2007. Web. 5 May 2007.

Lenhart, Amanda, and Mary Madden. "Social Networking Websites and Teens: An Overview." *Pew Internet and American Life Project*. Pew Research Center, 3 Jan. 2007. Web. 19 Feb. 2007.

Ludwig, Melissa. "LOOK@ME: Generation Next Is Living Out Loud and Online." *MySanAntonio.com*. San Antonio Express News, 15 Mar. 2007. Web. 15 Apr. 2007.

Matsuba, M. Kyle. "Searching for Self and Relationships Online." *CyberPsychology and Behavior* 9.3 (2006): 275–84. *Academic Search Complete*. Web. 14 Apr. 2007.

Start Works Cited list on a new page.

Center heading.

List sources alphabetically.

Use day-month-year format for dates.

Italicize database names.

Italicize periodical titles.

Use quotation marks for article titles.

Gardiner 9

"Research Links *MySpace* Use to Drop in Grades." *FresnoStateNews.com*.
California State U, 9 Mar. 2007. Web. 2 May 2007.

Scrabis, J. "*MySpace* Usage May Lower Grades in Both High School, College
Students." *Daily Collegian*. Pennsylvania State U, 23 Mar. 2007.
Web. 15 Apr. 2007.

"Top Sites for United States." *alexia.com*. N.p., n.d. Web. 2 May 2007.
<http://www.alexia.com/site/ds/
top_sites?cc=US&ts_mode=country&lang=none>.

Woods, Julia T. *Interpersonal Communication*: *Everyday Encounters*.
5th ed. New York: Wadsworth, 2007. Print.

Xiong, Chao. "Not Their Space." *Minneapolis Star Tribune* 16 Apr. 2007.
LexisNexis. Web. 2 May 2007.

Put URLs in angle brackets.

Italicize book titles.

Check that everything cited in paper is in Works Cited list.

SKILL 14.2   **Cite and document sources using APA style.**

In many respects, the APA style and the MLA style are similar and the basic logic is the same. In the APA system, the list where readers can find full bibliographic information is titled "References"; as in MLA format, it includes only the sources cited in the body of the paper. The distinguishing features of APA citation style are highlighted in the following sections.

For an example of a student paper in APA style, see the report by Shannon King on pp. 165–170.

In-Text Citations in APA Style

A typical APA-style in-text citation contains three elements: (1) the last name of the author, (2) the date of the publication, and (3) the page number of the quoted or paraphrased passage. Table 14.2 identifies some typical variations and shows again the one-to-one connection between the in-text citation and the References list.

TABLE 14.2   In-Text Citations in APA Style

Type of Source	References Entry at End of Paper	In-Text Citation in Body of Paper
One author	Pollan, M. (2006). *The omnivore's dilemma: A natural history of four meals.* New York, NY: Penguin.	…(Pollan, 2006, p. 256). OR According to Pollan (2006), … (p. 256).
Two authors	Kwon, O., & Wen, Y. (2010). An empirical study of the factors affecting social network service use. *Computers in Human Behavior, 26,* 254–263. doi:10.1016 /j.chb. 2009.04.011	…(Kwon & Wen, 2010, p. 262). OR Kwon and Wen (2010) claim that…(p. 262).
Three to five authors	Pollay, R. W., Lee, J. S., & Carter-Whitney, D. (1992). Separate, but not equal: Racial segmentation in cigarette advertising. *Journal of Advertising, 21*(1), 45–57.	…race" (Pollay, Lee, & Carter-Whitney, 1992, p. 52). OR Pollay, Lee, and Carter-Whitney have argued that "advertisers… race" (1992, p. 52). *For subsequent citations, use* Pollay et al. *For a quotation, use the specific page number, not the whole range of pages.*

(continued)

APA Style

TABLE 14.2 *continued*

Type of Source	References Entry at End of Paper	In-Text Citation in Body of Paper
Author has more than one work in References list	Dombrowski, D. A. (1984). *The philosophy of vegetarianism.* Amherst, MA: University of Massachusetts Press. Dombrowski, D. A. (1997). *Babies and beasts: The argument from marginal cases.* Urbana: University of Illinois Press.	…(Dombrowski, 1984, p. 207). …(Dombrowski, 1997, p. 328). OR Dombrowski (1984) claims that…(p. 207). According to Dombrowski (1997),…(p. 328).
Indirect citation of a source that you found in another source *You use a quotation from Peter Singer from a book by Dombrowski. Include Dombrowski, not Singer, in References.*	Dombrowski, D. A. (1997). *Babies and beasts: The argument from marginal cases.* Urbana: University of Illinois Press.	Animal rights activist Peter Singer argues that…(as cited in Dombrowski, 1997, p. 429). *Singer is used for the attributive tag, but the in-text citation is to Dombrowski.*

References List in APA Style

The APA References list at the end of a paper presents entries alphabetically. If you cite more than one item for an author, repeat the author's name each time and arrange the items in chronological order, beginning with the earliest. In cases where two works by an author appeared in the same year, arrange them in the list alphabetically by title, and then add a lowercase "a" or "b" (etc.) after the date so that you can distinguish between them in the in-text citations:

A formatted References list appears on p. 170.

Smith, R. (1999a). *Body image in non-Western cultures, 1750–present.* London, England: Bonanza Press.

Smith, R. (1999b). Eating disorders reconsidered. *Journal of Appetite Studies, 45,* 295–300.

APA Citation Models

Print Articles in Scholarly Journals

General Format for Print Article in Scholarly Journal

Author. (Year of Publication). Article title. *Journal Title, volume number,* page numbers. doi: xx.xxxx/x.xxxx.xx

If there is one, include the **DOI** (digital object identifier), a number that is uniquely assigned to many journal articles. Note the style for capitalizing article titles and for italicizing the volume number.

One author

Herrera-Sobek, M. (2006). Border aesthetics: The politics of Mexican immigration in
    film and art. *Western Humanities Review, 60,* 60–71. doi:10.1016/j.chb.2009.04.011

Two to seven authors

Kwon, O., & Wen, Y. (2010). An empirical study of the factors affecting social network
    service use. *Computers in Human Behavior, 26,* 254–263.

When a source has more than seven authors, list the first six and the last one
by name. Use ellipses (. . .) to indicate the authors whose names have been
omitted.

Scholarly journal that restarts page numbering with each issue

Pollay, R. W., Lee, J. S., & Carter-Whitney, D. (1992). Separate, but not equal: Racial
    segmentation in cigarette advertising. *Journal of Advertising, 21*(1), 45–57.

Note that the issue number and the parentheses are *not* italicized.

Print Articles in Magazines and Newspapers

General Format for Print Article in Magazine or Newspaper

Author. (Year, Month Day). Article title. *Periodical Title, volume number,* page numbers.

If page numbers are discontinuous, identify every page, separating numbers with
a comma.

Magazine article

Hall, S. S. (2001, March 11). Prescription for profit. *The New York Times Magazine,* 40–45,
    59, 91–92, 100.

Newspaper article

Henriques, D. B. (1998, September 27). Hero's fall teaches Wall Street a lesson. *Seattle
    Times,* pp. A1, A24.

Print Books

General Format for Print Books

Author. (Year of publication). *Book title: Subtitle.* City, State [abbreviated]: Name of
    Publisher.

Brumberg, J. J. (1997). *The body project: An intimate history of American girls.* New York,
    NY: Vintage.

If the publisher's name indicates the state in which it is located, list the city but
omit the state.

Reid, H., & Taylor, B. (2010). *Recovering the commons: Democracy, place, and global justice.*
    Champaign: University of Illinois Press.

Second, later, or revised edition

Montagu, A. (1986). *Touching: The human significance of the skin* (3rd ed.). New York, NY: Perennial Press.

Anthology article

Royer, A. (1994). The role of the transcendental meditation technique in promoting smoking cessation: A longitudinal study. In D. F. O'Connell & C. N. Alexander (Eds.), *Self recovery: Treating addictions using transcendental meditation and Maharishi Ayur-Veda* (pp. 221–239). New York, NY: Haworth Press.

Articles or Books from an Online Database

Article from database with digital object identifier (DOI)

Scharrer, E., Daniel, K. D., Lin, K.-M., & Liu, Z. (2006). Working hard or hardly working? Gender, humor, and the performance of domestic chores in television commercials. *Mass Communication and Society, 9*(2), 215–238. doi:10.1207/s15327825mcs0902_5

Omit the database name. If an article or other document has been assigned a digital object identifier (DOI), include the DOI at the end.

Article from database without DOI

Highland, R. A., & Dabney, D. A. (2009). Using Adlerian theory to shed light on drug dealer motivations. *Applied Psychology in Criminal Justice, 5*(2), 109–138. Retrieved from http://www.apcj.org

Omit the database name. Instead, use a search engine to locate the publication's home page, and cite that URL. If you need to break a URL at the end of a line, do not use a hyphen. Instead, break it *before* a punctuation mark or *after* http://.

Other Internet Sources

General Format for Web Documents

Author, editor, director, narrator, performer, compiler, or producer of the work, if available. (Year, Month Day of posting). *Title of web document, italicized.* Retrieved from Name of website if different from author or title: URL of home page

Barrett, J. (2007, January 17). *MySpace is a natural monopoly.* Retrieved from ECommerce Times website: http://www.ecommercetimes.com

Marks, J. (n.d.). "Overview: Letter from the president." Retrieved June 3, 2010, from the Search for Common Ground website: http://www.sfcg.org

Entire Web site

BlogPulse. (n.d.). Retrieved September 3, 2010, from the Intelliseek website: http://www.intelliseek.com

Article from a newspaper site

Bounds, A. (2007, June 26). Thinking like scientists. *Daily Camera* [Boulder]. Retrieved from http://www.dailycamera.com

Article from a scholarly e-journal

Welch, J. R., & Riley, R. (2001). Reclaiming land and spirit in the western Apache
homeland. *American Indian Quarterly, 25*, 5–14. Retrieved from
http://muse.jhu.edu/journals/american_indian_quarterly

E-book

Hoffman, F. W. (1981). *The literature of rock: 1954–1978*. Retrieved from
http://www.netlibrary.com

E-mail, interviews, and personal correspondence

Cite personal correspondence in the body of your text, but not in the References
list: "Daffinrud (personal communication, December 12, 2001) claims that . . . . "

Blog Posting

Dyer, B., & Barnes, E. (2008, October 7). The "greening" of the Arctic [Web log post].
Retrieved from http://blog.epa.gov/blog/2008/10/07/the-greening-of-the-arctic

Web video

Beck, R. (2006, November 2). Immigration gumballs [Video file]. Retrieved from
http://www.youtube.com/watch?v=n7WJeqxuOfQ

Miscellaneous Sources

Television program

Bochco, S., & Milch, D. (Directors). (2001, November 6). Lie like a rug [Television series
episode]. In *NYPD blue*. New York, NY: American Broadcasting Company.

Film

Madden, J. (Director). (1998). *Shakespeare in love* [Motion picture]. United States:
Universal Miramax.

Student Example of an APA-Style Research Paper

An example of a paper in APA style is shown on pages 165–170.

ACKNOWLEDGMENTS

Page 340. © 2007 Million Mom March Chapters of the Brady Campaign to Prevent Gun Violence. Used with permission. www.millionmommarch.org

Page 343. From *Gunfighters, Highwaymen, and Vigilantes: Violence on the Frontier* by Roger D. McGrath. Copyright © 1984 The Regents of the University of California. Used with permission.

Illustrations

Page 3. Bob Jacobson/Corbis

Page 14. Ennio Leanza/epa/Corbis

Page 52. Jon Carr

Page 60. Clockwise from top left: Tom Walker/Getty; Accent Alaska/Alamy; James Balog/Getty; Simon Bruty/Sports Illustrated/Getty

Page 62. Clockwise from top left: Jose Luis Pelaez Inc./Blend Images/Corbis; Corbis Premium RF/Alamy; Ken Seet Photography/Corbis; Richard G. Bingham II/ Alamy

Page 92. Thomas Hannich/Bransch/NY Times

Page 127. Mike Lane

Page 155. From left: Courtesy Manuel J. Cabrero; Courtesy Ron Taylor

Page 172. Clockwise from top left: Karen Kasmauski/Corbis; Guillermo Arias/AP; Carlos Barria/Corbis; J. Emilio Flores/Corbis

Page 174. Clockwise from top left: Steven James Silva/Reuters/Landov; Det. Greg Semendinger/NYPD/AP; David Turnley/Corbis

Page 180. Peter Turnley/Corbis

Page 181. Jean-Christophe Bott/Keystone/AP

Page 184. Scala/Art Resource, NY

Page 185. Albright-Knox Art Gallery/Art Resource, NY

Page 186. June Johnson (2 images)

Page 189. Lars Halbauer/DPA/Landov

Page 194. Coors Brewing Company

Page 196. Advertising Archives

Page 197. Advertising Archives (2 images)

Page 202. Stephen Crowley/The New York Times/Redux

Page 203. Dorothea Lange

Page 260. Top left: Bill Jacobus; top right: Spencer Platt/Getty; center left: Don Jon Red/Alamy

Page 340. MillionMomMarch.org

INDEX

Abstracts, 98. *See also* Summaries
Academic disciplines
  as field of inquiry and
    argument, 26–27
  scholarly questions for
    assorted, 26–28
Academic writing. *See also* Research
  source documentation;
  Scholarly publications
  closed-form prose for, 18, 21, 24
  document design for, 74–75
  examples of, 20
  graphics in, 328
  starting point for, 25
  titles for, 302–303
Ad hominem argument, 227
Advertisements
  advocacy, 245, 250
  analysis of, 191–199
  designing of, 190–191
  examples of, 186, 189, 194,
    196, 197
  goals of, 188
  media for, 187–188
  overview of, 186–187
  print ads, 191–193, 198
  strategies for effective, 188–190
  target audience for, 187, 188,
    193–195
Advocacy, degree of, 337
Advocacy advertisements, function
  of, 245, 250
all about writing, 294
Alley, Michael, 256
although clause, 38, 39
American Express ad, 197
American Psychological Association
  (APA). *See* APA style
Amis, Martin, 66
Analogy
  argument from, 249
  false, 226
Analysis
  of angle of vision, 54–55, 63–65
  explanation of, 171
and then chronology, 293–294
Anecdotal conclusions, 330
Angle of vision
  analysis of, 54–55, 63–65
  contrasts of same scene, 81–83

examples of, 55
explanation of, 51, 335
of images, 57–63, 175
persuasion through, 55–56
recognition of, 51–53
of research sources,
  335–337
strategies to construct, 54–55
thought exercise on, 51
Annotated bibliographies
  examples of annotations for,
    140–141
  explanation of, 128, 139
  features of, 140
  functions of, 139–140
  peer reviews for, 142–143
  shaping, drafting,
    and revising, 142
  writing critical preface for,
    141–142, 149–151
Anthologies
  APA style for citing, 374
  MLA style for citing, 358
APA style, 25*n*
  for anthologies, 374
  for articles in magazines and
    newspapers, 373, 374–375
  for articles in scholarly journals,
    372–373, 375
  for books, 373–374
  for citing online databases, 374
  for films, 375
  for interviews, 375
  in-text citations in, 371–372
  for manuscripts and papers, 76
  References list in, 372
  for television programs, 375
  for Web and Internet sources,
    374–375
Appeals
  bandwagon, 227
  to *ethos,* 20, 57, 58, 103,
    105, 224
  to false authority, 227
  to *logos,* 57, 58, 103, 104
  to *pathos,* 57–59, 103, 105,
    224–225
Arctic National Wildlife Refuge
  (ANWR) example, 55, 59–60,
    103, 106

Argument. *See also* Classical
  argument
  addressing objections and
    counterarguments in, 218–220
  appeals to *ethos* and *pathos* in,
    223–225
  articulating reasons in, 211–212
  articulating underlying
    assumptions in, 212–214
  audience-based reasons for,
    222–223
  components of, 206–207
  from consequence, 249
  evaluating evidence for, 217–218
  exploration of, 207–208
  fallacies in, 226–227
  finding issue for, 210–211
  framework for classical, 228
  generating and exploring ideas
    for, 229
  making concessions to, 221–222
  misleading views of, 207
  peer review for, 232–233
  from precedent or analogy, 249
  from principle, 248–249
  process of nutshelling, 296–297
  readings in, 234–244
  responding to objects, counterar-
    guments, and alternative views
    in, 221–223
  revision of, 232
  shaping and drafting, 230–232
  stages of development of, 208–210
  stating claim for, 211
  structure of, 213*n*
  truth seeking in, 206, 209
  types of evidence for, 214–217
  use of sources based on, 341–344
  visual, 250–251
Aristotle, 15, 57
Articles
  APA style for citing, 373
  MLA style for citing online
    databases, 358–359
  MLA style for citing print, 358
Assumptions, articulating
  underlying, 212–214
Attributive tags
  to avoid ambiguities, 346
  explanation of, 344–345